The Discipline of Law Schools

The Discipline of Law Schools

The Making of Modern Lawyers

Philip C. Kissam

CAROLINA ACADEMIC PRESS

Durham, North Carolina

ISBN: 0-89089-390-X
LCCN: 2003101471

Carolina Academic Press
700 Kent Street
Durham, North Carolina 27701
Telephone (919) 489-7486
Fax (919) 493-5668
E-mail: cap@cap-press.com
www.cap-press.com

Printed in the United States of America.

for Brenda, Jonathan

and Ariane

CONTENTS

ACKNOWLEDGMENTS

I owe thanks first of all to Dwight Kiel, who introduced me to the work of Michel Foucault a long time ago and encouraged us "to get down into the trenches" in order to apply Foucault's ideas to contemporary social institutions. My colleagues at the University of Kansas School of Law, Sandy McKenzie and Peter Schanck, read endless early drafts, provided helpful comments and other support in the rough and early going. John Covell, then at Yale Press, and two anonymous peer reviewers provided very substantial assistance in improving the manuscript. I am thankful also to many others for their helpful comments on this project. They include Richard Abel, Mike Davis, Kim Dayton, John Elson, Jay Feinman, Jerry Frug, Bryant Garth, Mike Hoeflich, Frank Levy, Allan Hanson, Lauren Hoopes, Rex Martin, Martha Minow, Jeremy Paul, Alexander Somek, Chris Suggs, Bill Staples, Carol Warren and Fred Woodward. The University of Kansas and University of Kansas School of Law provided research grants and a sabbatical to support this project. I am thankful as well to the publisher and editors of Carolina Academic Press, especially Bob Conrow, for their guidance and help in bringing this manuscript to publication.

The Discipline of Law Schools

INTRODUCTION

Law schools, as they educate and train lawyers, use routine practices and habits that in the aggregate fail to serve the best interests of lawyers and society. Consider, for example, these paradoxical situations in which intentions and practices seem to be at cross-purposes:

> Law and lawyers by and large serve wealth, property, power, order and stability, and yet modern law schools are full of teaching and scholarship that challenge the priority of these values over competing ones such as racial equality, ending sexism and economic justice;[1]

> The dominant "case method" of law teaching is often justified as an ideal way to teach lawyers both rigorous and imaginative thinking and public speaking;[2] yet many law students are bored, confused or made angry by this method,[3] and graduates of law schools can be shockingly deficient in even the most basic "case method skills;"[4]

> The law school curriculum appears to serve the interests of corporate law firms in hiring new lawyers who possess substantial doctrinal

---

1. For a recent account of debates in American law schools about the nature and politics of legal scholarship, see Arthur Austin, The Empire Strikes Back: Outsiders and the Struggle over Legal Education (1998); see also Chapter Four's description of the "Academic/Political Movements" in modern law schools.

2. See, e.g., Anthony T. Kronman, The Lost Lawyer: Failing Ideals of the Legal Profession 109–62 (1993); Paul Carrington, *Hail, Langdell!*, 20 Law & Social Inquiry 691 (1995).

3. On the well-recognized malaise among upper class law students, see, e.g., Kevin Clermont, *Resolving the Law School's Biggest Problem*, 5 Cornell L. F. 16 (1978); on confusions that the case method causes, see, e.g., John Makdisi, *The Problem with the Structure of Casebooks and Instruction*, 40 Clev. St. L. J. 437 (1992); on the anger or alienation that the case method can produce among students, see, e.g., Duncan Kennedy, *How the Law School Fails: A Polemic*, 1 Yale Rev. L. & Soc. Action 71 (1970); Catherine Weiss & Louise Melling, *The Legal Education of Twenty Women*, 40 Stan. L. Rev. 1299 (1988).

4. See David P. Bryden, *What Do Law Students Learn? A Pilot Study*, 34 J. Legal Educ. 479 (1984).

knowledge and skills; but lawyers in these firms complain today that the new law graduates they hire often perform quite poorly in basic aspects of written and oral communication.[5]

Law schools and the legal profession frequently advise law students and lawyers that lawyers have professional obligations to act as "ethical lawyers" and provide "public service;"[6] despite these pronouncements and law school courses aimed at this kind of instruction, law students by-and-large remain indifferent to ethical issues[7] and lawyers tend to ignore or resist the blandishments and proposals by leaders of their profession to pursue or codify these obligations in an effective manner.[8]

What causes these paradoxes? On first impression they may seem attributable to the greater diversity among today's law faculty, changes in modern law students, shifts in the nature of contemporary legal practices or the greater influence that practice has upon lawyers' attitudes and behavior. But throughout their history American law schools have been subject to disputes and discontents about teaching methods, the curriculum and scholarship.[9] Perhaps these disputes, discontents and dysfunctions are endemic to legal education. Perhaps the academic discipline of law, as a system of manifest intentions about the law, legal education and legal scholarship, rests upon a darker, more subterranean and habitual system of routine practices and tacit lessons, a latent disciplinary system we might call "the discipline of law schools."[10]

5. See Bryant G. Garth & Joanne Martin, *Law Schools and the Construction of Competence*, 43 J. Legal Educ. 469 (1993).

6. See, e.g., American Bar Assoc., In the Spirit of Public Service: A Blueprint for the Rekindling of Lawyer Professionalism (1986); American Bar Assoc., Teaching and Learning Professionalism: Report of the Professionalism Committee (1996).

7. See, e.g., Ian Johnstone & Mary Patricia Treuthart, *Doing the Right Thing: An Overview of Teaching Professional Responsibility*, 41 J. Legal Educ. 65, 88–92, 95–96 (1991).

8. See, e.g., Deborah L. Rhode, In the Interests of Justice: Reforming the Legal Profession (2000).

9. See, e.g., William Chase, American Law Schools and the Rise of Administrative Government (1982); Laura Kalman, Legal Realism at Yale, 1927–1960 (1986); Robert Stevens, Legal Education in America from the 1850s to the 1980s (1983).

10. Cf. Pierre Bourdieu, In Other Words: Essays on a Reflexive Sociology 9–14 (trans. 1990) (describing the concept of a habitus as a "system of dispositions" that are "socially constituted," "acquired through experience," and tend to reproduce the system, although the habitus is "indeterminate for particular instances of strategic behavior and can change in response to changes in material conditions"); Michel Foucault, Discipline and Punish (trans. 1977) (describing systems of disciplinary power in social institutions which "inscribe" tacit lessons upon the "bodies" and "souls" of persons in order to make them docile,

This book has a simple thesis. We must study *the routines, habits* and *tacit knowledge* of law schools if we are to comprehend American legal education, its paradoxes, and the law and lawyers that American law schools produce. We must study, that is, the full nature and tacit effects of the common core curriculum in law schools, the case method, the law school's final examination system and the institutions of conventional legal scholarship. Routine practices can shape our "non-conscious practical conscious" or "tacit knowledge" that affects behavior in unintended ways.[11] The routine practices of law schools can thus create habits and tacit concepts or predispositions in lawyers that quietly shape, reinforce or undermine the conscious ideas and beliefs about law and lawyering that law professors, law students, and lawyers discuss and hold. These habits, concepts and predispositions reinforce some learning that law professors and law students intentionally strive to provide or obtain. But they also tacitly disrupt, exclude or subordinate ideas and practices that legal education and legal educators would promote.

The discipline of law schools thus quietly empowers and constrains or limits students and lawyers, to say nothing of law professors who are the long-term denizens of law schools. This is not to say that individuals are unable to mitigate or escape the tacit lessons of the discipline. The discipline may not inscribe its lessons effectively in some persons. For others, personal reflection or the accident of particular instructive practices may cut against the discipline in ways that blunt or override its lessons. This is also not to say that the discipline operates in exactly the same way at each law school. Law schools accept different kinds of students, send their students to different legal markets, and are experimenting today with a variety of teaching methods, especially those that involve legal clinics and writing exercises. These variations can influence the precise operation and effects of the discipline from school to school, but these diverse practices rest upon an underlying structure of routines, habits and tacit conceptions of law and lawyering that constitute the discipline of law schools.

---

useful producers); Lars Bo Kaspersen, Anthony Giddens: An Introduction to a Social Theorist 31–65 (2000) (describing Giddens' theory of structuration as a theory of social behavior that focuses on practices that reproduce themselves with variation by means of the "practical consciousness" of individuals which can incorporate the "rules" and "resources" that are generated by "social systems").

11. See Anthony A. Giddens, Modernity and Self-Identity 35–36 (1991) (contrasting "non-conscious practical consciousness" with "discursive consciousness"); Donald A. Schon, Educating the Reflective Practitioner (1987); The Reflective Practitioner (1983) (describing the importance of various kinds of "tacit knowledge" to high quality professional practice and professional education).

The tendencies and predispositions taught by the discipline appear to be quite powerful, and many persons are likely to both benefit and suffer from the discipline's effects. The purpose of this book is to expose the discipline of law schools, to encourage reflections about the discipline and the lawyer's situation, and to suggest alternative practices that might counter the discipline's negative effects. These alternative practices, such as the decentering of the law school's final examination/grading/class ranking system by different kinds of writing exercises throughout the law school's core curriculum, will require a rethinking of the ethics of legal education, which is the topic of the last chapter in this book.

What are the tacit lessons of the discipline? One is the discipline's subtle promotion of a particular intellectual method at the cost of devaluing other intellectual methods that in legal practices will complement and at times compete with the favored method. The favored method is the method of *analysis*, that is, the mental practice and instinct of breaking things down and dividing them into many small discrete and useful parts. One consequence of the discipline's analytical tendency is the tacit disfavoring of other intellectual methods such as the interpretation or synthesis of complex legal materials and construction of complex or novel legal arguments.[12] The analytical tendencies of lawyers, of course, constitute an important legal skill, but the implicit devaluation of other important skills by the discipline should be worrisome. This devaluation appears, for example, in the apparent passion of many lawyers for focusing on the details of things without providing any conceptual or ethical understanding of their actions and statements. This devaluation also appears in the general disdain of many lawyers, law students and law professors for ethical questions about legal practices.[13]

The discipline also tacitly promotes *a rhetoric* of authority, complexity, confidence and closure[14] and *the related attitude* of a lawyer's "toughness."[15] This

---

12. Cf. Richard S. Markovits, *The Professional Assessment of Legal Academics: On the Shift from Evaluator Judgment to Market Evaluations*, 48 J. Legal Educ. 417, 418–27 (1998) (describing law student distaste for "legal arguments" as opposed to "legal conclusions" and how course evaluations by law students may encourage law professors to avoid teaching the construction of legal arguments).

13. On the presence of this disdain, see supra notes 7–8 and accompanying text.

14. Cf. Gerald Wetlaufer, *Rhetoric and Its Denial in Legal Discourse*, 76 Va. L. Rev. 1545 (1990) (describing the rhetoric in legal education, legal practice and judging as based upon legal authorities, objectivity, closure and the denial of rhetoric).

15. Cf. Austin Sarat, *Enactments of Professionalism: A Study of Judges' and Lawyers' Accounts of Ethics and Civility in Litigation*, 67 Ford. L. Rev. 809, 818–23 (1998) (describing "toughness" as a default norm for litigation work by lawyers).

attitude incorporates and communicates a coolness or studied indifference toward other persons, ethics, moral sentiment and the emotions. These rhetorical and stylistic traits of the discipline also subordinate risk-taking, more open-ended or tentative forms of rhetoric, and the possibilities for systematic deliberations about ethical, moral and other theoretical issues of law. To be sure, we want lawyers to attend persuasively to legal authority and complexity and to be zealous in the pursuit of client's interests. But good lawyers are also called upon to attend to complicated emotional and ethical situations,[16] and the discipline of law schools makes these kinds of considerations much more difficult than they otherwise might be. The discipline's general combative approach and emphasis upon impressing and winning surely set the stage, as it were, for the lawyer's "procedural pathologies" of undue coaching and intimidating witnesses, abusing the discovery process and concealing documents to guard against a client's losing the case.[17]

The discipline teaches *instrumentalist habits of reading and writing* that both empower and limit future lawyers.[18] These habits consist of quick, productive but often superficial ways of reading legal texts and writing about law, and they are linked to the law school's distinctive oral culture, which celebrates oral heroism and tacitly devalues complex reading and writing.[19] The law school's distinctive oral culture in turn rests upon the discipline's case method, its large amphitheatre classrooms, its Moot Court exercises and the speech-like forms of effective final examination writing. But this oral culture and the instrumentalist reading and writing habits of law schools tend to subordinate more complicated, more reflective, more critical and more imaginative ways of reading, writing and thinking about law.

---

16. See, e.g., D. Rhode, supra note 8; William H. Simon, The Practice of Justice: A Theory of Lawyers' Ethics (1998); Lynne N. Henderson, *Legality and Empathy*, 85 Mich. L. Rev. 1574 (1987).

17. On the widespread presence of such "procedural pathologies" among lawyers, see D. Rhode, supra note 8, at 82–105.

18. On these kinds of habits, see Elizabeth Fajans & Mary Falk, *Against the Tyranny of the Paraphrase: Talking Back to Texts*, 78 Corn. L. Rev. 163, 163–70 (1993) (describing the instrumentalist reading of law students); Philip C. Kissam, *Law School Examinations*, 42 Vand. L. Rev. 433 (1989) (describing the instrumentalist writing that is taught by law school examinations).

19. Cf. Lisa Eichhorn, *Writing in the Legal Academy: A Dangerous Supplement?*, 40 Ariz. L. Rev. 105 (1998); Philip C. Kissam, *Thinking (By Writing)About Legal Writing*, 40 Vand. L. Rev. 135, 141–48 (1987) (describing how the oral culture of law schools tacitly limits law student understanding of the writing process).

The discipline also generates *many unresolved contradictory messages* about law and lawyering through its diverse curriculum, fragmented casebooks, the multiple levels of analysis and relentless competition of arguments that occur in case method classrooms, and the recurrent uncertainties of classroom work and final examinations. A course in torts or personal injury law may present the law to first year students, implicitly or expressly, as a set of uncertain rules and methods to manipulate these rules while students are also studying contracts law as a set of relatively specific rules that can be used to give confident advice to clients.[20] In their second year, law students may study corporations law from an economic perspective that explains and assesses rules in relationship to economic efficiency, constitutional law from a perspective that explains particular rules as the result of the political preferences of judges or political assessments by judges of the relative competencies of different government agencies, and consumer protection or environmental law from various moral perspectives.[21] In individual classes these same students may often be left with a sense that law rests precariously on the fragile grounds of the persuasive arguments that are made on both sides of any difficult issue. Suppose, for instance, that students are asked to make arguments on both sides of a case where a battered woman has shot her ex-lover in circumstances where the threat of immediate harm was unclear.[22] Or suppose that students are asked, as may happen frequently, to construct competing arguments from the same precedents or same statutory language by interpreting the authorities either broadly or narrowly.[23] More generally, the discipline implicitly teaches that good judges are those who are "neutral" and "objective" and decide their cases only on "legal grounds," while bad judges are "political" and

---

20. Cf. James Boyle, *The Anatomy of a Torts Class*, 34 Am. U. L. Rev. 1003 (1985) (describing such a torts class and the common "plot" of legal education to present the law as both a set of definite rules and lawyers as adept at manipulation).

21. See Chapter One's discussion of the case method and Chapter Four's discussion of the academic/political movements in modern law schools.

22. See Duncan Kennedy, *Politicizing the Classroom*, 4 So. Cal. Rev. Law & Women's Studies 81, 88 (1994).

23. See, e.g., Karl Llewellyn, The Bramble Bush 72–75 (1930) (describing a "Janus-faced" or two-headed doctrine of precedent by which judges can read precedents narrowly by stating their rules in terms of the facts of prior cases or broadly by relying upon general statements in the opinions of prior cases); Boyle, supra note 20, at 1052–54 (describing methods for generating competing arguments from the same legal authority by using "formalist" and "purposive" methods to interpret a rule or the methods of narrow construction, by tying a case rule to the facts of prior cases, and broad construction, by characterizing the phenomena of prior cases in more abstract terms).

"subjective," but rarely is any systematic explanation provided or sought about how this can be.[24] This unresolved message, that judges in effect are two-faced, may help litigators explain to clients how they win or lose their cases, but it can leave students with limited or very unclear notions of how legal arguments are constructed or what law is.

These kinds of unresolved contradictory messages combine with the discipline's other tacit lessons of analysis, instrumentalist reading and writing, and rhetorical toughness to produce in law schools a deep skepticism about the possibility of binding legal or moral norms or, in other words, to teach the corrosive lesson that "there is no law there."[25] This skepticism reduces the practice of law to a toolkit of rhetorical devices or manipulable conventions. It supports the "dominant view" of legal ethics that the lawyer's role is only to provide technical, amoral services to clients,[26] and it produces pervasive doubt about any place for political ideals or moral obligations in the law. The discipline as a system of habits thus endorses the amoral use of technique while disfavoring politics, moral passion, legal theory and systematic arguments for legal change.[27]

The discipline's contradictory messages and ultimate lesson of "no law" may be seen as both empowering and limiting for American lawyers. On the one hand, the skepticism and doubt that is taught by this process may assist many lawyers in searching for legal ambiguities or testing the boundaries of legal rules in imaginative or novel ways that are useful to clients and the development of law. Instincts toward skepticism and doubt also may support more explicit lessons of tolerance for competing views. On the other hand, the many unresolved contradictory messages and the ultimate lesson of "no law" tacitly undercut many arguments about politics, legal ethics, legal theory and legal change by generating skepticism about the relative merits of different positions. They also seem to promote the conservative values of the *status quo* or, perhaps more precisely, the conservative values of political apathy or just let-

---

24. See Chapter Three's discussion of the discipline's generation of a Janus-faced image of judges under Rituals, Symbols, Myths.

25. Cf. Roger Cramton, *The Ordinary Religion of the Law School Classroom*, 29 J. Legal Educ. 247 (1978) (describing the moral skepticism that pervades law school classrooms).

26. William Simon describes this conception of the lawyer's role as "the Dominant View" in his recent book, The Practice of Justice, supra note 16. He also describes two competing conceptions of the lawyer's role as the "Public Interest" and "Contextual" views of lawyering. See id.

27. Cf. Robert Granfield, Making Elite Lawyers: Visions of Law at Harvard and Beyond (1992) (describing how emphasis upon legal technique in law school helps reconcile idealistic law students to practice in corporate law firms).

ting things be. In these ways students and lawyers can easily ignore many ideas about legal change and the ethical behavior of lawyers that are advanced by law professors and leaders of the legal profession.

The discipline supports *other conservative values* too, particularly by the emphasis on property rights and the maintenance of legal order in critical parts of the law school curriculum. The emphasis on teaching property rights in many first and second year courses tacitly privileges these rights over the competing claims of other individual and social values which only get emphasized, if at all, in public law courses and seminars that are scattered through the upper class law school curriculum.[28] Order is tacitly privileged over considerations of social justice by the discipline's silent emphasis on "the leading cases" and "the rules of law" in case method classes, and by the quiet reliance that law school examinations place upon understanding existing legal doctrines.[29] The discipline also promotes a professional ideology that includes strong beliefs, instincts and preferences for substantial professional autonomy, a legal expertise that is relatively independent of other kinds of intellectual work, deference within professional hierarchies, and a strong competitive individualism among lawyers.

To be sure, many of these conservative values may help lawyers progress in the practice of conservative law.[30] At the same time, these values are not shared by everyone, and reasonable arguments to limit these values are often made by law professors and leaders of the legal profession. But the discipline quietly or tacitly creates predispositions, presumptions or implicit privileges in favor of the conservative values. Learning is unfairly tilted, and legal education is made more conservative than it need be as a result of the discipline of law schools.

Most generally, the discipline produces *the powerful image* and *related predispositions* of the lawyer as a quick, productive, error-free, tough and combative intellectual worker. This image is produced, reconstituted and pursued in various ways throughout the routine practices of law schools, but it is produced and pursued most intensely in the large case method classes that dominate the first and second years of the curriculum and through the law schools' famous or infamous final examination system. This image reinforces the more specific lessons of the discipline and has other important consequences. This

---

28. See Chapter One's discussion of the core curriculum.

29. See Chapter One's discussion of casebooks, the case method and law school examinations.

30. See, e.g., R. Granfield, supra note 27.

image is best attained by law students and lawyers through the adoption of intellectually, socially and political conservative attitudes and behavior that tend to avoid and discourage open-ended, risk-taking deliberations about ethical, moral and political issues like those involved with ethical lawyering, judging hard cases and many sorts of controversial legal changes. The image thus symbolizes conceptions of the self and ethics that tend to detach the self from others and substantially restrict the domain of ethical questions that may be raised about the law, lawyering and legal education.

Ultimately, the discipline and its effects tend to entrench or privilege one model of legal training, that of training new associates for corporate law firms who are technically adept at productive doctrinal analysis. But this model fails to provide optimal training even for lawyers who work in corporate law firms,[31] and it discourages or subordinates valuable teaching methods that address a broader set of legal skills and different models of lawyering that are important to sectors of the legal profession such as the representation of personal clients, public agency work and small general practice law firms. In sum, the discipline's tacit lessons affect the education and politics of law schools, the inhabitants of law schools and America's lawyers in significant ways. While some of the discipline's tacit effects appear functional or desirable, others are less clearly valuable in terms of good education or effective deliberations by lawyers about questions of legal ethics, legal theory and legal change. The law school's disciplinary system of routines, habits and tacit knowledge would appear to deserve a careful examination and assessment.

This study of the latent discipline of law schools complements and is a necessary counterweight to the usual way of describing, explaining and interpreting law school experience. In most studies, such as the recent critiques of legal education by Mary Ann Glendon and Anthony Kronman,[32] the focus is on the intentions and writings of law professors. Professor Glendon and Dean Kronman have argued that the ideals of "the common law tradition" or "lawyer-statesmen" who exercise "practical wisdom" have been displaced in contemporary legal education by a commitment of the professoriate to a "theoretical analysis" of law, be this the theory of law and economics, critical legal studies or more traditional rule-oriented formalism. Glendon's and Kronman's arguments are thus based on their views of what law professors *intend to accomplish* in legal education and scholarship. This approach misses the *unin-*

---

31. See, e.g., Garth & Martin, supra note 5, and accompanying text.

32. Mary Ann Glendon, A Nation Under Lawyers: How the Crisis in the Legal Profession is Transforming American Society (1994); A.T. Kronman, supra note 2.

tended actions and *unintended effects* of actions that social institutions produce. These actions and effects are particularly important in specialized professional communities like law schools, where the intensity and conventions of work can generate powerful tacit norms. We need to examine how such norms influence what law professors in fact do and what law students in fact learn in order to obtain a better understanding of legal education and the possibilities for its reform, including reforms of the kind proposed by Glendon and Kronman.

Of course, many routines and relationships in the discipline of law schools have been established with specific intentions or have had intentions attached to them. So intentions have an explanatory role to play in analyzing the discipline. But intentions shift over time and are often contested or in conflict. Moreover, we know that substantial gaps exist between the intentions of legal educators and the effects of their actions. For example, law professors surely intend that classroom work should help students learn about the complex professional practices that are discussed and modeled in the classroom.[33] Yet in a study at three law schools, Roy Rickson discovered that students who score well on law school examinations quickly learn that they can prepare for final examinations more efficiently by studying legal treatises rather than attending classes.[34] Similarly, law professors surely intend their teaching to convey such basic skills as making distinctions between the "holdings" and "dicta" of judicial opinions, interpreting rules by reference to purposes, and interpreting statutes by paying careful attention to the words and phrases of statutes.[35] Yet David Bryden, in testing graduates from "three distinguished law schools," found that many new graduates of these schools were deficient in these basic skills.[36] Might the discipline of law schools explain these paradoxical or counter-productive results?

The first three chapters of this book examine the discipline's routine practices and their tacit effects. Chapter One analyzes the routine practices of law school in order to identify how distinctive practices such as the law school's large classes, its case method, its final examinations, conventional legal schol-

---

33. See, e.g., Mark Tushnet, *An Introduction*, to Symposium, *Academic Evaluations Focus*, 65 UMKC L. Rev. 643, 644 (1997).

34. Roy Rickson, *Faculty Control and the Structure of Student Competition: An Analysis of the Law Student Role*, 25 J. Legal Educ. 47 (1973).

35. See, e.g., Edmund M. Morgan, *The Case Method*, 4 J. Legal Educ. 379 (1952); Irwin Rutter, *Designing and Teaching the First-Degree Law Curriculum*, 37 U. Cinn. L. Rev. 7 (1968).

36. Bryden, supra note 4.

arship and the law school placement process generate powerful habits and tacit lessons that influence law school work and instruct future lawyers in particular visions of the law. Chapter Two analyses two pervasive structures of the discipline: the typical spatial and temporal relationships of law school life which tend to create or reinforce the discipline's lessons. Chapter Three then explores the more subtle and less tangible disciplinary practices such as the impersonal nature and "coolness" of law school relationships, the powerful rituals, symbols and myths that pervade law school activities, and the common or ordinary discourse of law schools. These techniques are central to the discipline's work and seem particularly impervious to change.

Chapter Four looks at the idea of reform that circulates within the discipline and the major reform movements that have emerged in law schools during the past few decades. These ideas and practices help disguise the discipline and its conservative values by presenting law schools and the law as progressive and always capable of improving by "working themselves pure." But these ideas and practices also promise change, even subversion of the discipline. Thus this chapter asks: how are the reform movements changing the discipline and how have the reforms themselves been affected by and incorporated within the discipline?

Chapter Five considers the organizational environment of the discipline. Intricate, often subtle connections exist between law schools and the American legal profession, corporate law firms, the judicial system, research universities, the State and American culture, and these connections help explain important aspects of the discipline. These other institutions have their own routine practices or disciplinary systems that intersect with the discipline of law schools. Throughout this study, but particularly in Chapter Five, we shall see that the discipline is influenced by its intersections with the competing disciplines of corporate law firms, the organized bar and the research university. For example, the placement process for law students that is shared between law schools and corporate law firms, the maintenance of bar examinations for licensing attorneys, and the American research university's interests in both productive scholarship and faculty accountability are all important to the discipline of law schools and help explain many of its functional and dysfunctional features.

Finally, Chapter Six explores the relationships between the discipline and different conceptions of ethics. The purposes of this inquiry are to assess how the discipline constructs or influences the ethical frameworks of law students, lawyers and law professors, to evaluate the discipline and its effects, to try to understand the ethical choices that persons are likely to make about the discipline, and to suggest some utopian but feasible changes that could make legal education more effective and more democratic.

We shall discover in Chapter Six that the discipline generates and rewards particular tacit conceptions of the self and ethics that help keep the discipline in place. These tacit conceptions of self and ethics support the generally conservative approach of lawyers to questions of legal ethics, legal theory and legal change, in particular by redefining ethical questions about law and legal education as mere technical questions and thus disguising the ethics of the discipline. These conceptions also help entrench a single overriding purpose for legal education, the acquisition of doctrinal knowledge and skill of doctrinal analysis, and the basic methods to accomplish this purpose, the law school's "core curriculum," its "case method," its final examination/grading/class ranking system, and the traditional institutions of legal scholarship.

From several ethical perspectives, it may be concluded that the discipline empowers lawyers in certain ways but also limits them in particular skills as well as influencing their ethical instincts, frameworks or character. The discipline provides many students in a low cost, hidden sort of way with basic skills, credentials, and a conservative ideology or style that all assist their entry into an economically successful, high status profession. The discipline also provides law professors with substantial opportunities, incentives and ideologies to pursue scholarship and consulting work as experts in legal doctrine. Thus many persons may consciously choose to embrace the discipline, or at least important aspects of it, in ways that would make significant reforms to the discipline impossible. At the same time, the discipline tends to limit the technical skills and ethical nature of American lawyers, especially by imposing a standard model of training that tends to ignore or discount three kinds of educational diversity: the diversity of intellectual methods which are important to the practice of law, the diversity of learning styles among law students, and the diversity of specific practical skills or models of lawyering that are important to different sectors of legal practice. Reforms of the discipline thus would seem to be desirable, and yet the discipline's powerful and inherent instincts for limiting and incorporating ideas of reform within itself and for its own purposes remain formidable.

There are, however, possibilities lurking within the discipline of law schools for more subversive conceptions of the self and ethics that could support substantial reforms of legal education by decentering the overriding purpose and basic methods of the discipline that promote the single model of a technical doctrinal expertise. Chapter Six sketches some tensions between the discipline and these more subversive conceptions of self and ethics, conceptions which could support more diverse, more effective, and more democratic forms of legal education. To be sure, the major effect of articulating subversive possibilities may be simply to confirm the attachment of many observers to the current form of the discipline. Moreover, such reform possibilities may just be another part of the long-standing reform tradition in American law schools, which sometimes modifies the discipline in small ways but whose main effect appears to be the pacification of discontented professors and law students.[37] In any event, as Arthur Leff once hoped, we can wish for "some beautiful innings" on the way to the likely defeat of these reform possibilities.[38] Furthermore, considering the ethics of reform is a good way to better understand the discipline of law schools and its powerful attractions.

This book in effect explains how the implicit logic of the routine practices and habits of American law schools helps produce American lawyers. The tendencies and predispositions promoted by the discipline will not affect everyone the same way, and they may be overcome by conscious effort in some or even many instances. But these tendencies and predispositions affect or regulate the behavior of persons in significant ways and they deserve careful attention. They constitute a matrix or environment, a "habitus" as Pierre Bourdieu has said,[39] which appears to condition the behavior of law students, lawyers and law professors in ways that both serve and disserve personal and social interests.[40] These tendencies and predispositions also help explain the paradoxes of American law schools. If we wish to comprehend legal education fully, we should try to understand the discipline of law schools, its tendencies and its predispositions.

---

37. See Chapter Four's discussion of the reform ideas and movements in law schools.

38. See Arthur Leff, *Law and*, 87 Yale L. J. 989, 1011 (1978).

39. See P. Bourdieu, supra note 10.

40. Cf. M. Foucault, supra note 10 (describing the functional and dysfunctional aspects of disciplinary systems in the 18th and 19th centuries in both Europe and the United States).

CHAPTER ONE

BASIC PRACTICES

The discipline of law schools incorporates a web of routine practices, expectations and relationships. This web is by no means a rigid or unchanging system. The history of law schools and contemporary practices reveal that the discipline's routines and relationships are often contested, either consciously or tacitly, and that this resistance can either alter or strengthen the discipline's practices.[1] Neither is the discipline's web seamless or perfectly coordinated. Its different sectors are "loosely coupled," which allows different practices in the web to support the expression and tacit construction of quite different ideas and images that can be unrelated or in conflict.[2] Thus, for example, both the discourse and images that are generated in law school classrooms are often substantially disconnected from the discourse and images that prevail in law school's final examinations, in legal scholarship, or even in the casebooks that constitute the basic reading for most law school classes. These disjunctions and conflicts invite our special attention for what they reveal about the complex mechanisms and tacit lessons of the discipline.

This chapter and the next two chapters examine the basic elements of the discipline in order to infer the tacit tendencies or predispositions that are generated by these elements. This chapter considers the basic expectations and routine practices that pervade legal education. Chapter Two examines the spa-

---

1. See Michel Foucault, *The Subject and Power*, in Herbert Dreyfus & Paul Rabinow, Michel Foucault: Beyond Structuralism and Hermeneutics 208, 210–12 (2d ed 1983) (Disciplinary power is exercised and revealed only at "points of resistance" where power is contested. In some cases resistance may subvert disciplinary power although typically resistance is incorporated within power and serves its goals.).

2. See John W. Meyer & Brian Rowan, *Institutionalized Organizations: Formal Structure as Myth and Ceremony*, 83 Am. J. Soc. 340 (1977) (contrasting the "loosely coupled" structures of "institutionalized organizations" whose behavior is influenced by "mythic properties" in their organizational environment with the more coordinated structures of "technical organizations" that produce goods and services in response to specific economic and technological demands).

tial and temporal contexts within which the routine practices of law school are conducted. Chapter Three looks at other pervasive but less tangible features of the disciplinary web such as the dominant style of impersonality, certain rituals and myths that are generated by law school practices, and the ordinary discourse or language of law schools. Only after we have viewed the interlocking elements of this complex system will we be in a position to understand the tacit knowledge and predispositions that the discipline is capable of inscribing in law students, lawyers and law professors.

The major practices of law school include the regular use of "casebooks" as primary reading materials, the regular use of the law school's "case method" in classroom discussions, and a very substantial reliance on end-of-the-semester final examinations to create discrete hierarchical rankings of law students, particularly during their first and second years of law school. These practices also include the practices and institutions of traditional legal scholarship, which include the publication of casebooks, treatises and law review articles that deal primarily or exclusively with appellate court opinions and student-managed law reviews as a major source of publication. The law school placement process, through which law students first seek summer employment and then permanent employment with law firms, is another major aspect of the discipline. These practices occur within a context of some powerful if often tacit expectations about law schools and legal education that both law students and law professors bring to their law school careers. These practices and expectations are the subject of this chapter.

These practices and expectations construct a number of significant tacit lessons about the nature of law and lawyers, but the most fundamental or most pervasive lesson of the discipline may be the powerful, relatively unshakeable tacit image that the law is agonistic or adversarial. The law is agonistic, *in part*, but this is certainly not what all law or lawyering is about, nor is this the message that most casebook authors or law professors intend to convey. But consider the fundamental image or message that must be conveyed by the many excerpts of appellate court opinions that are presented by casebooks and dissected in classrooms, by all the final examination questions that may be argued one way or another, by the often traumatic Moot Court experiences of first year students arguing appellate court issues against each other, and by the spacious, high-ceilinged, courtroom-like architecture of typical amphitheatre classrooms in which law students, like litigators, must make statements before professors who, like judges, may interrupt them, ask further questions, or comment critically on their statements. Surely the root idea generated by this process is that the law is argumentative, adversarial and combative.

Other more specific lessons of the discipline both flow from and support this root idea. The discipline's rhetoric of confidence, authority and closure, its basic attitude of "toughness," its ideological message of competitive individualism among lawyers, and its contradictory messages that "there is no law there" are each closely related to the constant adversarial process that is emphasized, suggested and practiced in the major routines of American law schools. The instrumentalist reading and writing habits inculcated by the discipline also come to be perceived as useful to the combat of law. The powerful image of combat also implicitly justifies a general disdain for ethics among law school inhabitants.

The discipline's basic practices contain diverse mechanisms that generate these tacit lessons, but two are especially prominent and influential. These are the dramaturgical techniques of the large case method classroom and the special intensity, gravity and gamesmanship of law school final examinations. Sometimes in obvious or explicit ways and other times in more complicated and subtle ways, these mechanisms extend their influence across the loosely coupled structures of the discipline to affect what is happening in other sectors. The dramaturgical aspects of classrooms can affect both the reading habits of law students and the writing habits of law professors. The special intensity and gamesmanship of the final examination system can affect almost everything, from law school admissions to faculty hiring, from the attention students pay to classroom work to the reading and writing habits of students and professors. Let us then begin our examination of the basic practices and expectations that constitute the discipline of law schools.

Elite and Non-Elite Law Schools

There is a basic distinction between elite and non-elite law schools that is a significant regulatory force in American legal education. This distinction, sometimes expressly and sometimes tacitly, influences the admission of students to law schools, the nature of their studies, and the appointments of new law faculty. This distinction also generally regulates behavior at both elite and non-elite law schools, albeit in somewhat different ways.

An elite law school satisfies four conditions. It is part of a prestigious research university which provides the law school with name recognition and reputation.[3] Its students must graduate from prestigious undergraduate col-

---

3. See W. Scott Van Alstyne, Jr., Joseph R. Julin & Larry D. Barnett, The Goals and Missions of Law Schools 3–9 (1990).

leges and have obtained "the top" or "best" scores on the Law School Aptitude Test (LSAT).[4] Corporate law firms must hire enough of the school's graduates so that all entering students can expect or hope to obtain prestigious or well-paid legal positions upon graduation.[5] Finally, the faculty must have exceptional credentials and engage in significant scholarship or consulting work that helps justify or legitimate the school's elite status.[6] The work of individual faculty at elite schools may involve different mixes of teaching, research, government service and private consulting, but this work must in some way help distinguish the elite school's reputation from non-elite schools.

Non-elite law schools fail to satisfy one or more of these conditions. But non-elite schools often strive to emulate elite schools. They may desire to obtain elite status or, perhaps more likely, to enhance the reputation and careers of the school, its faculty and its students. Or non-elite schools may emulate elite schools because elite school practices are taken to be the standards of excellence in legal education. In any event, this emulation occurs by trying to recruit students and faculty who have "outstanding credentials," by encouraging faculty at non-elite schools to publish reputation-enhancing scholarship, and by encouraging corporate law firms to employ the law school's graduates. Further, the dramatic expansion of large corporate firms and many law schools in recent decades has provided resources and incentives for many non-elite law schools to engage in this pursuit of excellence, this game of competition and emulation.

The precise nature of the distinction between elite and non-elite schools has changed over time, particularly with regard to differences between the work of elite and non-elite law faculties. As faculty at non-elite schools begin to emulate the work of elite faculty, a new generation of elite law school faculty tends to move towards new forms of innovative work. In general, elite faculty have been able to distinguish their work in terms of "the theory" of their teaching and scholarship and the "significance" of their scholarship and

---

4. See id. at 14–15.

5. See Robert Granfield, Making Elite Lawyers: Visions of Law at Harvard and Beyond 123–67 (1992); Frances Kahn Zemans & Victor G. Rosenblum, The Making of a Public Profession 91–122 (1981).

6. See Thomas H. Jackson, *Maintaining Quality in a Period of Recession*, in ABA, The Law School and the University: The Present and the Future 44, 46–48 (1993) (on the importance of scholarship to elite law schools); Deborah Jones Merritt & Barbara F. Reskin, *Sex, Race, and Credentialing: the Truth About Affirmative Action in Law Faculty Hiring*, 97 Colum. L. Rev. 199, 275–76 (1997) (on the importance of faculty credentials to elite schools); Van Alstyne et al., supra note 1, at 9–12 (on the importance of credentials and scholarship to elite schools).

consulting, especially public service consulting.[7] Thus, from 1870 to the 1920s, elite law faculty took the lead in implementing the case method of teaching installed at Harvard by Dean Langdell and in writing systematic treatises that attempted to organize, describe and rationalize law in a comprehensive manner.[8] Between the world wars Legal Realism emerged at Columbia and Yale to contest the prior era's commitment to doctrinal formalism in teaching and scholarship: in teaching, by trying to bring social contexts to the study of appellate cases, and in scholarship by emphasizing judicial indeterminacy and trying to explain what courts in fact do instead of focusing on doctrinal justifications for judicial decisions.[9] As realism was assimilated and dispersed throughout law schools, the theory of legal process, which emphasizes the principles, procedures and craft of judicial decision-making, surfaced after World War II to infuse teaching and scholarship at elite schools.[10] Then, as legal process became absorbed in routine practices, elite law faculty in recent decades have become the leaders in bringing systematic interdisciplinary work and the more overtly political work of critical legal studies, feminist jurisprudence and critical race theory into legal education.[11] These historical distinctions between faculty work at elite schools and non-elite schools have generated certain norms of "theory" and "significant scholarship" which, as we shall see, impose powerful regulatory though often tacit imperatives on law school practices and law school ethics.

Today, when a person applies to law school, she is confronted immediately by the distinction between elite and non-elite schools and by finer distinctions created by the discrete hierarchical rankings of individual schools. Many

---

7. See, e.g., Anthony T. Kronman, The Lost Lawyer: Failing Ideals of the Legal Profession 165–270 (describing elite law schools as theory-driven since the late nineteenth century, from Dean Christopher Columbus Langdell's theory about "legal science" which he implemented at Harvard Law School to the influential contemporary theories of law and economics and critical legal studies); Robert Stevens, Law School: Legal Education from the 1850s to the 1980s (1983) (describing the influence of Harvard on the development of American law schools).

8. See, e.g., R. Stevens, supra note 7, at 35–130; John Henry Schlegel, *Between the Harvard Founders and the American Legal Realists: The Professionalization of the American Law Professor*, 35 J. Legal Educ. 311 (1985).

9. See Laura Kalman, Legal Realism at Yale, 1927–1960 (1986); John Henry Schlegel, American Legal Realism and Empirical Social Science (1995); Brainerd Currie, *The Materials of Law Study, Parts I, II and III*, 3 J. Legal Educ. 331 (1951); 8 J. Legal Educ. 1 (1955).

10. See R. Stevens, supra note 7, at 271; G. Edward White, *The Evolution of Reasoned Elaboration: Jurisprudential Criticism and Social Change*, 59 Va. L. Rev. 279 (1973).

11. See R. Stevens, supra note 7, at 271–76; Chapter Four's discussion of the academic/political movements in contemporary legal education.

prospective law students consult and rely heavily on the ranking of law schools that has been published annually since 1987 by the *U.S. News & World Report*.[12] Prospective students then compete for acceptance by the most highly ranked schools largely on the basis of their undergraduate grades and LSAT scores. Law schools, of course, have ample incentives to compete for students with the highest undergraduate grades and LSAT scores in order to improve or maintain their annual ranking. These competitions surely create an atmosphere of powerful expectations, tacit or otherwise, that law school examinations and grades should be of the greatest if not exclusive importance in law school. If examinations and grades have been the basis of a student's (and school's) success, they will seem an excellent basis for future success as well.[13] Furthermore, the students and alumni at elite schools will expect their schools to maintain the practices that have made them elite, and students or alumni at non-elite schools may hold to similar expectations or promises that their schools will pursue elite school practices as a mark of quality.

The elite/non-elite distinction influences law faculty more directly as well. Teaching appointments are often sought in part on the basis of the hierarchical standing of law schools.[14] The appointments of new faculty are based heavily on applicants' grades and law review work at elite schools and their judicial clerking experience or work at prestigious law firms,[15] experience and work which typically result from excellent academic records at elite schools. The faculty at elite law schools must strive to maintain their exceptional credentials and "theoretical edge" by engaging in significant or innovative scholarship and important government consulting work. These commitments ensure intellectual excitement and a sense of dynamism in law schools and may

---

12. See Russell Korobkin, *In Praise of Law School Rankings: Solutions to Coordination and Collective Action Problems*, 77 Tex. L. Rev. 403 (1998); Frank Read, *Legal Education's Holy War over Regulation of Consumer Information: The Federal Trump Card*, 30 Wake For. L. Rev. 307, 307–08 (1995).

13. These expectations about examinations and grades are reinforced, of course, as law students discover that legal employers place great weight on the reputation of law schools and the relative grades or class ranks of individual law students.

14. See, e.g., Mark Tushnet, *Legal Scholarship: Its Causes and Cure*, 90 Yale L. J. 1205, 1207 n. 13 (1981) (discussing the circulation of faculty members among law schools and noting "I suspect…that faculty circulate within each stratum and that the most elite schools accept faculty members from the less elite schools, but faculty from the more elite schools do not move to the less elite schools").

15. See Robert J. Borthwick & Jordan R. Schau, *Gatekeepers of the Profession: An Empirical Profile of the Nation's Law Professors*, 25 U. Mich. J. Law Reform 191 (1991); Donna Fossum, *Law Professors: A Profile of the Teaching Branch of the Profession*, 1980 Am. Bar F. Res. J. 501, 513–18.

contribute much to improving or maintaining the coherence of American law.[16] But these commitments also may incline elite law schools to emphasize credentials more than performance or promise in appointing new faculty,[17] and they surely limit the time and motivations that elite law professors have to engage in extensive or innovative teaching activities that would limit their pursuit of prestigious scholarship and consulting work.[18] Meanwhile non-elite schools follow similar practices by hiring elite law school graduates as faculty, by maintaining a curriculum, teaching methods, final examinations and student-managed law reviews that replicate the practices at elite schools, and by encouraging their faculty to publish scholarship that enhances the school's reputation.[19] Thus the hierarchical distinctions between law schools and related expectations pressure all law schools to maintain their traditional conventional practices that ground and reproduce the discipline of law schools.

Professional Expectations

Law students famously enter law schools with only limited knowledge about the nature of legal practices.[20] They often bring with them ideas or attitudes that the law consists of "clear rules,"[21] and that good teachers should exercise a "professorial sovereignty" that provides orderly, clear and entertaining class discussions, absolute truths, and "fair" or "objective" evaluations.[22] Most law students are also young adults concerned about establishing their personal and

---

16. See Bryant G. Garth & Joanne Martin, *Law Schools and the Construction of Competence*, 43 J. Legal Educ. 469 (1993).

17. See Derrick Bell, Jr., Confronting Authority 44–45, 76–80 (1994); cf. Merritt & Reskin, supra note 6, at 275–76 (noting the importance of faculty credentials in the hiring of new faculty by elite law schools).

18. See, e.g., John S. Elson, *The Case Against Legal Scholarship or, If the Professor Must Publish, Must the Profession Perish?*, 39 J. Legal Educ. 343, 370–71 (1989); Marin R. Scordato, *The Dualist Model of Legal Teaching and Scholarship*, 40 Am. U. L. Rev. 367, 369–70 (1990).

19. See, e.g., Philip C. Kissam, *The Decline of Law School Professionalism*, 134 U. Pa. L. Rev. 251, 263–276 (1986).

20. See Olavi Maru, Research on the Legal Profession: A Review of Work Done 34–35 (2d ed. 1986); Zemans & Rosenblum, supra note 5, at 28.

21. See, e.g., John Henry Schlegel, *Searching for Archimedes—Legal Education, Legal Scholarship, and Liberal Ideology*, 34 J. Legal Educ. 103, 108 (1984).

22. See Mary Schmelzer, *Panopticism and Postmodern Pedagogy*, in Foucault and the Critique of Institutions 127, 129–33 (J. Caputo & M. Yount eds. 1993) (describing such expectations among undergraduate students).

professional identities,[23] and as such they may be particularly susceptible to symbolic assurances and role models about how they should conduct themselves as lawyers.[24] In these circumstances, many if not most students may expect that the primary if not only goal of law school is to obtain a rewarding job by earning high grades on examinations, and this expectation will be reinforced by the substantial emphasis that is placed on examinations, grades and obtaining legal employment during their years in law school.[25] Many students may also expect law professors to model the lawyering process. Moreover, pre-law school attachments to the notion that the law consists only of objective or formal rules can subject law students to two kinds of psychological deformation. On the one hand, an obsession with mastering the objective legal authorities that one uses on final examinations may generate in some formalists an excessive attachment to "the rules" and the associated idea that the rules can be applied "objectively" to generate all or most legal answers. On the other hand, if formalists become disillusioned with the objectivity of rules through their class discussions, casebook readings, the many contradictory messages about law, or disappointing results on their examinations, they may overreact in the other direction and become enamored with the idea that law is nothing but subjective, relativistic politics. The expectations of law students, then, are a fertile source of tacit disciplinary lessons.

The professional expectations of law professors are also significant for the discipline. New law professors quickly become aware that they must produce some kind of acceptable scholarship in their first years in order to acquire tenure.[26] More gradually they will become aware of the "implicit contract" that American research universities offer to their faculty: in exchange for teaching a small amount of time, you are funded to pursue research and scholarship.[27] Yet most law professors have nothing like the graduate training of PhDs to orient them towards teaching or scholarship, and their expectations about how to teach or do scholarship will surely be influenced by their experiences as "the best" students at elite law schools, as judicial clerks at prestigious appellate courts, and as young associates working in corporate

---

23. See Alan Stone, *Legal Education on the Couch*, 85 Harv. L. Rev. 392 (1971).

24. See Robert Redmount, *A Clinical View of Law Teaching*, 48 So. Cal. L. Rev. 705, 706 (1975).

25. See the discussions of law school examinations and the placement process in this chapter and Chapter Five's discussion of corporate law firms.

26. See, e.g., Robert H. Abrams, *Sing Muse: Legal Scholarship for New Law Teachers*, 37 J. Legal Educ. 1 (1987).

27. See Christopher Jencks & David Riesman, The Academic Revolution (1968).

law firms. These experiences, attitudes and instincts are likely to create tacit presumptions that the traditional practices of elite law schools, appellate courts and the work of young lawyers in corporate firms represent the standards of excellence for law teaching and legal scholarship. Since these practices emphasize the analysis of appellate court opinions, the expectations of professors, like those of students, tend to reproduce the routine practices of the discipline.

The Core Curriculum

Most law schools provide the same basic curriculum, which is not unlike the curriculum installed by Dean Langdell at Harvard in the late nineteenth century. First year students are required to take Contracts, Property, Torts, and Civil Procedure: three courses about different ways in which law protects property rights and a fourth that specifies rules of procedural justice. Criminal Law and Constitutional Law are usually required subjects although these subjects may often be taken in a later year. In the second and third years there are few or no requirements, but most students take "a recommended curriculum" which consists of business law and procedural law courses. These courses include Corporations, Federal Tax Law, the Uniform Commercial Code, Wills and Trusts, Evidence and Administrative Law.[28] First year students are also required to take a legal research and writing course and to practice making appellate arguments in a Moot Court program, although these exercises are different enough to warrant separate discussions.[29]

This core curriculum conveys several tacit messages. First, each course is designed to survey the basic rules of a specific field, and each course stands alone with little or no relationship to others.[30] This structure signals that useful law can be found in separate compartments and that one need only consult the

---

28. See, e.g., E. Gordon Gee & Donald Jackson, Following the Leader? The Unexamined Consensus in Law School Curricula (1975); cf. Comments of Roger Cramton, Proceedings of the Fifty-Third Judicial Conference of the District of Columbia Circuit, 145 F.R.D. 149, 211 (1992) ("The truth is that legal education is much the same as it was fifty years ago.").

29. See the discussion of Moot Court, under Courtrooms and Clinics in Chapter Two, and the discussion of legal writing programs in Chapter Four.

30. See Martin Horwitz, *Are Law Schools Fifty Years Out of Date?*, 54 UMKC L. Rev. 387, 398 (1986); Kristine Strachan, *Curricular Reform in the Second and Third Years: Structure, Progression, and Integration*, 39 J. Legal Educ. 523 (1989).

right compartment and right rule within the compartment to resolve legal disputes. In other words, situations must be *analyzed* or broken down until each element or "issue" can be matched to an appropriate rule from an appropriate compartment. The structure of the core curriculum thus suggests an image of law as sets of discrete rules that are embedded in a horizon of infinitely expanding compartments of rules, and that the basic legal method is some kind of analysis of the rules and facts to find an appropriate matchup. The core curriculum begins to promote the discipline's tacit lesson of analysis.

Second, as Duncan Kennedy says, the structure of the core curriculum focuses attention on the "hard courses" of "private law" that involve property rights and business organizations, while public law, family law, clinical education and interdisciplinary studies are consigned to the periphery of the curriculum as "soft subjects."[31] This structure greets law students in their first year, when they are most open to learning, with the implicit message that the protection of property rights is (and should be) the focus of legal practice and that economic individualism is (and should be) the basic justifying ethic of American law. The core curriculum, without explicit discussion, thus teaches that claims of property rights by persons or organizations are "natural" or privileged over any competing claims of unfairness or social good that are made about economic transactions, negligence law or substantive and procedural challenges to government regulations. Of course, in the intentional discourse of classrooms and legal scholarship, many arguments are made for different approaches to property rights, personal rights and organizations, but the discipline of law schools tacitly favors the arguments for property rights.[32]

Third, the core curriculum signals a sharp dichotomy between procedural law and substantive law. This division conveys the tacit message that procedural justice is sufficient to legitimate legal rules and that law in some important sense can be "neutral," "objective," and "nonpolitical." If procedural rules of fair play can be separated from substantive outcomes, as this division suggests, the law will appear to guaranty a nonpolitical resolution of disputes as long as substantive doctrines are applied in accordance with procedural rules.

---

31. See Duncan Kennedy, *The Political Significance of the Structure of the Law School Curriculum*, 14 Seton Hall L. Rev. 1 (1983).

32. See, e.g., James Boyle, *The Anatomy of a Torts Class*, 34 Am. U. L. Rev. 1003, 1023–34 (1985); Kennedy, supra note 31; Karl Klare, *The Law School Curriculum in the 1980s: What's Left?*, 32 J. Legal Educ. 336, 337–39 (1982). Cf. Meir Dan-Cohen, *Bureaucratic Organizations and the Theory of Adjudication*, 85 Colum. L. Rev. 1 (1985) (arguing that American law is wrong in its failure to distinguish between organizations and persons as different kinds of legal parties).

In this view, the rules of law are like the rules of games and one doesn't need to question the justice of outcomes. While one can argue that such procedural justice is the best sort of legal justice one may hope for, this is a contested question of legal theory.[33] But the core curriculum tacitly endorses one side in this debate: fair procedures are enough. The tacit endorsement of procedural justice also may play a significant role in sustaining the pervasive moral skepticism and moral relativism of law schools;[34] this endorsement permits the consideration of substantive rules to be limited to their uses, which are often quite manipulative, without any consideration given to their rightness or wrongness.

Finally, the core curriculum signals that there are "absolute truths" about law and a certain "professorial sovereignty" in the revelation of these truths. The requirements and expectations that all students study the same subjects in the first year or two years imply a certainty about values, truth, and how truth should be found.[35] Moreover, since the faculty is responsible for the curriculum which promises these absolute truths, at least initially law students may hold to a tacit presumption that their professors are or should be the ultimate arbiters, or sovereigns, of truth about the law.[36] To be sure, the intentional discourse of law schools may cause many students to modify or drop such beliefs, but the existence of the core curriculum tacitly favors these ideas, and these ideas help generate the special authority of law professors in the classroom and in grading the final examinations of their students.

The core curriculum has regularly been subject to challenges, alterations, and evasion or resistance. Most criticisms and proposed alternatives have tended to fall on deaf ears. The more subtle kinds of resistance to the core curriculum also get ignored or papered over, due apparently to the inherent attractions of the curriculum as a vehicle for other basic elements of the discipline, especially the case method of teaching, final examinations, and conventional legal scholarship.

---

33. Compare H.L.A. Hart, The Concept of Law (1961) with Ronald Dworkin, Taking Rights Seriously (1977).

34. See Roger Cramton, *The Ordinary Religion of the Law School Classroom*, 29 J. Legal Educ. 247 (1978).

35. Cf. Joseph F. Wall, *How the Grinnell Curriculum Runs the Course*, The Grinnell Magazine, Fall 1997, p. 2 (the "traditional classical education" in mid-nineteenth century American colleges was "an education designed by an age that knew what its values were, what truth was, and precisely where that truth could be found").

36. Cf. Schmelzer, supra note 22 (describing the expectations of "professorial sovereignty" among undergraduate students).

At least since the 1920s law professors and students have vigorously criticized the core curriculum's lack of relationship and progression, its lack of close connections to law practices, its autonomy from the social sciences, its emphasis on private law subjects and its repetitive or boring qualities.[37] Significantly, the Legal Realists at the Columbia and Yale Law Schools in the 1920s and 1930s criticized the Langdellian curriculum for its organization on the basis of rules rather than the factual situations that lawyers and clients regularly experience, its lack of close connections to lawyers' work, and its failure to use the social sciences to investigate and understand the contexts of lawyers' work. The Realists fashioned something of an alternative "functional curriculum" that was to be organized by different practice contexts and connected with the social sciences. These criticisms and changes were rejected or ignored by most law schools and law professors, often in a quite cursory manner, and ultimately Columbia and Yale abandoned their experiments, leaving but minor modifications to the core curriculum. The justifications for this rejection and abandonment may seem reasonable, if cursory, but the best explanation for the failure of the new curriculum may lie with its failure to incorporate fully the traditional case method and final examination techniques of law professors.[38] Bringing clinical and social science methods to the study of law, in other words, frustrated the special expertise and power of law professors. In the functional curriculum, law professors were less able to perform brilliantly before large classes by analyzing appellate court opinions[39] or to administer a "fair" and "objective" examination system that distributed many different grades to ambitious law students without producing embarrassing questions or other difficulties of grading.[40]

Today, both students and professors continue to resist the core curriculum in subtle, muted fashions. Students manifest resistance by spending much time working as law clerks or legal interns with private firms and public agencies,[41] by asking for more clinical work and simulated clinical courses, especially trial advocacy,[42] and by choosing to study law in interdisciplinary per-

---

37. See, e.g., L. Kalman, supra note 9; Currie, supra note 9; Kennedy, supra note 31; Strachan, supra note 30.

38. See L. Kalman, supra note 9; Currie, supra note 9.

39. See the discussion of the case method later in this chapter.

40. See the discussion of law school examinations later in this chapter.

41. See Ronald Pipkin, *Moonlighting in Law School: A Multischool Study of Part-Time Employment of Full-Time Law Students*, 1982 Am. Bar Found. Res. J. 1109.

42. See, e.g., *Report of the Committee on the Future of the In-House Clinic*, 42 J. Legal Educ. 508, 529–36 (1992).

spectives such as those of economics, history, moral theory or literature.[43] These forms of resistance may be viewed as intuitive searches for more effective forms of education that would add both practice-oriented and theoretical dimensions to the core curriculum's focus upon rules. At the same time, however, these forms of resistance reinforce the discipline in significant ways.

Law students who work on a part-time basis for law firms often engage in much routine, unsupervised work, and such work can reinforce the core curriculum's message that the solution of legal problems is based on matching facts to the right rules in the right legal compartments. Law school clinics, especially because of their limited resources, may involve similar routine, relatively unsupervised work that reinforces this message.[44] Less directly, the devotion of substantial time to outside work or clinical courses may cause many students to adopt blunt instrumentalist views to help them complete the core curriculum with minimum effort. These students are likely to concentrate on preparing for examinations, focusing on the knowledge of compartmentalized rules that they must match to the facts given on their final examinations.[45]

The new theoretical courses and seminars on such subjects as "law and literature" and "economic analysis of law" have serious intellectual purposes, to be sure. But these courses may provide many law students with little more than a dalliance between the "rigorous" or "hard" work of the core curriculum and their similar hard work in law firms.[46] These courses serve the discipline by giving disaffected, intellectually curious students safety valves to express their discon-

---

43. See, e.g., Cynthia L. Cooper, The Insider's Guide to the Top Fifteen law Schools (1990) (describing upper class curriculum offerings at 15 elite law schools); Harry Edwards, *The Growing Disjunction Between Legal Education and the Legal Profession*, 91 Michigan L. Rev. 34 (1992) (complaining that elite law schools are providing too much "theoretical education" to contemporary law students); Eleanor Fox, *The Good Law School, The Good Curriculum, and the Mind and the Heart*, 39 J. Legal Educ. 473, 476–81 (1989) (describing recent curriculum changes in American law schools); William Rothfield, "What Do Law Schools Teach? Almost Anything," NY Times, Dec. 23, 1988, p. 21 (describing the new "theoretical" law school seminars); Robert Weisberg, *Some Ways to Think About Law Reviews*, 47 Stan. L. Rev. 1147, 1154–56 (1995) (describing law school responses to the interdisciplinary interests of contemporary law students).

44. Cf. Robert Condlin, *Socrates' New Clothes: Substituting Persuasion for Learning in Clinical Practice Instruction*, 40 Md. L. Rev. 223 (1981) (arguing that many clinics are excessively oriented towards adversarial and doctrinal solutions to legal problems and thus inadequate in providing effective education in the types of practical knowledge involved in representing clients).

45. See the discussion of law school examinations later in this chapter.

46. See Weisberg, supra note 43, at 1154–56; Robin West, *The Literary Lawyer*, 27 Pac. L. J. 1187, 1191 (1996).

tents. Many such courses may also serve the discipline by celebrating or legitimating the law as it is rather than subversively questioning the law's premises by juxtaposing law with ideas and methods drawn from other academic disciplines.[47]

Several kinds of faculty resistance to the core curriculum also support the discipline of law schools. There are the recurring faculty debates about the curriculum that rarely produce anything but incremental changes.[48] These debates allow disaffected and discontented faculty members to air grievances about how law is taught, and they provide others with a useful platform to argue for the status quo based on "the need" to prepare students for bar examinations and their initial practices. These debates tacitly impose the idea that "faculty consensus" is necessary to produce even modest or incremental changes.[49] Such debates are an economical, ritualistic means of reinforcing the tacit disciplinary lessons of rule coverage, case method analysis and the priority of property rights while providing a safety valve for the disaffected. The debates themselves represent a kind of procedural justice, and in the periods between debates the most recent consensus can be used by administrators, committees and individual faculty members to help shape other, often more significant, curriculum decisions such as those involved in hiring new faculty.

Resistance to the discipline is also manifest in the recent efforts by particular schools to change the first year curriculum. Such efforts have consisted of three basic kinds: adding one or more "theory" courses to provide intellectual perspectives or diversity in the first year; combining subjects like torts and contracts to contest the compartmentalism of the core curriculum; and inserting clinical components into the first year.[50] These changes, while supplementing the core curriculum with good ideas, have left the structure of the core untouched. They seem likely to reinforce disciplinary lessons by helping teach the core subjects more effectively or, ironically, by causing new frustrations for those students who fail to appreciate the innovations and be-

---

47. See Robert Weisberg, *The Law-Literature Enterprise*, 1 Yale J. L. & Human. 1 (1988).

48. See, e.g., Robert Gorman, *Introduction* to *Curriculum Developments: A Symposium*, 39 J. Legal Educ. 469 (1989).

49. See, e.g., Curtis Berger, *A Pathway to Curricular Reform*, 39 J. Legal Educ. 547 (1989).

50. On adding theory courses, see, e.g., Berger, supra note 49; on combining first year courses, see Jay Feinman & Mark Feldman, *Pedagogy and Politics*, 73 Geo. L. J. 875 (1985); Todd Rakoff, *The Harvard First-Year Experiment*, 39 J. Legal Educ. 491 (1989); on adding clinical components, see, e.g., Paul Brest, *A First-Year Course in the "Lawyering Process"*, 32 J. Legal Educ. 344 (1982).

come even more strongly attached to traditional aspects of the core curriculum.[51]

The most significant faculty resistance to the core curriculum may be the flight of many experienced law professors from committing time or concern to teaching core courses. Law professors today appear to be primarily devoted to their scholarship, consulting work, or teaching doctrinal or theoretical specialties in upper class elective courses.[52] This flight from the core has several consequences for the discipline. If administrators have difficulty assigning experienced professors to teach core courses, they must turn to younger faculty and part-time faculty who are likely to replicate the disciplinary practices of casebooks, the case method and examinations, simply because this is what they know and have experienced. The flight from the core also promises more lecturing in large doctrinal courses and an increased use of objective, machine scored final examination questions to provide faculty with more time for other work.[53] Lecturing and multiple-choice examination questions are likely to enhance the core curriculum's tacit messages of analysis and rule coverage, for the analysis of judicial opinions and discussion of rules allow lectures to be constructed quickly and provide a sound basis for examination questions. In sum, the core curriculum's structure and major forms of resistance to the curriculum promote the tacit disciplinary lessons of rule coverage, analysis, property rights and procedural justice.

Casebooks

The primary texts in most core law school courses are "casebooks." These are large heavy books that are bound in serious, somber colors, blue, black or deep red, and carry serious, somber titles such as "Contracts Law: Cases and Materials" or "Federal Income Taxation." These books contain excerpts of appellate court opinions together with questions, notes and hypothetical problems related to the opinions, and they typically organize a field of legal princi-

---

51. See Jeremy Paul, *A Bedtime Story*, 74 Va. L. Rev. 915, 916–20 (1988) (describing frustrations that many students experience in innovative "legal methods" courses).

52. See, e.g., Richard Abel, American Lawyers 172–75 (1989); Terrance Sandalow, *The Moral Responsibility of Law Schools*, 34 J. Legal Educ. 163, 165 (1984).

53. There has been an increasing use of short answer and multiple-choice questions in law school examinations. See, e.g., Steven Nickles, *Examining and Grading in American Law Schools*, 30 Ark. L. Rev. 411, 434, 447–51 (1977).

ples and rules by categories that reflect the "major rules" or "leading cases" of the field.[54] Modern casebooks cover such a multiplicity of rules that they often present but one opinion to represent each major issue and indicate little apparent relationship between the rules.[55] Moreover, despite their many notes and questions, casebooks are notorious for providing little information about the doctrinal, social and historical contexts of judicial decisions that would help a reader understand, evaluate and criticize the excerpts of judicial opinions which constitute most of casebook reading.[56] The structure of casebooks makes it difficult to understand opinions as comprehensible narratives, as comprehensible parts of larger coherent doctrinal or social contexts, or as useful subjects for the development of legal arguments, counter-arguments and criticism.

Casebooks present complex information in highly fragmented and relatively isolated forms, and many students initially at least are overwhelmed and bewildered by these books.[57] Consider, for example, how three constitutional law casebooks present the issue of whether the right to free exercise of religion includes exemptions from state regulations that have no anti-religious purpose but adversely affect religious practices. In 23 pages (which is presumably a single day's assignment), Gunther and Sullivan's *Constitutional Law*[58] presents excerpts of the Court's majority opinions, concurring opinions and dissenting opinions in two principal cases,[59] summaries of 14 other cases that quote extensively from the opinions in these cases, two paragraphs of explanation, and a long paragraph of questions. There is also a substantial note in

---

54. See, e.g., Christopher Stone, *Towards a Theory of Constitutional Law Casebooks*, 41 So. Cal. L. Rev. 1 (1967).

55. See Duncan Kennedy, *Legal Education and the Reproduction of Hierarchy*, 32 J. Legal Educ. 591, 596 (1982).

56. See M.H. Hoeflich, *On Reading Cases: The Law Student in Wonderland*, 42 Syracuse L. Rev. 1163 (1991); John Makdisi, *Problems with the Structure of Casebooks and Instruction*, 40 Clev. St. L. Rev. 437 (1992).

57. See, e.g., Elizabeth Fajans & Mary R. Falk, *Against the Tyranny of the Paraphrase: Talking Back to Texts*, 78 Corn. L. Rev. 163, 163–170 (1993); Phillip Meyer, *Confessions of a Legal Writing Instructor*, 46 J. Legal Educ. 27, 29–31 (1996).

58. Gerald Gunther & Kathleen M. Sullivan, Constitutional Law 1477–1500 (13th ed. 1997).

59. Sherbert v. Verner, 374 U.S. 398 (1963) (holding that exemptions must be granted if the regulation burdens a person's religion and if there is no "compelling state interest" in enforcing the regulation against such persons); Employment Division, Dept. of Human Resources v. Smith, 494 U.S. 872 (1990) (limiting Sherbert v. Verner to the instance of unemployment compensation and holding, with this and one other exception for religious schooling, that states may enforce "religiously neutral" regulations that have "incidental effects" upon religious practices).

small type that summarizes five different perspectives on the leading case, *Employment Division v. Smith*,[60] and has more paragraphs of questions than paragraphs of statements about these perspectives. Rotunda's *Modern Constitutional Law*[61] uses 30 pages of larger type to present excerpts of the majority, concurring and dissenting opinions in six major cases, complex notes which summarize 15 other cases, and two paragraphs of questions about this material. Stone, Seidman, Sunstein and Tushnet's *Constitutional Law*[62] uses 22 pages to present summaries of four major cases, a note that describes other decisions pertaining to five different contexts, excerpts from *Employment Division v. Smith*, and a note asking questions about six different perspectives on the *Smith* case.

What is a beginning student to do when faced with such fragmented, decontextualized texts? Three options recommend themselves. She can read casebooks to extract what she needs or believes she will need for class discussions. She can read casebooks to extract what she needs or believes she will need for final examinations. Or she can turn to treatises, student hornbooks and "commercial outlines" to supplement or substitute for reading casebooks. Each option is likely to encourage an analytical, instrumentalist way of reading to obtain "the rules" of at least "the major" cases, for it is these rules that will seem most available and desirable to a bewildered, disoriented law student or to one who is simply pressed for time.[63] Understanding "the rules" will appear to be a rational means of preparing for class discussions and especially for examinations, where students need a grasp of many legal rules and case holdings in order to identify issues and apply such law quickly to novel situations.[64] This *instrumentalist reading* as a routine will focus students on a certain *analysis* of texts to discover the rules, but it ignores and tacitly discounts other ways of reading that would seek to ascertain the contexts of judicial decisions, solve underlying legal problems, interpret or synthesize complicated legal authori-

---

60. 494 U.S. 872 (1990) (described in note 59 supra).

61. Ronald D. Rotunda, Modern Constitutional Law: Cases and Notes 1381–1411 (6th ed. 2000).

62. Geoffrey R. Stone, Louis M. Seidman, Cass R. Sunstein & Mark V. Tushnet, Constitutional Law 1590–1612 (1996).

63. See Fajans & Falk, supra note 57 (describing the reading of judicial opinions by upper class law students as largely limited to "paraphrasing" the texts); cf. Leslie Bender, *Hidden Messages in the Required First-Year Law School Curriculum*, 40 Clev. St. L. Rev. 387, 392 (1992) (noting the hidden message in the law school curriculum of "fixed doctrinal categories and rules" that captures law students' attention and diverts them from other lessons of skills, method and theory).

64. See Philip C. Kissam, *Law School Examinations*, 42 Vand. L. Rev. 433 (1989).

ties, or use judicial texts to construct complex arguments.[65] To be sure, students may discover that successful work in classrooms or examinations requires these latter sorts of readings.[66] But the structure of casebooks erects tacit barriers to this discovery. This structure also encourages the discipline's lessons of analysis and a limited instrumentalist reading that observers of the reading process both in and outside law schools have labeled "inspectional" or "paraphrase" reading.[67]

The structure of casebooks promotes other tacit lessons as well. The organization of casebooks by rules reinforces the promise of the core curriculum that the law's compartments provide rules to resolve virtually every dispute, thus tacitly limiting the need to attend to complex arguments or interdisciplinary work The presence of fragmented, decontextualized excerpts of judicial opinions surely implies a need to defer to authority, whether this be found in judicial opinions or supplemental texts or the talk of law professors. The organization, fragmentation and decontextualization of casebooks also focus the attention of readers on concrete rights that are claimed by individuals or organizations as opposed to more general or abstract notions of public policy and social rights, thereby reinforcing the core curriculum's tacit privileging of property rights over competing values.

Casebooks also establish a basis for the discipline's contradictory messages about the nature and purposes of law. On the one hand, the casebook's organization by rules promises that the rules count, or at least that rules must figure heavily in the disposition of legal disputes. On the other hand, casebook questions and notes often raise brief, skeptical and fundamentally acontextual questions about the justification of a decision, the coherence of the case's rule with other rules or the coherence of an opinion's rationale, leaving readers to ponder or wonder whether there is any law of consequence to guide attorneys and judges. For example, on the issue whether the free exercise of religion requires exemptions from state regulations that have adverse effects

---

65. Cf. Richard Markovits, *The Professional Assessment of Legal Academics: On the Shift from Evaluator Judgment to Market Evaluations*, 48 J. Legal Educ. 417, 418–27 (1998) (suggesting that law students are often more interested in learning "legal conclusions" than in making complex legal arguments).

66. Cf. A. T. Kronman, supra note 7, at 109–62 (describing the ideal goals of the case method of law teaching as including these more complex behaviors).

67. See Mortimer Adler & Charles Van Doren, How To Read a Book (2d ed. 1976) (contrasting "inspectional reading" which scans texts quickly and preliminarily to search for frameworks or major themes in a text with more complex and richer "analytical," "synoptic" and "imaginative" readings); Fajans & Falk, supra note 57 (describing typical reading by law students as "the paraphrasing of texts").

on religious practices, consider the questions that Professors Gunther and Sullivan ask about just one of their five perspectives on *Employment Division v. Smith*, the leading case which held that such exemptions are generally not required:

> "Mainstream sects are likely to be able to obtain many exemptions through the political process. [two examples are given]....But are members of minority faiths similarly able to protect their religious practices through the political process? Should the Court presume minority religionists, like racial minorities and political dissenters, in need of judicial protection from majority prejudice? Justices Scalia and O'Connor answered this question quite differently in Smith. [short quotations from the two justices follow] Which of these views is more persuasive? Which one is borne out by the passage of [the Religious Freedom Restoration Act of 1993], below?
> Should religious exemptions be required to compensate for a structural disadvantage the religious suffer in politics—namely, that the establishment clause disables them from using religious arguments as a basis for legislation? [This question is followed by citations to seven scholars taking differing positions on the appropriate role of religious argument in public discourse and whether the establishment clause silences such arguments.]
> Consider the following observations on this issue by Justice Scalia. [There follows a lengthy quotation from an earlier dissenting opinion by Justice Scalia in which he defended the right of legislators to act upon their religious convictions.]"[68]

These questions are insightful about the Supreme Court's decision in *Employment Division v. Smith*. But the point here is that these kinds of questions, which are raised as only a small part of a complex reading assignment, are likely to create the tacit impression in many readers that there cannot be any guiding law on this subject, for one seemingly could easily go one way or the other. This impression, of course, will contradict the competing impression of binding legal rules that is generated by the basic organization of both the core curriculum and casebooks.

The resistance to casebooks illustrates the power of their tacit lessons over law school inhabitants. The original Langdellian casebooks in the late nineteenth century presented judicial opinions without introductory textual notes,

---

68. Gunther & Sullivan, supra note 58, at 1497–98.

questions or other materials to explain or criticize the opinions. Legal Realists in the 1920s, 1930s and 1940s attempted to reorganize casebooks by factual situations that are experienced in practice rather than by rules, and they tried to integrate legal doctrine with the social sciences.[69] These innovations were never widely accepted, although the Realist challenge did result in adding notes, questions and problems to casebooks and their renaming as "Cases and Materials."[70] More recently, the law and economics movement has inserted expositions about economics into many casebooks, especially those concerned with contracts, torts and economic regulation.[71] But even these books are usually organized by legal principles or rules, and one's sense is that these casebooks still encourage many readers to give precedence to the doctrine of rules over the integration of legal doctrine and economic analysis.[72]

The power of casebooks is also manifest in less formal sorts of resistance. One tendency, already noted, is to limit the reading of casebooks to "inspectional" or "paraphrase" reading that excludes the richer readings of opinions that may be intended by casebook authors or professors who assign the casebooks. Another form of resistance is not to read casebooks at all, but instead to read supplemental rule-oriented texts or take voluminous, perhaps verbatim notes of classroom discussions in order "to read the professor" in lieu of the casebook.[73] Yet another tendency is for professors to lecture about cases and rules in their classrooms, either directly or by answering their own questions, thus implicitly substituting their own reading of the law for student reading of casebooks.[74] These forms of resistance, of course, reinforce the dis-

---

69. See L. Kalman, supra note 9, at 46–97, 150–53; Currie, supra note 9.

70. See L. Kalman, supra note 9, at 95, 150–153.

71. See, e.g., Grady's Cases and Materials on Torts (1994); Posner and Easterbrook's Cases and Economic Notes on Antitrust, Second Edition (1981); Robert E. Scott & Douglas L. Leslie, Contract Law and Theory, Second Edition (1993).

72. See, e.g., the casebooks cited in note 71 supra. When law and economics casebooks succeed in displacing "the analysis of rules" with a thoroughgoing economic perspective, they still may reinforce the discipline of law schools by providing a substitute form of authority and analysis that parallels the authority of law professors and the discipline's analytic method. See Chapter Four's discussion of law and economics.

73. See, e.g., Cooper, supra note 43, at 21 (advising law students to "write down everything that is said in class" as a technique to prepare for final examinations). The modern availability of laptop computers has, of course, dramatically increased the possibility of taking voluminous or verbatim notes of classroom discussions.

74. The empirical studies of discourse in modern law school classrooms suggest that law professors do most of the talking, and some observers characterize much of this talk as "lecturing." See Thomas Shaffer & Robert Redmount, Lawyers, Law Students and People 162–167 (1977) (describing the discourse in classrooms at three Indiana law schools as

cipline's tacit messages of analysis, the idea that rules resolve disputes, and the idea that there is a unique expertise of lawyers based on relatively autonomous legal rules.

In sum, casebooks tacitly signify that the study of law is serious, relatively autonomous from other lines of inquiry, and perhaps intimidating as first year students contemplate their collections of massive casebooks. Casebooks also symbolize a complexity of many fragmented details while discounting, excluding or making difficult playfulness, imagination and critique. Casebooks thus create a material culture that encourages or demands analysis, the coverage of rules, and specific instrumentalist ways of reading, writing and using legal texts.

The Case Method

Class discussions in the core curriculum have several distinctive characteristics that help generate the discipline's tacit lessons. These discussions usually take place in large rooms among large numbers of students, who bring with them to class their expectations and uncertainties about professional education and professional practice. These discussions rely substantially on the law school's "case method," which involves an analysis or discussion of "cases" or judicial opinions and often takes the form, especially in first year courses, of some kind of question-and-answer dialogue between a law professor and individual students.[75] Law students and professors alike understand that the students will be evaluated by grades that are based only on their comparative performances on end-of-the-semester, time-limited, problem-solving final examinations. Law professors and most students also understand that the professor's teaching will be evaluated in written form by his or her students at the

---

lecturing); Elizabeth Mertz with Wamucii Njogu & Susan Gooding, *What Difference Does Difference Make? The Challenge for Legal Education*, 48 J. Legal Educ. 1, 56–57 (1998) (finding that the teachers of contract law to first year students at eight law schools do the majority of talking in their classrooms, although their talk is often in the form of questioning students and suggesting answers to their own questions).

75. See, e.g., Mertz, supra note 74. This question-and-answer dialogue is frequently, though often incorrectly, referred to as the "Socratic method." There is a popular perception that this method has been in decline since the 1950s and 60s. See, e.g., Phillip E. Areeda, *The Socratic Method (SM)*, 109 Harv. L. Rev. 911 (1996); Orin S. Kerr, *The Decline of the Socratic Method at Harvard*, 78 Neb. L. Rev. 113 (1999). In any event, the case method discussed in the text includes the "Socratic method," however defined, as well as other forms of question-and-answer dialogue about cases and professorial lecturing about cases.

end of the course.[76] These characteristics impose strong if tacit imperatives of control, entertainment, and expertise on typical case method classrooms, and these imperatives in turn generate or reinforce many disciplinary lessons.

The case method involves the discussion of judicial opinions presented by casebooks and the discussion of hypothetical problems that might be faced by courts or lawyers.[77] In the history of law schools this method has evolved considerably, especially by absorbing new ideas, shifting purposes and becoming more diverse and more complex. Langdell's case method studied groups of judicial opinions on each issue to ascertain by means of a "scientific" induction or logic a basic principle or rule that should govern the issue.[78] By the beginning of the twentieth century, however, Langdell's disciples were emphasizing the procedural rather than substantive values of the method by using opinions more to study legal reasoning and legal argument than to search for substantive rules.[79] Subsequently the Realists complicated the procedural aspects of the case method by adding social policy arguments and a corrosive skepticism about the meaning of words, the obligatory quality of legal rules and the causes of judicial behavior to the analysis of judicial opinions.[80] After World War II the Legal Process school promoted other procedural uses of the method, as they tried to restore the significance of legal doctrine, principles and rules with their understanding of doctrine as a matter of judicial craft, of how judges processed doctrinal arguments, rather than as something that can be scientifically correct.[81] The case method also has been affected by recent reform movements in legal education. Some versions now focus on providing economic explanations or critiques of leading cases.[82]

---

76. See Richard Abel, *Evaluating Evaluations: How Should Law Schools Judge Teaching?*, 40 J. Legal Educ. 407 (1990); Markovits, supra note 65, at 418–23; William Roth, *Student Evaluations of Law Teaching*, 17 Akron L. Rev. 609 (1984).

77. See, e.g., Charles D. Kelso, The AALS Study of Part-Time Legal Education: Final Report 179–87 (1972); A.T. Kronman, supra note 7, at 109–62; Areeda, supra note 75; Edmund M. Morgan, *The Case Method*, 4 J. Legal Educ. 379 (1952).

78. See, e.g., R. Stevens, supra note 7, at 52–54; Thomas Grey, *Langdell's Orthodoxy*, 45 U. Pitt. L. Rev. 1 (1983). For a revisionist view that credits Langdell with a more nuanced jurisprudence that recognized indeterminacy and normative opinions about what law should be, see Bruce A. Kimball, *"Warn Students That I Entertain Heretical Opinions, Which They Are Not to Take as Law": The Inception of Case Method Teaching in the Classrooms of the Early C.C. Langdell, 1870–1883*, 17 Law & Hist. Rev. 57 (1999).

79. See R. Stevens, supra note 7, at 54–57.

80. L. Kalman, supra note 9, at 67–97; R. Stevens, supra note 7, at 134–41, 155–63.

81. See, e.g., White, supra note 10.

82. See Chapter Four's discussion of Law and Economics; the casebooks cited in note 71 supra.

The political critiques of judicial opinions that have been developed by critical legal studies, feminist jurisprudence and critical race theory influence some class discussions as well.[83] Current forms of the case method have also been influenced by the Realist- and clinic-inspired "problem method" that focuses on discussing hypothetical problems, uses cases as precedents to make arguments about these problems, and pays less attention to judicial opinions standing alone.[84]

These shifts and accretions have produced a case method of many forms. All case method discussions spend time on the "briefing" or "analysis" of cases or assume that this work has been undertaken prior to class. In other words, students are expected to divide the excerpts of judicial opinions they read into their "relevant facts," their "issues," their "holdings" or "rules of law" and their "rationales." Some case method discussions may not progress much beyond this analysis of judicial opinions, but many forms of the method will interject doctrinal contexts, social policy arguments, methodological theory or economic, political and doctrinal critiques into discussions of the cases. The case method is thus capable of producing complex, multi-level discussions,[85] and the many components of these discussions will often, like the structure of casebooks, appear quite fragmented to beginning law students.

Here is Scott Turow describing case method discussions in a first-year contracts course at Harvard Law School in 1975:

> "The pattern of each class all week was more or less the same. First Perini would call on a student who would state the facts of the case; then Perini would ask the person under fire to identify the kernel issue in the decision. In one case, the plaintiff was suing for ground rent, so the narrower 'issue' was whether the word 'house' in the contract of sale meant the house alone, or also the land that sat beneath it. With that established, Perini would have the student consider the case's result, asking from whose point of view the judge seemed to have looked at things and what kind of interpretative standard that suggested. Then Perini would ask whomever he was questioning to compare that standard with what we'd seen in other cases. He'd ask the student to rec-

---

83. See, e.g., Duncan Kennedy, *Politicizing the Classroom*, 4 So. Cal. Rev. Law & Women's Studies 81 (1994).

84. See, e.g., Gregory L. Ogden, *The Problem Method in Legal Education*, 34 J. Legal Educ. 654 (1984).

85. See, e.g., C.D. Kelso, supra note 77, at 179–87; Karl Llewellyn, The Bramble Bush 39–57 (1930); A.T. Kronman, supra note 7, at 109–62.

oncile the decisions, to explain the ways they seemed to establish consistent principles of interpretation, and to account for differences through the varying circumstances and facts of each case....Finally, Perini would touch on what he sometimes refers to as 'the deep-thought issues,' and what students usually call 'policy questions.' How much discretion do we want judges to have in interpreting contracts? Too much, and the judge, in essence, can compose the agreement himself, rather than the parties. Too little, and the judge may have to accept without question all kinds of perjury and injustice."[86]

Turow, of course, is describing the case method as conducted by a master of the art, and as understood by a perceptive student. But notice the many intersecting levels of analysis, the complexity of subjects and the frequent contemplation of contradictory ideas in these discussions. Moreover, law professors are not all equally skilled in the case method, and students can cause discussions to deteriorate due to their misunderstandings, lack of preparation or other proclivities. In considering the tacit effects of complex, multi-level case discussions, then, we should also look at the way things can go wrong. Phillip Areeda, an apparent master in using the case method,[87] recently outlined some "common mistakes" that occur:

"The greatest source of confusion and boredom is unfocused class discussion—speeches by class members rather than discussion—especially in response to vague or mega-questions....

Classroom questions and hypotheticals can be unduly complicated in two ways: too intricate for quick oral comprehension and/or implicating too many issues....Most questions in class will be oral rather than written. Yet, I have heard instructors offer lengthy hypotheticals with many parties and a complex succession of facts....But even a simply stated and readily absorbed hypo may be too complex in a different sense: it may implicate too many issues....[I]f the subordinate pieces are too many or too complex, the development of each will be too episodic to follow as different students respond to different pieces of the puzzle. Alternatively, the instructor will waste much time and suppress spontaneity by repeatedly telling a student that his point is out of sequence and will have to be repeated later.

---

86. Scott Turow, One L 70–71 (1977).

87. See, e.g., Areeda, supra note 75; Robert C. Clark, *In Memoriam: Phillip E. Areeda,* 109 Harv. L. Rev. 897, 898–99 (1996).

Even the perfect hypothetical will not produce perfect answers. That's fine; exploring an answer's imperfection is often very helpful to the class.... But one student's formulation may be expressed in a way that the rest of the class will not readily understand.... Or it may take him forever to make his point.... Or the student's point might not then be worth class time because it's premature, quite special, or one whose exploration will not illuminate the issue before the class.... In these situations, the 'good guy' professor makes a serious mistake. He fears that it would be rude to interrupt the unclear, prolix, or irrelevant student and so loses class momentum, wastes class time, and allows the rest of the class to be bored.

Student confusion results from another feature of the 'good guy' instructor, who is so fearful of 'putting students down' that he never hints that a response might be imperfect...With a variety of contradictory answers provided by the class, this instructor says 'fine' to each, offering no follow up to guide the class. That's bad socratic teaching; indeed, it's bad teaching period because it neither exhibits nor induces rigorous analysis."[88]

We can see from these illustrations by Areeda and Turow how the case method itself can fragment a student's understanding, leave many unresolved contradictory messages about the law, and implicitly inscribe lessons that law at its best must be complex and authority-ridden. In order to understand the full impact of the case method, however, we should examine how this method combines with other prominent aspects of law school classes to produce many of the significant mechanisms and tacit lessons of the discipline.

Consider first the impact of large classes. Virtually all core classes are relatively large, say from 60 to 150 students, and this context imposes the tacit imperatives of control and entertainment. The control imperative demands that class communications be clearly relevant to the purposes of professional education, that the law professor control the discussion and that student comments should be closely aligned to the classroom's norms of relevance. This imperative appears both in statements about the purposes of case method discussions and in the typical techniques or maneuvers by which case method discussions are implemented in the core curriculum.

Let us listen to two eminent professors speaking about their ideals or norms for classroom communication. First, Paul Bator, addressing first-year law students at the University of Chicago:

---

88. Areeda, supra note 75, at 919–21.

"[Y]ou will notice, very soon, that the First Year classroom is, in a sense, instruction about *the moral constraints on the right to speak*. To speak is to exercise power. It follows, therefore, that you are not entitled to say anything you please. *It is our moral duty to ask ourselves, before we speak: have I reflected enough about this? Have I thought it through? Is it truthful? Is it fair?* The First Year class, at its best, with its unrelenting insistence that you explain and justify, is moral instruction designed to make you learn the habit of thinking about consequences even before you speak. To learn and feel the morality of responsibility and care in speech and argumentation is one of the inner excellences of the law."[89]

Now here is Robert Summers addressing his class in commercial law at Cornell Law School:

"I will call on students each day. This means that during the semester I will get around to each student at least once, and to a few twice. I will call on two or three students per day—and I will call on you to speak up so all can hear. As lawyers, you will often be judged by the heard word! *And I will be in charge of the questions.* The class hour must not collapse into a series of random and unrelated questions from students, (however good the questions individually). Coherence requires structure, and structure requires some centralized control. I will stay after every class to take questions and to continue the argument. *I will, of course, usually take questions during class when 'in point.'*"[90]

These statements evidence three significant norms. First, each professor declares his control of the discussion, Professor Summers explicitly and Professor Bator indirectly by referring to "the moral constraints on the right to speak." Secondly, each professor states the importance of students speaking in class. Thirdly, perhaps contradictorily, each professor insists also on the student's responsibility to be relevant, thorough and truthful when speaking or, in other words, on the student's duty "to get it right" under close surveillance by the professor and the student's peers. These norms are surely intended to

---

89. Paul Bator, *Talk to the First Year Class*, Univ. of Chicago, The Law School Record, Vol. 35/Spring 1989, p. 5, 6 (emphasis added).

90. Robert Summers, *The First Hour of the Course in Commercial Law, Spring Semester 1990*, Cornell Law Alumni Bulletin, p. 12 (1991) (emphasis added).

educate lawyers in effective legal analysis and public speaking. But what *tacit messages* do they convey? Do they not suggest the potential silencing of many students—by requirements that class speech be error-free and excellent, as Paul Bator demands, or always "in point" as Roberts Summers insists, or by the substantial lecturing of law professors when they become impatient with the imperfect talk of others?[91] Furthermore, among students who are not silenced, the case method seems capable at times of generating a special sort of speech that is problematic in its own right and constitutes yet another silencing tactic. At least at some schools, student talk in classrooms can often approximate a kind of speech-making or "nonconversational speech" that tries to impress audiences by its brilliance or authority while essentially ignoring what others are saying or have said.[92] The control imperative in case method classrooms is thus likely to promote the detailed analysis of judicial opinions, a rhetoric of confidence, complexity, authority and closure, and a discourse of both rules and skepticism as speakers attempt to impress their large audiences with a blend of brilliance and authority.

There are several devices of case method discussions that also implement the control imperative and its tacit messages. Elizabeth Mertz's study of first-year contracts classes at eight law schools reveals several of these devices. They include an "insistent channeling" of all discussion through the professor, the professor's frequent repetition of questions, the "common" practice of professors interrupting students, the imposition of ideas and words on students by professors, and a sometimes marked tendency of law professors to limit their express and tacit feedback on student comments to the technical aspects of subjects under discussion.[93] Several of these devices, interruption, the repetition of questions, and limiting of positive feedback to the use of technical language, as well as humor employed at the expense of the interrogated student, are on display in this classroom exchange taped by Mertz and her colleagues:

---

91. On the substantial talk by law professors in core curriculum classrooms, see supra note 74.

92. See Catherine Weiss & Louise Melling, *The Legal Education of Twenty Women*, 40 Stan. L. Rev. 1299, 1332–45 (1988); cf. Areeda, supra note 75, at 919 (noting "speeches by class members rather than discussion").

93. See Elizabeth Mertz, *Linguistic Ideology and Praxis in the U.S. Law School Classrooms*, in Language Ideologies: Practice and Theory 149 (Bambi B. Schieffelin, Kathryn A. Woolard, Paul V. Kroskrity eds, 1998); Elizabeth Mertz, *Recontextualization as Socialization: Text and Pragmatics in the Law School Classroom*, in Natural Histories of Discourse 229 (Michael Silverstein & Greg Urban, eds, 1996).

"P: What errors were alleged in the appeal of Sullivan v. O'Connor…
Ms. A? (pause) What errors were alleged in the appeal of Sullivan v.
O'Connor?

A: Um, the defense claimed that um the judge failed in allowing the
jury to take into account for damages anything but a claim for out-
of-pocket expenses.

P: Well, that's a rather general statement. How did this get to the appellate court?

A: Well the um the the patient was a woman who wanted a—

P: How did this case get to the appellate court?

A: The defendant disagreed with the way the damages were awarded
in the trial court.

P: How did this case get to the appellate court? The Supreme Court
once a—I think this is true—they asked some guy who'd never argued
a case before the Supreme Court before—they said to him—he was a
Southerner—and they said to him—ah—counsel how did you get
here? (Laughter) Well, he said, I came on the Chesapeake and Ohio
River (Louder laughter). How did this case get to the appellate court?

A: It was appealed.

P: It was appealed, you say. Did you find that word anywhere except
in my problem?"[94]

Elizabeth Mertz has concluded that such exchanges in law school classrooms model the correct use of technical legal language and a rhetorical style
of controlling interactions among many people by the invocation of some of
"the more powerful linguistic socialization techniques available in the human
repertoire."[95] The case method professor thus tacitly instructs her students in
the need to control discussions by becoming the center of attention, asking
frequent questions, interrupting others and assuming or stating what others
may or should be thinking. This surely is tacit instruction in a rhetorical style
of confidence, control and closure.[96]

---

94. Mertz, *Recontextualization as Socialization*, supra note 93, at 243.

95. See Mertz, *Linguistic Ideology*, supra note 93, at 154–56; see also Susan Phillips,
The Language Socialization of Lawyers: Acquiring the "Cant", in Doing the Ethnography of
Schooling 177, 192 (G. Spindler ed. 1982).

96. Scott Turow described his internalization of such lessons during his first year at
Harvard Law School in the following way:

"At home, Annette told me that I had started to 'lawyer' her when we quarreled,
badgering and cross-examining her much as the professors did students in class."
S. Turow, supra note 86, at 75.

Case method classes also invite entertainment as a means of maintaining control, attention and enthusiasm among large audiences of law students. One entertaining move is to emphasize or exaggerate factual situations reported by judicial opinions or used in hypothetical problems that present morally sympathetic, morally bizarre or morally contentious behavior. For example, a case in criminal law or torts involving a battered woman who kills her abuser in some particularly cold-blooded way might illustrate all three types of behavior to different members of the class.[97] The ability to characterize or interpret facts is an important legal skill, to be sure, but classroom exaggeration of this sort also serves more entertaining and subterranean disciplinary purposes. These bits of humor can lighten tensions, intensity, or stress and make routine classroom practices more acceptable. They help establish the professor as a charismatic performer or expert authority by providing a kind of rhetorical backdrop for her claims about legal doctrine or social policies. Humor can also aestheticize morally troublesome legal rules or procedures by making them seem pleasurable, deflecting potential criticisms and thus helping legitimate the status quo.

Entertainment in the case method classroom is also provided by the frequent criticism of judicial opinions as students and (more often) professors claim that a decision is inconsistent with other decisions or fails to serve some social policy. This kind of entertaining criticism of cases is a relatively easy task in light of the professor's superior knowledge of relevant legal doctrines, the fragmented, decontextualized excerpts of opinions in casebooks, and the fragmented, multi-layered aspects of case method discussions. This criticism serves several latent functions. It encourages students to feel superior to the parties, lawyers and judges "who got it wrong," thus satisfying their innate sense of wanting to become good technical lawyers.[98] It helps establish a professor's authority as an expert and the professor's image as an "ideal judge." Such images and authority satisfy student expectations about professorial sovereignty, assure them that their examinations will be graded "objectively," and help validate their choice of law schools by demonstrating the brilliance of the school's faculty. The criticism of particular cases is also a subtle way of legitimating legal norms, as the specific instance of the case is used simply to *as-*

---

97. Cf. Kennedy, supra note 55, at 594–95 (describing the use of "hot" cases to engage law students' emotions in order to teach them that law does not respect emotion); Kennedy, supra note 83, at 88 (using hypothetical cases involving battered women to encourage students to argue both sides of close, indeterminate legal issues).

98. See Carrie Menkel-Meadow, *Feminist Legal Theory, Critical Legal Studies, and Legal Education or "The Fem-Crits Go to law School"*, 38 J. Legal Educ. 61, 67–68 (1988).

sert the rightness or wrongness of a particular legal norm.[99] Judicial criticism of particular cases thus tacitly legitimates the routine practices of classrooms and the discipline's general ideas of legal authority and a relatively autonomous professional expertise.

There is also the distinctive *agon* or contest of wits between professors and their students. This occurs whenever students are invited to compare their partial, fragmentary understandings of law with the more comprehensive understandings of a professor.[100] While many students dislike these contests, especially when they must participate, observing the winners and losers of these one-sided affairs can be enjoyable to observers for many of the reasons that victories by one's home team, action movies or the law school criticism of judicial opinions are satisfying. The special contest of wits in the law school classroom, intentionally or not, thus engenders a competitive atmosphere that tacitly justifies what goes on in case method classrooms and makes classroom work consistent with the competitive process of law school examinations. Yet the entertainment features of the case method also disguise the significant disjunction between much case method classroom work, where individual cases and issues are analyzed, and most final examination work, where students must identify the right issues in novel fact situations and apply rules to resolve these issues. The tacit imperatives of the case method thus help establish another significant fragmentation in the discipline: the "loose coupling" between course work and examinations which makes it easier in the end for law professors to impose many different grades on final examination answers.

The entertainment imperative has other consequences for the discipline as well. Judicial criticism and the contest of wits in case method classes require the deployment of brief, quickly constructed, persuasive and authoritative arguments, and these practices rely on and model a rhetoric of confidence and closure, a rhetoric of "correct answers" that is based on some sort of objective foundational principles.[101] Moreover, entertaining practices by law professors help establish them as suasive models or images of the lawyer as an expert who is always quick, precise and error-free in analyzing situations, applying rules or policy arguments, and dismissing "wrong an-

---

99. See Nikolaus Benke, *Women in the Courts: An Old Thorn in Men's Sides*, 3 Mich. J. of Gender & Law 195, 202–03 (1995).

100. See Bradley Dillon, *Paper Chase and the Socratic Method of Teaching Law*, 30 J. Legal Educ. 529 (1980); Kennedy, supra note 55, at 593–95; Menkel-Meadow, supra note 98, at 67.

101. See Gerald Wetlaufer, *Rhetoric and Its Denial in Legal Discourse*, 76 Va. L. Rev. 1545 (1990).

swers." The entertainment imperative thus elaborates the tacit rhetorical style that is promoted initially by the control imperative of large case method classes.

The professional expectations of law students should also be considered. Students expect to learn not only legal doctrine but also how to deal with the uncertainties of professional work, prospective clients and complicated legal problems. In the uncertain, mysterious and competitive environment of core curriculum classrooms, professors become "special persons with whom students may identify as a source of strength, competence, style and purpose."[102] These expectations enhance a law professor's opportunities to model theories, rhetoric and lawyering styles.[103] In view of the diverse forms of the case method, we can expect that law professors collectively model a variety of legal theories and styles. As a matter of *intentions* to expose students to different theories and styles this would seem admirable in our pluralistic world, but since this modeling is *mostly tacit* its effects upon students may be problematical.[104] The most likely consequence of tacitly modeled diverse theories and methods where there is no chance for systematic comparisons or resolution of conflicts may be the conclusion that law simply is what those with power say it is or, in other words, that there is no law there. Furthermore, many professors are likely to model a certain kind of litigator's or judge's rhetoric that is impersonal, authoritative and combative in light of the case method's large classes, its focus on appellate court opinions, and its control and entertainment imperatives. The inevitable dramatic role of the law professor in case method classrooms is thus likely to suggest that adversarial litigation is the essence of legal practice—in contrast to the many different legal practices and skills such as legal planning, counseling, negotiations, legislation and administration.[105]

Student expectations about final examinations are another critical influence on the case method. Students sense and soon learn that their end-of-the-semester, comparatively graded final examinations will demand some kind of internalization or memorization of a comprehensive set of legal rules.[106] This causes many students to expect that class discussions should "cover" all aspects

---

102. Redmount, supra note 24, at 706.

103. See T. Shaffer & R. Redmount, supra note 74, at 153–62; Abel, supra note 76, at 411; Menkel-Meadow, supra note 98, at 77.

104. Cf. Richard Markovits, *Legal Scholarship: The Course*, 48 J. Legal Educ. 539 (1998) (suggesting that law professors should make their theories of law explicit).

105. See Bender, supra note 63, at 392–93.

106. See Kissam, supra note 64; the discussion of examinations in the next section.

of the course that are important or, in other words, all the rules that may be useful on final examinations.[107] Many faculty understandably if implicitly may try to satisfy this expectation in view of the pending student evaluations of their teaching.[108] In addition, many law faculty, understanding the competitive pressures faced by students to earn top grades on comparatively graded examinations, will strive to present a sufficiently demanding set of rules during class sessions to assure themselves they have done the best they can to place each student at "the same starting place" in the race for law school grades. These tacit expectations and obligations appear to encourage many professors to supplement their students' readings of fragmented casebooks, treatises and outlines by substantial lecturing about the legal rules of their subjects.[109] Thus, as an important part of the case method many professors "write" the same kinds of semi-abstract statements of legal doctrine that are found in treatises, student hornbooks, law review articles and casebook outlines, and these statements from authoritative professors help entrench the discipline's promises of rule coverage and a compartment of rules for every occasion.

Student evaluations of law teachers influence the case method, perhaps significantly. Law school deans and many professors may say that these evaluations play little role in determining the *material interests* of law teachers, which depend they say far more heavily upon their scholarship and peer reviews of their teaching.[110] This may be,[111] but student evaluations surely affect the *psychological interests* of law professors, who in general may be persons particularly in need of public applause. These evaluations, moreover, invite students to evaluate law professors on a unidimensional scale, which allows the con-

---

107. See James Boyd White, *Doctrine in a Vacuum: Reflections on What a Law School Ought (and Ought Not) to Be*, 36 J. Legal Educ. 155, 164 (1986) ("The first assumption that should go is that everything of importance in the field, or for the exam, will be covered in class.").

108. See, e.g., Markovits, supra note 65, at 418–23.

109. On the vast amount of lecturing that occurs in modern law schools, whether in the form of direct lectures, question-and-answer dialogues or "Socratic monologues," see T. Shaffer & R. Redmount, supra note 74, at 162–67; Roger Cramton, *The Current State of the Law Curriculum*, 32 J. Legal Educ. 321, 328 (1982); Walter Gellhorn, *The Second and Third Years of Law Study*, 17 J. Legal Educ.1, 3 (1964). Cf. Mertz, supra note 74, at 56–57 (describing the predominance of professorial talk in first-year contracts classrooms).

110. See Abel, supra note 76, at 412–17.

111. But cf. NY Times, June 9, 1987, at A-14, col. 2 (quoting Robert Clark of Harvard Law School on the denial of tenure to two critical legal studies professors: "Neither of those people were very good teachers...[b]oth were among the bottom ten percent in student ratings.").

struction of league tables that rank law professors comparatively and hierarchically just as final examinations and class ranking systems rank law students.[112] Student evaluations thus impose tacit forces on law professors to satisfy student expectations about their legal education and final examinations. These evaluations thereby help enforce the tacit lessons of rule coverage, law as compartments of rules, and a legal rhetoric of confidence, authority and closure since these lessons or images will fit with significant student expectations about what they need for their final examinations and practices. [113]

Students resist the case method by not going to class, by not preparing for class discussions, by "passing" or declining to respond when called on, and by more subtle forms of behavior that indicate frustration, indifference or malaise.[114] This resistance is likely to reinforce the discipline's lessons of analysis and rule coverage. As students diminish their attention to class work, they are likely to compensate by preparing more intensively for their final examinations.[115] Meanwhile faculty are likely to respond to this resistance by implementing additional disciplinary techniques such as relying only on volunteers, lecturing, assigning students to participate in particular discussions (the "rolling boulder method," which "rolls along" rows of seated students) or imposing attendance requirements. These responses in their ways tend to focus the attention of law students on the basic disciplinary lessons of "analysis" and "rule coverage." For example, when students volunteer or are assigned discussion responsibilities, they are likely to rely heavily on what they've learned to do: to analyze judicial opinions to disclose their rules. Moreover, these techniques leave other students more freedom to ignore the case method and focus on their final examinations. Other responses, like declaring the rules more clearly or requiring student attendance, are almost by definition aimed at making the discipline's lessons effective.

Law faculty are less likely to resist the case method. They have been successful at this method, first as excellent law students and then as teachers. Still, especially at elite schools, there are traces of resistance in the tendencies of some professors to focus their class discussions on theoretical considerations

---

112. See Abel, supra note 76, at 412–13; Kissam, supra note 19, at 272–75.

113. Cf. Julius Getman, In the Company of Scholars 24–25 (1992) ("One of the most important lessons I learned as a teaching fellow (at Harvard Law School) was the importance of developing and communicating a point of view about the assigned material. Most texts are open to interpretations, and it is up to the teacher to attach a meaning to them.").

114. See Cramton, supra note 109, at 328–29, 332; Pipkin, supra note 41, at 1161; Roy Rickson, *Faculty Control and the Structure of Student Competition: An Analysis of the Student Role*, 25 J. Legal Educ. 47 (1973).

115. See Rickson, supra note 114.

or the social contexts of law instead of the case method.[116] Core courses like Contracts, Torts and Corporation Law are now taught from economic perspectives that ask about the economic effects of legal rules or whether legal rules should be changed to promote some concept of economic efficiency.[117] A critical legal studies professor may teach a doctrinal course with intent to reveal the law's contradictions and ideological consequences.[118] But these developments are ambiguous in their relationship to the discipline. On the one hand, like faculty flights from the core curriculum, they portend limits to the discipline and possible grounds for transformative changes. On the other hand, these developments may only refine, modify and strengthen the discipline by providing a discourse that makes the discipline more palatable for those students and faculty who desire to apply intellectual curiosity, social passions or political restlessness to the study of law. We shall consider these ambiguous situations in Chapter Four, but first we must complete our study of the discipline's basic components and techniques in this and the following two chapters.

Law School Examinations

Final examinations occur at the end of virtually all core curriculum courses, and these examinations are rarely preceded by practice exams, mid-term exams or other graded exercises. Although the questions vary in form, law school examinations ordinarily confront students with novel fact situations and ask them to identify legal issues and apply rules or other legal authority to these issues or, in other words, to solve potential legal problems.[119] In essay questions, rather lengthy narratives of factual situations are often used to introduce false leads and disguise multiple interrelated issues.[120] Law school ex-

---

116. See, e.g., Kronman, supra note 7, at 225–75; Graham Lilly, *Law Schools Without Lawyers? Winds of Change in Legal Education*, 81 Va. L. Rev. 1341 (1995).

117. See, e.g., Symposium, *The Place of Economics in Legal Education*, 33 J. Legal Educ. 183 et seq. (1983); the casebooks cited in note 71 supra.

118. See Kennedy, supra note 83.

119. See Nickles, supra note 53; Steve Sheppard, *An Informal History of How Law Schools Evaluate Students, With A Predictable Emphasis On Law School Final Exams*, 65 UMKC L. Rev. 657 (1997).

120. See, e.g., S. Turow, supra note 86, at 168–69, 260 (describing a four-hour examination in Torts involving three questions described in four single-spaced pages and a four-hour examination in Contracts involving five questions described in nine single-spaced pages); Sheppard, supra note 119, at 754–76 (reproducing recent exam questions from elite

aminations are also famous for giving students very little time in which to complete their answers.[121] These examinations, among other things, seem designed—often quite deliberately—to ensure that no student can address all the issues adequately and that law professors will have a relatively easy time in establishing the multiple grading distinctions that are required by the law school's grading curve, whether it is mandatory or an implicit norm.[122]

Scott Turow has provided a sharp description of the law student's experience taking final examinations during the first year of law school, and how this process demands that a student analyze complicated situations, identify many issues, recall rules and apply the rules quickly:

> "The typical law-school test is what's usually referred to as an 'issue spotter.' A long narrative is presented, involving a complicated series of events and a number of actors. The exam generally instructs the student to put himself in the position of a law-firm associate who has been asked by a senior partner for a memo describing the legal issues raised.... Inevitably, the narrative has been constructed in such a way that its facts straddle the boundaries of dozens of legal categories. A varying interpretation of a single detail can produce a Merlin-like change in the issues, and often the outcome of the case. For the student, the job is to sort quickly through the situation to try to name the endless skein of applicable rules and also to describe the implications of using one rule rather than another. Like a good lawyer, the student is expected to be able to argue both sides of the issue."[123]

The second part of the formal examination process is the grading of examinations and consequences of this grading. Examination questions may be short answer or essay type, but law school examinations are usually graded

---

law schools, which include Professor Rotunda's one hour constitutional law question described in two single-spaced pages, Professor Kauper's three hour property exam described in five and one-half single-spaced pages, and Professor Brown's two-hour constitutional law exam described in two single-spaced pages).

121. See, e.g., S. Turow, supra note 86, at 167–71, 257–60 (describing the experience of severe time constraints on writing final examinations in Torts, Criminal Law, Property and Contracts during the author's first year at Harvard Law School).

122. See Kissam, supra note 64, at 437–61. On the increasing and widespread use of mandatory grading curves in law schools, see Robert C. Downs & Nancy Levit, *If It Can't Be Lake Woebegone...A Nationwide Survey of Law School Grading and Grade Normalization Practices*, 65 UMKC L. Rev. 819, 835–48 (1997).

123. S. Turow, supra note 86, at 163.

"objectively" in the sense that some kind of overall complex numerical grading scale is employed to establish a hierarchy of numerical scores.[124] This hierarchy of scores then becomes the justification for distributing the many different grades that are required by the mandatory or implicit grading curves which exist at most law schools.[125]

When examinations have been graded, most law schools average the grades of each student and rank the students in each class by percentile categories or from the highest to lowest grade average.[126] Thus, after only one semester in law school, most law students obtain either an ordinal or percentile rank such as 1st, 97th, 163rd or third quartile, a ranking which compares their examination performances with those of every other student in the class. This rank constitutes the primary if not exclusive evaluation of most law students' work and their potential as lawyers. These comparative grades and class ranks are also important because legal employers—especially larger and more prestigious law firms—rely heavily on class rankings to screen their prospective applicants and because law school grade averages are usually a critical factor in selecting law students for the honor and status of serving on a school's law review. This grading/ class ranking system clearly has material consequences for students and can have psychological consequences too, especially when one's rank is stated as an individual number, say, 127th.[127] The grading/class ranking system symbolizes the power and influence that final examinations have within the discipline of law schools.

Law school examinations seem to have evolved rather gradually in the twentieth century towards a greater diversity of forms and increasing complexity

---

124. See Kissam, supra note 64, at 444–52.

125. See id.; see also Downs & Levit, supra note 122 (on the prevalence of mandatory grading curves at American law schools).

126. See Douglas A. Henderson, *Uncivil Procedure: Ranking Law Students Among Their Peers*, 27 U. Mich. J. L. Reform 399, 404–06 (1994); Nickles, supra note 53, at 426–27 (noting that as of 1975, 84% of reporting law schools used class ranking systems and approximately 4/5 of these schools, or 60% of the reporting schools, ranked students individually).

127. See Henderson, supra note 126. See also S. Turow, supra note 86 (describing the passionate attention that first year students at Harvard in 1975–76 paid to their examinations and grades due to their general competitiveness, their interest in law review, and their growing knowledge of the placement process, and noting an "atomizing effect" that divided students into categories by grades); Kissam, supra note 64, at 464–65, 479–85 (describing what the examination/grading/class ranking system of law schools can "do to persons," both students and professors).

and length in the factual narratives that are presented by essay questions.[128] Three trends are noteworthy for the evidence they provide of the discipline's presence and power in contemporary law schools. In the second half of the twentieth century, multiple-choice and other short answer questions have increasingly been substituted for essay questions.[129] Short answer questions inevitably probe for the analysis of factual situations, identification of issues, a recall of rules and a quick application of rules to facts, and they diminish the possibility of using examinations to measure a student's abilities at more complex or more open-ended tasks such as the interpretation of problematic legal authorities or the construction of legal arguments. Law schools in recent years also have tended to make their grading scales more discrete and their grading curves mandatory.[130] This development surely enhances the expectations of both students and professors that final examinations will be graded "objectively," presumably by using some hierarchy of "points" or numerical scores. This numerical grading, like the use of multiple-choice questions, diminishes the possibility of testing for more open-ended tasks that invite if they do not require more holistic grading methods. Thirdly, the dramatic expansion of corporate law firms in recent decades has produced more widespread attention to class ranks in the hiring process and thus increased the material consequences of class ranks for many law students, both those in the lower ranks at elite schools and many at non-elite schools which now send a significant number of their graduates to these firms.[131] These three trends point towards an expanded influence of final examinations over other routine practices.

This formal description cannot do justice to the intensity, competitive pressures and gamesmanship involved in taking law school examinations. To un-

---

128. See Sheppard, supra note 119, at 672–80 (noting the increasing complexity and length of essay questions and the "profound similarity in the construction of the essay questions offered by different professors in different faculties"), 697–776 (reprinting final examination questions at elite law schools from the late 19th century through the 1990s); compare Benjamin Wood, *The Measurement of Law School Work*, 24 Colum. L. Rev. 224 (1924) (describing final examinations at Columbia Law School in the 1920s), with Kissam, supra note 64 (describing law school examinations in the 1980s as similar to those at Columbia in the 1920s).

129. See Nickles, supra note 53, at 447–51; Sheppard, supra note 119, at 682–86.

130. See Downs & Levit, supra note 122, at 835–48; Kissam, supra note 64, at 448–49.

131. See Linda Wightman, Legal Education at the Close of the Twentieth Century: Descriptions and Analyses of Students, Financing, and Professional Expectations and Attitudes 60–84 (1995) (Law School Admission Council) ("The most coveted work settings are large and mid-sized firms, with a full third of the entering (law school) class identifying these as their first choice."); Chapter Four's discussion of corporate law firms.

derstand these aspects, one must appreciate the student's long run-up to final examinations, at least during the first year, as outlines of the course material are prepared, study groups organized and implemented, and last minute often frenzied reviews of the material conducted right before the examination.[132] One must also appreciate the increasing knowledge that law students acquire during their first and second years about the importance of grades for making law review and obtaining prestigious legal employment.[133] One must appreciate too the special intensity of writing law school final examinations under substantial time pressure, which Scott Turow has described:

> "I read the questions. The first was a straight issue spotter. An M.D. had given a patient a drug still in experimental stages and the series of disasters you come to expect in a Torts course had followed: blindness, car crashes, paralysis—the world, in general, falling apart. We were asked what torts had occurred. The second question was wide open. It was another kind of issue-spotting narrative about a gardener and a tree falling on a neighbor's house, but we were instructed to emphasize theory and policy in our answer. The final question cited three well-known cases of nuisance law and asked for an essay about them. We had four hours.
>
> What had never quite struck home with me about a law exam was the importance of time. I had realized that we would be tested over a few hours on a knowledge which had taken months to acquire. And I'd looked at past exams. But I'd never really tried to write out an answer. It was only now that I saw that there was not a quarter of the time I'd need to frame a reasonably thorough response. The questions themselves covered four single-spaced pages and even after reading them twice I knew I hadn't recognized half of what was there. As it was, I couldn't figure out how I'd ever write down all of what I had seen. It was all split-second reaction, instantaneous stuff; there'd be no deep contemplation."[134]

Surely it is here, in the examination process, that the discipline best teaches its tacit lessons of analysis, quickness or productivity, a focus upon relatively autonomous legal rules, a legal rhetoric of authority and complexity (if not

---

132. For dramatic descriptions of this run-up, see S. Turow, supra note 86, at 150–67, 233–58.

133. See supra note 127 and accompanying text.

134. S. Turow, supra note 86, at 168–69.

also confidence and closure) and the skeptical doubts or uncertainties that flow from unresolved contradictory messages about the presence or absence of legal obligations. Students must "analyze" factual situations ferociously to determine issues and apply "the rules" in conditions of uncertainty about whether they have identified the correct issues or applied the correct rules. The good examination taker will be skeptical or flexible about the meanings of words, rules or specific facts because flexibility will help her identify ambiguities, which can support arguments on both sides of issues. The good examination taker must convey her ideas quickly, clearly, precisely and confidently to her readers, which invites some sort of instrumentalist writing.[135] Many if not most examination takers will also confront substantial uncertainties and apparently arbitrary discrepancies between their efforts to prepare for and write particular final examinations and the variable grades they receive for these efforts.[136]

The examination process teaches basic instincts towards productivity to both students and professors. Students must engage in quick if superficial analysis and write precisely but quickly, especially if they hope to obtain one of the few high grades that are allowed by grading curves.[137] Moreover, since students soon learn that their grades are not much influenced by the time they spend preparing for examinations,[138] their examination work may often be aimed at producing the same output with fewer resources rather than more or better output from given resources. Law professors meanwhile learn to read and judge the examination answers in large classes quickly, "objectively" and in a negative or critical state of mind. They must employ complex quantitative criteria based on many rules and must search as much for "weak" answers as "strong" ones in order to impose a grading curve that requires many average and low grades to establish the law school's class ranking system. Law school examinations thus invite a rough sort of productivity at "legal analysis" from law students and law professors alike.

---

135. See W. Lawrence Church, *Law School Grading*, 1991 Wisc. L. Rev. 825, 828–29; Kissam, supra note 64, at 440–44, 452–61.

136. For good discussions of the uncertainty and doubt among law students about the grades they receive, see S. Turow, supra note 86, at 202–11, 267–68; Markovits, supra note 104, at 543.

137. See Church, supra note 135, at 828 (reporting that "legible handwriting" and "the length of answers (the longer the better)" were found to be positively correlated with high grades on one law school essay examination).

138. Henderson, supra note 126, at 415, 424; James Lofton, *Study Habits and Their Effectiveness in Legal Education*, 27 J. Legal Educ. 418, 431–33, 445–46 (1975).

Significantly, the structure of law school examinations privileges particular features of law and legal inquiry over others. Although the intentions and discourse in casebooks, law school classrooms and even in the construction of examinations may be quite different, the routine process of setting, writing and objectively grading large numbers of final examinations inevitably emphasizes the analysis of problems into precisely identified issues and manipulation of positive legal rules to generate basic answers to the issues. Thus the examination process, more than any other aspect of the discipline, tacitly privileges the "analysis" of rules and facts and an advocacy that relies heavily on these rules and other legal authority over competing values or arguments of policy, moral principle, practical judgments, theory and politics. Moreover, while this privileging may be tempered or corrected by other discourse, including the writing of so-called "policy questions" for final examinations, this privileging of analysis and rules takes place in a deep latent manner that exercises its influence no matter how much attention is paid to competing values.

The law school examination process also inscribes an instrumentalist style of thinking and writing about legal problems. This style aims to produce a series of loosely related but well constructed (if not well written) paragraphs, each of which identifies an issue, states a relevant rule and describes the application of this rule to given facts in order to "analyze" or "resolve" the issue. This style aims to record many answers in a productive manner and incorporates the discipline's lessons of analysis, the flexible manipulation of formal rules and a confident objectivist rhetoric that depends upon legal authority. We might call this style "the paradigm of good paragraph thinking/writing."[139] This paradigm may not be a good way to think or write about many complicated legal problems or other aspects of legal practice, but it is a useful tool for writing law school examinations. The paradigm, moreover, tacitly protects and promotes the discipline by discouraging or penalizing students who try to make unnecessary or marginal arguments about social policies or moral rights that do not fit easily within the paradigm. The paradigm of good paragraph thinking/writing empowers prospective lawyers to be efficient and productive in certain limited ways, but at the same time it tacitly limits them with regard to more imaginative and more critical aspects of legal practice.

This paradigm writing may also be viewed as quite similar to a student's ideal response to a surprising question in the case method classroom, or to a

---

139. See Kissam, supra note 64, at 443, 477–78.

lawyer's ideal response to a judge's novel question during oral argument in a courtroom. That is, a first sentence grasps or clarifies the issue. A second sentence states some relevant legal authority. Then two or three additional sentences show how the authority applies to resolve the question asked. Thus, while the case method and final examination are but loosely coupled in terms of their intellectual work, at a more profound level they both tend to privilege certain kinds of "oral performances" over more systematic, more imaginative and more critical types of thinking and writing.

Law professors are very much subject to the disciplinary lessons of examinations, for they must repeatedly construct examination questions and then productively or quickly read and grade many answers to these questions in their large classes. This process typically entails reading large numbers of essay answers to the same question, and this is apparently a traumatic though tedious experience for most professors.[140] The tacit disciplinary lessons of precise analysis, avoiding error, an objectivist rhetoric of authority and complexity, raw productivity and doubts about the existence of binding legal obligations may thus shape the thought of many law professors if not also their personal characters.[141]

Resistance to law school examinations is understated but manifest in two distinct phenomena. One is the well-recognized malaise or despondency among upper class law students as they come to accept their places in class ranking systems.[142] The other is the proliferating taste of many upper class students and faculty for courses that do not require examinations, courses which include representing clients in law school clinics, conducting simulated practice exercises and writing research papers instead of final examinations. The malaise effect may diminish the acquisition of well-honed examination skills, but malaise itself does not encourage change or any search for richer forms of education. The taste for non-examination courses may be a more subversive kind of resistance, but we have already seen that clinics and seminars have ambiguous consequences for the discipline.[143] In any event, the resistance to final examinations does not seem especially marked or powerful within law school communities.

---

140. See Clark Byse, *Fifty Years of Legal Education*, 71 Iowa L. Rev. 1063, 1086 (1986); George Christie, *The Recruitment of Law Faculty*, 1987 Duke L. J. 306, 310, 315; David Vernon, *Ethics in Academe—Afton Dekanal*, 34 J. Legal Educ. 205, 205 (1984).

141. See Kissam, supra note 64, at 483–85.

142. See. e.g., Cramton, supra note 109, at 328–29.

143. See supra text accompanying notes 41–47; see also Chapter Four's discussion of the professional reforms and academic/political movements in law schools.

The Institutions of Scholarship

Most law professors and some students engage in legal scholarship. On first impression this work may appear to have a paradoxical relationship to the discipline. Legal scholarship is generally perceived as "cutting edge" work that is different in kind from the training of students and more concerned with reforms, theory and the discovery of new knowledge than with the study of conventional rules and legal rhetoric.[144] Yet much legal scholarship is of the conventional sort that organizes, reports on and criticizes legal doctrine,[145] and this scholarship overlaps the discipline's basic subjects and values. There are other relationships too between the institutions of scholarship and law school teaching practices that constitute integral parts of the discipline.

The unique law school phenomenon of student-managed academic journals[146] builds on and reinforces other disciplinary elements. Virtually every law school has a principal law review and many schools have begun to publish other specialized journals as well.[147] Second and third year students are selected to work on these publications, usually on the basis of their grades and their relative scores on "writing competitions" that are much like take-home final examinations.[148] The editors of law reviews are third year students selected by the staff or the previous editors. The business of these journals is to select, edit and publish articles written by professors or lawyers and shorter student-authored "notes" or "comments" that typically "analyze" a recent judicial decision or series of decisions. Law review offices, like faculty offices,

---

144. See, e.g., Thomas Bergin, *The Law Teacher: A Man Divided Against Himself*, 54 Va. L. Rev. 646 (1968); Anthony T. Kronman, *Foreward: Legal Scholarship and Moral Education*, 90 Yale L. J. 955 (1981).

145. See, e.g., Michael J. Saks, Howard Larsen & Carol J. Hodne, *Is There a Growing Gap Among Law, Law Practice, and Legal Scholarship?: A Systematic Comparison of Law Review Articles One Generation Apart*, 30 Suffolk U. L. Rev. 353 (1996) (documenting the vast increase in law review publications between 1960 and 1985 and concluding, on the basis of their review of randomly selected articles, that conventional scholarship about legal doctrine or rules, scholarship "that would resonate with practitioners," is still vibrant and expanding despite the new "theoretical scholarship" that has also proliferated in recent decades.).

146. See generally Roger Cramton, *"The Most Remarkable Institution": The American Law Review*, 36 J. Legal Educ. 1 (1986).

147. See Saks, Larsen & Hodne, supra note 145, at 363.

148. See Church, supra note 135, at 831; Josh E. Fidler, *Law Review Operations and Management*, 33 J. Legal Educ. 48, 52–54 (1983); Joshua Rosenkranz, *Law Review's Empire*, 39 Hast. L. J. 859, 892–99 (1988).

are set apart from other student spaces in the law school, signifying special honor and prestige. The selection of a review's new officers and members is announced publicly and is among the few public events in law schools that recognize student excellence. Law reviews symbolize and reward excellence in the case method/final examination law school.

Law reviews serve the discipline in obvious and subtle ways. They reward and promote excellence in the values of final examinations: the analysis of complex situations, the rapid and comprehensive use of legal rules, and the deployment of a confident, objectivist rhetoric. They symbolize both professional competition and professional hierarchy as indicia of good legal practices, and they help socialize their student members in these values.[149] Law reviews are an important site for producing law professors since their alumni constitute a large and influential component of most law faculties.[150] Law reviews also influence, filter and cabin much writing by law professors, and the relative prestige of the reviews at different law schools reinforces the discipline's basic distinction between elite and non-elite law schools.

Consider first the nature of student work on law reviews. Much of this work revolves around the writing and editing of "notes" and "comments" by student members. A typical note might discuss a recent Supreme Court decision, say the Court's validation of a municipal ban on nude dancing,[151] by describing 30 years of relevant Supreme Court precedents, summarizing the plurality opinion, concurring opinion and two dissenting opinions, and then offering the student's assessment based on her interpretation of the decision's consistency with precedents or on some favored policy value, such as artistic freedom or preserving quiet and order on municipal streets. Student comments usually attempt to reconcile a series of judicial decisions with each other, to

---

149. Cf. Thomas L. Haskell, *The New Aristocracy*, NY Rev. of Books, Dec. 4, 1997, pp. 47, 51 (noting that professions intensify competition in non-pecuniary kinds of achievement "as a means of encouraging individual practitioners to live up to whatever standards of conduct and technical performance may be thought important within a particular community of practitioners" and that "every authentic profession stages competitive exercises to socialize novices").

150. Currently about 50% of all law professors with tenure-track positions have served on law reviews as students, see Borthwick & Schau, supra note 15, at 205–06, but this undoubtedly understates the influence of former law review members on the construction of the ethos at most law schools. A higher percentage of senior faculty are likely to have been on law reviews, and law review status, especially editorial positions, has always been a significant credential for faculty appointments at the elite schools which set the trends in legal education. See Fossum, supra note 15, at 518; Merritt & Reskin, supra note 6, 275–76.

151. City of Erie v. Pap's A.M. 529 U.S. 277 (2000).

resolve conflicts between the decisions, or to use the decisions to recommend judicial outcomes in new legal cases.[152] This kind of work is likely to be influenced if not controlled by the discipline's core curriculum, case method and final examinations, for this is what law review students will know about the law, or what they will know best.[153] The subjects investigated by student members are likely to be closely related to core curriculum subjects, and their writing is likely to make extensive use of the case analysis, judicial criticisms and paradigm of good paragraph thinking/ writing that they have experienced in case method classrooms and writing final examinations. Furthermore, the law review experience is often intense and memorable for many students.[154] The collaborative nature of the work, its relative freedom from professorial control or sovereignty, the excitement of working on changing law, the joy of individually constructed projects and the honor or glory of law review are all factors that explain this enjoyment. The law review's tacit lessons of analysis, a complex, objectivist rhetoric, the productive use of rules to fashion comprehensive if superficial discussions, and the skepticism from contemplating unresolved contradictory messages about law are likely to be deeply inscribed by the experiences of law review work.

The tacit messages of law review work become more significant for the discipline when former law review members become law professors. As these professors contemplate teaching and scholarship, their experience on law reviews with legal analysis and the use of legal rules in a relatively autonomous way will constitute a tacit if not express guide to the kinds of teaching and scholarship they pursue. Like all university professors, they must earn some kind of favorable student evaluations of their teaching and produce sufficient scholarship to obtain tenure, and law professors usually do not have extended graduate study or work as a teaching assistant to help them prepare for these tasks. After tenure, to be sure, a law professor's goals may become more diffuse or ambitious. But even then one's memorable experiences on a law review are

---

152. See, e.g., Robert Vaught, *The Debate over Evolution: A Constitutional Analysis of the Kansas Board of Education*, 48 Kan. L. Rev. 1013 (2000) (using the Supreme Court's establishment clause decisions to argue that a 1999 decision by the Kansas Board of Education that deleted evolution subjects from statewide tests of public school students might violate the Establishment Clause of the First Amendment).

153. Cf. John Henry Schlegel, American Legal Realism and the Social Sciences 11 (1995) (noting that the common structure of the law school classroom and scholarly legal article maintains a "dialogue of justification" of legal rules).

154. See, e.g., Douglas Cane, *The Role of Law Review in Legal Education*, 31 J. Legal Educ. 215, 220 n.33 (1981) ("everyone, quite correctly, recalls law review as the most valuable part of their legal education").

available to guide one's choices.[155] Since law reviews constitute the essential graduate school for a significant portion of law professors, it is not surprising that much law teaching and much legal scholarship imitate the student notes and comments that law professors originally wrote for their law reviews. The student-managed law review thus reproduces the discipline of law schools.

Law reviews also have a more direct influence on legal writing. Because third-year students select and edit articles written by law professors, the experienced writers of law review articles are bound to understand, at least tacitly, that the legal training of an audience they must reach consists of studying core curriculum subjects, engaging with the case method and its judicial criticisms, and writing "comprehensive" examination answers by using the paradigm of good paragraph thinking/writing. Law professors are thus likely to write, and law reviews to publish, those many "pieces that recite prior developments at great length, contain voluminous and largely meaningless citations for every proposition, and deal with topics that are either safe and standard, on the one hand, or currently faddish on the other."[156] In other words, much law review writing by law professors will be like student notes and comments, only longer and more comprehensive. Law reviews thereby extend the influences of the core curriculum, the case method and paradigm of good paragraph thinking/writing into the research and writing habits of law professors. Moreover, since publication decisions are usually made by editorial committees, by consensus, and perhaps at times on recommendations from faculty members, a law review's publication policy may often rely on the current intellectual trends at its school. This conformity will tacitly convey the current ideas of elite law school faculty to other legal scholars, and thus law reviews also circulate disciplinary values by translating, transmitting and incorporating the new theoretical ideas and interests of elite law faculty into the routine practices of other law professors.

A second institution of legal scholarship that helps maintain the discipline is the writing of conventional doctrinal scholarship by law professors. This scholarship consists of researching and writing legal treatises, short treatises for students called hornbooks, casebooks and casebook outlines, and the many law review articles that organize, report on and criticize judicial decisions. In the late nineteenth and early twentieth centuries, this scholarship was done mostly by faculty at elite law schools, and the major treatises and case-

---

155. Cf. Philip C. Kissam, *The Evaluation of Legal Scholarship*, 63 Wash. L. Rev. 221, 244–47 (1988) (describing the two career stages of law professors and pressures on law professors to keep writing in the mode of student writing for law reviews).

156. Cramton, supra note 146, at 8.

books of this period created the basic branches or fields of modern law.[157] Today this kind of scholarship is scattered more widely throughout the legal academy and serves to integrate the major preoccupation of many law professors with the discipline's routine practices that instruct students directly. This scholarship is grounded in the analysis of judicial opinions, the description and criticism of judicial decisions and caselaw rules, and the rights of parties under positive legal rules, especially the manifold rights of property. Each of the different strands of conventional doctrinal scholarship illustrates this grounding and the relationships of this scholarship to other elements of the discipline.

Legal treatises organize and analyze judicial decisions in order to describe a field of law in a relatively comprehensive manner.[158] A treatise in essence attempts to organize and describe a large number of judicial precedents in related areas of the law in a way that will be useful to legal practitioners who face a variety of highly particularized problems. Treatises thus contain many relatively abstract statements of legal principles and rules, and they must be updated frequently to take account of all new judicial decisions in the field. Treatise writers also rely heavily on the authority of judicial decisions, although the American tradition of treatise writing also includes some use of reason and argument by authors to criticize particular judicial decisions and articulate "the best law" on a subject.[159] Law professors who write treatises or student hornbooks must therefore engage deeply *and frequently* in case analysis that focuses on the rules of cases rather than their facts, and to a lesser extent may engage in judicial criticisms that typically depend on making arguments about the consistency or inconsistency between different judicial decisions. Treatise writing fits very well with the case method and more subtly replicates the comprehensive qualities of law school examinations.

Casebooks as the texts that students read and professors teach are a basic element of the discipline themselves. The writing of casebooks and casebook outlines that law students use to reduce the confusion and fragmentation of

---

157. See Schlegel, supra note 8.

158. See A.W.B. Simpson, *The Rise and Fall of the Legal Treatise: Legal Principles and the Form of Legal Literature*, 48 U. Chi. L. Rev. 632 (1981).

159. See id. at 671–74 (describing the desire of American treatise writers in the early 19th century to rely on natural law theories to distinguish American law from English law, and citing the early 20th century treatises of Wigmore on evidence, Williston on contracts, Corbin on contracts, and Scott on trusts and estates as exemplars of the American tradition). For a contemporary treatise that continues the tradition, see Lawrence Tribe, American Constitutional Law (3rd ed. 2000).

their case method classes is not a dissimilar process from treatise writing, and it is not uncommon for law professors to author both a treatise or hornbook and a casebook in the same or related fields. The main distinction between the two kinds of writing is that casebooks concentrate on analyzing (by excerpting or summarizing) a relatively small number of "leading cases" and raising questions about these cases.[160] Writing casebooks clearly helps commit law professors to the discipline's case method.

Conventional doctrinal articles in law reviews organize and analyze smaller batches of judicial decisions for any of several purposes. Consider, for example, an array of articles on the Supreme Court's recent decisions under the Eleventh Amendment of the Constitution that have recognized an immunity of state governments from judicial remedies imposed by the national government. William Fletcher discusses these decisions to explain their doctrinal antecedents, clarify their rulings and identify the open issues within this rapidly changing jurisprudence.[161] Carlos Vasquez organizes and analyzes these same decisions to identify contradictions in their rationales, to predict several future developments and to criticize some of these developments.[162] Ann Woolhandler provides an extensive examination of historical precedents to defend the recent decisions expanding state immunities.[163] On the other hand, Vicki Jackson relies on her reading of Framers' Intent and some traditional principles of constitutional jurisprudence to criticize the Court's recent decisions, Woolhandler's defense of them, and a position taken by Vazquez.[164] The writers of such articles, like the writers of treatises and casebooks, surely must develop at least tacit commitments to the discipline's case method and the comprehensive qualities of final examinations. Conventional doctrinal scholarship is more varied, more comprehensive, more directly related to legal reforms and perhaps often more intellectually challenging than standard forms of the case method and final examinations. But the loose coupling between these practices of similar intellectual work helps maintain the discipline of law schools. The intellectual or political excitement of doing conventional doctri-

---

160. See supra text accompanying notes 54–68.

161. William A. Fletcher, *The Eleventh Amendment: Unfinished Business*, 75 Notre Dame L. Rev. 843 (2000).

162. Carlos Manuel Vazquez, *Eleventh Amendment Schizophrenia*, 75 Notre Dame L. Rev. 859 (2000).

163. Ann Woolhandler, *Old Property, New Property, and Sovereign Immunity*, 75 Notre Dame L. Rev. 9191 (2000).

164. Vicki C. Jackson, *Principle and Compromise in Constitutional Adjudication: The Eleventh Amendment and State Sovereign Immunity*, 75 Notre Dame L. Rev. 953 (2000).

nal scholarship is another enforcing mechanism, of course, since this interest encourages law professors to maintain routine disciplinary practices in their teaching in order to support their scholarship.

A third practice of scholarship which is integral to the discipline is the evaluation of legal writing by law professors. These evaluations are made frequently in the course of one's research or teaching and in connection with decisions to grant tenure, make promotions, increase salaries or appoint experienced professors to new positions. The methods by which these evaluations are conducted can buttress disciplinary values. If a law faculty desires scholarship that is original or reveals new knowledge, they may place considerable emphasis on publications in prestigious law reviews, especially in making their tenure decisions or appointing professors with experience.[165] This approach encourages writers to take special account of student editors at elite law reviews and the law review conventions of case analysis, exhaustive or comprehensive research and a rhetoric of "correct answers" based on foundational principles if they wish to publish in prestigious law reviews. The same law review conventions will also help a legal scholar convey her ideas to the many different kinds of specialists who may participate in a faculty's decision about her tenure, promotion or appointment. Other law faculties may care more about the quantity of scholarship that a professor produces and measure this quantity by the number and length of books and articles published.[166] A sound way to satisfy this goal, especially for new professors, is to reproduce the discipline's methods of case analysis and judicial criticism in one's scholarship in order to write quickly and productively about many issues.[167] In addition, law professors who want to produce significant scholarship of any kind may, at least instinctively, tend to favor the discipline's routine methods of case teaching and final examinations in order to conserve their time and energy for research and writing.

Resistance to the practices of conventional legal scholarship assumes three forms. One is simply the withdrawal from scholarship, which leaves an ambitious law professor with more time for teaching or consulting. Consulting work, although it may be more sophisticated, can reinforce tacit commitments to the values of classroom and examination practices since much consulting by law professors involves the application of doctrinal expertise. The alloca-

---

165. See Markovits, supra note 65, at 423.

166. Numbers of publications are a good device for quickly conveying an impression of a law school faculty's "high quality" to outsiders such as university administrators, legislators or alumni.

167. See Kissam, supra note 155, at 244–47.

tion of additional time to teaching is more ambiguous with regard to the discipline. On the one hand, this may engage the professor more effectively in using the case method and final examinations; on the other hand, more time spent teaching core curriculum subjects could lead to productive experiments with law teaching that moves beyond the case method/final examination procedures to explore alternative educational methods such as "the problem method of law teaching"[168] or "teaching by writing."[169] These methods are generally believed to take more time than the traditional case method/final examination system, but they could promote a much broader and richer set of legal skills.

A second form of resistance to conventional legal scholarship, usually temporary but surprisingly frequent, is to turn (as this book does) to writing about legal education. Much of this writing attempts to explain technical aspects of legal education and better ways to accomplish these aspects.[170] But a good deal of this writing constitutes a "scholarship of complaint" that speaks to the perceived limits or ineffectuality of particular kinds of teaching, scholarship, law students or law professors and proposes some kind of utopian reform.[171] Writing about legal education has a long history in any event, and it has been well served by the West Publishing Company's subsidization of the Journal of Legal Education since 1948. This writing by-and-large serves the discipline by celebrating or justifying its major features and, in the case of complaints or proposed reforms, by offering an emotional outlet for discontented professors.

The third form of resistance to conventional doctrinal scholarship is to turn to other kinds of research and writing, be this interdisciplinary scholarship, political writing or journalism. The current reform movements in legal scholarship such as law and economics, critical legal studies and feminist jurisprudence are major instances, but this resistance assumes many forms and includes much "non-scholarly" writing such as investigative reports for public or professional agencies and columns about law or politics in newspapers and magazines. The relationships between this non-conventional writing and the discipline are complex, and they will be examined in Chapter Four. In general this work may appear to be a source of subversion to the discipline, but

---

168. See, e.g., Ogden, supra note 84.

169. See, e.g., Carol McCrehan Parker, *Writing Throughout the Curriculum: Why Law Schools Need It and How to Achieve It*, 76 Neb. L. Rev. 561 (1997).

170. See, e.g., Areeda, supra note 75; Morgan, supra note 77.

171. I owe this observation to an anonymous reviewer of the manuscript of this book, who among other things was encouraging some self-reflection about this book.

we shall see that the discipline also informs, limits and has cabined or captured the subversive ideas in this scholarship and turned much of this scholarship to the discipline's purposes.

The institutions of legal scholarship thus have intricate tacit relationships with teaching that help entrench the discipline of law schools and protect it from significant incursions. These institutions produce many scholars who, in the words of Roger Cramton, tend to be "threatened by anything new, disdainful of the practice of law, and inclined to be intolerant of any research other than the manipulation of doctrine or abstract theory."[172] In general the institutions of scholarship subtly enforce disciplinary values throughout the law school.

The Placement Process

The placement of students in legal employment as a law school activity constitutes another set of regularized practices that are an important part of the disciplinary web. These practices differ between elite and non-elite law schools, but there are common effects of the placement process that help entrench the discipline. At elite schools most students will expect and obtain jobs with high paying, relatively prestigious corporate law firms, while at non-elite schools only a fraction of the students obtain these types of jobs. Yet the time consumed in job-hunting, the apparent rewards that are granted to high class ranks and law review status in obtaining more prestigious positions and other more subtle influences of the placement process encourage conformity with the discipline's other practices at both elite and non-elite schools.

Many law students begin searching for legal employment as early as their first semester in law school. At elite schools many students start looking for their first summer jobs in the fall semester of their first year, and by the autumn of their second year virtually all students will be heavily engaged in on-campus interviews and elaborate call-back visits to corporate law firms.[173] At non-elite schools fewer students may search for or obtain summer jobs after their first year and fewer upper-class students are likely to participate in on-campus interviews with corporate firms. But placement offices at these schools begin coaching their students on the nature of job hunting during the first

---

172. Cramton, supra note 109, at 329.

173. See, e.g., Ann D. Turnicky, How to Get the Job You Want in a Law Firm 8–88, 100–04 (1997) (advising law students to prepare resumes and begin researching law firms in November and December of their first year, and then taking students through the elaborate and time-consuming process of second year interviewing).

year of law school, and many students will commit large amounts of time in their second and third years to the complicated process of searching for jobs with smaller law firms, with firms located outside their school's market area and with other kinds of employers.[174] The time and intensity of these activities surely encourage many students at elite and non-elite schools to take shortcuts in preparing for their classes and examinations, which of course will tend to reinforce the discipline's tacit lessons of analysis, a rule-oriented discourse and rapid productivity.

The placement process also rewards law students who have the top grades and provides positive feedback, unlike much of law school, to all students who obtain satisfactory employment opportunities while they are attending law school.[175] At elite schools the importance of class rank or grades to obtaining "the very best jobs" may often be muted in discussions and public signals, but there is a very clear awareness among students at these schools that the students with top grades will obtain the most distinguished judicial clerkships or teaching positions or employment at the most famous and prestigious law firms.[176] At non-elite schools the significance of class rank, grades and law review status is even more pronounced since only the students with these credentials will even qualify for interviews or obtain positions with certain corporate law firms. Thus the tacit values of law school examinations are reinforced symbolically and materially by the regular operations of law school placement. Furthermore, the dramatic or psychological contrast between the positive, often enthusiastic feedback that many students receive from successful job hunting and the limited positive feedback that only a relatively few law students receive from the discipline's other routine practices may contribute significantly to the malaise of upper-class law students.[177] As we have seen, this malaise enforces the discipline quite smartly.[178]

---

174. See Catherine K. Fitch, *The Placement Search and Employment Opportunities for Law School Graduates*, 29 Stet. L. Rev. 1285 (2000); Turnicky, supra note 173, at 125–40 (advising that time be spent on researching law firms and "networking" with lawyers in relevant fields). At non-elite schools many students also take part-time clerkships during the school year to obtain experience and connections that may help them find employment after graduation. See Pipkin, supra note 41.

175. See Note, *Making Docile Lawyers: An Essay on the Pacification of Law Students*, 111 Harv. L. Rev. 2027 (1998).

176. See id. at 2033–35.

177. See id. (arguing that the contrast in positive feedback between the placement process and academic process makes many Harvard law students experience "a sense of loss, anger and impotence").

178. See supra text accompanying notes 114–15.

Finally, the interviewing process itself sends subtle but powerful disciplinary messages. The brief on-campus interviews with corporate law firms that begin the process for many students are designed to allow a law firm and a student to sell themselves to each other, and to allow the firm's representative to make a preliminary assessment of the student's motivations and fit with the work and personnel of the firm.[179] Thus a typical interview will contain many statements about the nature of the firm's work for corporate clients, responses by the student about her interests in such work, and talk that examines the student's credentials—as either the interviewer or student tries to elucidate qualities that lie beneath the student's grades or other credentials. There also may be talk about courses in the law school curriculum that relate to the law firm's work—perhaps as a means of assessing the student's motivations or simply because this is a topic about which both the interviewer and student can easily talk. This kind of talk then gets repeated in multiple on-campus interviews and in more extensive subsequent interviews at law firms. Furthermore, as a technique for selling themselves, law students are often advised or learn to avoid "negative impressions," "opinions," "emotions," "mistakes" or "disagreements" as a way of making a favorable impression quickly with large numbers of unknown interviewers.[180]

The law school placement process thus engages law students with the best paying and most prestigious employers early in the students' law school careers. This process pays attention, much of it flattering attention, to law school examinations and grades, law review status or its absence, and the attractions and power of representing corporate clients. The process tacitly steers students towards law school courses that emphasize the property rights of corporations and other wealthy clients. It also signals that good lawyers should defer to professional hierarchies, and be careful, precise and error-free in their work and personality. The placement process thus symbolizes and reinforces the discipline's emphasis upon the values of final examinations, that is, upon the values of analysis, quick productive writing, obtaining good grades and high class ranks, and it also reinforces the discipline's rhetorical lessons of "coolness" and "toughness," its tacit instruction in professional deference, and its emphasis on property rights as law's center.[181]

We have now completed our examination of the basic practices and expectations that constitute American legal education. These disciplinary ele-

---

179. See Clifford R. Ennico, The Legal Job Interview 17–33 (1992).

180. See, e.g., id. at 67–112.

181. For discussion of the law school's pervasive "examinatorial regime" and its tacit lessons of "coolness" as a personal style, see Chapter Three.

ments and their lessons are also shaped by the physical facilities of law schools, and they are shaped or organized as well by the special temporal rhythms that are generally followed by law students and law professors alike. Chapter Two considers these critical aspects of the discipline.

CHAPTER TWO

SPACE AND TIME

Space and time matter to the discipline of law schools. Most importantly, the case method is typically practiced within relatively large amphitheatre classrooms that affect the ways in which this method works and is understood by both professors and students. Case method classes and final examinations take place within two sets of complicated temporal rhythms that substantially affect how these procedures work and are understood. More generally, the typical physical facilities and time patterns of law schools reinforce many of the discipline's lessons in subtle, elaborate ways. Let us consider the spatial relationships of law schools first and then the temporal relationships.

Spatial Relationships

Architecture can influence social behavior by expressing ideals, organizing habits or relationships, and conditioning the ways in which persons present themselves to others.[1] In this perspective, law school buildings construct and symbolize professional importance, professional autonomy and a formalist sort of expertise. More specifically, the amphitheatre classrooms and courtrooms of law schools idealize litigation and heroic oral practices. Law school architecture also facilitates a meticulous surveillance of students and professors, separates persons and groups from each other, imposes hierarchies, and helps make legal education and the discipline invisible.

---

1. See Murray Edelman, The Symbolic Uses of Politics 108 (1964) ("Settings not only condition political acts. They mold the very personalities of the actors."); Susanne Langer, Feeling and Form: A Theory of Art 100 (1953) ("the primary illusion of plastic art, visual space, appears in architecture as envisagement of an ethnic domain"); Daphne Spain, Gendered Spaces 6 (1992) ("Although space is constructed by social behavior at a particular point in time, its legacy may persist (seemingly as an absolute) to shape the behavior of future generations.").

The Buildings

The exterior designs of law schools range from the collegiate gothic to neo-classical to late modernist and international styles. But whatever its style, a law school building's prominent size and location, its rich materials, imposing formal lines and formal or distancing relationships with other buildings are likely to signal that law work is important, serious, a formal enterprise and quite different from work in the rest of the university.[2] These tacit signals are reinforced by the geographic isolation of many law schools from other sites of the university such as the main library, the humanities and social science departments and the administrative center.[3] Thus law school buildings both symbolize exclusivity and establish barriers to outsiders that enhance the autonomy of legal education. They might be said to resemble the sacred spaces of early Christian monasteries, which were located on the margins of urban civilization, inaccessible to ordinary persons, while inviting and celebrating the contemplation and production of spiritually and socially significant knowledge.[4]

---

2. See Ilene H. Forsyth, The Use of Art: Medieval Metaphor in the Michigan Law Quadrangle (describing the neo-gothic University of Michigan law buildings); Mona Harrington, Women Lawyers: Rewriting the Rules 41–42 (1993) (describing the cloistral qualities of Harvard Law School that block out its neighborhood); Susan McLeod, *Architecture and Politics in the Reagan Era: From Postmodernism to Deconstructivism*, 8 Assemblage, Feb. 1989, pp. 23, 45–50 (describing the hermeticism or exclusionary qualities of Frank Gehry's deconstructivist plan for Loyola Law School in Los Angeles); University of Dayton School of Law, Joseph E. Keller Hall (brochure), p. 2 ("Situated at the face of the University, Keller Hall dramatically reflects the importance of legal and professional education at the University"). Cf. Richard P. Dober, Campus Architecture: Building in the Groves of Academe 177 (1996) (arguing that American university architecture emphasizes "grand projects" that fail to contribute to their surroundings but are "usually intended to signify institutional advancement, solemnize special causes three dimensionally, ennoble benefactors, and provide publicity, if not prestige, to the sponsoring college and university").

3. See David Sokolow, *From Kurosawa to (Duncan) Kennedy: The Lessons of Rashomon for Current Legal Education*, 1991 Wisc. L. Rev. 969, 980 ("Like most law schools, the University of Texas School of Law is an island unto itself; set at the northeast corner of the campus, it has its own library, classrooms, cafeteria and study areas. One could attend law school there for three years and never set foot anywhere else on the campus.").

4. See, e.g., R. P. Dober, supra note 2, at 99 (picture of the University of Missouri's law school courtyard); I. H. Forsyth, supra note 2 (describing the neo-collegiate gothic style and cloistral qualities of Michigan Law School); Quinnipiac College School of Law Magazine, Vol. 1, Issue 1 (Fall 1994), pp. 8–9 (comparing new law school buildings at Quinnipiac to religious spaces).

The interiors of law school buildings also focus the mind on the discipline of law schools. Somber colors, windowless spaces, the muted sounds of carpeted halls, lobbies, classrooms and offices, and the neutral, homogenizing qualities of artificial climate and lighting all tend to exclude social contexts, focus attention on the special forms of classroom work and scholarship and symbolize an autonomous, disciplined sort of speech and thought.[5] The large-scale public areas for entryways, hallways and student commons, which often are adorned by conservative portraits of former law professors and distinguished alumni, also express seriousness, an ideal professional manner, status, expertise, and power.[6] The massive, formal and hermetic qualities of law school interiors are like the inner sanctums of Buddhist temples or the chapels in gothic cathedrals which signal a marked and honored departure from the outside world.

Amphitheatre Classrooms

Amphitheatre classrooms are pervasive in law schools. They seat 50 to 200 or more students to accommodate the large classes of the core curriculum. There is usually a small stage or space with a desk or table at the well of the room, which places the professor at dead center of the class discussions, and students are seated in semi-circular terraced rows that rise considerably above the professor's location. The audio and sight lines between the professor and students and among the students are usually quite good, and the typical high ceilings of these rooms invite robust speech and imply grandeur. These rooms are efficient instruments of the discipline.

The structure of the amphitheatre classroom conveys tacit messages that serve the discipline. Amphitheatre classrooms simulate inverted courtrooms, with professors in the place of detached, neutral judges and students in the place of attorneys assembled before an interrogating, all-powerful judge. In this space, however, the professor/judge is below the student/attorneys, and the professor/judge, not the student/attorneys, occupies the exploitable space in which to move, gesticulate and make dramatic interventions.

---

5. See Victor Papanek, Sensing a Dwelling (1993; manuscript on file with author).

6. See Harrington, supra note 2, at 45 (describing the portraits of male judges, professors and other notable lawyers at Harvard Law School: "Almost everyone mentions the portraits. Clearly, they haunt the imaginations of many alumnae."); cf. Leslie Kanes Weisman, Discrimination by Design: A Feminist Critique of the Man-Made Environment 35–64 (1992) (describing the status and power that are expressed and promoted by large-scale American public architecture).

Michel Foucault once observed about courtrooms that

"The very least that can be said is that this implies an ideology. What is this arrangement? A table, and behind this table, which distances them from the two litigants, the 'third party,' that is, the judges. Their position indicates firstly that they are *neutral* with respect to each litigant, and secondly this implies that their decision is not already arrived at in advance, that it will be made after an aural investigation of the two parties, on the basis of a certain conception of *truth* and a certain number of ideas concerning what is just and unjust, and thirdly that they have the *authority* to enforce their decision. This is ultimately the meaning of this simple arrangement."[7]

What then is the ideology of the law school's *inverted courtroom*? The desk or podium and rows of terraced student chairs create distance between the professor and her students, suggesting that the professor will be "neutral with respect to each (student)," that she will be conveying "the truth and a certain number of ideas about what is just and unjust," and that she has "the authority to enforce (her) decision(s)" about class discussions, judicial opinions and final examinations. But the law professor, unlike the judge, has the exploitable space in this courtroom and thus may also be expected to function as something of an advocate as well as a judge. Moreover, student expectations that legal doctrine will be explained and legal work modeled by their professors suggest that the law professor, unlike a judge, is not expected to reserve her decisions but instead to make many immediate statements about the law, lawyers and law students. The classroom's architecture thus combines with these expectations to produce a tacit ideal of the law professor as a very quick and very productive "advocate/judge/expositor" who is capable of moving seamlessly back and forth between these three rather different functions. Fragmentation and confusion can ensue from professorial attempts to fulfill these three roles in combination.

The physical placement of students above the professor also signals a consumer-producer relationship that tacitly reverses the power of students and professors. This reversal implies that "dominant" professors will satisfy the expectations of "dominated" students. Locating professors in a depressed, detached position in the classroom also reinforces student expectations that law professors will model the different roles of the persuasive legal advocate, the

---

7. Michel Foucault, *On Popular Justice: Debate with the Maos*, in Power/ Knowledge: Selected Interviews and Other Writings, 1972–77, pp. 1, 8 (Colin Gordon, ed., 1980) (emphasis added).

rationalistic, neutral judge who assesses both ideas and students quickly and authoritatively and the expert who explains legal doctrine in ways that make students feel comfortable for their examinations.

The amphitheatre classroom also facilitates a meticulous and reciprocal surveillance of professors and students that enforces the discipline and its lessons of analysis, a rule-oriented discourse and autonomous expertise. The relatively unimpeded audio and sight lines between each student and the professor allow students to focus carefully on the professor's behavior and allow the professor to find and observe individual students with maximum efficiency. The semi-circular rows of student chairs also provide good audio and sight lines among students, enhancing a peer control of class discussions which quietly insists that student contributions be relevant to what students want to hear. The windowless character of most law school classrooms helps students focus on the professor and each other as well. These surveillance mechanisms enforce conformity to conventional norms, especially the classroom ideal of a precise, careful, objective analysis of judicial opinions, the use of many rules as the basis of a confident, objectivist rhetoric, and the modeling of a unique professional expertise.

In large classes, law professors typically employ "seating charts" to identify student locations, another device which enhances the supervisory power of professors. Assigned seats assure conformity in the distribution of bodies, forestall resistance to interrogation, and remind students of their place within the hierarchy. The seating chart together with the professor's authority to call on any student at any time produces a one-way visibility of students in which they are aware that the professor *might be* observing them—even though he can observe only a few students at one time. This one-way visibility mimics Jeremy Bentham's "Panopticon," which was designed to be a low cost, utility-maximizing surveillance device for prisons and other institutions that desire to impose feigned observations on their inmates at all times.[8] Thus the am-

---

8. See Michel Foucault, Discipline and Punish 195–228 (1977). Bentham's design featured a central tower with cleverly shielded observation positions that would provide "continuous" and "one way" observations of inmates economically since the inmates could never be sure whether they were under observation. The inmates were to be housed in wings surrounding the tower in rooms shielded from each other but illuminated from the outside to provide maximum visibility of inmates to observers in the tower. Id. For descriptions of panopticon plans implemented by non-carceral institutions other than law schools, see L.K. Weisman, supra note 6, at 39 (depicting the "open landscape" office design of Frank Lloyd Wright's Larkin Company Building in Buffalo, New York, which allowed supervisors to oversee their "regimented, hierarchical, sexually segregated work force"); Thomas Greenhouse, "With Shoe on Capitalist Foot, Czechs Woo Old Industrialist," NY Times, April 30, 1990, pp. A1, C3 (describing Thomas Bata's nineteenth century shoe plant in Zlin, Czecho-

phitheatre classroom of law schools creates a marvelous "examination space" in which the disciplinary practices of casebooks and the case method are conducted with intensity at relatively low cost.

The amphitheatre classroom also creates a marvelous "theatrical space" that plays a subtle role in the law school's construction of law and lawyers. These classrooms are not only large but also typically high ceilinged, thus providing stately qualities that bespeak grandeur or power and invite vigorous, robust speech making. The acoustic qualities of these rooms privilege the aural qualities of persons who speak with robust charismatic tones, dramatic modulations and majestic or sensual timbres.[9] These conditions favor the deeper registers of male voices, constituting an unstated male norm of classroom performance.[10] Large, high-ceilinged rooms also encourage and reward visually charismatic behavior, especially when a professor's dress, physical gestures and other body language are perceived as professionally appropriate.[11] The dramatic, panoptic spaces of the amphitheatre strengthen the vividness and intensity of the face-to-face interactions by which most law students first experience "the law" and "lawyers," tacitly enhancing the discipline's basic lessons of analysis, a rule-oriented discourse and a focus upon technical concepts.[12]

Amphitheatre classrooms also help privilege oral practices over reading and writing. These classrooms invite acts of oral heroism in which a lecturing professor, a question-asking professor or students can try to engage in brilliant charismatic speech that declares what the law is or argues what the law should be in confident, rapid-fire assertive styles.[13] These classrooms also invite stu-

---

slovakia, with its "unusual 16-story headquarters in which the chairman's office was placed in an elevator so that it could move from floor to floor, allowing the boss to keep an eye on his workers.").

9. Cf. Morton Filler, *He's the Top*, NY Review of Books, Feb. 11, 1993, pp. 16, 17 (quoting the architect Louis Kahn: "If you look at the Baths of Caracalla...we know that we can bathe just as well under an 8-foot ceiling as we can under a 150-foot ceiling, but I believe there's something about a 150-foot ceiling that makes a man a different kind of man.").

10. Cf. Catherine MacKinnon, Feminism Unmodified 36 (1989) (describing unstated male norms that are pervasive in American society).

11. Cf. Carrie Menkel-Meadow, *Feminist Legal Theory, Critical Legal Studies, and Legal Education or "The Fem-Crits Go to Law School*, 38 J. Legal Educ. 61, 67–68 (1988) (describing the implicit professional modeling that law professors do).

12. See Peter L. Berger & Thomas Luckmann, The Social Construction of Reality: A Treatise in the Sociology of Knowledge 28–34 (1967) (the most important experience of "others" takes place in face-to-face situations).

13. For evidence of such classroom behavior by both professors and students, see, e.g., Chris Goodrich, Anarchy and Elegance: Confessions of a Journalist at Yale Law School (1991); Scott Turow, One L (1977); Catherine Weiss & Louise Melling, 40 Stan. L. Rev.

dent attention to careful note-taking, especially of what the professor says, simply as a normalizing or stabilizing technique if not also a good technique to prepare for examinations. The physical structure of amphitheatre classrooms thus fuses with the discipline's routine practices, especially the case method, Moot Court and oral-like writing of final examinations, to honor oral skills and make oral communications appear most important to the study and practice of law. The law school classroom engenders productive, brilliant and authoritative speech-making as a tacit ideal of law and lawyering while tacitly devaluing both reading and writing.

Courtrooms and Clinics

Law schools have formal courtrooms in which mock trials and appellate arguments are staged. These rooms are used primarily for "moot court" exercises in appellate and trial advocacy courses. Judges also may bring their courts "on circuit" to use law school courtrooms. Law school clinics, in which upper class students represent actual clients, are typically located in law school buildings as well. These spaces symbolize the primacy of litigation and adversarial conflict and reinforce the privileging of these ideas in the discipline's tacit concepts of law and lawyers. Furthermore, the contrast between prominently situated, expensively furnished courtrooms and more utilitarian, marginally located clinic spaces tacitly signals that appellate law and "theory" are more important than the "practice" of applying rules to concrete situations.[14]

Moot court exercises are usually required in the first year of law school, and the most successful competitors in these exercises subsequently may represent their schools in external competitions with moot court teams from other schools. Trial practice courses are usually elective and available only to upper class students. These programs provide many students with their major (or only) opportunities to talk law publicly outside the confines of the case method, and these programs provide a kind of public recognition and rewards that are something of an alternative to law review membership. These exercises are also traumatic experiences for many students since they pose initial

---

1299, 1332–45 (1988) (describing "non-conversational speeches" in Yale law school classrooms). Cf. Shaffer & Redmount, Lawyers, Law Students and People 165 (1977) ("It appears that each participant [in law school class discussions] makes his or her own speech.").

14. Cf. Mark Spiegel, *Theory and Practice in Legal Education: An Essay on Clinical Education*, 34 UCLA L. Rev. 577 (1987) (describing how concepts of "theory" implicitly dominate legal education and devalue "practical" aspects like clinics).

challenges "to act like lawyers," especially to dress, look and sound like lawyers. The aura, richness and formality of the courtrooms in which these exercises occur enhance their special qualities, and thus the lessons of adversarial conflict, competitive individualism, and a combative rule-oriented rhetoric are tacitly inscribed in law students. Many students understandably may graduate from law school with vivid images of courtroom litigation as "the way" to practice law?[15]

Law school clinics are a different matter. Clinics typically provide offices for clinical faculty, client interview rooms and a work area for students, and these utilitarian spaces are usually located in peripheral areas of the school, in out-of-the-way spots convenient to clients or simply residual spaces, far removed from the more honored locations of courtrooms and core curriculum classrooms.[16] These locations and the inexpensive furnishings of clinic spaces symbolize the lesser importance of the practical or applied aspects of legal education and practice. These locations and furnishings may discourage students from taking clinical courses. In any event, clinical locations tend to separate clinical faculty and the clinical work of students from the mainstream of the law school. Clinic architecture quietly privileges "theory" over "practice"[17] and helps protect the discipline's basic elements of casebooks, the case method and the final examination from subversion by more practice-oriented educational methods.[18]

Other Spaces

Other law school spaces also enforce lessons of the discipline. For example, student commons are usually large areas in which students can banter com-

---

15. Cf. Robert A. Kagan, *Do Lawyers Cause Adversarial Legalism? A Preliminary Inquiry*, 19 Law & Soc. Inquiry 1, 23–28 (1994); E. Walter Van Valkenburg, *Law Teachers, Law Students and Litigation*, 34 J. Legal Educ. 584 (1984) (suggesting that law teaching and legal scholarship promote excessive litigation).

16. See Pierre Schlag, *Normativity and the Politics of Form*, 139 U. Pa. L. Rev. 801, 926–29 (1991); Mark Tushnet, *Scenes from the Metropolitan Underground: A Critical Perspective on the Status of Clinical Education*, 52 Geo. Wash. L. Rev. 272, 273 (1984).

17. See Spiegel, supra note 14 (describing the use of the theory/practice distinction in law schools to limit clinical education unfairly).

18. Cf. Joanne Martin & Bryant G. Garth, *Clinical Education as a Bridge Between Law School and Practice: Mitigating the Misery*, 1 Clinical L. Rev. 443, 444 (1994) (arguing that "distinctions between clinical education and the traditional curriculum must blur rather than be maintained, whether by clinicians or non-clinicians").

petitively about brilliant and not-so-brilliant classroom performances, await nervously to begin examinations, and exclaim with relief or joy when classes or examinations end, thus continuing to circulate disciplinary values. Law review offices, by their separate, sometimes prominent locations, symbolize the hierarchy among students that is grounded in final examination performances and class ranks. These spaces can also replicate the hierarchy of corporate law firms by providing offices for the editors but not staff members. Placement offices, where law firms interview students for summer and permanent positions, quietly indicate the prestige and economic opportunities that await those who have mastered the discipline. These offices tend to be simple, sparely furnished rooms in which students learn to appreciate directly the function of final examinations and grades as they obtain their initial impressions of employment prospects that so often are hinged upon class rank.[19]

Faculty offices symbolize and facilitate autonomy, authority, productivity and law school achievement. These offices divide professors from students, professors from each other, and professors from any collective mission a law school might have. They are symbolic sites of productivity and also sites of occasional confrontations between professors and students that help enforce the discipline in subtle but effective ways. Faculty offices are typically separated from student spaces, and at many schools they are protected by the symbolic or actual guardianship of secretarial stations and secretaries who work there.[20] Law faculty are also separated from students and each other by the elaborate word processing/internet apparatuses that dominate the modern professor's office. The occupants of these offices often seem literally attached to their word processors as they attend to producing the "pieces" of scholarship, government reports, committee reports and private consulting work that are staples of the law professor's work.[21] These humming, blinking machines invite "productivity" as their superb electronic qualities seduce the writer into producing longer sentences, longer articles, longer books and more articles and books.[22] Moreover, when a person's eyes are glued to a word processing

---

19. See Chapter One's discussion of the placement process.

20. Cf. Thomas Shaffer, *Moral Implications and Effects of Legal Education or: Brother Justinian Goes to Law School*, 34 J. Legal Educ. 190, 192–94 (1984) (describing other ways in which law school architecture separates faculty from students).

21. Cf. Mark Rohr, *A Law School for the Consumer*, 13 Nova Law Review 101, 101 (1988) (there is "a deeply-rooted expectation that the professors regularly produce scholarly writings").

22. Cf. Jeff Madrick, *Computers: Waiting for the Revolution*, NY Rev., March 26, 1998, pp. 29, 31 ("Why haven't computers dramatically augmented productivity? Some analysts

screen, her back to the door and her word processor on, any interruption or unplanned conversation with a colleague or student may appear as an unpleasant interference rather than joint educational venture—either to the office's occupant, for whom the word processing machine often seems an extension of self, or to anyone who would dare to venture into the sanctuary of the busy, productive legal scholar.[23]

Faculty offices also provide a kind of "confessional space" by reason of their formality, their orientations towards productivity and their arrays of authoritative texts aligned on the walls. Here individual students can bare their souls, expectations, achievements and class ranks to professors while seeking advice or information about examinations, research projects or possible employment opportunities.[24] In this event the professor may choose between or combine the distinctive but conflicting roles of personal confidant, doctrinal expert, and tough examiner of a student's "analytical abilities" and other aspects of her work or life. The law professor now resembles a priest and the law student a mendicant, stripped of all her personal possessions and self other than her law school self. The primal qualities of this space, its seriousness signified by the blinking word processor, email messages on screen or other visible projects, and its authority signified by the detached professor and his authoritative texts, help inscribe the discipline's messages of analysis, examinations, productivity and hierarchy. Faculty offices thus facilitate quick, revealing confessions by students about their insecurities or law school failures and quick confident statements by professors or students that would demonstrate a flawless professional expertise. In the ambiguous world of professional education, the discipline of law schools imposes its norms subtly and efficiently.[25]

The most symbolic disciplinary space in law schools may be the law library. Here, in an environment reminiscent of university libraries but more intimate, more specialized and quite autonomous from the university library, students and professors are surrounded by armies of case reporters and law reviews that occupy the most visible shelves in a library, which itself occupies a major part

---

believe that the enormous power of computers is often superfluous. For example, law briefs are now much thicker and more detailed than they once were, thanks to word processing and the greater ease in obtaining supporting documents. But this does not mean that law is being practiced more efficiently; perhaps just the opposite is true.").

23. Cf. Alan Stone, *Legal Education on the Couch*, 85 Harv. L. Rev. 392, 404 (1971) (describing the "harried, unapproachable, forbidding demeanor" that many law professors adopt as a response to large classes and their desire for autonomy from students).

24. See generally Philip C. Kissam, *Conferring with Students*, 65 UMKC L. Rev. 917 (1997).

25. See also Chapter Three's discussion of the law school's confessional technology.

of the law school building. These signs surely affirm the regular use of case-books, the case method and the institutions of conventional legal scholarship.

Temporal Relationships

Law school time is organized by the special rhythms of student time and faculty time. These rhythms overlap and infiltrate each other, although the most striking relationship between them may be a certain chaos, or discord, which signals and facilitates the essential separation of students from faculty. In any event, these rhythms separately and together generate timetables that regulate the routine work of law schools.

Student Rhythms

Law students are notoriously pressed for time, especially in their first and second years.[26] They face a relatively full schedule of class hours, complicated reading assignments which demand substantial time at least initially, an examination/grading system that encourages extensive review or cramming before examinations, and the often time-consuming search for legal employment. Many students also spend time working to obtain financial support, practical experience or permanent employment.[27] The pressures of time encourage much instrumentalist behavior that tacitly reinforces the discipline's basic lessons.

Five basic rhythms regulate student time. Several of these have their greatest influence during the first year of law school, when student work is most traumatic, most competitive, most uncertain, and learning is most likely to take place.[28] But even after the first year, when grades and class ranks have distributed students to their places in the law school hierarchy, these rhythms persist and encourage patterns of reading, writing and thinking that help entrench the discipline's lessons of analysis, a rule-oriented discourse and a rhetoric of authority and complexity.

---

26. See, e.g., Benjamin, Kasniak, Sales & Shanfield, *The Role of Legal Education in Producing Psychological Stress Among Law Students and Lawyers*, 1986 Am. Bar Found. Res. J. 225, 247–49.

27. See Ronald Pipkin, *Moonlighting in Law School: A Multischool Study of Part-Time Employment of Full-Time Law Students*, 1982 Am. Bar Found. Res. J. 1109.

28. See Aubrey Schwartz, *Law, Lawyers, and Law School: Perspectives From the First-Year Class*, 30 J. Legal Educ. 437, 439 (1980).

The rhythm of weekly time is organized by a formal schedule of class hours and informal schedule of class preparations. The class schedules of law students are more similar to those of undergraduates than graduate students, and in their first and second years law students are generally expected to attend from 12 to 15 class hours per week.[29] The novelty and complexity of reading fragmented casebooks to prepare for multi-layered discussions in the case method classroom can also demand much time of students, at least initially. A commitment to these schedules can be time-consuming until the student becomes comfortable with classroom expectations or acquires more efficient methods. During this initial period, the insistent pace of routine law school work promotes the habits of "analyzing" judicial opinions for their rules or holdings and "reading" casebooks, other texts and class discussions to determine the legal rules and other tools that may be useful on law school examinations. These habits, by giving students something they expect from the law and by emulating the professional work in casebooks and classrooms which they easily understand, provide a kind of stability or certainty in the uncertain professional world that surrounds new law students.

The rhythm of semester time becomes apparent to students, especially first year students, as they begin to sense or understand that they must master relatively large numbers of doctrinal rules and case holdings to prepare for their examinations. This rhythm engages many students in intricate combinations of reviewing reading assignments, reviewing class notes and constructing outlines to help them memorize or internalize the objective bases of examination answers.[30] At this point, reading supplemental texts increases dramatically as students begin to sense their limited understanding of what may be expected of them on examinations. The rhythm of semester time thus enforces a student's commitment to doctrinal details and to instrumentalist methods of reading and class preparation. This rhythm is not unlike the ballooning work schedules that lawyers often employ to meet deadlines, and thus it may have practical value in addition to encouraging a productive review of legal subjects. But this rhythm clearly enforces the tacit lessons of analysis, rule coverage, and the in-

---

29. See E. Gordon Gee & Donald Jackson, Following the Leader? The Unexamined Consensus in Law School Curricula 12 (1975) (reporting that most law schools require 80 to 90 credit hours for graduation or, in other words, an average of 13.3 to 15 credit hours per semester); see also ABA, Standards for Approval of Law Schools and Interpretations, sec. 305 (a) & (b), interpretation #3 (unless the exceptions for clinical education or writing work apply, a semester credit hour at an approved school requires one 50 minute class session each week for 15 weeks).

30. See Janet Motley, *A Foolish Consistency: The Law School Exam*, 10 Nova L. J. 723, 749–60 (1986).

strumentalist habit of "inspectional" or "paraphrase" readings of legal texts in order to determine their rules and holdings quickly if superficially.

The rhythm of examination time arrives at the end of the semester. This is a distinctive three-part rhythm, of last minute cramming, the rapid press of thought and writing during each examination, and a momentary lull before beginning preparations for the next exam.[31] This rhythm demands sustained competitive work after a semester of mastering complicated doctrinal details, and it approximates the rhythm of many lawyering projects. Significantly, this rhythm imprints habits of analyzing complex problems quickly by employing conventional rules and methods and writing confident, authoritative, rule-based essays in a rapid, instrumentalist manner. This rhythm also facilitates and promotes the paradigm of good paragraph thinking/writing. How else is one to get through a battery of examinations at the end of the semester with some measure of competitive success? The paradigm conveys a rule-oriented analysis of legal problems in a confident, productive fashion. But this paradigm excludes non-conventional, non-formalist values and discourages reflective or critical thought that requires more time and space for deliberation, feedback and revisions to the problems one is addressing or the texts one is writing.[32] The rhythm of examination time thus tacitly teaches and privileges analysis, a rule-oriented discourse, rapid-fire productivity, and a confident, assertive rhetoric by exposing students to an especially intense, traumatic, and memorable pace for several weeks of their law school lives.

The rhythms of weekly, semester and examination time shift during a student's three years in law school. Weekly time and semester time may become more intense as faculty in upper class courses impose longer reading assignments and students engage in job searches, law review work or part-time work outside the school. But these rhythms relax for many students as they discover shortcuts to prepare for their classes or examinations. In most cases, however, these rhythmic shifts point towards simpler, more efficient ways to prepare for final examinations, for example by relying more heavily on commercially published "course outlines" to reduce their review time or by reducing their class attendance to prepare for final examinations.[33] These

---

31. For descriptions of this rhythm, see S. Turow, supra note 13, at 187–96, 289–93.

32. See Philip C. Kissam, *Thinking (By Writing) About Legal Writing*, 40 Vand. L. Rev. 135, 138–41 (1987); *Law School Examinations*, 42 Vand. L. Rev. 433, 477–79 (1989).

33. See James Lofton, *Study Habits and Their Effectiveness in Legal Education*, 27 J. Legal Educ. 418, 431–33, 445–46 (1975); Roy Rickson, *Faculty Control and the Structure of Student Competition: An Analysis of the Student Role*, 25 J. Legal Educ. 47 (1973).

shifts reinforce the focus of first year rhythms on the discipline's tacit lessons of analysis, a rule-oriented discourse, and instrumentalist reading habits.

Law students also experience the less regular but insistent rhythm of "career time." This rhythm marks the different stages in the law student's progression from law school towards legal employment and incorporates the shifts between a student's studies and her new experiences with legal workplaces. These shifts occur episodically as the student moves back-and-forth between her law school work, on-campus interviews with law firms that often require absence from class, the more sustained "call-back" visits with firms for summer, part-time or permanent employment and finally work during the summers or part-time work at a firm or firms.[34] The patterns of this rhythm differ somewhat between elite and non-elite law schools, but this rhythm can become all consuming at times for students at both kinds of schools.

The obvious consequence of this career rhythm is the decreasing availability of time for legal study, which invites students to use short-cuts in preparing for classes and examinations that rely on the disciplinary values of analysis and a rule-oriented discourse. More subtly, this rhythm can reinforce the twin psychological deformations of excessive formalism and excessive relativism or apathy. The periodic and frequent shifts between the discipline of legal study, the rewards of obtaining legal jobs and the diffuse, quite different experiences of early legal work may convince many students that there is little connection between their studies and legal practice.[35] In this uncertain space about what it is that lawyers do, what might students turn to for their (implicit) theories of law? It seems plausible that this uncertainty or tension between legal studies and legal practice may induce many students to return (tacitly of course) to something like their initial pre-law school views—that the law consists primarily of rules. Other students may gravitate towards the relativistic view that law is simply a bag of rhetorical tools.

The most irregular rhythm of student time is the rhythm of "festival time," which consists of those times and events at which students collectively attempt to escape the discipline. These festivities include intense student parties and other gatherings at which law school personalities, classroom rituals, examinations or placement opportunities become the principal or only subjects of

---

34. See Chapter One's discussion of the placement process.

35. See Ronald Pipkin, *Legal Education: The Consumers' Perspective*, 1976 Am. Bar F. Res. J. 1161, 1167–73 (measuring the increasing disenchantment of upper class students at five law schools in their perceptions of the rationality of law school pedagogy and how well legal education prepares them for practice).

discussion.[36] They include informal faculty-student gatherings too that introduce students to professional schmoozing and more formal law school events at which festival-like role shifts, reversals and satire celebrate the local law school culture and construct a sense of professional bonhomie. Depending on their circumstances, these festivals can generate either fascination and celebration or criticism of disciplinary practices. Either way, such festivals focus attention on the discipline's elements, its lessons and values, thus completing a circle of the somewhat monastic-like rhythms that keep law students attuned to the discipline of law schools.

Faculty Rhythms

The rhythms of faculty time are quite different. These rhythms harness the diverse perspectives of law professors to the discipline's basic routines and values. In addition, the difference between student and faculty rhythms creates a particular "invisibility" of faculty and students to each other that erodes the possibilities for genuine individualized communication between them and enhances the basic elements of the discipline.

There is, first, the three or four step rhythm of classroom performances. This rhythm approximates those of athletes or entertainers and is perhaps something like the law student's examination rhythm. First, law professors must not be disturbed and will not change their routines for an hour or two before each class, or at least before each class in a doctrinal course with a large number of students. A last-minute immersion or cramming of doctrinal details that may need explication in the classroom and, more pervasively, a constructive focusing of nervous energy before one's performance in a large amphitheatre classroom mark this initial phase.[37] The next phase involves performing before a large number of students, typically seated in an amphitheatre, who, the professor understands, are searching for professionally useful knowledge, judgments about their progress towards this goal, and the resolution of puzzles embedded in the readings or raised by class discussion.

---

36. Scott Turow describes a number of these events in the description of his first year at Harvard Law School. See S. Turow, supra note 13.

37. See, e.g., Lillian R. Bevier, *As Law Professor: The Practically Perfect Job* in Women Lawyers: Perspectives on Success 213, 223–24 (Emily Courcic, ed. 1984) ("During the time right before class I am at my least graceful....The feeling is a little like stage fright, just as law teaching is a little like acting. Only with law teaching, there's no script and no director— no prompter and no fellow actors. There's just you and the audience of students.").

Ideally, there is a maximum rush of adrenalin at this point, which lasts fifty minutes, to allow the professor to profess her expertise by demonstrating mastery of the complex, sometimes contradictory classroom imperatives of control, entertainment and rigorous or sophisticated case method analysis. At the end of each performance there is the possibility of "applause" from interested or admiring students who surround the professor in the well of the amphitheatre classroom for a few minutes of camaraderie or other repartee.[38] This applause is not available to everyone, to be sure, but when it occurs it forms a pleasant prelude to those brief moments of letdown, relaxation and post-performance critique that seem inevitable aspects of public performances. In any event, both after-class applause and post-performance lulls are limited substantially by the other more insistent rhythms of law faculty time.[39]

Law faculty are also subject to a semester rhythm, although one which is markedly different from that of students. This is a complicated, multi-part beat that is constructed by the constraints that doctrinal courses must "cover" a significant number of rules and issues and that the law professor must write, read, and grade large numbers of final examinations. This rhythm produces two rather odd but substantial moments of release from the routines of classroom work: first, at the moment the last class of the semester ends, and again when grades are handed to the registrar. Within this subtle rhythm of disciplined repetitive acts and eruptive moments of release, the analytical, rule-oriented, authoritative and productive law professor is constructed. The constraint of rule coverage in doctrinal classes is imposed by the expectations of students and by explicit or implicit norms of the core curriculum, and it is satisfied in either of two basic ways. There is the even pace, which ensures throughout the semester that a planned amount of doctrinal material is thoroughly covered at each class. This pace maximizes the intentional control of the professor over class discussions and imposes special demands on law students to make their contributions brief, "to the point" and aimed at "right an-

---

38. See, e.g., Robert Summers, *The First Hour of the Course in Commercial Law, Spring Semester 1990*, Cornell Law Alumni Bulletin, p. 12 (1991) ("I will stay after every class to take questions and to continue the argument."); Weiss & Melling, supra note 13, at 1337 ("Women also weren't 'important enough' for most after-class discussions with the professor. Almost invariably, when the professor is a man, the cluster around the professor consists only of men.")

39. See, e.g., Weiss & Melling, supra note 13, at 1337 (quoting a first year student at Yale: "I went up to talk to [the professor] after class. He was surrounded by five men. I tried to wait my turn. Twenty minutes later, they were finally done, and [the professor] seemed ready to go. By the time he got to talk to me he was impatient, and my confidence was diminished further.").

swers."[40] There is also the irregular pace, which considers a subject more slowly and in more open-ended ways during the early parts of the semester but aims at rule coverage by increasing the length of reading assignments and lecturing later in the semester. This pace enforces a rule-oriented discourse by paying attention to the rules just as students are beginning to do the same in preparing for their examinations. This pace also allows professors to lecture at the end of the semester, thus presenting themselves as unchallenged and unchallengeable experts just as they are evaluated by their students in end-of-the-semester formal course evaluations. Each pace, in its different way, focuses the law professor and law students on tacit values of the discipline.

As the semester progresses, law professors become increasingly aware of their need to write effective final examinations. Exams must be "effective" in terms of separating students into the different grading categories that are demanded by the law school's mandatory grading curve, and they must be "fair" in terms of providing a relatively thorough coverage of issues considered during the semester. Novel, ingenious problems consisting of complex situations must be constructed in ways that relate to course materials but disguise issues sufficiently to ensure that some kind of "objective" grading can easily distinguish many categories of performance in terms of student abilities to spot issues, recollect rules and apply rules under severe time constraints.[41] In effect, new jigsaw puzzles must be constructed each semester in order to divide students efficiently into A, B, and C students. Making examinations entrenches the imperatives of analysis and rule coverage in professors, tacitly reminding them of these essential disciplinary lessons.

Law faculty must then read and grade the student answers. This is time-consuming if many students have written essay answers over a three or four hour period, and everyone agrees that this is boring tedious work.[42] This can be a depressing experience too unless denial mechanisms are summoned to explain why the poor qualities of most student answers do not implicate the professor's teaching.[43] Boredom and depression may stem not only from the repetitiveness of the task but also from the professor's need to impose a grad-

---

40. See Chapter One's discussion of the case method.

41. See, e.g., David Chambers, *The First-Year Courses: What's There and What's Not*, in Looking at Law School: A Student Guide from the Society of American Law Teachers 39, 41 (S. Gillers ed. 1977); Chapter One's discussion of law school examinations.

42. See, e.g., Clark Byse, *Fifty Years of Legal Education*, 71 Iowa L. Rev. 1063, 1086 (1986); George Christie, *The Recruitment of Law Faculty*, 1987 Duke L. J. 306, 310, 315.

43. Cf. Jay Feinman & Marc Feldman, *Pedagogy and Politics*, 73 Georgetown Law Journal 875, 879–81 (1985) (describing the dismal perspectives that many law professors de-

ing curve, many low grades, and persuasive numerical distinctions between the higher and lower examination scores. But then, at the end of the grading process, resolution or dissipation of disharmonies is at hand, for the professor will have reproduced a hierarchy of examination scores that reflects the hierarchy which originally produced the professor as an excellent student and lawyer. The many grades arrayed along a professor's grading curve will constitute evidence that he too has produced a few brilliant analysts, like himself, and a much larger number of more modest journeymen. Any doubts about the quality of one's teaching can subside.

We are now in a position to understand two special moments in this rhythm of semester time. The first occurs shortly after the final class. Why do so many law professors profess to love teaching large classes and yet revel as the last class ends?[44] This seems paradoxical but for the fact that the last class represents an end to the disciplinary pressures of implementing analysis and rule coverage, writing an effective examination, and engaging in the daily if unintentional business of "preparing" or "setting up" students to write examination answers that will grade easily under the law school's grading curve.[45]

The second moment occurs at the end of the grading process. Why do so many law professors discourse bitterly about the process of reading essay examinations and yet continue to believe, in the face of obvious evidence to the contrary, that essay questions are the best way to test the skills of legal analysis or good legal writing?[46] This seems paradoxical but for the fact that the essay examination reproduces the law school hierarchy in a form that signifies a special expertise and satisfaction: to wit, writing and thinking like a

---

velop about their students' potential abilities as lawyers as a result of reading examination essays).

44. See David Vernon, *Ethics in Academe—Afton Dekanal*, 34 J. Legal Educ. 205, 205 (1984) ("All of us in law teaching remember Afton Dekanal with affection and admiration....He was killed by a bolt of lightning immediately after having taught the last class of the semester and before he had the opportunity to write or grade the final examination, achieving the dream most of us have.").

45. The business of "setting up" law students for examinations involves focusing class discussions on "theory" or on the analysis of "pivotal" or "test" cases that are only tangentially related to what is expected of students on final examinations: the application of conventional rules to novel factual problems. It also involves the failure to provide much supervised practice in writing examination problems. See Chapter One's discussion of the case method and law school examinations.

46. For some evidence of this belief, see W. Lawrence Church, *Law School Grading*, 1991 Wisc. L. Rev. 825; Michael Jacobs, *Law School Examinations and Churchillian Democracy: A Reply to Professors Redlich and Friedland*, 41 DePaul Law Review 159 (1991).

lawyer via the paradigm of good paragraph thinking/writing. In contrast, objective examinations and individualized papers test for knowledge of legal doctrine and the ability to apply it in forms that are used throughout the academic world. Thus the second moment of revel or release, which ends the semester's rhythm, makes the semester worthwhile, and reinvigorates professors for the future is the distribution of hierarchically-ordered grades based on a specialized form of professional writing.

Two other rhythms complete the circle of faculty time. Most comprehensively, law professors appear subject to "a lawyer's rhythm" of working constantly to meet deadlines. Although many professors may leave practice in order to escape the constraints of this lawyer's rhythm, many or most have been exposed not only to the insistent rhythms of law student time but also to the more intense, deadline-oriented rhythms of judicial clerking or working as a young associate in a corporate law firm.[47] In contemporary law schools, the pressures of teaching large classes under the rhythms of classroom and semester time, especially at the beginning of a career, publishing articles or books to earn tenure, a chaired professorship or the applause of one's peers, and meeting the deadlines of consulting work appear to generate a rhythm of work not unlike the insistent pace of work in corporate law firms. This rhythm makes the law professor seem at least as pressed for time as her students are.[48] This tendency to labor at the lawyer's pace suggests that many professors remain loyal to the paradigm of good paragraph thinking/writing that served them well in writing their final examinations, their comments for law reviews and their law firm briefs or memorandums.[49] This lawyer's rhythm may also explain how professorial minds can remain locked within the analytical, rule-oriented and rhetorical dimensions of the discipline, and this rhythm certainly reinforces the discipline's tacit lesson of productivity as well.

The final rhythm of faculty time consists of longer-term patterns that span a professor's career. These patterns vary among individuals and schools but only a few standard options are available. The first years of a career typically

---

47. Many law professors clerk for judges and practice law, typically for a few years as an associate in a law firm, before they enter teaching. See Robert J. Borthwick & Jordan R. Schau, *Gatekeepers of the Profession: An Empirical Profile of the Nation's Law Professors*, 25 U. Mich. J. Law Reform 191 (1991).

48. See Stone, supra note 23, at 404.

49. Cf. Philip C. Kissam, *The Evaluation of Legal Scholarship*, 63 Wash. L. Rev. 221, 244–46 (1988) (describing the tendencies of law professors in their scholarship to replicate the same kinds of legal analysis that worked for them as law students and as student members of law reviews).

involve earning tenure. In the modern research university, with its bureaucratic accountability requirements for good teaching evaluations and good publication records, earning tenure usually means mastering the art of teaching doctrine to large classes and publishing a few "comprehensive" or "exhaustive" articles in student-edited law reviews.[50] These articles typically analyze topical doctrinal issues in ways that will satisfy tenured colleagues and any specialist experts who may provide external reviews. This experience seems analogous to the law student's first year, and as a set of paradigmatic or traumatic events may have similar capabilities of committing persons tacitly to the basic elements of the discipline.

After tenure, the choices of law professors expand and they may escape from pre-tenure rhythms. But the main options for many law professors involve capitalizing on one's doctrinal expertise by extensive consulting or extending one's scholarship into more substantial doctrinal work by writing casebooks, treatises or more sophisticated articles for law reviews. There is scholarly resistance to these options today, particularly at elite schools,[51] but the career rhythms of many law professors continue to dictate doctrinal work in teaching, scholarship and consulting that replicates and reinforces the basic routines of law school life.

There is, finally, the significant discordance between student and faculty rhythms. The "stressed" law student and "busy, harried" law professor have little time to meet outside the classroom. Thus individual student-faculty conferences and more casual meetings are infrequent and, when they occur, are often as intense, as narrowly focused, as controlled and as fast paced as classroom discussions. These meetings quickly become focused on disciplinary matters such as case method discussions, final examinations or the relevance of particular courses or a student's class rank to employment opportunities. They tacitly signal deference to professional authority, the ideal lawyer's quickness or productivity and an ideal rhetoric of confidence and closure.[52] This discordance between faculty and student rhythms thus reinforces *the mutual invisibility* of law students to professors and professors to law students *as persons.*[53] This invisibility along with other disciplinary techniques constitutes an-

---

50. See Philip C. Kissam, *The Decline of Law School Professionalism*, 134 U. Pa. L. Rev. 251, 271–76 (1986).

51. See, e.g., Richard Posner, *Legal Scholarship Today*, 45 Stan. L. Rev. 1647 (1993); Symposium, *Legal Scholarship: Its Nature and Purposes*, 90 Yale L. J. 955 et seq. (1981); Chapter Four's discussion of Academic/Political Movements.

52. See Kissam, supra note 24, for a fuller discussion of these meetings.

53. See Robert Nagel, *Invisible Teachers: A Comment on Perceptions in the Classroom*, 32 J. Legal Educ. 357 (1982) (arguing that many law students fail to perceive their law professors as persons due to a misunderstanding of the law teacher's instructional intentions);

other significant aspect of the discipline that we shall consider in the next chapter.

Chapter Three's discussion of the "invisibilities" in law school (arguing that law professors fail to perceive their students as persons).

CHAPTER THREE

DISCIPLINARY TECHNIQUES

The routines, habits, spatial relationships and rhythms of law school life facilitate a number of more general practices and attitudes we might call "disciplinary techniques." These techniques reinforce the discipline's tacit lessons and are so ineffable, so impervious to change, that they seem the most insidious of disciplinary elements. These techniques include the invisibility of law school persons to each other as persons, a distinctive emotional style of coolness or impersonality, a collection of pervasive rituals, symbols and myths that nourishes powerful disciplinary images, an examinatorial regime, a special confessional technology, and the ordinary discourse of law schools. These techniques reinforce each other and the lessons of the discipline while tacitly excluding or subjugating other ways of thinking about law, lawyers and legal education. We shall need to excavate these techniques in order to complete our understanding of the discipline's basic elements.

Invisibilities

The routine practices, spatial relationships and insistent pace of law school life make legal education relatively invisible to outsiders. Law schools incorporate internal invisibilities as well—in relationships among persons, educational practices, and the dissemination of legal knowledge. These different invisibilities are mostly unintentional but they become part of the tacit or "practical consciousness" of law school inhabitants and are only rarely questioned.[1] These invisibilities help protect the discipline from interrogation by outsiders and insiders alike.

Law students and law professors are relatively invisible to each other as persons.[2] Students are invisible to their professors in several ways. In large classes

---

1. On the distinction between "discursive consciousness" and "non-conscious practical consciousness," see Anthony Giddens, Modernity and Self-Identity 35–36 (1991).

2. Cf. Robert F. Nagel, *Invisible Teachers: A Comment on Perceptions in the Classroom*, 32 J. Legal Educ. 357 (1982) (arguing that law students mistakenly perceive that their pro-

professors can identify students by means of seating charts but at any single moment a professor is unlikely to focus on more than one or a few students, leaving most outside the professorial gaze most of the time. Even students participating in class discussions are unlikely to be perceived as persons, for the professor's primary interest and attention, especially in large classes, will be aimed at instructing the class rather than the person by eliciting useful statements about legal subjects.[3] The large size of amphitheatre classrooms limits the chances for eye contact, thus also reducing the possibility of personal relationships.[4] In addition, most professors read and grade their final examinations on an "anonymous" or "blind" basis without knowledge of student names.[5] This method guards against favoritism but eases the conscience by allowing law professors to distribute many low grades to examination numbers rather than persons. Law school grading under a mandatory grading curve also limits the incentives of professors to get to know their students as persons, for if they did, they would have to explain many low grades to *persons* rather than to mere "students" who appear before them, in essence, as *anonymous numbers.*

The invisibility of law students as persons has consequences. This helps law professors communicate with students in formal, impersonal tones, tacitly modeling a lawyer's rhetoric or style as formal, impassive, and uncaring for others. The invisibility of students as persons allows professors to dispense harsh classroom criticisms, low grades, and the minimal feedback of a single symbol as the grade for the course with psychological ease, since the professor need not be concerned *personally* about the effects of her actions. Student anonymity also discourages the discussion of examination performances with individual students, and focuses the discussions that do occur on a professor's "model answer" or "grading scale" instead of the student's particular strengths, weaknesses and opportunities for improvement.[6] Student-

---

fessors "do not notice them or care about them" and, in turn, that law students intentionally ignore their teachers as persons).

3. See Chapter One's discussion of the case method and Chapter Two's discussion of amphitheatre classrooms.

4. I owe this observation to Lauren Hoopes.

5. See Paul Carrington, *One Law: The Role of Legal Education in the Opening of the Legal Profession Since 1776,* 44 Fla. L. Rev. 501, 560–65 (1992).

6. On the limited nature of individual discussions about law school examinations, see Monroe H. Freedman, *The Professional Responsibility of the Law Professor: Three Neglected Questions,* 39 Vand. L. Rev. 275, 282 (1986); Steven H. Nickles, *Examining and Grading in American Law Schools,* 30 Ark. L. Rev. 411, 426, 463–66 (1977); Philip C. Kissam, *Conferring With Students,* 65 UMKC L. Rev. 917, 918–26 (1997).

faculty conferences about examinations, papers, professional opportunities and other mentoring issues are also constrained by the impersonal or critical tones or stances that law professors tend to adopt towards students who are not perceived as persons.[7]

Law professors also become invisible as persons. This invisibility is generated by student expectations about professorial sovereignty, the impersonal, critical stances of many professors, their "harried, forbidding" demeanor[8] and defensive reactions by students to their own invisibility.[9] This invisibility helps establish an aura of mystery about the law professor's expertise and strengthens perceptions of professors as role-models or symbols of what judges or lawyers do, since students perceive their professors in roles rather than as persons. Professorial invisibility also facilitates the discipline of law school by allowing professors to manage their complex classroom and examination tasks more easily and perhaps by inducing students to limit their commitment to academic work in the absence of personal relationships with mentors.[10]

The case method establishes other invisibilities that inform the discipline. Clients as persons are largely absent from casebooks and classroom discussions in the core curriculum, although clients do appear at strategic moments as a kind of standard client or ghost-in-the-machine who communicates clear goals to lawyers (win this case or, maximize profits).[11] The mostly invisible figure of the standard client reinforces the idea that lawyers should be amoral servants of clients who determine their goals independent of any legal advice.[12] The standard client also avoids more realistic conceptions of clients that would take account of the unruly messiness of life situations, of clients who lack power or respect in society,[13] and of clients who desire or need ethical or business advice from lawyers as well as legal advice.[14] The mostly invisible standard client and related conception of lawyers as amoral servants help the dis-

---

7. See Kissam, supra note 6; Chapter Two's discussion of faculty offices under Other Spaces.

8. See Alan Stone, *Legal Education on the Couch*, 85 Harv. L. Rev. 392, 404 (1971).

9. See Nagel, supra note 2.

10. See id.

11. See Ann Shalleck, *Constructions of the Client Within Legal Education*, 45 Stan. L. Rev. 1731 (1993).

12. For discussions of the law school notion of the lawyer as amoral servant, see Anthony T. Kronman, The Lost Lawyer: Failing Ideals of the Legal Profession (1993); Roger Cramton, *The Ordinary Religion of the Law School Classroom*, 29 J. Legal Educ. 247 (1978).

13. See Shalleck, supra note 11.

14. See Robert Gordon, *The Independence of Lawyers*, 68 Bost. U. L. Rev. 1 (1988); William Simon, *Ethical Discretion in Lawyering*, 101 Harv. L. Rev. 1083 (1988).

cipline generate its tacit lessons of analysis, an assertive, rule-oriented rhetoric and law that is nothing or virtually nothing but manipulable rules.

The case method also promotes the invisibility of the social, historical and moral contexts of judicial opinions. Casebooks and class discussions often introduce these contexts into the consideration of particular cases and rules, but the discipline's deep structure of fragmented casebooks, multi-layered class discussions and final examinations tends to discount or subordinate these contexts.[15] This exclusion or tacit subordination of contexts supports an ideology of autonomous professional expertise. By discounting the meaningful contexts from which one can argue for legal distinctions between persons and organizations, it also tacitly supports an ideology of economic liberty that would grant the same rights and liberties to profit-making corporations and other organizations as it would grant to persons.[16] The relative invisibility of clients and non-doctrinal contexts in routine law school practices help promote several of the discipline's lessons.

Coolness

The disciplinary practices of law schools, including the invisibility of persons, fit well with a distinctive emotional style that has been prescribed for and is prevalent within the middle classes and bureaucratic workplaces of twentieth century America. As described by Peter Stearns in American Cool, this is a style of caution, muted emotions, impersonality and "strategic" or "uninvolved" friendliness.[17] Many law professors and law students may acquire this style elsewhere, but the discipline builds upon this style and refines or refurbishes it, schooling the inhabitants of law schools to practice coolness in more perfect ways.[18] This style makes other discipli-

---

15. See Chapter One's discussion of casebooks, the case method and law school examinations.

16. Cf. Randall Bezanson, *Institutional Speech*, 80 Iowa L. Rev. 735 (1995) (arguing that free speech doctrine should recognize distinctions between persons and organizations); Meir Dan-Cohen, *Bureaucratic Organizations and the Theory of Adjudication*, 85 Colum. L. Rev. 1 (1985) (arguing that American law and legal theory should draw express distinctions between organizations and individuals).

17. Peter N. Stearns, American Cool: Constructing a 20th Century Emotional Style (1994).

18. Cf. Jennifer L. Pierce, Gender Trials: Emotional Lives in Contemporary Law Firms 59 (1995) (describing how masculinized forms of emotional labor such as "strategic friendliness" permeate the training and workplace culture of litigators).

nary practices psychologically attractive and more resistant to change. This style is also an integral component of the discipline's tacit lessons of competitiveness and toughness towards other persons, ethical deliberations and emotions. Coolness is a basic disciplinary maneuver in the American law school.

Consider the relentless rationality of casebooks, classroom discussions and most legal scholarship, the peculiar visibilities of students and professors in amphitheatre classrooms, the objectiveness of examination grading, the discrete hierarchical positions in class ranking systems, and the competitiveness among both students and faculty to obtain the applause and rewards that are granted for excellence in law school work.[19] In these contexts, an impersonal friendliness that emphasizes workplace harmony and displaces or conceals the "positive emotions" of love, rage, empathy, grief and guilt and "negative emotions" of anger, fear and jealousy would seem to be extremely functional.[20] Avoiding emotion, personal relationships and any passion for ethics, religion, social justice or caring relationships will help professors and students work comfortably with positive legal rules without concern for the consequences of these rules for persons or society. Emotional coolness can also help professors and students survive and achieve in their competitions for grades, class rank, law review honors or the recognition of their teaching and scholarship. Caution and coolness are helpful as well in avoiding "professional mistakes" and in navigating the law school's hierarchies of authority, status and power.

There are, of course, exceptions to law school coolness. Authentic friendships do flourish in law schools, and individual professors or students are quite capable of expressing their passion for ethics, justice or disadvantaged persons. The negative emotions of anger, fear and jealousy surface from time-to-time as well. But there are many practices where coolness is helpful. Law professors need to manage large numbers of students in their classes, earn praise for their teaching on student evaluations, and dispense variable and many disappointing grades to students, all without endangering the time one needs to engage in scholarship, public service or consulting work. Law professors need to manage their relationships with each other within a competitive system that consists of comparative student evaluations of their teaching, comparative peer reviews of their scholarship, and the competition for prestigious teach-

---

19. See Chapter One and Chapter Two's discussion of amphitheatre classrooms.

20. Cf. P. Stearns, supra note 18, at 95–228 (describing the functionality of such muted emotions in American bureaucratic workplaces and middle class families).

ing appointments.[21] Similarly students need to manage their time carefully and develop their adult identities and social lives within a competitive evaluation system that measures each student against other students and positions each student within a hierarchical ranking system.[22] In these competitive contexts emotional coolness is useful in managing one's daily life and it is useful too in managing the law student's often complex search for legal employment.

The style of coolness, then, is a technique which empowers law school inhabitants by limiting and discouraging the play of emotions that might interfere with disciplinary tasks. Yet many emotions, for example, love, rage, empathy, sympathy and caring for others, are important to effective listening, teaching, acquiring knowledge, judging and questioning or reforming the status quo.[23] A judge's sympathy or empathy for parties who argue before her may be important to understanding their arguments and thus to good judging.[24] A teacher's empathy for his students may help him perceive and work with particular obstacles to learning that individual students have and, conversely, a student's empathy for his teachers may encourage him to seek individual instruction or help teachers communicate with other students.[25] The love of others and rage at social injustice can be important motivations to learn, to question the law critically and to work for reforms.[26] The emotions, especially caring for others, can form an important part of reasoned moral and legal arguments about what the law should be.[27] But the discipline's coolness tacitly directs law school inhabitants away from emotions and towards "toughness" instead.

---

21. See, e.g., Richard Abel, *Evaluating Evaluations: How Should Law Schools Judge Teaching?*, 40 J. Legal Educ. 407 (1990); Philip C. Kissam, *The Decline of Law School Professionalism*, 134 U. Pa. L. Rev. 251, 271–76 (1986).

22. See Stone, supra note 8.

23. See A. Kronman, supra note 12, at 66–74; Nel Noddings, Caring: A Feminine Approach to Ethics and Moral Education (1984); Lynne Henderson, *Legality and Empathy*, 85 Mich. L. Rev. 1574 (1987); Alison Jagger, *Love and Knowledge: Emotion in Feminist Epistemology* in A.M. Jagger & S.R. Bordo (eds), Gender/Body/Knowledge: Feminist Reconstructions of Being and Knowing 145 (1989); Martha Nussbaum, *The Use and Abuse of Philosophy in Legal Education*, 45 Stan. L. Rev. 1627, 1633–34 (1993); Robin West, *Love, Rage and Legal Theory*, 1 Yale J. Law & Feminism 101 (1989).

24. See A. Kronman, supra note 12, at 66–74; Henderson, supra note 23.

25. See N. Noddings, supra note 23.

26. See Jagger, supra note 23; West, supra note 23.

27. See, e.g., Plyler v. Doe, 457 U.S. 202 (1982) (holding that a state may not deny free public education to children as a means of punishing their parents for illegal entry into the United States); Henderson, supra note 22; Nussbaum, supra note 22, at 1633–34. See also Martha Nussbaum, Poetic Justice (1995); Robin West, Caring for Justice (1997).

Rituals, Symbols, Myths

Murray Edelman has described how rituals, symbols and myths in political discourse can provide "symbolic assurance" to anxious spectators of political events.[28] The inhabitants of law schools are somewhat like the anxious spectators of political events. Students face the particular anxieties of performing in amphitheatre and other large forums before professional experts and large numbers of their peers, and performing on examinations in ways that will satisfy their expectations for employment upon graduation.[29] Law professors may be subject to anxieties too about the inherent uncertainties of teaching or about the competitions among professors for recognition, applause and possible appointments to chaired professorships or more prestigious faculties.[30] The discipline addresses these anxieties by providing a series of recurrent rituals, symbols and myths that offer assurance to those who teach or study within the discipline.

A ritual is "a motor activity that involves its participants symbolically in a common enterprise, calling their attention to their relatedness and joint interests in a compelling way."[31] Ritual imposes meaning and order on "confusing or ambiguous situations" by simplifying reality, screening out anomalous facts and reassuring its participants that "there are no dissenters."[32] Ritual, in other words, is a mode of collective behavior that constructs suasive symbols or myths which are important to the cohesive functioning and welfare of social groups.

The discipline incorporates four basic rituals. One is the ritual or ordeal of the first year classroom. Beginning, anxious and often confused students con-

---

28. Murray Edelman, The Symbolic Uses of Politics (1964).

29. See Benjamin, Kasniak, Sales & Shanfield, *The Role of Legal Education in Producing Psychological Stress Among Law Students and Lawyers*, 1986 Am. Bar F. Res. J. 225, 247–49 (attributing law student stress to the frenetic or competitive pace of law school life); Heins, Fahey & Henderson, *Law Students and Medical Students: A Comparison of Perceived Stress*, 33 J. Legal Educ. 511 (1983) (attributing higher stress found among law students to law school examinations); Stone, supra note 8, at 398–401, 423–28 (describing the "identity crisis" of young adult law students and the impact of law school grading upon their "ego-ideals").

30. See Martha Minow, *Law Turning Outward*, 73 Telos 79 (1986) (describing the uncertainty of contemporary law professors about issues of legal knowledge); Stone, supra note 8, at 401–05 (describing the law professor's perfectionist syndrome that guards against the commitment of any mistake).

31. M. Edelman, supra note 28, at 16.

32. Id. at 16–17.

front professional experts in face-to-face social interactions that optimize "the social construction of reality."[33] These interactions occur in amphi*theatres* which provide dramatic backdrops for actions that can involve "hostility, competition, exhibitionism, and other emotional reactions"[34] and that almost always involve the case method's mechanisms of control, entertainment and expertise.[35] The first year classroom thus appears to be a ritualistic site capable of generating powerful assuring symbols.

This site generates images or symbols of lawyers and judges that revolve around the law professor's tripartite role as an expositor of legal doctrine, a "model advocate" capable of making arguments for any standard figure client, and a "model judge" of legal doctrine, law students and the performance of real judges. Lawyers are thus depicted or symbolized as masters of complex legal rules, as authoritative judges of legal matters, as consummate actors, and as amoral advocates who are capable of serving any client's interests. Intriguingly, the flow of classroom criticisms of "right" and "wrong" judicial decisions together with student perceptions of "arbitrary judgments" by professors in grading examinations or in classrooms also appears to generate a Janus-faced image of judges. Judges, in this image, are independent, objective, rational and honorable when they make "correct" decisions pursuant to positive legal rules or, in fewer cases, according to some notion of "wise policy." But judges are "biased" or "political" when they make "illogical" or "incorrect" decisions, which can be any decision with which professors, students or lawyers and their clients happen to disagree. This dualistic image performs important functions for both legal education and the profession. The image of an independent, objective, rational, wise judge supports and claims honor for the legal profession by presenting judges as honorable, ethical and socially beneficent.[36] But the opposite face of this image simultaneously helps professors, students and lawyers establish or maintain their status as professional experts, by allowing them to make quick yet inaccessible criticisms of particular decisions as "political" or as decisions by "political judges." Thus the dark side of this Janus-faced image pro-

---

33. See Peter L. Berger & Thomas Luckmann, The Social Construction of Reality 28–34 (1967) (the vividness and intensity of face-to-face situations provide our most important experiences of "others" and thus help implement the construction of social reality).

34. Stone, supra note 8, at 413.

35. See Chapter One's discussion of the case method.

36. On the importance of public perception of judges as independent and wise to the honor and status of the American legal profession, see Samuel Haber, The Quest for Authority and Honor in the American Professions 206–239 (1991); Maureen Cain, *The Symbol Traders*, in Lawyers in a Postmodern World: Translation and Transgression 11, 22–23 (M. Cain & C.B. Harrington eds, 1994).

vides lawyers with an easy explanation for why they failed to win a particular case: the judge was "biased" or "political." This Janus-faced image of judges also symbolizes the fundamental if blurred distinction in law schools between "rules" and "law," on the one hand, and "policy" and "politics," on the other. This distinction reinforces the discipline's lessons of rule-oriented discourse, authority-laden rhetoric, and autonomous professional expertise, but it is sufficiently blurred to promote the lessons of amoral advocacy and manipulable law that encourage making all kinds of arguments.

The second ritual consists of final examinations. This ritual begins with the intensive or extensive preparations for exams by individual students and small study groups. It then involves taking competitive time-limited examinations collectively in large rooms and student gatherings before and after these examinations to gossip about or compare possible questions and answers. This ritual includes subsequent gatherings around a bulletin board or registrar's office in order to examine any information about law school grades that a school publishes.[37] These activities surely generate tacit images or symbols of lawyers as productive analysts, as competitive workers, and as highly credentialed professionals. These images, in turn, reinforce the discipline's tacit norms of analysis, a rule-oriented discourse, and a competitive individualism among lawyers.

The third ritual is Moot Court. This exercise typically requires first year students to write mock appellate court briefs and make mock oral arguments before a group of tough-minded questioners (professors, upper class students and sometimes local attorneys) who are free to simulate their own ideas about ideal judging. This dramatic and competitive activity usually engages first-year students at a time when many are still struggling to master the case method and final examinations. Moot Court is thus likely to symbolize for many students some idea of legal rhetoric as a rhetoric of confidence, domination, authority and closure that is necessary to ward off aggressive rule-oriented questioners. Together with the drama of large case method classes, the intense Moot Court experience of many students is also likely to symbolize the discipline's privileging of heroic oral performances over complex reading and writing.[38]

---

37. While law schools no longer publish grades by the names of students, they do sometimes list individual grades by numbers assigned to students for the purpose of anonymous grading and they often publish grade distribution data for courses.

38. Moot Court judges do not have to decide the merits of the case before them; they must decide instead which advocates are better than the others and offer critiques of the advocacy presented to them. This change in function may help explain the particularly aggressive questioning of students by many Moot Court judges.

The discipline's fourth ritual consists of the placement interviews by law firms that occur at law schools. These interviews occur frequently during the fall semester, and they involve the sudden appearance of law students in formal conservative dress who must engage representatives of corporate law firms in serious, deferential, "hushed" conversations about the student's credentials and her motivations to work at a particular firm.[39] The seriousness of student dress, transformed from the casual unisex clothing of most law students, and the seriousness of the conversations provide the ultimate symbolic assurance that legal education is worthwhile in material and symbolic terms. Meanwhile this ritual reinforces the discipline's values of professional deference, analysis and examinations since everyone in the school understands that the more successful participants in this activity will generally be the students who have enjoyed the greatest success on final examinations and law reviews.[40]

The discipline also generates powerful myths about law, lawyers and legal education which reassure students and professors that their work is purposeful and worthwhile. Myths are stories of origins and group identities that help us deal with uncertainties, reconcile inconsistencies and mystify or disguise the contradictions and other troublesome features of our social worlds.[41] The myths in modern social institutions can also take the form of "rational myths." These are beliefs which assume a rational form, that particular methods will promote particular goals, even though there are no empirical demonstrations of the means-ends relationships. These myths "depend for their efficacy, for their reality, on the fact that they are widely shared, or are promulgated by individuals or groups that have been granted the right to determine such matters."[42] The disciplinary practices of law school generate three rational myths that help construct the discipline's lessons, cushion the discipline from criticism, and establish images and ideas about progressive law, lawyers and legal education.

One myth is the law school's Whiggish story about how autonomous law is always being improved by powerful, independent judges who somehow understand complex legal doctrine, society's needs for just and compassionate

---

39. See Chapter One's discussion of the placement process. Cf. Mona Harrington, Women Lawyers: Rewriting the Rules 123 (1993) (describing the "noticeable hush" at sites of corporate law firms).

40. On the importance of law school credentials to corporate law firms, see David B. Wilkins & G. Mitu Gulati, *Reconceiving the Tournament of Lawyers: Tracking, Seeding, and Information Control in the Internal Labor Markets of Elite Law Firms*, 84 Va. L. Rev. 1581, 1654–57 (1998).

41. See Peter Fitzpatrick, The Mythology of Modern Law 13–27 (1992).

42. John W. Meyer & W. Richard Scott, Organizational Environments: Ritual and Rationality 14 (1983).

law, and the appropriate ways to adjust legal doctrine in order to meet society's needs. This story is generated by the steady diet of casebook readings, case method analysis, which includes "judicial criticism," the image of apparently powerful and omniscient law professors as judges, the law school practice of honoring judges while criticizing their opinions, and the frequent talk in both classrooms and scholarship about reforming law.[43] This story of improvement helps mystify and reconcile contradictions between the competing rules and legal theories that appear in law school discourse and the contradictions or inconsistencies between the law's ideas of certainty, uncertainty, indeterminacy and satisfaction of social needs. For example, in this myth we can trust judges to make pragmatic interventions that temper the undue harshness or unfairness of formal rules, and we can trust them to know when to apply bright-line formal rules whenever certainty and order are required. The Whiggish myth alleviates doubts among those who attach themselves to positivist theories of law and among those who believe in the discipline's more basic message that there is no law there. More generally, if the law improves itself, as this Whiggish myth suggests, there is simply no need to abandon the discipline of law schools.

A second myth presents lawyers as both autonomous thinkers and client-bound advocates, as both ethical practitioners and amoral technicians, as objectivists who denigrate rhetoric and as persuasive rhetoricians,[44] and as skilled at advocacy about what law should be as at counseling clients about what law is. This myth of the "judicious lawyer" is generated by suasive images throughout the curriculum of lawyers working both sides of these divisions. For example, personal injury law may be taught essentially as a course in litigation advocacy and persuasive rhetoric, while contract law is taught as a course in legal positivism, objectivity and client counseling. Talk about connections between the ethical and material aspects of lawyering may be infrequent, but law school deans, distinguished alumni and visiting judges are prone to make "remarks" about these connections at ceremonial occasions like orientations for new students and commencements. This myth is also nourished by keeping students distant from actual practice situations and engaged in case method analysis for as long as the discipline can.[45] The myth of the balanced or judi-

---

43. See Chapter One's discussion of the case method, especially its use of judicial criticisms, and of the normative nature of most conventional scholarship.

44. See Gerald Wetlaufer, *Rhetoric and Its Denial in Legal Discourse*, 76 Va. L. Rev. 1545 (1990).

45. Law school clinics expose students to limited kinds of practice situations but are usually limited to third year students. See Chapter Four's discussion of clinical education.

cious lawyer, like the myth of progressive law, reassures law school inhabitants that ethical, intellectual and material rewards can be obtained rather easily from legal practice without conflict, and this myth too cautions against abandoning the discipline.

The discipline's third rational myth is the relatively widespread belief, among professors and graduates if not students, that the law school's case method is the best educational method for training lawyers. While many *students* appear to be confused by the case method, or dislike it, or avoid it, *law graduates* in general hold high opinions of their training in "the analysis of legal doctrine."[46] Moreover, while there is no unanimity among contemporary law faculty about the values of the case method, a general consensus sanctions significant use of the method.[47] This method is "rational" in the sense that it appears to be a means to train lawyers in using law, and the method "works" as long as most professors employ it, most students pass their examinations, and major firms continue to hire students who obtain the highest grades on examinations in case method courses. Yet there are no empirical studies which show the case method to be an effective educational strategy by comparison to other methods.[48] We also know little about how students understand this method or the effects the method has upon them.[49] Strong beliefs in the case method are thus a rational myth that is generated by widespread practices in successful institutions and maintained as a matter of inertia or tacit faculty interests in maximizing classroom performances while saving time to engage in other faculty work.[50]

---

46. See Frances Zemans & Victor Rosenblum, The Making of a Public Profession 123–164 (1981); Bryant G. Garth & Joanne Martin, *Law Schools and the Construction of Competence*, 43 J. Legal Educ. 469 (1993).

47. See, e.g., A. Kronman, supra note 12, at 109–62; Paul Carrington, *Hail! Langdell!*, 20 Law & Social Inquiry 691 (1995).

48. See Paul F. Teich, *Research on American Law Teaching: Is There a Case Against the Case System?*, 36 J. Legal Educ. 167 (1986).

49. See David P. Bryden, *What Do Law Students Learn? A Pilot Study*, 34 J. Legal Educ. 479 (1984) (reporting on the general failure of graduates from "three distinguished law schools" to execute satisfactorily basic legal skills like those of statutory interpretation); Roy E. Rickson, *Faculty Control and the Structure of Student Competition: An Analysis of the Law Student Role*, 25 J. Legal Educ. 47 (1973) (reporting that the better students at three Minnesota law schools learn to avoid going to classes and to prepare for final examinations in other ways).

50. See Rickson, supra note 49, at 47 ("Faculty attitudes about the student role reflect their own professional involvement and they work to define the student role so that it fits the needs of the profession, as they define those needs. Law students, on the other hand,

These three myths, of progressive law, judicious lawyers and case method rationality, like the rituals and symbols of the discipline, may affect the behavior of lawyers in beneficial ways. But these myths also are comforting ideas that fit into the intricate web of disciplinary practices, tacitly encourage compliance with these practices, and protect them from criticism. These myths are likely to be attractive to law professors who are uncertain or anxious about their prospects or status as elite professionals, scholars, teachers or political activists and to those many students who are anxious about their personal or professional identities.[51] These myths, especially those about progressive law and judicious lawyers, are likely to be comforting to future lawyers as well, and these myths certainly can help reconcile law students and lawyers to the discipline's overall image of the lawyer as a quick, productive, combative and amoral technician. The discipline's rituals, symbols and myths are salient features of the discipline's dramaturgical nature.

The Examinatorial Regime

Law students and law professors learn to examine everything critically under precise if often unstated standards of excellence, usefulness and acceptable or deviant conduct. The subjects examined range from excerpts of judicial opinions in casebooks, to student and professorial comments in classrooms, to final examination answers and legal scholarship, to law students and law professors themselves. This examinatorial regime consumes much energy and reinforces the tacit lessons of the discipline, especially its messages of analysis, a rule-oriented discourse, a rhetoric of confidence, and professional autonomy. This regime also tacitly controls, limits and informs the opportunities in law school for non-disciplinary or anti-disciplinary inquiry.[52]

---

are often more responsive to the needs of their immediate status than they are to the problems of the relatively distant role.")

51. See Stone, supra note 8.

52. Cf. Michel Foucault, Discipline and Punish 135–228 (Alan Sheridan trans. 1977). Foucault describes how military organizations, factories, schools, prisons and asylums invented practices in the late eighteenth and early nineteenth centuries to require recruits, workers, students and inmates to perform precisely articulated, easily observed and precisely measured tasks under economical supervision. In Foucault's account, these examinations combined the techniques of "an observing hierarchy" with those of "normalizing judgments." Id. at 184. Hierarchically positioned observers were to inspect persons and performances carefully and precisely as "a means of correct training" in a way that measured "non-observance, that which does not measure up to the rule" (where the rule or

Law school work involves a relatively uninterrupted series of examinations. Students are observed, judged and measured under precise norms of conduct in several arenas. In classrooms their comments are evaluated by professors and other students under conventions of precision, relevance, and authority.[53] On final examinations student answers are evaluated comparatively by means of norms about the proper definition of legal issues, precise statements and the application of legal rules or case holdings, by complex grading scales that award many points for relevant or right answers, and by a mandatory grading curve that requires many distinctions between grades.[54] Students are then measured ultimately by means of their class ranks, their positions within the hierarchy of law reviews, and their success in other competitive endeavors such as Moot Court. All these examinations and measurements are driven by the discipline's basic values of analysis, a rule-oriented discourse, a confident rhetoric, and insistent productivity, and they tend to produce the rather common evaluative talk among law faculty about "outstanding students," "A students" and "A examination papers." Other descriptions of students and student performances pale in comparison by reason of the apparently substantial "gap" or "distance" between these other descriptions and the powerful symbolic value of the "A."[55]

Law school grades and class ranks constitute a critical part of the normalizing gaze that the discipline imposes on students. Each student's grades are averaged and class ranks are constructed by comparing these average grades. This ranking measures, reifies and reduces each student's talents, skills and knowledge into a single, hard statistic: the student's number or rank in class. This ranking achieves disciplinary perfection as each student is measured and compared against every other student in his class by means of a single "rigor-

---

norm is often established by the best performances) and "marks the gaps, hierarchizes qualities, skills and aptitudes" in order to punish non-conforming acts and reward conforming acts. Id. at 177–84. These examinations cast a *normalizing gaze* on their subjects that "in a sense imposes homogeneity" and, in yet another sense, "individualizes by making it possible to measure gaps, to determine levels, to fix specialties and to render the differences useful by fitting them together." Id. at 184–85. The purposes of these examinations were to empower persons by teaching them useful skills, to generate detailed individualized knowledge about each person under supervision, and to inscribe the disciplinary lessons of modern social institutions into military recruits, factory workers, school pupils, patients and inmates in order to produce "docile, useful bodies." See id. at 170–94.

53. See Chapter One's discussion of the case method.

54. See Philip C. Kissam, *Law School Examinations*, 42 Vand. L. Rev. 433 (1989).

55. Cf. id. at 480 (describing law student interpretations of their different positions within the class ranking hierarchy that is established by law school grades).

ous" or "objective" number, and each student but one is "penalized" by the symbolic importance of the gap or distance between her rank and the rank of First in the Class. Each student but one is thus given an inferior evaluation which signals one's relative deficiencies as a legal producer. Class ranks also symbolize the competitive or tournament-like qualities of legal education, since a student's rank is often the most important credential that law firms and other employers will use to sort their applicants, and this rank is often the only measure that students have to define themselves, their self-worth, or their potential as lawyers.[56] The grading and class ranking process at most law schools thus tacitly teaches the values of hierarchy and competitive individualism as it rewards and punishes students for their comparative proficiencies in basic legal analysis and a confident rule-oriented rhetoric.

Law professors too are observed and measured by normalizing judgments. The professor's work in classrooms is regularly observed, discussed and measured by her students, first in accordance with their expectations about ideal university professors and then, as their law school experience develops, in accordance with their perceptions of the ideal law professor. Professors are also measured formally by the course evaluations of students. These evaluations usually invite students to employ a common measuring scale that evaluates professors on a unidimensional basis of say, A, B or C,[57] and this scale allows for the construction of league tables that rank professors as teachers just as class ranks are imposed on students. In more episodic but possibly more significant events, law students as the editors of law reviews observe, measure and compare the articles submitted to them by professors, making judgments that determine where scholarship is published within the hierarchy of American law reviews.[58] These examinations of professors by students necessarily rely on the discipline's values of analysis, a rule-oriented discourse and a confident, authoritative rhetoric, and they contribute much to the common talk within law schools about "outstanding teachers" and "brilliant," "original" or "intellectually powerful" scholars.[59] Faculty members who fail to obtain the highest evaluations of their teaching or to publish in the most prestigious law

---

56. See id. at 464–65, 480–83.

57. See Abel, supra note 21, at 412–13; Kissam, supra note 21, at 272–75.

58. On the importance to law professors of the prestige of the law reviews in which they publish, see Richard S. Markovits, *The Professional Assessment of Legal Academics: On the Shift from Evaluator Judgement to Market Evaluations*, 48 J. Legal Educ. 417 (1998).

59. On the abstract norms conventionally used by law professors to evaluate legal scholarship, see, e.g., Philip C. Kissam, *The Evaluation of Legal Scholarship*, 63 Wash. L. Rev. 221, 221–22 (1988).

reviews will, of course, be described in less glowing terms, thus receiving gentle reminders of the importance of professional hierarchies and competitive individualism within the discipline.

Law students and law professors also learn to make precise normalizing judgments about the judicial opinions they read, discuss and write about. Students are expected to analyze opinions and reduce them to their component parts of "relevant facts," "issues," "holdings," "rules," and the "rationale" or "policy" that would justify the decision. This process inculcates conventional norms about what is expected of good judicial writing, and the practice of judicial criticism in classrooms adds more academic and more mysterious norms such as the principle of doctrinal consistency or a professor's, casebook author's or student's particular notions of good policy arguments. These evaluations by students may be *intended* to accomplish many purposes, but the process also tacitly commits law students to the discipline's examinatorial regime.

As students prepare for their examinations, they will concentrate on understanding the particular conceptions of law and argument that are held by the professors of their courses. Their basic norms for evaluating legal authorities may coalesce around the professor's evaluations in each course. This disciplinary examination of opinions tacitly teaches the lesson of independent, all-powerful judges, as modeled by law professors, who are able to make authoritative statements about any legal material or, in other words, the lesson that the law is what judges say it is. But the discipline's practice of judicial criticisms in the case method classroom also allows professors and students to condemn quickly judicial decisions that may depart from the observer's own view of what constitutes "sound legal reasoning."[60] These condemnations encourage professors and students to feel superior to the parties and judges who "got things wrong," thus constructing a sense of expertise, solidarity and elitism among law school inhabitants.[61] Such condemnations also implicitly teach skepticism about the legitimacy of judicial holdings and rules, a skepticism that reinforces the discipline's basic message that there is no law there.

Law students learn to make judgments about many hypothetical problems too, first in classroom discussions and then on examinations. This process in-

---

60. See Chapter One's discussion of judicial criticisms as part of the case method.

61. See Carrie Menkel-Meadow, *Feminist Legal Theory, Critical Legal Studies, and Legal Education or "The Fem-Crits Go to Law School"*, 38 J. Legal Educ. 61, 67–68 (1988). The technique of judicial criticism and its tacit message of superiority may be compared to the somewhat analogous technique in business schools of placing students in the role of decision-making CEOs, which tacitly teaches students superiority, objectivism, and an indifference to workers as persons.

volves analyzing and evaluating novel situations by applying the conventional rules of a particular legal field, and this process must almost always be undertaken quickly and productively. In examining and resolving hypothetical problems, even more than with judicial opinions, law students have little to rely on but the limited rules and case holdings they have already studied together with the discipline's skepticism about rules and its lesson of judicial discretion. The examination of hypotheticals thus tends to reinforce the discipline's tacit message that there is no law there.

Law professors make many hierarchical observations and normalizing judgments about judicial opinions. They must examine opinions to teach doctrinal courses by the case method, to write casebooks and treatises, and to write scholarship that makes normative recommendations based on a writer's assessment of a decision's or outcome's consistency with prior opinions or with policies that are express or implicit in these opinions. To be sure, individual professors may bring other perspectives to their reading and thinking about judicial decisions, for example, political, economic or literary perspectives.[62] In general, however, the law professor's commitments to the basic elements of the discipline emphasize making hierarchical normalizing judgments about judicial opinions—and this may be so even when other perspectives are in play.

Law professors also spend a considerable amount of time making observations and judgments about law students and their writing. This work occurs most regularly in grading examinations, but it also occurs in monitoring classroom performances and in less formal contacts with students. The structure of these situations typically commits the professor to evaluating a student or her work in accordance with the discipline's tacit norms of analysis, a rule-oriented discourse and a confident authoritative rhetoric. These observations and judgments are propelled more than anything by the discipline's grundnorm, the class ranking system, as faculty members construct and use this system to evaluate law students and their work.

Thus, in evaluating answers to examination questions, faculty are continually aware of their need to make many distinctions in grades to comply with the school's grading curve. In advising a student about employment prospects, the faculty member will be continually aware of the student's class rank in order to give reasonable advice in terms of the credentials that different employers may require. Class ranks and the examinatorial regime are also in play whenever a professor is asked to explain a grade to a disappointed, hostile or simply curious law student. This is an unpleasant, tedious and potentially

---

62. See Chapter Four's discussion of Academic/Political Reforms.

time-consuming task for many professors, and the most effective way to limit these discussions is simply to "re-examine" the student's examination performance. Such "re-examinations" can be performed in different ways, but often they involve merely restating or emphasizing the student's point score on the examination relative to other scores, or trying to illustrate deficiencies in the student's work by quickly reciting some relevant rule and its conventional application to one or two issues.[63] Or a professor may seek to avoid these discussions entirely by distributing "model answers" or "check lists" that demonstrate a perfect score, a technique which often seems to overwhelm confused, uncertain students and may be more effective than re-examinations in enforcing the tacit lessons of analysis, a rule-oriented discourse and law school productivity. In sum, the many discrete judgments that faculty make of students and student work tend to enforce disciplinary values not only among students but also among the faculty who make these judgments. These precise, hierarchizing judgments also help explain the common despair observed among so many law professors about the potential abilities of most students or, in other words, the potential abilities of those who are not "A students."[64] This corrosive negativism serves the discipline by assuring uncertain professors that they can make effective distinctions about "legal matters" and that they can be good judges not only of student work but of legal or political issues as well. Indeed, the law professor's commitment to "normativity," that is, to making recommendations to judges and legislatures, may be grounded in the routinized hierarchical observations and normalizing judgments that law professors constantly are making about law students and their work.[65]

Law faculty also make hierarchical observations and normalizing judgments about each other and each other's work. Formally, these examinations occur in making faculty appointments, in granting tenure, promotion, research awards or chaired professorships, and in making salary decisions by law school deans or faculty committees. This scrutiny of other faculty and their work can range from an intense focus upon the comparative rankings recorded by the student evaluations of faculty teaching,[66] to episodic if often traumatic peer

---

63. See Freedman, supra note 6, at 282–86; Kissam, supra note 54, at 471–73.

64. On the presence of such despair among law faculty, see Jay Feinman & Marc Feldman, *Pedagogy and Politics*, 73 Geo. L. J. 875, 881–82 (1985); Andrew Watson, *The Quest for Professional Competence: Psychological Aspects of Legal Education*, 37 U. Cin. L. Rev. 91, 107–08, 111–12 (1968).

65. On the prevalence of this normativity in general law school discourse, see Pierre Schlag, Laying Down the Law: Mysticism, Fetishism and the American Legal Mind (1996).

66. See, e.g., "Harvard Professor Protests Colleagues' Tenure Denials," NY Times, June 9, 1987, p. 14 (Robert Clark, commenting on Harvard University's denial of tenure to two

reviews of a faculty member's teaching, to reading a faculty member's scholarship or surveying the quantity and prestige of her publications,[67] to relying (carefully) on a candidate's credentials and personality in making appointments to the faculty.[68] Law professors examine each other and each other's work in less formal situations as well. These include our casual conversations about teaching experiences or techniques, conversations about the scholarly developments in one's field and simply reading the scholarship of others to find information, ideas and authorities that can be applied to one's own teaching or scholarship.[69]

These many examinatorial situations present manifold opportunities for the tacit enforcement of the discipline's norms. Reading and evaluating the scholarship of others to help one's teaching or scholarship, under the press of law school time, is likely to produce readings and evaluations that focus on a work's provision of "analysis," "useful authorities" and "normative recommendations" since this is what any productive-minded faculty reader needs most in teaching doctrinal courses or writing conventional legal scholarship. In turn, scholars who seek influence and applause from this audience will understand these interests, at least tacitly, and strive to provide much analysis, authorities and normative recommendations by writing "clearly" and "exhaustively" on doctrinal topics to articulate many such ideas under the paradigm of good paragraph thinking/writing.[70] Tenure and promotion decisions involve more formal evaluations that engage faculty members from different specialties at the candidate's school and faculty from the candidate's own specialty at other schools. The writers of this scholarship will understand, at least tacitly, that they should write simultaneously for three different audiences: the specialists in their field, the tenured members of their own faculty, and the student editors who make decisions that affect the quantity and prestige of law

---

critical legal studies professors: "Neither of those people were very good teachers. Both were among the bottom ten percent in student ratings."); see also Abel, supra note 21; Markovits, supra note 58.

67. See Kissam, supra note 59; Markovits, supra note 58; Edward L. Rubin, *On Beyond Truth: A Theory for Evaluating Legal Scholarship*, 80 Cal. L. Rev. 889 (1992).

68. See, e.g., Derrick Bell, Jr., Confronting Authority 4, 44–45, 76–80 (1994) (describing the "elitist" hiring standards, which depend heavily upon credential and personality, that American law schools use in hiring new faculty members).

69. See Rubin, supra note 67, at 935–40 (suggesting that "applicability" is an important criterion for evaluating legal scholarship within legal sub-disciplines).

70. Cf. Pierre Schlag, *Normativity and the Politics of Form*, 139 U. Pa. L. Rev. 801 (1991) (providing a psychological/linguistic explanation of how normative legal thought circulates among law professors).

review publications. Writing articles that present a lot of analysis, a lot of legal authorities and a lot of normative recommendations in a confident rhetorical style is likely to seem the best or safest strategy for satisfying this mix of audiences.

The examinatorial regime of law schools thus produces much individualized knowledge about law students and law professors and it produces this knowledge by employing various conformity-inducing norms that enforce the tacit lessons of the discipline efficiently, and lightly. The foremost lessons of the regime would appear to be the teaching or reinforcement of the discipline's basic intellectual method, analysis, and its rule-oriented discourse, with the rules or norms of this examinatorial regime varying among legal rules, conventional legal methods, norms of law school grading and evaluating law teaching, and the norms or rules of related academic disciplines such as economics or analytical philosophy. More generally, this examinatorial regime appears to induce a special sense of professional expertise in law school inhabitants, a sense of the need to critically examine or cross-examine just about everything.

The examinatorial regime does entail some obvious costs. For example, if law professors carefully observe and critique student performances in the classroom, there are costs to the professor in terms of extra preparation time and perhaps also in terms of less favorable student evaluations if his students choose to repay what they may perceive as professorial hostility.[71] Reading essay answers to final examinations is costly in terms of time and boredom, and such costs are probably an important factor in the increased use of machine-graded multiple choice examinations.[72] Reading a colleague's writings to evaluate them for purposes of tenure, salary increases or promotion or to provide critical assistance is also costly at least in terms of time.[73] The discipline of law schools, however, alleviates these examinatorial costs by providing a special sort of "confessional technology" that operates in a virtually costless or effortless way. This technology internalizes the enforcement of disciplinary norms by inducing a deep self-knowledge, guilt and shame in law school inhabitants about their relative positions within the discipline's hierarchies among law schools, law professors and law students.

---

71. See, e.g., Anthony D'Amato, *The Decline and Fall of Law Teaching in the Age of Student Consumerism*, 37 J. Legal Educ. 461, 461–62 (1987).

72. On the increasing use of these examinations, see Nickles, supra note 6, at 447–51.

73. Cf. Markovits, supra note 59 (describing a shift from such evaluations to reliance upon the prestige of publication sites as the measure of good legal scholarship).

A Confessional Technology

"There is no need for arms, physical violence, material constraints. Just a gaze. An inspecting gaze, a gaze which each individual under its weight will end by interiorising to the point that he is his own overseer, each individual thus exercising surveillance over, and against, himself. A superb formula: power exercised continuously and for what turns out to be a minimal cost."
— Michel Foucault[74]

Confessions, like examinations, reveal a lack of harmony between one's conduct and the accepted norms or standards in a community, but confessions also generate personal regret about this disharmony and the will or desire to restore harmony and to construct a more coherent self in light of the power or community which establishes the standards.[75] Confessional procedures, of course, are not only religious or individual in nature but also serve important social functions.[76] In American law schools, certain kinds of confessions transform or interiorize the *normalizing gaze* of the examinatorial regime into a more economical, more insidious and lighter *confessing gaze*, a

---

74. M. Foucault, Power/Knowledge 155 (1980).

75. See, e.g., Sissela Bok, Secrets 73–77 (1982); Romand Coles, Self/Power/Other: Political Theory and Dialogical Ethics 14–53 (1992).

76. In the Middle Ages, the Catholic Church began to orient confessions "toward the discovery of internal dispositions to sin and redemption, dispositions rooted in concrete social and professional situations," to provide means by which individuals could recognize and express "internal contrition" about their sins or shortcomings that would promote "a unification of conscience" about conflicts between their commercial and religious lifeworlds. See Jacques Le Goff, *Merchant's Time and Church's Time in the Middle Ages*, in Time, Work, and Culture in the Middle Ages 29, 38–42 (A. Goldhammer trans. 1980). In Michel Foucault's account, confessional procedures emigrated from the Church to modern social institutions such as the asylum, criminal law, social work and psychoanalysis, and today the confession has become an important technique or ritual for producing truth and self-knowledge in these and other social institutions. See Michel Foucault, The History of Sexuality, Vol. I, pp. 58–68 (1976). In Foucault's words, the confession
"plays a part...in the most ordinary affairs of everyday life, and in the most solemn rites; one confesses one's crimes, one's sins, one's thoughts and desires, one's illnesses and troubles; *one goes about telling, with the greatest precision, whatever is most difficult to tell.* One confesses in public and in private, to one's parents, to one's educators, one's doctor, to those one loves; *one admits to oneself, in pleasure and pain, things it would be impossible to tell to anyone else,* the things people write books about." Id. at 59 (emphasis added).

gaze that helps maintain harmony between the discipline's norms of analysis, a rule-oriented discourse, a confident rhetoric, productivity and the competitive rankings between law students and between law professors.[77] This technology quietly or silently generates attractions to, or at least a calm acquiescence in, many disciplinary norms and practices.

The discipline, in keeping with its techniques of invisibility and coolness, employs a special truncated confessional technology, one which relies heavily upon self-confessions and only rarely involves confessions to others. But modern law schools seem like fertile ground for confessional practices. Both students and professors can face conflicts between the commercial practices of law and the ethical or spiritual demands of their politics, religion or public service ideals, and these conflicts might be resolved or mitigated by making confessions to other students, to oneself or to a sympathetic professor in ways that produce a "unification of conscience" which stabilizes one's work or one's career.[78] There is a dense network of accepted norms in law schools, and law school inhabitants certainly have many opportunities to confess to "shortcomings" under these norms. The invisibility of others *as persons* and the discipline's style of coolness and impersonal friendliness mean that most of these confessions will be self-confessions, but these qualities of the discipline, which tend to present all the others around you as supremely self-confident, surely heighten the need for and traumatic quality of such confessions.

In law school classrooms the tension between the ideal of lawyerly perfection and the new student's struggles or frustrations in acquiring a new language provides many opportunities and requirements for students to confess (to themselves or their teachers) about their insufficient understanding of the assigned readings, the class discussions or "what the professor wants." This tension also permeates informal discussions of law school work, where there are opportunities for confessions about one's insufficient understanding of reading materials, classroom discussions or examinations. These confessions may not reveal precise norms of good law school performance. But they strengthen the resolve of students to determine what these standards are, or

---

77. On Michel Foucault's distinction between the "normalizing gaze" of a discipline's power or examinatorial regime and the "confessing gaze" which "peers deep into the soul," see R. Coles, supra note 75, at 54–98.

78. See supra note 76. See also Robert Granfield, Making Elite Lawyers: Visions of Law at Harvard and Beyond (1992) (exploring how left law students at Harvard Law School come to reconcile their liberal or radical political ideals with working in corporate law firms by engaging in certain "ideological work" that is supported by law school practices).

at least to master them implicitly, and they make students more receptive to the discipline's basic norms.

The discipline's confessional technology operates more elegantly once course grades and class ranks have been generated and distributed to first year students. Now there is a clear norm by which each student can measure his or her deviance from law school excellence and confess to oneself or to others about one's feared shortcomings as a lawyer.[79] These confessions may strengthen the resolve of many to improve and may serve "as an added control for those who are not certain that they will be capable of keeping the temptations of their past lives subdued."[80] Alternatively, the confessions induced by first year grades may help cause the substantial inattention and malaise of many upper class students, a resistance which paradoxically reinforces the discipline's lessons.[81] The confessional practices associated with law school grades also help students develop realistic expectations about their future employment prospects.[82]

When individual students ask faculty members for advice or instruction about coursework, final examinations or employment prospects, further opportunities are presented for confession. How often do deferential students preface these requests with a confession of their limited understanding of a subject or a confession of their class rank or law school standing when they seek employment advice or a recommendation? These situations tremble with the possibility of choices by the confessing student about what to reveal, what to hold back, and of choices by the listening professor about how far to inquire into this student's shortcomings, what information to use, and what not to use in giving advice or providing recommendations.[83] What more effective device could there be for students to comprehend the tacit lessons of the discipline than to confess their law school shortcomings individually before the ideal judge/advocate of the classroom?

The ultimate confessional experience for law students is provided by their interviews for employment when they discover precisely how their grades,

---

79. See Kissam, supra note 54, at 480–483 (describing law student interpretations of their experiences with final examinations, grades and class ranks).

80. S. Bok, supra note 75, at 76–77.

81. See Chapter One's discussion of student resistance to the core curriculum.

82. Cf. Duncan Kennedy, *Legal Education and the Reproduction of Hierarchy*, 32 J. Legal Educ. 591, 600 (1982) ("Grading as practiced teaches the inevitability and also the justice of hierarchy, a hierarchy that is at once false and unnecessary.").

83. See S. Bok, supra note 75, at 81–88 (discussing the moral considerations of such choices by both confessors and listeners in confessional situations).

class rank, comportment and style make them eligible or not eligible for particular opportunities. The placement process is an elaborate scheme of discovery and self-measurement in accordance with the discipline's norms, especially as students compare their different opportunities. Law students first match their qualifications with publicly announced or rumored qualifications for different law firms, and then engage in interviews with law firm representatives, where grades and the presence or absence of law review status are important topics. They then obtain rejection letters or "call-backs" for further interviews, and they subsequently receive offers or rejections for summer employment, after the first and second years of law school or for permanent employment after graduation. Comparisons with other students are made throughout this process, and there are manifold opportunities to ponder the ways in which a student has failed to satisfy the discipline's norms.

The discipline also allows law professors to confess to shortcomings. In teaching there can be confessions about one's imperfect statements in class, one's inability to control or direct student discussion in productive or perfect ways, or one's failure to establish a good rapport with large numbers of students. These confessions frequently are made to one's self, especially during those brief post-class moments of self-critique that form part of the rhythm of classroom time, or when reviewing course evaluations. Conversations about course evaluations with law school deans and other faculty (especially before tenure is awarded) provide additional opportunities for confession. To be sure, most law professors never *appear* to experience moments of self-doubt about achieving the discipline's norms for excellent classroom performance. But appearances are a function of the discipline's cool style, its confident rhetoric, and the ability of many law professors to master these disciplinary norms.

With scholarship there can be confessions about one's limited productivity, about the limited quality or prestige of one's scholarship and, perhaps most frequently, about the failure to produce scholarship that gains applause from the appropriate specialists at elite law schools. These confessions may be less regular than confessions about teaching but they can be more traumatic and more important, especially because they are often associated with decisions on tenure, promotion or appointment to a more distinguished law school. These confessions occur as one's writings are accepted or rejected by particular law reviews or publishers whose prestige marks the quality of scholarship within the hierarchical world of law schools. They also can occur when comments of peers are obtained on a draft manuscript or published work. Like student confessions about employment prospects, faculty confessions provide many opportunities to ponder one's deficiencies at legal analysis, the manipulation of positive rules, or the deployment of a confident, authoritative, engaging rhetoric.

Most faculty confessions are undoubtedly self-confessions. This interiorization is easily explained. Upon close viewing, many law professors who participate in discussions about law teaching or scholarship seem to display powerful mixtures or combinations of aggressiveness, abrasiveness, insecurity, defensiveness and other distancing behavior that would make public confessions of failure quite painful.[84] Yet these self-confessions are likely to inscribe lessons that are similar to those imprinted in law students: impulses, thoughts and tacit dispositions towards the analysis of things, a rule-oriented discourse, individualized competition and productivity. These confessions of failures to meet the discipline's norms can also promote "unifications of conscience" that help ameliorate conflicts between the commercial and ethical life worlds of law professors—by inducing disciplinary teaching and scholarship to assuage feelings of guilt.

The Discourse of Law Schools

The discipline's most pervasive and complex technique is "the discourse of law schools." In Michel Foucault's view, a professional discourse consists of all the statements that are made by the members of a professional group and the tacit formative rules that provide order or coherence among the statements by legitimating particular statements as "truth statements."[85] The discourse of law schools then may be said to consist of the statements that are made within the law school's different forums, especially classrooms, final examinations and specialist scholarship, and the tacit "rules of formation" that generate order, coherence and truth statements in these forums. This multi-forum, multi-

---

84. See, e.g., David Riesman, *Law and Sociology: Recruitment, Training and Colleagueship*, 9 Stan. L. Rev. 643, 652 (1957):

"Speaking for myself, I must say that the atmosphere of a law school is too abrasive, too cocky, to make for an easy colleagueship on matters which are subject to scathing self-doubt at the frontiers of intellectual work. If one is working along an already laid-out track—as one can so readily do in many fields of psychology—it is one thing, but if one is exploring rather new areas, with all the misgivings to which pioneering intellectual work is prone, then to meet constantly the really quite amiable needling of the skeptical law-man may be tiresome."

See also Stone, supra note 8, at 403–04 (law professors "have internalized a legal standard of perfection which requires that they anticipate every possible counterargument before they advance a positive thesis of any sort").

85. See Michel Foucault, The Archaeology of Knowledge and The Discourse on Language (A.M. Sheridan-Smith, trans. 1972).

level discourse appears to produce several tacit messages or signals that constitute important aspects of the discipline.

Consider first the ensemble of statements about law to which students are exposed during three years of law school. This ensemble will include many relatively concrete statements about the objects of legal study: judicial opinions, rules and related practices. It will include many diffuse, often implicit and often conflicting statements about the nature of law, legal methods, legal rhetoric or legal styles and about the justifications or criticisms of legal rules, concepts, theories and strategies that may be based on the principle of doctrinal consistency, principles of social science, different conceptions of political philosophy, and so on. Coherence among such statements may be provided by particular courses or particular projects. But in general the contemporary discourse of law schools contains substantial amounts of uncertainty and unresolved contradictions among its diffuse statements about legal theories, legal methods, legal concepts, legal rhetoric and the appropriate sources or appropriate nature of justifications and criticisms. To take two examples: some courses, say a contracts course or tax course, may be taught from a perspective of legal counseling that emphasizes the ascertainment of certain rules and results that can guide corporate clients in making business decisions. But other courses may be taught from a litigator's perspective which emphasizes legal uncertainty and the manipulable qualities of legal rules. As a second example, some law school courses may be taught by professors who believe or appear to believe in the theory of legal positivism, the idea that law consists essentially of binding rules that are established by government tribunals. Other courses, however, may be taught by professors who are or appear to be legal skeptics, who believe that legal authorities always or almost always may be manipulated to serve a client's, a lawyer's or a judge's values or interests.[86] The overall ensemble of statements in the discourse of law schools is thus likely to produce the significant latent message that law and legal practices are just full of contradictions or, in other words, that "there is no law there" in the sense of any principles or rules that are capable of obligating or binding judges, lawyers and other persons.

---

86. See, e.g., Austin Sarat, *Law's Two Lives: Humanist Visions and Professional Education*, 5 Yale J. Law & Humanities 201 (1993) (describing the professional education of law schools as a combination of "*positivism*, the view that law is distinct, self-contained, and bears no necessary connection to any ethical values, and *realism*, the belief that legal rules and decisions are not compelled by logic but are rather the products of artful manipulations, skillful interpretive moves, plays of rhetoric, and political motivations") (author's emphasis).

The tacit rules of formation which organize and legitimate truth statements in different forums of law school discourse may differ from each other, sometimes quite radically, and this difference provides additional implicit support to the message that law is full of contradictions. More significant, though, is the likelihood that at most schools at least the tacit rules for making legitimate statements in the core curriculum and on final examinations will be quite similar. Core courses and examinations obtain a major share of student attention, of course, and thus common rules of formation for the discourse in these forums are likely to produce tacit messages or instincts that are integral and important parts of the discipline of law schools.

What are these tacit rules? One is related to the discipline's basic method, analysis, and we might call this "the rule of analysis." Legitimate statements in core curriculum classrooms and on examinations generally must be based on some prior analysis or reduction of judicial opinions or factual situations into separate components that allow one to speak or write about "the issues," the "holdings" or "rules" of cases, and the precise application of often complex rules to novel fact situations. A second rule of formation would appear to be "the rule of legal authority" or, in other words, a tacit proposition that legitimate statements about law in core curriculum classrooms and on examinations must be grounded in some recognized legal authority as provided by legal texts or law professors. This rule involves a commitment to stating legal authorities no matter how complex or conflicted they may be, and this rule grounds the rhetoric of law school discourse in complexity and teaches the implicit norm that lawyers should be deferential to legal authorities, especially animate authorities like judges or professors. A third common rule would seem to be "the rule of confidence," which helps legitimate analytical and authoritative statements both in core curriculum classrooms, through brilliant, charismatic or determined declarations, and on examinations through a productive use of the paradigm of good paragraph thinking/writing that produces many clear precise statements about relevant issues, relevant rules, and the possible application of the rules to complicated factual situations.[87]

This discourse and its basic rules reinforce the discipline's web of routine practices, expectations and techniques in important ways. They support the discipline's methodological message that all things should be analyzed or reduced into component parts. They support the discipline's rhetorical message

---

87. See Chapter One's discussion of the case method and law school examinations.

that lawyers should strive for a rhetoric of confidence, complexity, authority and closure. And they support the discipline's tacit philosophical message that, no matter how paradoxical it seems, there may be "no law" in the sense of binding principles and rules. More generally, the discourse of law schools also reinforces the notion that law is a relatively autonomous subject, at least as law is conceived in core curriculum courses and on final examinations. This discourse, we might say, grounds a circle of pervasive techniques that binds law school inhabitants to the discipline of law schools.

Coda: The Pleasures of the Discipline

Legal education, nonetheless, faces this dilemma or paradox. How can students be trained to dominate the many subtleties and complexities of legal work when they first must be dominated themselves during the initial stages of their education? The discipline's answer is a hedonism of power, which instructs students by dominating them while subtly inviting, attracting or seducing them into assuming dominating styles as a matter of pleasure or desire.

The ostensible pleasures of routine law school practices may seem superficial on first impression, but these pleasures are varied and this variety seems designed to attract many persons to the discipline of law schools. The pleasure begins for many law students with the odd, compelling and sometimes humorous nature of stories in the cases in first year casebooks. Contracts casebooks may begin with "the case of the hairy hand."[88] And Torts cases are replete with odd or bizarre stories, such as the scales that fell so accidentally on poor Mrs. Palsgraf,[89] the plaintiffs who stepped on different kinds of banana peels,[90] and the outdoor privy that did not hold.[91] Considerable pleasure also

---

88. Hawkins v. McGee, 146 Atl. 641 (N.H. 1929), in such casebooks as John P. Dawson, William Burnett Harvey & Standley D. Henderson, Contracts (6th ed, 1993); Thomas D. Crandall & Douglas J. Whaley, Contracts (1987); Robert W. Hamilton, Alan Scott Ray & Russell J. Weintraub, Contracts (2d ed. 1992).

89. See Palsgraf v. Long Island R.R. Co, 162 N.E. 99 (1928), in such casebooks as Prosser, Wade and Schwartz's Cases and Materials on Torts 304 (9th ed. 1994).

90. See Goddard v. Boston & Maine R.R. Co., 60 N.E. 486 (1901); Anjou v. Boston Elevated Ry. Co., 94 N.E. 386 (1911); Joye v. Great Atlantic & Pacific Tea Co., 405 F.2d 464 (4th Cir. 1968), in Prosser, Wade & Schwartz, supra note 89, at 227–28.

91. See Rush v. Commercial Realty Co., 145 A. 476 (1929), in Prosser, Wade & Schwartz, supra note 89, at 589.

may be found in the classroom wit or brilliance of particular professors.[92] The steady flow of judicial criticism in classrooms and law review writing also can give pleasure by providing law students with feelings of superiority and expertise in viewing the "mistakes" of judges and lawyers.[93] The visual and aural charisma of particular professors and students working in large amphitheatre classrooms is another source of disciplinary pleasure.[94] And for persons with instincts or tastes for competition, pleasure is provided by the *agon* of classroom practices,[95] by the competition for grades among the members of each law school class, and by other law school competitions for honors such as Moot Court and selection to law review.

The discipline of law schools also provides deeper hedonic pleasures. One of these is the pleasure that can result from trusting another or submitting oneself to another's care or control.[96] The discipline's examinatorial and confessional technologies provide opportunities for this kind of trust or submission as students, collectively in large classrooms, seminars, student lounges and carnival-like parties or individually in meetings with faculty or upper class students, attempt to divine the ways by which law students or lawyers confront uncertainty. Conferences, talks and other meetings that individual students may have with professors, clinical supervisors, law review editors or teaching assistants about examinations, writing exercises, Moot Court, clinical work and future employment are particularly good events at which students may submit their ideas, hopes, fears and even selves into the care or control of others. The pleasures of trust and submission thus inculcate tacit attachments to the discipline as well as help teach the disciplinary lesson of deference to superiors within a professional hierarchy.

A second deep hedonic theme concerns the pleasures of a peculiar sort of voyeurism or, more prosaically, the joy of observing the skillful exercise of power and dominance by experts. This may be an especially masculine sort of

---

92. For insightful descriptions of such wit and brilliance as perceived by law students, see Scott Turow, One L (1976); Robin West, *The Hedonic Difference in Women's Lives: A Phenomenological Critique of Feminist Legal Theory*, 3 Wisc. Women's L. J. 81,108–111 (1987).

93. See Chapter One's discussion of judicial criticism as part of the case method.

94. See Chapter Two's discussion of amphitheatre classrooms.

95. See, e.g., Lani Guinier, Michelle Fine & Jane Balin, *Becoming Gentlemen: Women's Experiences at One Ivy League Law School*, 143 U. Pa. L. Rev. 1, 51 n. 128 (discussing the law school game of "asshole bingo" in which students rate the classroom performances of other students).

96. Cf. West, supra note 92, at 89 (describing pleasures that some women experience in the "controlled erotic submission" of their selves to others).

pleasure, like that of spectators at athletic events, but in any event there are abundant opportunities for this pleasure in law schools. Such opportunities exist in classrooms whenever students and professors enjoy the spectacle of criticisms made of a judge's, a lawyer's, or a student's performance.[97] They also exist whenever a disinterested party (say a professor, or a student who has obtained employment) contemplates the aesthetics of a grading curve, of class ranks, or the relative employment opportunities for different students who have achieved relatively different professional status within the hierarchy of the law school.

A third hedonic theme consists of pleasures in the discipline's distinctive oral culture. In classrooms, moot courts and clinics, there is a particular kind of talk about human rights and wrongs within the legal disposition of complex disputes that, as the novelist Nathalie Sarraute once observed, expresses "the quivering of human beings" and makes the law school experience pleasurable.[98] There are, in addition, opportunities to exercise or observe the "charismatic" or "brilliant" expositions in amphitheatre classrooms and courtrooms.[99] Even final examinations, although formally in writing and somber forms of writing at that, approximate a sort of one-way courtroom-like oral discourse as students are expected to "think quickly on their feet" and provide quick responses to questions set by severe judges.[100] The combat of competition for grades also assures the pleasure of competitive adrenalin flow for some students.

In essence, then, the discipline generates an heroic oral culture that may tacitly attract many persons. The pleasures of this heroic oral culture also privilege oral communications over writing, and this may be a cause of so many law school inhabitants discounting the educational and legal values of writing and learning law by writing.[101]

---

97. See Menkel-Meadow, supra note 61, at 67–68; Chapter One's discussion of the case method.

98. See "Cafe Complet" (interview of Nathalie Sarraute), Guardian Weekly, Mar. 14, 1993, p. 15 ("Curiously, like many writers, I studied law. I decided to become a barrister because I loved talking. To start with, I didn't realize that the everyday business of a lawyer involved more law than speeches....I have excellent memories of law lectures. They taught me to tear myself away from the written language and to get into the spoken language, the only one which can express the quivering of human beings that interests me in writing.").

99. See Chapter One's discussion of the case method and Chapter Two's discussion of amphitheatre classrooms and courtrooms.

100. See Kissam, supra note 54; Chapter One's discussion of final examinations.

101. On the importance of writing to legal education, see Leigh Hunt Greenshaw, "To Say What The Law Is": Learning the Practice of Legal Rhetoric, 29 Val. U. L. Rev. 861 (1995); Carol McCrehan Parker, Writing Throughout the Curriculum: Why Law Schools Need It and

Other aesthetic pleasures also tacitly attach persons to the discipline and its lessons. One of these is the aestheticization of morally troublesome rules. This can occur by casebook or classroom emphasis on bizarre or extraordinary facts in cases which present rules[102] or by the suasive justification of legal rules simply from "the historical bulk of precedent and prescription, of theory and practice, of sheer *legitimacy*" that supports the rules.[103] Another aesthetic pleasure resides in the subtle identification between law students and legal rules that seems to be promoted by case method dialogues which, as John Henry Schlegel says, "bring the student into the process of crafting a justification for a rule of law (even vicariously through the action of others)."[104] Finally, there is the basic but powerful pleasure of accomplishing complex and difficult tasks. By the third year of law school, the repetitive nature of casebook readings, case discussions and final examinations surely allows most law students at least a modicum of pleasure in completing these seemingly difficult, mysterious tasks. Herein, perhaps, lies a sound functional reason why legal education should last three years. Perhaps it is not that students need three years of instruction in substantive doctrine and basic analytical skills, or that the legal profession needs costly barriers to entry, or that law professors need three year-law schools to protect their jobs and incomes. Rather three years may be just about the right amount of time for generating substantial pleasures in the discipline of law schools before lawyers begin to practice. Such pleasures may validate the disciplinary experience of law schools, serve law school interests by producing more contented students and alumni, and help validate the complex, often frustrating work of legal practitioners, thus serving the profession's interests in maintaining esprit, solidarity and a docile motivated workforce for legal employers. In any event, the assorted pleasures of the discipline complete our inventory of the relatively pervasive techniques that help construct and enforce the tacit lessons of the discipline, its routine practices and its habits.

How to Achieve It, 76 Neb. L. Rev. 561 (1997); on the typical discounting of writing by the inhabitants of law schools, see Lisa Eichhorn, *Writing in the Legal Academy: A Dangerous Supplement?*, 40 Ariz. L. Rev. 105 (1998); Philip C. Kissam, *Thinking (By Writing) About Legal Writing*, 40 Vand. L. Rev. 135 (1987).

102. See Chapter One's discussion of the entertainment imperative in the case method.

103. Mary O'Brien & Sheila McIntyre, *Patriarchal Hegemony and Legal Education*, 2 Can. J. Women & Law 69, 78 (1986).

104. John Henry Schlegel, *Damn! Langdell!*, 20 Law & Social Inquiry 765, 768 (1995).

CHAPTER FOUR

REFORM

"power is tolerable only on condition that it mask a substantial part of itself. Its success is proportional to its ability to hide its own mechanisms."
— Michel Foucault, The History of Sexuality, Vol. I, 86

The idea of reform circulates insistently within the discipline of law schools. Many law professors believe in re-forming the perceptions and thought if not the minds of their students.[1] At least since the 1930s, much conventional legal scholarship has been aimed at reforming judicial doctrines.[2] Reform also gets talked about when professors criticize judicial opinions in their classrooms, when "new theory" appears in legal scholarship, casebooks or teaching and when law faculties debate curriculum changes.[3] The legal profession regularly proposes reforms of legal education to enhance the legitimacy and marketability of lawyers.[4] Universities seek to increase their prestige and the prestige of their law schools by encouraging law professors to engage in "better scholarship," which is often measured by the quantity or prestige of a professor's publications, and in "better teaching," which typically is assessed by averaging and comparing the numerical results of student course evaluations.[5]

---

1. See, e.g., Oliver Wendell Holmes, Jr., *The Use of Law Schools*, in The Essential Holmes 224 (R. Posner ed. 1992) (the essential function of law schools is moral education in restraining democratic excess).

2. See, e.g., Edward F. White, *Reflections on the "Republican Revival": Interdisciplinary Scholarship in the Legal Academy*, 6 Yale J. of Law & Humanities 1, 12–35 (1994).

3. See Chapter One's discussion of elite and non-elite law schools, the core curriculum, the case method and the institutions of scholarship.

4. See, e.g., Rayman Solomon, *Five Crises or One: The Concept of Legal Professionalism, 1925–1960*, in Lawyers' Ideals/Lawyers' Practices 144 (R.L. Nelson, D.M. Trubek & R.L. Solomon, eds, 1992).

5. See Richard L. Abel, *Evaluating Evaluations: How Should Law Schools Judge Teaching?*, 40 J. Legal Educ. 407 (1990); Philip C. Kissam, *The Decline of Law School Professionalism*, 134 U. Pa. L. Rev. 251, 271–276 (1986); Richard S. Markovits, *The Professional As-*

There is also a tradition of complaint and reform proposals that question elements of the discipline like the case method[6] and final examinations.[7] These many reform ideas provide energy to law schools and at the same time disguise the discipline's power. They generate new ideas and recirculate old ones, all the while protecting the discipline from criticism by tacitly assuring audiences that the law, legal education, and legal scholarship are flexible instruments and capable of reforming themselves to serve the public good.

Law schools in recent decades have experienced a proliferation of reform movements. The "professional reforms" of clinical legal education, legal writing programs and teaching professional ethics and several "academic/political reforms" such as law and economics, critical legal studies and feminist jurisprudence have become institutionalized in law schools, and each movement has generated significant support.[8] These movements challenge different aspects of the discipline, expressly or implicitly, and in the aggregate they would seem to have the potential, at least in principle, to transform the discipline. This potential is merely implicit or tacit, however, because the discipline has incorporated these reform movements within itself in both obvious and not-so-obvious ways that tend to limit their subversive threats—just as the discipline has treated the earlier and more diffuse ideas of reform that have traversed law school discourse.

Reform ideas and movements that challenge the discipline's elements can modify the discourse of law schools and alter law school practices. Some reforms might even transform the discipline's basic structures such as the case method or examinations if they were left uncabined to expand throughout legal education. But the discipline checks these reforms and mitigates their threats by fragmenting, marginalizing and infiltrating them, by enfolding them within itself and by ensuring that reforms serve rather than subvert the discipline's values and practices.[9] Nor have participants in these diverse reform

---

sessment of Legal Academics: On the Shift from Evaluator Judgment to Market Evaluations, 48 J. Legal Educ. 417 (1998).

6. See, e.g., Jerome Frank, *Why Not a Clinical Law School?*, 81 U. Pa. L. Rev. 907 (1933).

7. See, e.g., Philip C. Kissam, *Law School Examinations*, 42 Vand. L. Rev. 433 (1989); Janet Motley, *A Foolish Consistency: The Law School Exam*, 10 Nova L. J. 723 (1986).

8. See Gary Minda, Postmodern Legal Movements (1995); Philip C. Kissam, *Lurching Towards the Millennium: The Law School, the Research University, and the Professional Reforms of Legal Education*, 60 Ohio St. L. J. 1965 (1999).

9. Cf. Christine Boyle, *Teaching Law As If Women Really Mattered, or, What About the Washrooms?*, 2 Can. J. Women & Law 96, 108–09 (1986) (suggesting that the study of "fairly obvious" women's legal issues may help marginalize women in law schools).

movements shown much interest or ability in establishing "counter-hegemonic" alliances to challenge the discipline's structures.[10] Perhaps the tacit incentives and constraints of the discipline are too powerful to permit these alliances. In any event, the discipline continues to produce its routines, habits
and tacit conceptions, at times modifying the statements in its discourse but
generally proceeding on a steady course.

This chapter examines the law school's reform tradition and the contemporary reform movements to determine their relationships to other aspects of
the discipline. The prevailing sense one gets from this analysis is that the discipline, through a variety of devices, has captured these reforms sufficiently
to orient them towards the discipline's purposes and structures. The more radical motivations and ideals that often explain the origin of reform ideas have
thus become corrupted or tainted by the discipline's power. At the same time,
the concepts and motivations of these reforms remain a source of possible
change and, more obscurely, a possible source for transforming the discipline
of law schools.

The Reform Tradition

The modern American law school was constructed on ideas of reform. At
Harvard in the late nineteenth century, Christopher Columbus Langdell replaced the prevailing lecture system of teaching with a case method/final examination system that drew upon or merged practices taken from training
legal apprentices, such as reading judicial opinions and practicing "moots" or
mock appellate arguments, and practices borrowed from the research university, such as the "scientific" study of subjects, final examinations, and full time
professors who become "scientific experts" in teaching, research and scholarship. Although subsequently modified in many respects, Langdell's general
ideas about the core curriculum, the case method, final examinations and conventional legal scholarship have remained basic elements of the discipline of
law schools.[11]

---

10. See generally David Trubek, *Back to the Future: The Short, Happy Life of the Law
and Society Movement*, 18 Fla. St. L. Rev. 1 (1990) (describing a need for counter-hegemonic alliances to promote more progressive legal education).

11. See, e.g., William LaPiana, Logic and Experience: The Origin of Modern American Legal Education (1994); Robert Stevens, Legal Education in America from the 1850s
to the 1980s, pp. 35–199 (1983); Arthur E. Sutherland, The Law at Harvard: A History of
Ideas and Men, 1817–1967 (1967); Chapter One.

Since its beginning the Langdellian system has provoked dissenting views and reform proposals. The discipline of law schools has overcome these threats to its elements by deploying a variety of techniques, and three in particular illustrate the discipline's power and adaptability. One technique has been simply to ignore the reform proposal, to treat it by silence. A second has been to reject the reform proposal in an open but conclusory fashion, by fiat as it were or by angry declamations. Both of these techniques indicate an implicit confidence in the values of the discipline, particularly in its capacity to establish a unique kind of professional expertise for law professors and successful economic opportunities for graduates of the case method/final examination law school. A third, more complicated technique has been to respond to reforms through various combinations of direct resistance, adaptations, infiltrations and the incorporation of modified reforms into the discipline's system of routine practices and tacit values. This technique employs both rational arguments against the reform ideas and an instinctive confidence in the values of the discipline. We shall see these techniques at work, both individually and collectively, as we examine both the reform tradition and modern reform movements that have challenged basic elements of the discipline.

Langdell's original curriculum focused almost exclusively on the study of private law doctrine as revealed by judicial opinions, and this structure of the core curriculum has been the subject of criticism throughout the history of law schools. Early on, in the late nineteenth and early twentieth centuries, critics argued that this curriculum was either too practical, too unsuited for university study, or too academic and too far removed from the practices of lawyers in diverse local environments.[12] It was also argued that Langdell's curriculum paid inadequate attention to office counseling in contrast to litigation, to public law subjects such as administrative and constitutional law, and to social science explanations and evaluations of the law.[13] These seemingly reasonable complaints or reforms were given short shrift at the time, most apparently because of the private law curriculum's excellent fit with the case method, which was providing law professors with many explicit and implicit values that supported their professionalization.[14] Moreover, the changes recommended by criticisms that were implemented in law schools were implemented only after relatively long periods of silence, rejection, and substantial

---

12. See R. Stevens, supra note 11, at 40–41, 55, 61.

13. See id. at 40, 57–59.

14. See id. at 57–59 (describing Langdell's case method as "a brilliant teaching device" that allowed a wide spectrum of opinions to be expressed and fit implicitly with the prevailing Darwinian, "scientific" and "practical" attitudes of the times).

adaptation of the reform proposals. For example, public law subjects were added to the curriculum only as upper class elective courses in the 1920s and 1930s.[15] The clinical education of lawyers, although started at a few schools in the first half of the twentieth century,[16] became a major presence in legal education only in the past three decades.[17] The introduction of social sciences into legal training followed a complicated path as well, beginning with the failure of the Legal Realists to incorporate social science into law during the interwar period[18] and continuing today with the checkered successes and failures of both law and economics and the law and society movement.[19]

The Realists at Columbia Law School in the 1920s mounted the most sustained effort to reform the Langdellian curriculum when they introduced their ideas of a "functional curriculum" that would study law in the context of practice situations rather than appellate courts.[20] As we have seen this effort failed to change the Langdellian curriculum, in essence because of its uneasy fit with the case method and final examinations or, in other words, because of the tacit power of the discipline's structures.[21]

Since World War II reform ideas about the law school curriculum have consisted mainly of two kinds. One type proposes technical adjustments to the core curriculum, which is a normal kind of resistance to the discipline that serves its purposes.[22] The other kind of reform has been to supplement the curriculum by adding the "professional reforms" of legal writing programs, clinical education, and training in professional ethics. We shall examine these latter movements in some detail later in this chapter in order to discover the nature of their latent threats to the discipline and the manifold ways in which the discipline has responded to ensure that these programs are implemented as useful rather than dangerous supplements.[23]

The case method has also been subject to complaints since its beginning. This method was criticized early on by law professors committed to the lec-

---

15. See id. at 159–60.

16. See id. at 162.

17. See infra at notes 47–48, 56–58.

18. See Laura Kalman, Legal Realism at Yale, 1927–1960 (1986); John Henry Schlegel, American Legal Realism and Empirical Social Science (1995).

19. See infra at notes 187–212.

20. See L. Kalman, supra note 18, at 67–96; Brainerd Currie, *The Materials of Law Study, Parts I, II and III*, 3 J. Legal Educ 331 (1951); 8 J. Legal Educ. 1 (1955).

21. See L. Kalman, supra note 18, at 78–96; Chapter One's discussion of the core curriculum, the case method and law school examinations.

22. See Chapter One's discussion of the core curriculum.

23. See infra at notes 46–172; see also Kissam, supra note 8.

ture method, lawyers and law students as wasteful of time, fragmentary and "unsuited to the average student."[24] The method received more systematic critiques from outside, disinterested observers in the Redlich and Reed Reports on American legal education in 1914 and 1921.[25] Josef Redlich, an Austrian law professor, criticized the case method's orientation towards the common law, its destructive effects upon legal history and legal theory, its limited connection to practice situations, its repetitive or boring nature, and its observed tendency to encourage "only the particularly quick or talented students (to) take place in the debates."[26] Alfred Reed, an accountant hired by the Carnegie Commission to study law schools, was more charitable but he too criticized the case method's limited coverage of subjects, its attraction for legal scholars to produce casebooks rather than more visionary scholarship and, most pointedly, the method's apparent educational failures in the hands of ordinary or "mediocre" teachers.[27] Harvard law students, asked to evaluate their education in 1935, reiterated some of the same complaints: that the case method becomes too repetitive, too wasteful of their time and too conducive to laziness after the first year, and that class discussions under the case method tended to "degenerate into a dialogue between the professor and a few students, to which the remainder of the class paid little attention."[28]

Since World War II complaints about the case method have continued to appear, with two themes especially apparent. Law students have begun to articulate perceptions of the hostility, competitiveness, alienation and discrimination that this method appears to generate.[29] In addition, a few small empirical studies have suggested rather consistently that the case method may not often achieve its goals of teaching analytical skills effectively.[30] Yet the case

---

24. See R. Stevens, supra note 11, at 57, 62.

25. Josef Redlich, Common Law and the Case Method in American University Law Schools (1914); Alfred Z. Reed, Training for the Public Profession of the Law (1921); see R. Stevens, supra note 11, at 112–23.

26. See Redlich, supra note 25, at 16, 40–41, 46, 49–50; Stevens, supra note 11, at 118–19.

27. See Reed, supra note 25, at 371–382; Stevens, supra note 11, at 120–21.

28. See Arthur E. Sutherland, The Law at Harvard 283–84 (1967).

29. See, e.g., Lani Guinier, Michelle Fine & Jane Balin, *Becoming Gentlemen: Women's Experiences at One Ivy League Law School*, 143 U. Pa. L. Rev. 1 (1994); Duncan Kennedy, *How the Law School Fails: A Polemic*, 1 Yale Rev. L. & Soc. Action 71 (1970); Catherine Weiss & Louise Melling, *The Legal Education of Twenty Women*, 40 Stan. L. Rev. 1299 (1988).

30. See David Bryden, *What Do Law Students Learn? A Pilot Study*, 34 J. Legal Educ. 479 (1984); Roy Rickson, *Faculty Control and the Structure of Student Competition: An*

method remains securely in place, protected by the silence of many who administer this system and by some elegant justifications as well.[31] Perhaps we can conclude only that the case method is defended by those who master its intricacies or otherwise benefit from the method and criticized by those who are less comfortable or less skillful at the game. Still, there remain the early studies by outsiders, Redlich and Reed, and the more recent empirical studies that suggest good reasons to continue to question the case method. Moreover, there remains the silence of those many law professors who continue to administer versions of the case method without making inquiries into the complaints, a situation which suggests that the instinctive confidence of law professors in the discipline of law schools in fact runs deep.

Reform ideas if not complaints about the final examination system have been less prevalent than criticisms of the curriculum or case method in the history of American law schools. To be sure, a few schools like Yale, California-Berkeley and Buffalo have restructured their grading scales to attempt an escape from hierarchical class rankings, mandatory grading curves, and the constraints this system imposes on setting, writing and evaluating final examinations.[32] Also, an increased use of practice examinations, mid-term exams and take-home exams may be mitigating the severity of final examinations, and the proliferation of clinics and seminars permits students to substitute a number of practice and writing projects for examinations in their upper class years.[33] But the time-limited, problem-solving, hierarchically graded final examination remains the primary instrument and model of law school evaluation. Moreover, the unquestioned tacit power of this system is evident in the focus and intensity that law students and law faculty bring to preparing for, writing and grading final examinations,[34] in the silence, simple shrugging of shoulders or cursory rejections of reasoned criticisms of the system[35] and in the ample capacity of law faculties to quickly sanction any at-

---

Analysis of the Student Role, 25 J. Legal Educ. 47 (1973); Paul F. Teich, *Research on American Law Teaching: Is There a Case Against the Case System?,* 36 J. Legal Educ. 167 (1986).

31. See, e.g., Anthony T. Kronman, The Lost Lawyer: Failing Ideals of the Legal Profession 109–62 (1993); Phillip E. Areeda, *The Socratic Method (SM),* 109 Harv. L. Rev. 911 (1996).

32. See Kissam, supra note 7, at 497 n. 239.

33. See, e.g., Jay Feinman, *The Future History of Legal Education,* 29 Rutgers L. J. 475, 482 (1998).

34. See Chapter One's discussion of law school examinations and Chapter Two's discussion of the rhythms of faculty and student time.

35. See, e.g., Mark Tushnet, *An Introduction,* 65 UMKC L. Rev. 673 (1997) (summarizing symposium articles on law school grading methods).

tempt to deviate significantly from the system.[36] The final examination system stands virtually unscathed by the reform tradition of American law schools.

Complaints about conventional legal scholarship and challenges to its institutions have also been relatively sporadic, at least until the emergence of the modern academic/political reform movements we shall examine later in this chapter. The attempt by certain Legal Realists to base legal scholarship on social science is a notable exception, and the rise and decline of this reform effort is instructive about the discipline's power to resist and limit reforms. As described by John Henry Schlegel,[37] one group of Realists tried to integrate law with empirical social science in ways that would explain the empirical causes and the consequences of law, implicitly questioning the doctrinal basis of conventional scholarship. On Schlegel's account these Realists developed a number of valuable or promising ideas and projects but their efforts were hampered by many factors, including some that reveal the tacit attractiveness of the discipline's practices and values. These Realists often were distracted from their social science orientations by their law professor's attachments to law reform or doctrinal exegesis,[38] and they were limited by the inattention, lack of comprehension, and occasional mean-spiritedness shown towards their work by colleagues in the legal academy.[39] The discipline thus infiltrated and quietly influenced the work of these Realists and tacitly informed the legal academy's rejection of their more subversive work.[40]

---

36. See, e.g., Jay Feinman & Marc Feldman, *Pedagogy and Politics*, 73 Geo. L. J. 875 (1985) (describing the shut-down of an experiment with "mastery teaching" of first year subjects because this method distributed higher grades than those permitted by the grading curve).

37. J.H. Schlegel, supra note 18.

38. See id. at 81–114 (describing the projects of Charles Clark and William Douglas at Yale and how both Clark and Douglas allowed their reform interests to overcome their efforts at social science research); 147–210 (describing the work of the Johns Hopkins Institute of Law and its ultimate failure to develop a coherent research program, due in good part apparently to the continuing doctrinal research interests of several of its faculty members, Walter Wheeler Cook, Herman Oliphant and Hassel Yntema).

39. See, e.g., id. at 175, 183, 198, 209, 339–40 (on Felix Frankfurter's antagonism towards the Johns Hopkins Institute of Law); id. at 120, 146, 200, 294, 296, 211, 234, 237 (on Karl Llewellyn's generally negative response to the empirical social science work of other Legal Realists).

40. William Chase describes a similar story of how attachments to the case method in both teaching and scholarship among Harvard law faculty, and particularly in Felix Frankfurter, limited the development of administrative law scholarship during the first decades of the twentieth century. William C. Chase, The American Law School and the Rise of Administrative Government (1982).

Other Realists like Jerome Frank and Fred Rodell relied more speculatively on social science concepts to attack the trust of legal scholars in judicial doctrine and, in Rodell's case, the basic institution of law review scholarship.[41] While noticed at the time, these attacks were never sustained on a broad front and could be safely ignored by mainstream law professors as the Realist movement failed to obtain sufficient adherents and diminished through the 1930s.[42] The Realists, to be sure, changed the nature of conventional legal scholarship by questioning the determinacy and value-neutrality of judicial doctrine and adding reform-oriented policy arguments to the critique of judicial doctrine.[43] Moreover, although not directly influenced by Realism, it was during the Realist period of the 1920s and 1930s that student-edited law reviews expanded in number and became institutionalized in American law schools.[44] On balance, then, the Realist reform efforts modified and strengthened the institutions of conventional legal scholarship but failed in the critical effort by some to transform this scholarship in ways that would decenter the case method and diminish legal scholarship's autonomy from other forms of intellectual inquiry.

In summary, the tradition of criticizing legal education from within has provided certain energies and modifications to the discipline but left its basic structures essentially intact. This tradition of internal criticism has by-and-large served the discipline well—by constituting a safety valve for the expression of individual discontents and by protecting the discipline from external observations and criticisms of the kind it received in the Redlich and Reed reports in the early twentieth century. Perhaps the same may be said about this book as well. In any event, the next two sections of this chapter consider the contemporary reform movements in law schools. These movements have often been stimulated by external sources, and they are more collective in nature than the general reform tradition we have just surveyed. We shall discover, however, that the relationships between the discipline and these movements tend to replicate relationships between the discipline and the reform tradition. The reform movements, in other words, also tend to serve as outlets for discontented individuals, or malcontents,[45] and to disguise and protect the power of the discipline from observation or criticism. These movements accomplish

---

41. See Jerome Frank, Law and the Modern Mind (1930); Fred Rodell, *Goodbye to Law Reviews*, 23 U. Va. L. Rev. 38 (1936).

42. See L. Kalman, supra note 18, at 120–44; R. Stevens, supra note 11, at 155–63.

43. See, e.g., R. Stevens, supra note 11, at 156; White, supra note 2.

44. See R. Stevens, supra note 11, at 157, 164–65 n. 13.

45. Cf. J.H. Schlegel, supra note 18, at 224 (describing three leading Realist reformers as "classic malcontents").

other things as well, for they clearly have modified the discourse of law schools and altered or shifted some of the discipline's other routine practices. They represent sources of potential transformative changes. But the discipline's integration or capture of these reform movements remains a salient theme.

The Professional Reforms

In the latter part of the twentieth century three professionally oriented reforms to legal education became institutionalized in American law schools. In response to both internal and external criticisms that the case method/final examination law school is pedagogically limited, overly elitist or inegalitarian, and too far removed from actual legal practices, law schools have gradually installed, modified and expanded legal writing programs, law school clinics in which supervised students represent clients, and new courses in legal ethics. In principle, each of these reforms organizes legal knowledge differently from the discipline in ways that implicitly question and threaten to displace or transform the discipline's basic methods. In practice, however, the discipline's subtle tactics of compartmentalization, marginalization and infiltration have helped limit and splinter these reforms while keeping them cabined within niches in the law school curriculum. In essence, each of the reform movements promotes certain *ideals* of legal education which help legitimate the discipline. At the same time, the *reality* of each program is substantially different from the program's ideals, and this reality tacitly reinforces the discipline. We shall need to look at the history or genealogy of these professional reforms to understand their original promises or ideals, their implicit challenges to the discipline, and the complex ways in which the discipline has worked to compromise or distort the ideals of these reforms.

American law schools operated throughout the first half of the twentieth century with a relatively simple program based on Langdell's innovations at Harvard. Courses on legal doctrine were taught by the case method with a final examination at the end of each course. Law students were required to take a legal bibliography course, to help them do research in practice. Moot Courts were available on an optional or required basis, and at elite schools a student-edited, student-managed law review provided opportunities for sustained research and expository writing by the few students who obtained top grades on first year examinations and were admitted to the law review. Apart from these minimal supplements, legal education was devoted to case method courses and final examinations that engaged students in applying appellate law to given situations. Scholarship was performed mostly by professors at elite schools, and this was case method scholarship about legal doctrine, published in law reviews, casebooks and treatises, until the Legal Realists introduced social contexts and interdisciplinary study into the margins of scholarship.[46]

There were, to be sure, stirrings of change in law teaching before World War II. In the interwar period John Bradway and Jerome Frank argued for learning law by representing clients[47] and a few schools followed Denver's and Pennsylvania's examples by opening legal aid clinics.[48] In 1938 the University of Chicago began its innovative research and writing program for first year law students.[49] But case method classes and final examinations remained the basic program at most law schools (at least for students not on law review) throughout the first half of the twentieth century and well into its second half.

After World War II the expansion of American universities and law schools and influx of war veterans to law schools generated new resources, new democratic motivations and renewed criticisms to make changes to the basic program.[50] The major professional reform initiated at this time was a first year course in "legal writing," which then was combined with legal bibliography to constitute a required first year "research and writing" course.[51] These programs initially were designed to expose law students to thought and writing not included within case method courses and to provide opportunities for extensive research, legal analysis and writing comparable to the opportunities of law review students.[52] But the first year writing course has been in a state of considerable flux at most law schools ever since, as experiments with a great variety of structures have been tried in order to obtain better results from limited resources.[53] Many schools have also created an upper class research and writing requirement, which usually is

---

46. See R. Stevens, supra note 11, at 35–199; J.H. Schlegel, supra note 18; Marjorie Rombauer, *First-Year Legal Research and Writing: Then and Now*, 25 J. Legal Educ. 538, 539–40 (1973).

47. See John Bradway, *Some Distinctive Features of a Legal Aid Clinic Course*, 1 U. Chi. L. Rev. 469 (1933); Frank, supra note 6.

48. See R. Stevens, supra note 11, at 162.

49. See Harry Kalven, *Law School Training in Research and Exposition: The University of Chicago Program*, 1 J. Legal Educ. 107, 108 (1948).

50. See, e.g., Report of the AALS Committee on Curriculum, *The Place of Skills in Legal Education*, 45 Colum. L. Rev. 345 (1945) (Karl Llewellyn, chair); Kalven, supra note 49.

51. See Rombauer, supra note 46, at 540–42.

52. See Kalven, supra note 49; Howard Westwood, *The Law Review Should Become the Law School*, 31 Va. L. Rev. 913 (1945).

53. See, e.g., Allen Boyer, *Legal Writing Programs Reviewed*, 62 Chicago-Kent L. Rev. 23 (1985) (describing three basic models for the first year writing course); Helene Shapo, *The Frontiers of Legal Writing: Challenges for Teaching Research*, 78 Law Library J. 719, 721–724 (1986) (describing eight models of instruction for legal writing courses).

satisfied by completion of a seminar paper, clinical work or law review work.[54] The growth of seminars and multiple law reviews may also be viewed as part of the expansion of writing opportunities in law schools.[55]

In the 1960s clinical education became another significant presence as law schools opened legal clinics to make legal education "more relevant" to students and to help the legal profession meet its new constitutional duties to provide legal services to the poor.[56] Subsequently, simulated clinical courses, especially in trial advocacy, were developed to respond to allegations by judges and professional organizations that new lawyers were deficient in trial skills.[57] The development of these clinical programs has more-or-less continued in the 1980s and 1990s, limited by available resources but stimulated by new ABA accreditation standards and several task force studies, most recently the MacCrate Report.[58]

Then in the 1970s the Watergate affair aroused both public and professional concerns about the ethical behavior of lawyers. The profession responded by establishing a "legal ethics" part to state bar examinations and by requiring law schools to teach this subject.[59] Law schools traditionally had adopted a minimalist approach to teaching legal or professional ethics, and now they simply added a new required course.[60] But the profession's interest in promoting training in legal ethics has continued and, if anything, increased as evidenced by several task force and committee reports expressing concerns about the state of "professionalism" among lawyers.[61]

---

54. See William J. Bridge, *Legal Writing After the First Year of Law School*, 5 Ohio N. L. Rev. 411 (1978); George D. Gopen, *The State of Legal Writing: Res Ipsa Loquiter*, 86 Mich. L. Rev. 333, 355–56 (1987); S. Blair Kauffman, *Advanced Legal Research Courses: A New Trend in American Legal Education*, 6 L. Ref. Servs. Q. 123 (1986).

55. On the proliferation of seminars, see, e.g., Elinor Fox, *The Good Law School, The Good Curriculum, and the Mind and the Heart*, 39 J. Legal Educ. 473, 476–81 (1989); on the proliferation of multiple law reviews at many law schools, see Michael J. Saks, Howard Larsen & Carol J. Hodne, *Is There A Growing Gap Among Law, Law Practice, and Legal Scholarship? A Systematic Comparison of Law Review Articles One Generation Apart*, 30 Suffolk L. Rev. 353, 363 (1996).

56. See, e.g., William Pincus, *Clinical Legal Education in the United States, 1968–1975*, 49 Australian L. J. 420 (1975); Report of the AALS—ABA Committee on Guidelines for Clinical Legal Education 7–8 (1980).

57. See id. at 8; Roger Cramton & Eric Jensen, *The State of Trial Advocacy and Legal Education: Three New Studies*, 30 J. Legal Educ. 253 (1979).

58. See note 61 infra.

59. See Michael Kelly, Legal Ethics and Legal Education 2 (1980).

60. See id. at 5–21.

61. See ABA, In the Spirit of Public Service: A Blueprint for the Rekindling of Lawyer Professionalism (1986) (the Stanley Commission's Report); ABA, Teaching and Learn-

These three reforms, in their ideal forms, challenge basic elements and techniques of the discipline on three fundamental grounds. They promote *student-centered learning* in contrast to the professor-centered learning that structures the case method/final examination system.[62] They promote *practical rationality* and *making contextualized judgments* by comparison to the technical rationality or rule-oriented discourse and rule-oriented judgments that are prominent features of the discipline's practices and methods, especially in final examinations.[63] Less obviously, these reforms also promote the acquisition of various kinds of *tacit professional knowledge* (in other words, knowledge we know but cannot speak) by comparison to the express technical knowledge that is the central feature of the case method/final examination system.[64] These three forms of education seem essential to training good lawyers, but each form challenges the professional expertise of classroom law professors, the objectivity of law school evaluations, and even the basic sense of a relatively autonomous or unique expertise of lawyers. It should not be surprising then that many law professors and many students instinctively shy away from the full or ideal implications of these professional reforms, or that the discipline has employed certain implicit tactics or strategies to limit these reforms and assimilate them to its basic structures.

---

ing Professionalism: Report of the Professionalism Committee (1996); ABA: Teaching and Learning Professionalism: Symposium Proceedings (1997).

62. This contrast is obvious in clinical education and legal writing programs but perhaps less so in the case of legal ethics. Ethics training in its ideal form, however, will engage law students in applying their own moral values and perspectives to legal situations. Ethics training also may be developed in clinical situations. In both senses ethics training may be said to involve student-centered learning in ways that diverge from the case method.

63. On the tendency of university-based professional training, including law schools, to favor technical rationality over practical rationality, see Donald A. Schon, *Educating the Reflective Legal Practitioner*, 2 Clinical L. Rev. 231, 236–42 (1995). Of course, the case method (and presumably final examinations) may be employed intentionally by professors to emphasize practical rationality and the making of contextualized judgments, see, e.g., A. T. Kronman, supra note 31. But the contrast here is between the practical rationality and contextualized judgments that are a necessary part of the writing process, clinical work and ethical judgments and the discipline's habitual, nonintentional features that for a host of reasons tend to favor or privilege the technical rationality of rules and rule-oriented judgments. See Chapters One, Two and Three.

64. On the importance to legal practice and legal training of acquiring various kinds of tacit professional knowledge, which is best achieved by repeated practice, supervision and feedback, see Schon, supra note 63. See also Donald A. Schon, The Reflective Practitioner (1983); Educating the Reflective Practitioner (1987).

The discipline's common response to the professional reforms, in addition to silence or grudging acceptance, has consisted of four basic strategies. Each reform has been developed as a specialized compartment within the already highly compartmentalized structure of the law school curriculum, thus keeping the major lessons of each reform separate from the core curriculum and from other aspects of legal education, including the other professional reforms. The political and administrative structures of these programs have been splintered, particularly by the employment of part-time teachers, contract teachers, faculty with "special" tenure status and student teachers in lieu of full-time tenure-track professors, thus insuring that specialists in these fields are without political power or incentives to do much more than establish their own niches within law schools. The concurrent development of the reforms since the 1970s has meant that these programs compete with each other for new resources, tending to make their proponents competitors rather than allies in reforming the curriculum.[65] Basic ideas of the case method/final examination system have also infiltrated the professional reforms in ways that limit their reformist qualities and ensure their ultimate loyalty to the discipline's purposes and structures.

We need to explore the history and practices of the professional reforms in some detail in order to discover the promise of their ideals, the power and effects of the discipline's embrace, and the fragmented realities of each movement as it has developed within the discipline's web of routine practices, habits and tacit knowledge.

Legal Writing Programs

"It is curious that law schools only recently have paid curricular attention to education in writing for lawyers. This is a particular anomaly in the legal profession, in which communication is essential and words are 'the skin of a living thought.'"
Helene Shapo[66]

"Perhaps ideally, all faculty members would devote the major portion of their time to teaching writing, research, and analytical skills to each

---

65. See Beverly Balos, *Conferring on the MacCrate Report: A Clinical Gaze*, 1 Clinical L. Rev. 349, 353–354 (1994).

66. Shapo, supra note 53, at 719 (footnotes omitted).

student individually. Needless to say, this would be a more time-consuming program than most faculties would tolerate."

—Stewart Macaulay & Henry G. Manne[67]

Law schools began to introduce writing programs into the curriculum under two rather different influences. One was the Legal Realist critique of legal education, which called for "some realism" about professional training and the provision of more comprehensive education in the activities of practicing lawyers.[68] The second consisted of the egalitarian or democratic values of the New Deal and World War II, which invited or demanded that more attention and resources be paid to the majority of students who do not obtain the benefits of a law review experience.[69] The initial writing programs after World War II were designed to provide legal writing opportunities that would be "other than the writing of examinations," would entail individualized feedback from more experienced legal writers, and would involve much re-writing, especially of memorandums that attempted to resolve client problems.[70] As writing programs developed, however, they soon became subject to a host of competing purposes, competing conceptions about writing or how best to implement writing practices for law students, to say nothing of limited resources and the unwillingness of most law faculty to supervise student writing. Experienced observers agree that most law school writing programs have failed to come close to their basic goal of providing substantial, meaningful, student-centered learning experiences based on the writing process.[71]

---

67. Stewart Macaulay & Henry G. Manne, *A Low-Cost Legal Writing Program—The Wisconsin Experience*, 11 J. Legal Educ. 387, 388 (1959).

68. See, e.g., Karl Llewellyn, The Bramble Bush (1930) (noting the limited professional value of case method training); *On What is Wrong with So-Called Legal Education*, 35 Colum. L. Rev. 651 (1935) (recommending better training of lawyers in "reading and writing"); Frank, supra note 6 (recommending clinical training for law students).

69. See Kalven, supra note 49, at 107–08; Ray Moreland, *Legal Writing and Research in the Smaller Schools*, 7 J. Legal Educ. 49, 52–53 (1954); Westwood, supra note 52.

70. See Burton Kanter, *Effective Legal Writing—Some Thoughts and Reflections on Learning and Teaching*, 1960 Chicago Bar Record 113; Kalven, supra note 49; Moreland, supra note 69.

71. See Gopen, supra note 54, at 355–62; George Rideout & Jill Ramsfield, *Legal Writing: A Revised View*, 69 Wash. L. Rev. 35, 36–37 (1994); Shapo, supra note 53, at 725. A short list of exceptional law school writing programs might include those at Brooklyn, Chicago-Kent, Montana, NYU and Chicago. See Bari Burke, *Legal Writing (Groups) at the University of Montana: Professional Voice Lessons in a Communal Context*, 52 Mont. L. Rev. 373 (1991); Elizabeth Fajans & Mary Falk, *Against the Tyranny of the Paraphrase: Talking Back to Texts*, 78 Cornell L. Rev. 163 (1993); Gopen, supra note 54, at 357–58; Kalven,

The ideal conception of law school writing can be summarized by a set of principles that articulate ways to use writing as an experience-based learning process. The most fundamental principle states that legal research, legal thought and writing should be integrated exercises in order that students experience and understand the vital, often tacit interconnections between effective research, the analysis of problems which shifts as research and writing progresses, and the re-thinking and re-writing of texts that so often informs effective research and analysis.[72] These integrated exercises, moreover, should be continued and intensified throughout the three-year curriculum to take advantage of the increasing knowledge and confidence of students in applying legal techniques.[73] This practice should provide many opportunities for *re-vising* texts on the basis of feedback from more experienced writers and, more frequently, from the basic fact of re-reading one's own text.[74] Such feedback is necessary to help students acquire the capacity to reflect about and evaluate their work on their own and to make adjustments, a capacity which seems essential for many kinds of demanding professional tasks.[75] Law school writing also should involve writing many different kinds of documents (for example, opinion letters, contracts, wills, pleadings, and legislation) to introduce students to the varied contexts and diverse audiences for whom lawyers write.[76] Substantial feedback from more experienced writers together with much re-vising and re-writing also implies a need for much "collaborative" or "joint" work between students and their supervisors as a good, perhaps essential means by which more experienced supervisors convey their understandings of tacit professional knowledge to students.[77]

---

supra note 49; Lewis Solomon, *Perspectives on Curriculum Reform in Law Schools: A Critical Assessment*, 24 U. Toledo L. Rev. 1, 19–27 (1992).

72. See Rombauer, supra note 46; Shapo, supra note 53.

73. See, e.g., Robert C. Berring & Kathleen Vanden Heuvel, *Legal Research: Should Students Learn It or Wing It?*, 81 Law Library J. 431 (1989) (genuine instruction in legal research can only be accomplished during the second and third years of law school).

74. See Kalven, supra note 49; Moreland, supra note 69; Harry Pratter & Burton Kanter, *Expanding the Tutorial Program: A Bloodless Revolution*, 7 J. Legal Educ. 395 (1955); Rideout & Ramsfield, supra note 71, at 61–93.

75. See generally D. A. Schon, The Reflective Practitioner, supra note 64.

76. See Leigh Hunt Greenshaw, *"To Say What The Law Is": Learning the Practice of Legal Rhetoric*, 29 Val. U. L. Rev. 861 (1995) (emphasizing writing for varied contexts and audiences as critical aspects of acquiring skills in legal rhetoric).

77. See Rideout & Ramsfield, supra note 71, at 61–93. See also D.A. Schon, Educating the Reflective Practitioner, supra note 64 (describing the collaborative transmission of tacit professional knowledge in the studio classes of architecture schools).

More generally, law school writing should be governed by two principles drawn from contemporary composition theory. One is that good substantive writing should be learned and taught as a *process* in which the writer generates substantive and stylistic knowledge by the act of writing itself, and thus benefits from re-readings, feedback, revisions and re-writings. The second principle is that writing should be learned and taught as a *social act* in which the writer enters into a complex discourse between her own ideas and texts, the texts of others, readers of her texts and her imagined ideal audiences for each kind of writing.[78] This conception of writing as a process and a social activity holds that it is a mistake to think of writing merely as a *product* by which one instrumentally conveys independently conceived thoughts in a clear and neutral manner.[79]

This ideal conception of the writing process serves the discipline by enhancing claims about the effectiveness of law school training. Were this ideal widely implemented, however, it would seriously challenge the case method/final examination system. If legal writing "is basically 85% analysis and 15 percent composition,"[80] students and faculty who began to use the writing process to learn the law would soon discover that writing is a far better means of learning the basic skills of legal analysis, synthesis and rhetoric than by oral exchanges in the case method classroom and the instrumentalist writing demanded by final examinations. Simply put, the writing process both provides and invites concrete individualized feedback to the thought of law students in ways that the case method and final examinations cannot. The writing process also provides many opportunities to place complex legal materials into coherent relationships in ways that the case method and final examinations simply cannot match.[81]

The discipline has deployed several strategies to devalue or subjugate writing knowledge and the writing process. First, attention to writing has been limited primarily to a single required course in the first-year curriculum, and

---

78. See, e.g., Carol McCrehan Parker, *Writing Throughout the Curriculum: Why Law Schools Need It and How to Achieve It*, 76 Neb. L. Rev. 561, 565–67 (1997); Rideout and Ramsfield, supra note 71, at 51–61.

79. See Parker, supra note 78; Rideout & Ramsfield, supra note 71.

80. Peter Gross, *On Law School Training in Analytic Skill*, 25 J. Legal Educ. 261, 266 (1973) (quoting W.C. Warren, *The Teaching of Legal Writing and Legal Research*, 52 Law Library J. 350, 352 (1959)).

81. See, e.g., Boyer, supra note 53, at 324; Gross, supra note 80. On a successful experiment that employed frequent writing exercises to help teach legal analysis, see Jay Feinman & Marc Feldman, *Achieving Excellence: Mastery Learning in Legal Education*, 35 J. Legal Educ. 528 (1985); on the crude instrumentalist nature of the writing that is demanded by law school final examinations, see Kissam, supra note 7.

this is usually taught separately from doctrinal subjects.[82] This separation signals that legal writing is a "skill" separate and independent from legal analysis. The course's location in the first year engages students in writing law at that moment when they are least capable of perceiving the possibilities of using the writing process to acquire and generate substantive and procedural legal knowledge. Moreover, the course's usual location in the fall semester of the first year means that highly motivated, high achieving law students are given their first detailed, concrete negative criticisms and feedback in their writing course, thus possibly discouraging many from the writing process.[83] To be sure, the proliferation of elective seminars, upper class writing requirements and new law reviews has increased opportunities for student writing in upper class years. But the lack of formal institutional endorsement continues to signal that writing is an episodic, separate skill that is less important than the analysis, thought and oral brilliance of case method classrooms, and that writing in law school is essentially a matter of personal choice. In sum, the separate and limited first-year writing course reflects and reinforces the widespread assumption in law schools that writing is merely a neutral instrument or skill for transferring independently conceived thoughts and that the only relevance of "legal writing" therefore is the finished product.[84] This assumption misses or detracts from the possibility of acquiring invaluable professional knowledge by employing writing as a learning process,[85] and thus protects the discipline's basic structures from significant change.

Second, many law schools today are investing additional resources in research and writing programs, and there is a marked attempt in these programs to integrate research, methods of legal reasoning, and writing.[86] But limited

---

82. See Rideout & Ramsfield, supra note 71, at 77; Shapo, supra note 53, at 720–21.

83. See Lisa Eichorn, *Writing in the Legal Academy: A Dangerous Supplement?*, 40 Ariz. L. Rev. 105, 123–24 (1998).

84. Cf. Maxine Hairston, *The Winds of Change: Thomas Kuhn and the Revolution in the Teaching of Writing*, 33 College Composition and Communication 76, 77–79 (Feb. 1982), reprinted in Rhetoric and Composition: A Sourcebook for Teachers and Writers 3, 4–6 (Richard L. Graves, ed. 3rd ed., 1990) (teaching English composition as a separate skills course emphasizes writing as a finished product and denigrates the values of writing, teaching writing, and understanding writing as a basic method or process for acquiring substantive knowledge).

85. See Reed Dickerson, *Teaching Legal Writing in Law Schools: Drafting*, 16 Idaho L. Rev. 85, 85–86 (1979); Philip C. Kissam, *Thinking (By Writing) About Legal Writing*, 40 Vand. L. Rev. 135 (1987); Rideout & Ramsfield, supra note 71.

86. See, e.g., Neil Feigenson, *Legal Writing Texts Today*, 41 J. Legal Educ. 503, 511–16 (1991); Shapo, supra note 53, at 721–25.

resources and the fragmented administrative structures of writing programs diminish the opportunities for effective integrated experiences and contribute to the common law school view that writing is merely a neutral instrument to convey independently conceived thoughts and therefore ought to be confined to subordinate places. Many legal writing courses are taught by part-time instructors or third-year students who work under the variable supervision of full-time faculty and are unlikely to have much experience in teaching the process of legal thinking/writing.[87] When full-time instructors are employed, they are often young lawyers or writing instructors who are neither recognized nor paid as law professors, nor as experienced, and they tend to turn over rapidly.[88] The absence of full-time tenure-track professors and the basic fact that the research and writing course "typically carries less academic credit than any other first-year offering" surely signal to students that writing is not to be taken as seriously as substantive doctrinal courses.[89] Furthermore, some courses still provide instruction in legal bibliography, legal reasoning and legal writing in separate units, thus reducing the possibility of tacit learning from integrated exercises and reinforcing the perception that legal writing's mission "is to perfect [the] production of specific written forms."[90] Research instruction by part-time adjuncts and third-year students also tends "to be more idiosyncratic and anecdotal than instruction informed by a more comprehensive study of the types of research materials available in the law school library."[91] The limited resources and fragmented structures of writing programs thus help eliminate the challenge of the writing process to the discipline.

Third, the first year research and writing course is often perceived as practice or training in performing the same analysis that is demanded in law school classrooms and, more significantly, by final examinations.[92] Legal writing texts sometimes promise this,[93] and typical problems for research memorandums and other assignments are often similar to final examination problems.[94] Thus many law students may perceive research and writing courses merely as a

---

87. See Gopen, supra note 54, at 355; Shapo, supra note 53, at 725.
88. See Rideout & Ramsfield, supra note 71, at 39, 87–88; Shapo, supra note 53, at 725.
89. See Douglas Abrams, *Integrating Legal Writing into Civil Procedure*, 24 Conn. L. Rev. 813, 817–18 (1992); Rideout & Ramsfield, supra note 71, at 77–78.
90. Feigenson, supra note 86, at 510.
91. Shapo, supra note 53, at 725.
92. See Mary Ellen Gale, *Legal Writing: The Impossible Takes a Little Longer*, 44 Albany L. Rev. 298 (1980); Macauley & Manne, supra note 67, at 390.
93. See Eichorn, supra note 83, at 113–14.
94. See, e.g., Kalven, supra note 73; Macauley & Manne, supra note 88.

means to help them negotiate the case method/ final examination system. In this perspective, legal writing becomes an integral part of the discipline of law schools.

Finally, the discipline's values infiltrate writing programs and otherwise cabin them in numerous subtle ways. Most directly, the law school often insists upon typical law school grading of law student writing, particularly in first year courses when the distribution of competitive grades is most important to establishing the class rank of students.[95] The imposition of competitive grading curves on the writing process diminishes the possibilities for sympathetic, constructive, individualized feedback from writing instructors to law students, who must in view of the competitive grading make their finished products "by themselves" in order to ensure a fair race for grades. Under the regime of law school grading curves, then, where many low grades must be dispensed and justified, there is diminished incentive for genuine collaborative work between instructors and students, diminished incentive to create revision assignments (for a revised document will constitute work of both the instructor and the student), and a marked tendency to provide only negative or Delphic sorts of feedback on revision assignments as ways for instructors to tacitly avoid participating in the revision of documents they must grade.[96]

A common explanation for the fragmented, limited reality of law school writing programs is scarce economic resources. But this explanation disguises a more fundamental if less attractive explanation: the unwillingness or distaste of most full-time law professors for "teaching writing, research, and analytical skills to each student individually."[97] The discipline supports this unwillingness, intolerance and indifference by several means. The discipline's pressure on law faculty to publish frequently and to think of themselves primarily as scholars rather than teachers may cause many professors to fear the *possible* commitment of *any* additional time to supervising individual students.[98] Many faculty may also sense or fear the personal risk to their sense of professional expertise and the painfulness that can be involved in trying to articulate to students what is wrong with particular written texts and how these

---

95. Cf. ABA, Section of Legal Education and Admissions to the Bar, Sourcebook on Legal Writing Programs 53–55 (1997) (reporting that as of 1994 73% of law schools grade first year writing courses "similarly" to other first year courses).

96. See Kissam, supra note 85, at 169–79; Rideout & Ramsfield, supra note 71, at 91–93.

97. Macauley & Manne, supra note 67, at 388.

98. See Chapter Three's discussion of the law school's examinatorial regime and confessional technology.

texts might be improved.[99] Many faculty may fear too that if they must read many versions of student writing on the same problem, they will simply experience the same substantial boredom that they discover in reading final exam papers.[100]

In addition, many professors and students in the disciplinary law school appear to hold misperceptions about the writing process that limit education by writing.[101] One view is that good legal writing is just good writing and that there is no need to teach "legal writing" as such beyond teaching particular forms or remedial writing skills.[102] Another is that good writing is based on "natural talent" and cannot be taught, a view which also limits writing programs to teaching legal bibliography, legal forms and remedial grammar and syntax. Others perceive legal writing merely as an ancillary means to the more important "analysis" that is taught by the case method, a view which relegates the teaching of legal writing to writing instructors or practicing lawyers instead of full-time professors. As a consequence of these views, many law professors seem to believe that teaching by writing is "anti-intellectual" or "low value" work by comparison to their classroom performances, scholarship and consulting work; they thus ignore the values of learning by writing and tend to keep specialized writing instructors out of law schools or cabined within a special subordinate role.[103] These beliefs are understandable in light of the paradigmatic significance that the case method, final examinations, and much instrumentalist writing by law students and law professors assumes within the discipline. They also are relatively powerful, unshakeable beliefs

---

99. Cf. Kissam, supra note 7, at 472–73 (describing the problems that the presence of tacit knowledge creates for discussing final examinations with law students).

100. On the boredom that law professors experience reading final examination answers, see Clark Byse, *Fifty Years of Legal Education*, 71 Iowa L. Rev. 1063, 1086 (1986); George Christie, *The Recruitment of Law Faculty*, 1987 Duke L. J. 306, 310, 315.

101. See Eichorn, supra note 83, at 106–117; Rideout & Ramsfield, supra note 71, at 40–48.

102. See, e.g., "Beyond Small Groups: Legal Writing Instruction at Yale", Yale Law Report, Spring 1995, pp. 8, 9 (interview with Robert Harrison, a legal writing instructor at Yale Law School) ("A few members of the faculty think we should devote even more time to legal writing instruction, but most don't. Many see three years as too short a time to give a proper grounding in the substantive areas of the law and to develop a feel for legal theory and policy, which is our special mission. Still others, I am sure, view legal writing instruction as essentially remedial in nature, and hardly necessary at a law school that admits only the best and the brightest."). See also Kissam, supra note 85, at 141–48 (a similar discussion of faculty expertise inclining law professors away from writing).

103. See Rideout & Ramsfield, supra note 71, at 47–48.

that are grounded in the discipline's web of routine practices, habits and tacit conceptions.

In sum, the instinctive confidence of law school inhabitants in the discipline's structures, especially the case method and final examinations, conspires to keep legal writing in a subordinate location. The ideal of law school writing programs allows law schools to market themselves as the producers of excellent education,[104] while the fragmented reality of the programs maintains the status quo of the case method/final examination law school as "the superior form" of education.

Clinical Education

"But is it not plain that, without giving up entirely the case-book system or the growing and valuable alliance with the so-called social sciences, the law schools should once more get in intimate contact with what clients need and with what courts and lawyers actually do?"
Jerome Frank[105]

"'Clinics' were a frightening prospect to the traditional academic teachers."

—William Pincus[106]

Clinical education, broadly defined, involves the performance of legal roles by students in some kind of supervised setting.[107] Students may represent clients in either in-house clinics or externships, and they may participate in simulated clinical work in subjects such as trial advocacy, negotiations, interviewing or counseling.[108] The basic point of clinical education is to integrate doctrinal knowledge with skills in ways that involve the complicated unruly domains of clients, facts, and problems to be solved. Clinical education, like writ-

---

104. See, e.g., Eichorn, supra note 83, at 116–17.

105. Frank, supra note 6, at 913.

106. Pincus, supra note 56, at 422.

107. See, e.g., *Report of the Committee on the Future of the In-House Clinic*, 42 J. Legal Educ. 508, 511 (1992) (hereafter "In-House Clinic Report"); Marc Feldman, *On the Margins of Legal Education*, 13 NYU Rev. Law & Soc. Change 607, 612–17 (1984–85).

108. See, e.g., In-House Clinic Report, supra note 107; Michael Grossman, *Clinical Legal Education: History and Diagnosis*, 26 J. Legal Educ. 162, 173–91 (1974); Nina Tarr, *Current Issues in Clinical Legal Education*, 37 Howard L. J. 31, 32–39 (1993).

ing, immerses law students in a world of practical rationality, contextualized judgments, tacit knowledge and student-centered learning that is fundamentally dissimilar from the world of the case method and final examinations.

Law school clinics arrived in the 1960s, although a few models and clinical critiques of legal education existed much earlier.[109] Several forces combined to provide a mixture of ideas, resources, and regulatory pressures that encouraged law schools to develop clinics. Many clinics were established with the purpose of providing student-centered, practice-oriented kinds of learning as a model for what good legal education should be.[110] Some clinics were also initiated with the object of providing better legal services to low income persons through direct services, law reform projects, and the training of future lawyers to represent persons with low incomes or other disadvantages.[111] Clinics were thus designed to make legal education "more relevant" both educationally and politically. The legal profession too helped promote law school clinics. Initially the profession sought help in serving the increasing numbers of indigent persons who sought free or low-cost legal services under the mandate and influence of judicial decisions and the federal government's War on Poverty in the 1960s.[112] More recently the organized bar has used accreditation measures and reform studies to increase the pressure on law schools to provide at least minimum amounts of clinic training to all students who seek it.[113] In addition, private foundations, especially the Ford Foundation, and the federal government made substantial grants to help law schools initiate and develop their clinical programs, although this support now appears to be receding with the general institutionalization of clinics.[114]

---

109. See, e.g., Philip G. Schrag & Michael Meltsner, Reflections on Clinical Legal Education 3–7 (1998); Grossman, supra note 108, at 168–69. A major critique advocating clinical education in the 1930s was Jerome Frank's, supra note 6.

110. See P. Schrag & M. Meltsner, supra note 109, at 5–6; Grossman, supra note 108, at 186–93; Pincus, supra note 56.

111. See Grossman, supra note 108, at 173–80; Tarr, supra note 108, at 32.

112. See Grossman, supra note 108, at 173–78.

113. See, e.g., ABA, Standards for Approval of Law Schools and Interpretations, Standard 302 (a) (iii) (the approved "law school shall...offer instruction in professional skills"); Standard 405 (e) (the approved "law school should afford to full-time faculty members whose primary responsibilities are in its professional skills program a form of security of position reasonably similar to tenure and perquisites reasonably similar to those provided other full-time faculty members") (Oct. 1992); ABA, Legal Education and Professional Development—An Educational Continuum (1992) (the "MacCrate Report") (urging law schools to expand their training in "professional skills and values").

114. See P. Schrag & M. Meltsner, supra note 109, at 4–7; Pincus, supra note 56.

The basic instincts of the discipline have been to resist clinics, limit them and incorporate them in fragmented, compromised ways. Clinical education has thus become a closely watched and regulated domain, especially since its methods and philosophy contrast so markedly with the case method/final examination system. The discipline has constrained clinical education by separating clinics from the core curriculum, by marginalizing clinics in terms of their space, budget allocations, prestige and conceptualization, and by infiltrating clinic programs with disciplinary values.[115] Thus limited and tamed, clinics help legitimate the law school as a provider of excellent education, and they provide transitional bridges to practice for some students. They also provide a temporary place of refuge for those upper class students who desire relief or escape from the routines of the core curriculum, case method and final examinations.

The diffuse nature, purposes and methods of clinical training make it difficult to generalize about the movement.[116] Nonetheless, a basic ideal conception or tacit jurisprudence of clinical education might be described by the following principles.[117] First, students are asked to perform roles in legal practice contexts that are quite different from the case method's primary context of appellate court opinions. In these different contexts, facts are uncertain, contested, unknown, and in some cases unknowable, and facts must be established through the instruments of the imperfect memories, judgments or intuitions of human agents. Clients have goals that are often diffuse, unclear and changeable, and these goals must be pursued and clarified through an ongoing discourse between attorneys and clients. Clients, witnesses and opposing parties also have emotions and ideas about law of their own that enter into client-attorney interactions. The clinical experience thus exposes students to interactions with complex subjectivity and humanity, unruly factual situations, practical judgments and ethical issues that are basically absent from the case method and final examinations, which typically assume or stipulate facts and assume "a standard" abstract client who has the clear goal of winning a lawsuit in appellate court.[118]

---

115. On the marginalization of clinics in general, see Feldman, supra note 107; Tarr, supra note 108, at 40–43; Mark Tushnet, *Scenes from the Metropolitan Underground: A Critical Perspective on the Status of Clinical Education*, 52 Geo. Wash. L. Rev. 272 (1984).

116. See In-House Clinic Report, supra note 107, at 611–617; Tarr, supra note 108, at 32–39.

117. The following description draws heavily from Anthony Amsterdam, *Clinical Legal Education—A 21st-Century Perspective*, 34 J. Legal Educ. 612 (1984); Feldman, supra note 107, at 612–17; Frank, supra note 6; Schon, supra note 63.

118. See Ann Shalleck, *Constructions of the Client Within Legal Education*, 45 Stan. L. Rev. 1731 (1993).

Secondly, students perform under the supervision of experienced instructors who try to provide helpful kinds of feedback and evaluation of the student's work that will both promote a client's interests and enhance the student's learning. This supervision in principle guides students, but does not control them, through varied exercises in which doctrinal knowledge and multiple skills are applied in an integrated fashion to obtain practical results. At its best this work involves both sensitive supervision and much collective reflection upon the kinds of ethical issues, situational evaluations and practical judgments that inform high quality professional practice.[119]

The specific purposes of clinics are so many, so often in conflict or competition, and so complex, that any particular clinical program is unlikely to achieve them all.[120] In general, however, clinics ideally attempt to provide individually supervised student-centered experiences that help students acquire the experience and knowledge to make sound practical, rhetorical and ethical judgments under the stress of actual or simulated practice conditions.[121] In their ideal form clinics also will help students establish useful "perspectives" on the complex interrelationships between lawyers, uncertain clients, unruly facts, legal problems and social institutions.[122]

This ideal conception of clinical training threatens important aspects of the discipline. From a clinical perspective, the case method's elimination of

---

119. See, e.g., Kenneth R. Kreiling, *Clinical Education and Lawyer Competency: The Process of Learning to Learn from Experience Through Properly Structured Clinical Supervision*, 40 Md. L. Rev. 284 (1981); Michael Meltsner, James V. Rowan & Daniel J. Givelber, *The Bike Tour Leader's Dilemma: Talking About Supervision*, 13 Vt. L. Rev. 399 (1989); Schon, supra note 63; Nina Tarr, *The Skill of Evaluation as an Explicit Goal of Clinical Training*, 21 Pac. L. J. 967 (1990); Amy L. Ziegler, *Developing a System of Evaluation in Clinical Legal Teaching*, 42 J. Legal Educ. 575 (1992).

120. See In-House Clinic Report, supra note 107, at 511–517 (describing nine "principal goals" of live client in-house clinics and arguing that "clinics provide the best opportunity in the curriculum to integrate these manifold teaching goals," but recognizing too that "none of us can be perfect exemplars of all of these qualities, and no one can teach all of these goals in our clinic with perfect emphasis").

121. On the nature of sound practical judgments and the educational methods that seem helpful or necessary to instruct law students in making such judgments, compare A. T. Kronman, supra note 31, at 11–162 (on employing the case method to promote practical judgment); with D. A. Schon, Educating the Reflective Practitioner, supra note 64; *Educating the Reflective Legal Practitioner*, supra note 63 (on using clinical methods and individualized supervision of professional students as the best way to promote practical judgment).

122. See John O. Mudd, *The Place of Perspective in Law and Legal Education*, 26 Gonz. L. Rev. 277 (1990/91).

most aspects of the client can be perceived as artificial and misleading education[123] The relentless insistence of the case method and final examinations on rule-oriented analysis and judgments also might be perceived as a poor way to train professionals for work that involves much tacit knowledge and making practical judgments in uncertain, constantly varying situations. Should these perceptions take hold, the case method/final examination system might be limited to a small part of the curriculum, to teach case analysis and provide practice for bar examinations, and more effective techniques such as lectures, out-of-class readings, various types of non-examination writings and computerized exercises might be employed to teach most doctrinal knowledge and legal skills.[124] "Pre-clinical" or "quasi-clinical" methods and courses that included much writing and individually supervised student work could then replace most case method classes. Law professors might even begin to devote more time to professional instruction and less to producing the quantities of scholarship that are emphasized by the assumptions and practices of the discipline.[125]

This has not happened, of course, and economics, inertia and the "frightening prospect" of clinics to "traditional" law professors constitute the usual explanation (or justification) for the limited place of clinics.[126] Underlying this explanation, one can perceive three distinct strategies by which the discipline has acted to limit the clinical threat. These strategies consist of dividing tactics, which keep clinical education separate from the case method/final examination system, tactics that marginalize and subordinate clinical programs, and infiltrating tactics by which clinics are turned to serve the discipline's purposes.

Clinical education has been kept separate, even invisible, from the rest of legal education as a matter of curriculum, space, and time, thereby preventing contamination of the discipline's basic structures. Clinics are found mostly

---

123. See Shalleck, supra note 118.

124. See Frank, supra note 6 (recommending reduction of the case method to a small part of the curriculum); Walter Gellhorn, *The Second and Third Years of Law Study*, 17 J. Legal Educ. 1, 3 (1964) (recommending lecturing in upper class courses to cover doctrine); Kissam, supra note 8, at 2005–16 (recommending non-examination kinds of writings); James Boyd White, *Doctrine in a Vacuum: Reflections on What a Law School Ought (and Ought Not) to Be*, 36 J. Legal Educ. 155, 164 (1986) (recommending readings that are not discussed in class as a means of covering necessary doctrinal materials).

125. Cf. John S. Elson, *The Case Against Legal Scholarship or, If the Profession Must Publish, Must the Professional Perish?*, 39 J. Legal Educ. 343 (1989) (arguing that law teaching is relatively more valuable than most current legal scholarship).

126. See, e.g., Pincus, supra note 56, at 422.

in the third year curriculum, where clinical learning occurs only after the case method/final examination system has socialized students to the law.[127] Live-client clinics typically operate in spaces located on the periphery of law school buildings, in basements or at greater distances from the main halls of learning, thus keeping clinical faculty, clinic students and their learning spatially as well as temporally separate from non-clinical faculty and students.[128] Many students also become fully engaged in clinical work as they spend more hours working in clinics than in other courses,[129] and rather extreme time demands are placed on clinical faculty by their need to supervise many students, publish as well as teach, and manage what in effect are medium-size law firms with limited resources.[130] Thus the discipline's curricular organization, its spatial relationships, and its temporal rhythms tend to keep nonclinical faculty and students from attending to clinical education, and these dividing factors also diminish the possibility that clinical faculty and students will have the resources or incentives to try to educate non-clinicians in the values of clinical learning.

The discipline marginalizes clinical education by tacitly subordinating clinical knowledge and values in several subtle ways. Most clinics provide services to indigent clients who are among the "low status" clients of the profession,[131] signaling that clinical knowledge is inferior to or less important than the doctrinal knowledge and analytical skills that are to be acquired in case method classrooms.[132] The distant, crowded and utilitarian spaces within which clinical work proceeds[133] symbolize a vulnerability, an otherness or inferiority of clinical work, especially when clinic spaces are compared to the rather grand or imperial nature of the architecture within which the core curriculum is

---

127. The practice rules of courts that limit law student litigators to third year students make this a necessity for many clinics, and most clinics are litigation clinics.

128. See Marjorie McDiarmid, *What's Going on Down There in the Basement: In-House Clinics Expand Their Beachhead*, 35 N.Y.L. Sch. L. Rev. 239 (1990); Pierre Schlag, *Normativity and the Politics of Form*, 139 U. Pa. L. Rev. 801, 926–29 (1991).

129. See In-House Clinic Report, supra note 107, at 546–48.

130. See id. at 551–560.

131. See John Heinz & Edward Laumann, *The Legal Profession: Client Interests, Professional Roles, and Social Hierarchies*, 76 Mich. L. Rev. 1111 (1978); Edward Laumann & John Heinz, *Specialization and Prestige in the Legal Profession: The Structure of Deference*, 1977 Am. Bar Found. Res. J. 155 (describing how the prestige of lawyers correlates with the social success of their clients).

132. See Tushnet, supra note 115, at 274.

133. See In-House Clinic Report, supra note 107, at 527; McDiarmid, supra note 128; Schlag, supra note 128, at 926–27.

studied.[134] Limited academic credit for clinical work and different grading practices may signal to students and faculty that clinical education is on the margins of legal education.[135] Finally, the unwillingness of most law schools to provide substantial economic compensation, status or security of tenure to clinical faculty marginalizes clinics in both fact and symbol within law school communities.[136]

The discipline infiltrates clinical programs by imposing its tacit concepts and values on clinics and their participants. Both non-clinical and clinical faculty may try to impose "academic rigor" on clinical work by insisting upon faculty-controlled rather than student-centered learning experiences in order to emulate the particular rigors of the case method/final examination system. Thus law schools may favor the development of simulated clinic courses over live clinics because the former provide more predictability and more faculty control than live client clinics.[137] Some schools or individual faculty may try to maintain academic rigor by imposing typical law school grading patterns on clinic work, which can diminish the incentives for close supervision or joint work between students and their supervisors.[138] Ideas of academic rigor, of grading and close faculty supervision, may also encourage law faculties to impose undue restrictions on the less expensive, more diverse opportunities of attorney-supervised externships.[139] Clinical faculty themselves may incorporate the discipline's ideal of the law professor as a paragon of doctrinal expertise into their work as clinical supervisors, tending to limit student opportunities for the exercise of discretion and tending to treat ambiguous situations as opportunities to exercise an expert's persuasive rhetoric rather than as opportunities for inquiries that advance the student's acquisition of professional knowledge.[140] These various infiltrations limit or interfere with

---

134. See Chapter Two's discussion of the law school's spatial relationships.

135. See Tarr, supra note 108, at 40.

136. See, e.g., In-House Clinic Report, supra note 107, at 536–41, 551–60; Tarr, supra note 108, at 40–43.

137. See Grossman, supra note 108, at 170–72, 184–86; Tarr, supra note 108, at 35–36.

138. Cf. supra text at notes 95–96 (discussing grading of legal writing courses).

139. Compare Steven Maher, *Clinical Legal Education in the Age of Unreason*, 40 Buffalo L. Rev. 809 (1992) (arguing that clinical faculty in law schools have tended to exclude external live client clinics for political reasons), with Tarr, supra note 108, at 38–39 (arguing that the "main disadvantage" of external clinics is "the lack of control over the quality of the educational experience").

140. See Robert Condlin, *Socrates' New Clothes: Substituting Persuasion for Learning in Clinical Practice Instruction*, 40 Md. L. Rev. 223 (1980). Compare Robert Condlin, *Clinical Education in the Seventies: An Appraisal of the Decade*, 33 J. Legal Educ. 604 (1983) with

opportunities for students and instructors to concentrate on that delicate interplay among student performances, sympathetic but constructive feedback, collective reflections, self-evaluations and the acquisition of tacit knowledge that constitute the ideals of clinical training.

The discipline also establishes certain incentives for clinic participants to seek status within law school communities in ways that detract from the optimum clinical experience and discourage expansion of the clinical influence. Clinical faculty may become concerned that "their more intimate relationships with students negatively influence the perceptions of students and faculty toward clinicians"[141] or that "students who participate in the clinic are not given the stature of law review participants by their academic community,"[142] thus implicitly limiting or discounting their most effective work with students. The discipline also creates incentives for clinical faculty to concentrate their scholarly efforts on conventional forms of scholarship, since this is a good way to produce the quantities of scholarship demanded by the discipline's examinatorial regime. This incentive, however, limits the development of a potentially more subversive literature about the nature of good lawyering practices and effective clinical education.[143]

More generally, the discipline infiltrates the clinic conceptually. Today, thirty years after the birth of the law school clinic, most law professors, including clinicians, many or most law students, and perhaps many practicing lawyers *still* characterize and discount clinical programs as "practical skills" education in contrast to the "theoretical education" of the case method and final examinations.[144] This is a mischaracterization, but it is an effective way of tacitly devaluing or subordinating clinical knowledge. The association of clinics with vocationalism, with the interests of students in using clinics to obtain professional employment, supports this theory-practice distinction and quietly denigrates or subordinates clinical knowledge. These distinctions of theory/practice and academic/vocational tacitly limit the possibility of clinics

---

Norman Redlich, *The Moral Value of Legal Education: A Reply*, 33 J. Legal Educ. 613 (questioning the extent or applicability of Condlin's findings and theory), and Gary Bellow, *On Talking Tough to Each Other: Comments on Condlin*, 33 J. Legal Educ. 619 (agreeing with Condlin's findings but expressing reservations about their implications).

141. In-House Clinic Report, supra note 107, at 554.

142. Tarr, supra note 108, at 40.

143. See Chapter Three's description of the examinatorial regime. Cf. In-House Clinics Report, supra note 107, at 557–58 (arguing that law schools should encourage scholarly writing about clinical methods, legal pedagogy and legal practices).

144. See Mark Spiegel, *Theory and Practice in Legal Education: An Essay on Clinical Education*, 34 UCLA L. Rev. 577 (1987).

and privilege the case method/final examination system among many law professors and students. After all, once a person has become recognized as one of the very best, or even sufficient, experts in the case method or in final examinations, it may be quite painful to put this expertise at risk.

Thus divided, marginalized and infiltrated, clinical education serves the discipline in significant ways. As Mark Tushnet explains:

> "Clinical education pacifies student demand for practical experience and social productivity. It also eases the conscience of liberal law professors who are uncomfortable because few of their students practice the public interest law that those professors consider important."[145]

Clinical training also helps to legitimate American lawyers. It suggests to regulators and the public that legal education produces sufficient practical legal competence in our new lawyers, and it provides services to indigent clients that help the profession profess its ideal of public service. Thus, as an integral part of the discipline, the ideal conception of clinical education serves law school interests and the status quo while the clinical movement in fact is limited to a fragmented reality that avoids any subversive challenge to the discipline's basic structures.

Professional Ethics

> "We take up lawyer ethics because we have an unarticulated sense that something is wrong, that we are drifting, and being pulled by strong currents into dangerous waters."
>
> —James R. Elkins[146]

"Legal ethics," "professional ethics," "professional responsibility" and "professionalism" are protean terms in law school discourse and there are good reasons for this malleability. On the one hand, the organized profession, like other professions, has historically sought to legitimate lawyers, legal services and statutory monopolies for lawyers by promoting ideals of public service and professional self-regulation that assure the public and external regulators

---

145. Tushnet, supra note 115, at 273. On the nature of a similar kind of "ideological work" that law schools provide for left law students to help them reconcile their values with taking jobs at large corporate law firms, see Robert Granfield, Making Elite Lawyers: Visions of Law at Harvard and Beyond (1992).

146. James R. Elkins, *Symptoms Exposed When Legalists Engage in Moral Discourse: Reflections on the Difficulties of Talking Ethics*, 17 Vt. L. Rev. 353, 361 (1993).

that lawyers provide high quality services.[147] In pursuit of this end the organized bar has sought to improve "ethical training" by law schools throughout the twentieth century, and since Watergate this interest has intensified substantially.[148] On the other hand, law schools and law faculty have resisted the profession's calls for ethics training. They have tended to ignore or dismiss the profession's proposals as irrelevant or counter-productive to the business of teaching doctrine and analytical skills; they also have raised the common if contradictory objections that ethics training will be ineffective because ethical values are acquired as a personal matter and that teaching ethics effectively will constitute impermissible "indoctrination" or a violation of "academic neutrality."[149] Both sides to the debate over legal ethics have a common interest, then, in employing open-ended terms to describe what they want or oppose in legal education. But there is also a story here of implicit threats to the discipline and the discipline's measured response that is quite similar to the stories of writing programs and clinical education in law schools.

Conceived expansively professional ethics education has at least five dimensions, and these dimensions may be taken as an ideal conception of ethics training in law schools.[150] One dimension is teaching the statutes, regulations, judicial decisions and ethics committee opinions that regulate lawyer practices with regard to representing client interests, conflicts of interest, keeping client information confidential, and the management of client properties. A second dimension consists of studying the practices of lawyers and regulatory bodies in managing and responding to the specific duties and aspirational aspects of the lawyer's "role morality" as a zealous advocate of clients and as an officer of the court. A third dimension concerns studying the ethical dilemmas that the role morality of lawyers imposes on individual lawyers.[151] A fourth looks at the substantial "ethical discretion" that lawyers can have vis-à-vis their clients when law is uncertain, open or contested, and how lawyers in these situations often need or are invited to advise clients about their own business or

---

147. See, e.g., Richard L. Abel, American Lawyers (1989); Magali Sarfatti Larson, The Rise of Professionalism: A Sociological Analysis (1977).

148. See, e.g., M. Kelly, supra note 59; Deborah Rhode, *Ethics by the Pervasive Method*, 42 J. Legal Educ. 31, 34–41 (1992).

149. See M. Kelly, supra note 59, at 23–27; Rhode, supra note 148, at 36–41, 44.

150. See M. Kelly, supra note 59, at 29–43; Ian Johnstone & Mary Patricia Treuthart, *Doing the Right Thing: An Overview of Teaching Professional Responsibility*, 41 J. Legal Educ. 75, 75-86 (1991); Rhode, supra note 148, at 38–50.

151. See William H. Simon, *The Trouble with Legal Ethics*, 41 J. Legal Educ. 65, 65–67 (1991). See also David Luban, Lawyers and Justice: An Ethical Study (1988); William H. Simon, The Practice of Justice: A Theory of Lawyers' Ethics (1998).

personal goals and methods as well as the law.[152] Finally, normative questions about the legal system as a whole, its rules, its adversarial practices and its capacity or incapacity to provide effective services to all sectors of society constitute yet another dimension to ethics training in law schools.[153]

The implementation of this ideal conception is complicated by the range of possible purposes and methods for teaching ethics and by controversies that surround the choices among these purposes and methods. Least controversial are the goals of making students aware of professional ethics issues and sharpening their analytical skills for dealing with them, especially when the issues involve the codified rules of legal ethics covered on bar examinations.[154] More controversial are the more complicated goals of enhancing students' "capacity for reflective moral judgment," providing systematic instruction in ethical reasoning, and attempting if indirectly to influence the moral attitudes and conduct of lawyers.[155] There is also contention about the proper methods of instruction, which range from providing special courses, to teaching ethics in clinics, to employing a "pervasive method" of teaching ethics throughout the law curriculum.[156] This controversy helps reduce the implementation of ethics training in law schools to a bare minimum.

The history of ethics training in law schools is relatively clear. From the late 1890s through the 1960s law schools made only minimal efforts to consider ethics. They provided lectures by visiting judges or attorneys or a single low-credit, ungraded course that might or might not be required and was often taught by adjunct faculty.[157] The organized bar and conferences of law school leaders expressed concerns "lamenting the inadequacy of ethics instruction," but it was not until Watergate implicated many lawyers in unethical and illegal behavior that the bar and law schools took action to reform ethics train-

---

152. See, e.g., Robert Gordon, *The Independence of Lawyers*, 68 Boston Univ. L. Rev. 1 (1988); *Corporate Law Practice as a Public Calling*, 49 Md. L. Rev. 255 (1990); Austin Sarat, *Lawyers and Clients: Putting Professional Service on the Agenda of Legal Education*, 41 J. Legal Educ. 43 (1991); William H. Simon, *Ethical Discretion in Lawyering*, 101 Harv. L. Rev. 1083 (1988).

153. See Kelly, supra note 59, at 35–37; Johnstone & Treuthart, supra note 150, at 86.

154. See Rhode, supra note 148, at 42–43; Simon, supra note 151.

155. See Johnstone & Treuthart, supra note 150, at 84–85; Rhode, supra note 148, at 42–43.

156. See Johnstone & Treuthart, supra note 150, at 86–97; see also Rhode, supra note 148, (recommending that both special courses and a modified pervasive method be used as necessary elements in a "continuing method" of law school instruction in ethics).

157. See M. Kelly, supra note 59, at 5–21; Rhode, supra note 148, at 35–36.

ing in law schools.[158] In 1974 the ABA mandated law schools to require "instruction in the duties and responsibilities of the legal profession."[159] States soon began to require an examination on professional ethics for admission to the bar, and today most states require candidates for licensure to pass a multistate multiple-choice examination.[160] As a result virtually all law schools offer a required course in ethics, usually for two credits, and this course concentrates on preparing students to pass the bar exam. This course generally is perceived as ineffective instruction, is treated as an unattractive teaching assignment by faculty, and is often if not always staffed "by a reluctant, rotating cadre of junior faculty and outside lecturers."[161] The resistance of the discipline to ethics training remains firmly in place.

The modern interest in ethics training has, however, engaged some full-time faculty in both teaching and scholarship within this field, and this work is producing new insights into lawyers' ethics and possible reforms to ethics instruction in law schools.[162] The new scholarship in ethics emphasizes conflicts in legal practice between the role morality of lawyers and human morality.[163] It also focuses on relationships between lawyers and clients and the ethical discretion that lawyers may exercise in advising clients about appropriate ways to act under legal uncertainty.[164] The new scholarship also points to ways in which legal educators provide tacit instruction in a certain kind of amoral ethical behavior, and to reasons why law schools ought to provide more comprehensive instruction in ethics throughout the curriculum.[165]

Taking ethics seriously could constitute a substantial threat to the discipline's structures. For example, providing sustained instruction in the major traditions of ethical thought might have percolating effects throughout the curriculum, adding systematic moral analysis and moral arguments which surely would disrupt the flow of rule-oriented case method discourse that pertains to final examinations in doctrinal subjects. Raising pervasive questions about lawyers' ethics could threaten the law school's tacit conception of the

---

158. See Rhode, supra note 148, at 36–39.

159. ABA Standards for the Approval of Law Schools, Standard 302(a)(iii) (1974).

160. See Rhode, supra note 148, at 40–41.

161. Id. at 39–41.

162. For an overview of the new scholarship on legal ethics, see David Luban, *Reason and Passion in Legal Ethics*, 51 Stan. L. Rev. 873 (1998); for an overview of possible reforms to ethics training in law schools, see Johnstone & Treuthart, supra note 150.

163. See, e.g., D. Luban, supra note 151.

164. See, e.g., W.H. Simon, supra note 151; Gordon, supra note 152.

165. See, e.g., Elkins, supra note 146; Carrie Menkel-Meadow, *Can a Law Teacher Avoid Teaching Legal Ethics?*, 41 J. Legal Educ. 3 (1991); Rhode, supra note 148.

good lawyer as an amoral, client-bound technician who employs an objectivist, discussion-closing rhetoric and dominating style. Raising pervasive questions about lawyers' ethics might also question how law professors and legal education model or instruct their students in "ethical behavior."[166] Such questions would constitute a serious challenge to the ideal of the case method professor as both an impersonal, authoritative, critical, rule-oriented judge and charismatic, tough-minded advocate, and again the routine practices of the case method classroom could be disrupted.

The discipline, however, has divided, splintered, marginalized and infiltrated ethics training in much the same way it has treated law school writing and clinics. The multi-faceted nature of legal ethics and its teaching methods has made ethics training a relatively easy target. Faculty indifference or unwillingness to appreciate the importance of ethical questions or how law teaching tacitly instructs students in amoral advocacy can best be explained by the tacit power and attractiveness of the case method and final examinations. The case method analysis of judicial opinions has worked well for faculty, and they understandably may have difficulty conceiving of legal education as anything but the case method's rough amalgam of a skeptical, flexible legal positivism and ad hoc policy arguments. In this perspective, ethical questions and any systematic moral analysis of law or lawyers' behavior will seem incidental, marginal or even invisible.

Law student indifference to ethics training is also well recognized,[167] and this indifference has causes that are rooted in the discipline. In the case method/final examination system, law students learn tacitly to perceive of law as mostly rules, a lesson which helps prepare them to take their final examinations and bar examinations.[168] This lesson encourages students to focus on ethics instruction merely as preparation for their bar examinations, and may help explain their indifference to broader, more complex and less certain issues of professional ethics. Thus the discipline tacitly generates student interests that match faculty interests in limiting ethics training to the study of the codified rules of legal ethics in a separate course.

---

166. See Menkel-Meadow, supra note 165.

167. See Johnstone & Treuthart, supra note 150, at 88–92, 95–96; Ronald Pipkin, *Law School Instruction in Professional Responsibility: A Curricular Paradox*, 1979 Am. B. Found. Res. J. 247; Rhode, supra note 5, at 40. Clinical instruction in professional ethics may be an exception, since law students are often enthusiastic about their experiential learning in clinics. However the elective nature, relative costs and other objectives and needs of clinics undoubtedly limit their practical effectiveness in providing ethics instruction.

168. See Chapter One's discussion of law school examinations.

The discipline discourages the consideration of ethical issues in more pervasive ways. The "rigor" and "impersonality" of case method classrooms, the fierce competitiveness of the law school's examination/grading/class ranking system, and the discipline's cool style tacitly teach the division and separation of human agents from each other and the limitation of relationships between human agents to formal, impersonal, hierarchical terms. Effective deliberation about ethics, especially talk about the moral sentiments that are involved in ethical judgments,[169] requires a more open, more egalitarian, risk-taking and relatively unbounded discourse between persons, and this sort of deliberation puts one's self at substantial risk.[170] The disciplinary law school fails to provide a supportive environment for this kind of deliberation and reflection.

Thus cabined in a single upper class course of low status, ethics instruction incorporates the discipline's values and serves the discipline's interests. The single course typically is oriented towards teaching doctrinal rules as a matter of design and student interest, and ethics is kept separate from the core curriculum. This focus on doctrinal rules avoids the more complicated, less certain, more creative and more embarrassing ethical questions that occur in legal practices, helping preserve the unclouded rationalism of the case method.[171] This course is often taught by adjunct faculty or unhappy junior faculty, and ethics is thus quietly subordinated to the more important work of teaching the core curriculum. There is little chance that questions about ethics will emerge throughout the curriculum in any systematic way or that the discipline's overall image of the law as an amoral technician will be questioned effectively.

At the same time, the presence of a required course in "legal ethics" as well as the new scholarship on legal ethics allows law schools to profess a good faith commitment to the legal profession's ideals of public service and professional self-regulation. Furthermore, the emphasis on the rules of legal ethics and the zealous advocacy of client interests in the typical legal ethics course reinforces the moral indifference that is implicitly taught in the case method classroom.[172] Thus the discipline has enfolded professional ethics into itself to serve its purposes, in training and legitimation, much as it has incorporated legal writing programs and law school clinics.

---

169. See Luban, supra note 162, at 893–901.
170. See Elkins, supra note 146.
171. See Simon, *The Trouble with Legal Ethics*, supra note 151.
172. See Debra Schleef, *Empty Ethics and Reasonable Responsibility: Vocabularies of Motive among Law and Business Students* 23 Law & Soc. Inquiry 619 (1998).

Academic/Political Movements

Since the 1960s several movements have emerged in legal scholarship that challenge conventional legal scholarship and legal thought. These movements include law and economics,[173] the law and society movement,[174] the law and literature movement,[175] critical legal studies,[176] feminist jurisprudence[177] and critical race theory.[178] These movements are "academic" in the sense that they rely on interdisciplinary work that bridges law with other disciplines, non-legal thought and social contexts. They are "political" in at least three senses. Each would make political values more prominent within the discourse of law schools. Each would reform the methods and substance of legal scholarship and law teaching. Each movement also seeks to reform the law by its scholarship, its public service and its influence on lawyers, law professors and students.[179]

These movements have for the most part focused on scholarship about law, and the relationships between these movements and other elements of the discipline are relatively limited, speculative and difficult to trace. Nonetheless, each of the academic/political movements has generated writing about aspects of legal education, and each movement has produced casebooks or other teaching materials. Furthermore, the discourse of the new legal scholarship undoubtedly influences the classroom discourse of many law professors. We need to explore the relationships between these reform movements and the

---

173. See, e.g., Symposium, *The Place of Economics in Legal Education*, 33 J. Legal Educ. 183 et seq. (1983).

174. See, e.g., Lawrence Friedman, *The Law and Society Movement*, 38 Stan. L. Rev. 763 (1986); Trubek, supra note 10.

175. See, e.g., James Boyd White, *Law and Literature: "No Manifesto"*, 39 Mercer L. Rev. 739 (1988); *Interpretation Symposium*, 58 So. Cal. L. Rev. Issues # 1 & 2 (1985).

176. See, e.g., Mark Kelman, A Guide to Critical Legal Studies (1987); *Critical Legal Studies Symposium*, 36 Stan. L. Rev., Issues #1 & 2 (1984).

177. See, e.g., Katharine T. Bartlett & Rosanne Kennedy (eds), Feminist Legal Theory: Readings in Gender and Law (1991); Symposium, *Women in Legal Education—Pedagogy, Law, Theory, and Practice*, 38 J. Legal Educ., Issues # 1 & 2 (1988).

178. See, e.g., Critical Race Theory: The Key Writings That Formed the Movement (1995) (K. Crenshaw, N. Gotanda, G. Peller & K. Thomas eds); Symposium, *LATCRIT: LATINAS/OS and the Law*, 85 Cal. L. Rev. 1087 et seq. (1997) Richard Delgado & Jean Stefanic, *Critical Race Theory: An Annotated Bibliography*, 79 Va. L. Rev. 461 (1993); Steven Goldberg, "The Law, a New Theory Holds, Has a White Voice," NY Times, July 17, 1992, B8.

179. See generally G. Minda, supra note 8.

discipline's other elements in order to ascertain the threats or challenges to the discipline's basic structures, the discipline's responses, and the current ways in which the academic/political movements appear to serve the discipline.

The academic/political movements have brought new contexts, new methods and new perspectives to the study of law. Some of these developments challenge central practices and lessons of the discipline expressly or implicitly. For example, the law and literature movement emphasizes interpretive activities in law, an emphasis which could put in question the discipline's commitment to analysis as its primary intellectual method. Similarly, the emphasis in the law and society movement on factual contexts, or law in action, and the reliance on factual narratives in feminist jurisprudence and critical race theory could question the discipline's commitment to rule-oriented discourses. More generally, the interdisciplinary, political and ethical contexts, methods and perspectives of the academic/political movements question the discipline's tacit messages of the law's autonomy and the lawyer's unique expertise.[180]

At the same time, aspects of the academic/political reform movements fit well with particular elements or lessons of the discipline. The application of economic theory to legal rules can provide a new formalistic analysis that parallels or supports the positivist analysis of rules, and economic theory provides a new kind of authority, albeit interdisciplinary authority, that can support or substitute for doctrinal authority.[181] The emphasis placed by critical legal studies on skepticism, competing legal arguments, legal indeterminacy and legal politics[182] fits well with the discipline's skepticism about the meaning of words, its classroom and moot court practices of making arguments on both sides of issues, and the discipline's tacit message that legal rules are manipulable. The emphasis of law and literature on the power and authority of texts may simply reinforce the discipline's focus upon authoritative legal texts and their rules. In general, the many non-doctrinal contexts, ideas and perspectives of the academic/political movements in the aggregate surely contribute new contradictory messages about the nature of law and legal rules which reinforce the discipline's other contradictory messages that tacitly prom-

---

180. See id. at 191–198 (on the new movements in legal scholarship questioning the law's autonomy).

181. See id. at 78–79; Pierre Schlag, *"Le Hors De Texte, C'est Moi"; The Politics of Form and the Domestication of Deconstruction*, 11 Cardozo L. Rev. 1631, 1653–57 (1990).

182. See, e.g., Duncan Kennedy, *Form and Substance in Private Law Adjudication*, 89 Harv. L. Rev. 1685 (1976); *Politicizing the Classroom*, 4 S. Cal. Rev. Law & Women's Studies 81 (1994); James Boyle, *The Anatomy of a Torts Class*, 34 Am. U. L. Rev. 1003 (1985); Jeremy Paul, *The Politics of Legal Semiotics*, 69 Tex. L. Rev. 1779 (1991).

ise both binding law and manipulable non-law. The relationships between the new academic/political movements and other aspects of the discipline of law schools thus appear complex and ambiguous.

The discipline's response has been to accept and use those aspects of the new movements that fit its basic structures and otherwise to compartmentalize, marginalize and infiltrate these movements. Several tactics have been employed. The imperatives of the case method classroom and the final examination/grading/class ranking system have certainly discouraged any pervasive use of the more radical concepts and methods promoted by the new movements, since these concepts and methods tend to complicate classroom control, classroom expertise and objective grading of large numbers of examinations. The loose or weak relationships between the discipline's different structures have also limited the influence of the reform movements by making it difficult to transfer ideas from scholarship or classroom discussions to the core curriculum or final examinations. The discipline has thus tended to cabin the new movements by limiting them to the domains of scholarship, upper class seminars and occasional discourse in larger courses and by engaging their adherents in the routines of the core curriculum, the case method and final examinations.[183] Moreover, as scholarship that would reform the law, these movements add to the discipline's legitimacy within the research university, legal profession and society by promoting the insistent circulation of reform ideas. The new movements also serve to satisfy diverse intellectual inclinations among today's law professors and law students, offering those who need them rich opportunities for restorative dalliances or "ideological work" that allows one to reconcile or disguise any cognitive dissonance or schizophrenic tendencies they may experience between their ideals, which they can pursue in scholarship or seminars, and the instrumentalist, routine work of training or studying to be lawyers.[184]

---

183. See, e.g., Friedman, supra note 174, at 773–77 (discussing the limited influence of the law and society movement); Elisabeth Gemmette, *Law and Literature: An Unnecessarily Suspect Class in the Liberal Arts Component of the Law School Curriculum*, 23 Valparaiso U. L. Rev. 267 (1989); Mark Tushnet, *Critical Legal Studies: A Political History*, 100 Yale L. J. 1515, 1519–23 (1991) (discussing the limited institutionalization of critical legal studies in law schools).

184. On the nature of the cognitive dissonance or "schizophrenic tendencies" that may stem from the dichotomy between academically-oriented scholarship and professionally-oriented law teaching, see Thomas Bergin, *The Law Teacher: A Man Divided Against Himself*, 54 Va. L. Rev. 646 (1968). On the nature of "ideological work" that allows individuals to reconcile or disguise dichotomies between their ideals and their reality, see Robert Granfield, Making Elite Lawyers: Visions of Law at Harvard and Beyond 143–67 (1992)

The discipline has marginalized and infiltrated the new reform movements too. The limitation of these movements to the periphery of the curriculum tacitly signals the lesser importance of these perspectives within the discipline. The imperatives and tacit lessons of the discipline seem to cause both a marked animus and general ignorance or silence about the new movements among law school disciplinarians. More subtly, the discipline can help us understand the perhaps more surprising animus, disdain and ignorance that is displayed so often by adherents of one movement towards other movements.[185] This tendency may result from a modern decline in civility or that "revolutionary fervor" which seems to sustain revolutions or revisionist movements, especially in their formative stages.[186] Or perhaps it results from the fact that the new academic/political movements advance competing conceptions of law, politics and truth that often bring their proponents into sharply opposing positions. But a deeper explanation may be that the proponents of these reforms also act as disciplinarian law professors, with tacit images dancing before them of the ideal classroom law professor as a complete expert and master of persuasive, charismatic rhetoric who always wins, or at least always closes, the debate. In any event, the negative attacks between the new academic/ political movements surely limit the thrust of their challenges to the discipline.

Let us examine these movements separately. We shall consider them more-or-less in the order of their historical appearance as distinct movements within

---

(describing how law students on the left at Harvard reconcile their political values with taking jobs in corporate law firms).

185. For examples of this animus, see Friedman, supra note 174, at 777 ("Legal economists have a tendency to claim too much; they are notoriously imperial."); Richard Posner, *The Decline of Law as an Autonomous Discipline: 1962–1987*, 100 Harv. L. Rev. 761, 768 (1987) (expressing skepticism about the authoritative interpretation of texts, political radicalism and the "sheer infantilism" that has fueled the movement "known as" critical legal studies). Compare Richard Posner, Law and Literature: A Misunderstood Relation (1988) (reading literature and other literary skills, except for questions of style, are unimportant for law), with Richard Weisberg, *Entering With a Vengeance: Posner on Law and Literature*, 41 Stan. L. Rev. 1597, 1598 (1989) ("Never have so many of the world's most distinguished imaginative works left so bright a reader so unmoved. Rarely has assertion so prevailed over demonstration in so well-researched a scholarly endeavor."); James Boyd White, *What Can a Lawyer Learn from Literature?*, 102 Harv. L. Rev. 2014, 2015 (1989) ("It is obvious that [Judge Posner] has read a good many literary texts, but from what he says here it is far from clear why he has done so.").

186. Cf. Miloslovan Djilas, Rise and Fall 6 (Eng. trans. 1985) ("We had embarked on that course characteristic of every revolution: inspired fervor directing a reckoning of accounts. The more exalted the fervor, the more merciless the reckoning.").

law schools. This will provide a certain economy in describing their influence on each other as well as upon the discipline.

Law and Economics

Law and economics, or the "economic analysis of law,"[187] is concerned with the economic dimensions of legal phenomena. As Lewis Kornhauser says, law and economics is centered around four basic questions. In a world of limited resources, how do persons and organizations respond to legal rules and institutions? How are laws constructed? Are legal rules efficient? Should the law or particular rules be made efficient?[188]

Over the past 40 years law and economics has become solidly institutionalized in law schools. Law and economics scholars have been appointed to virtually all distinguished faculties, law and economics journals have been established, and there are law and economics courses at many law schools. Economic reasoning has become a well-recognized part of legal scholarship and has influenced the writing of casebooks for many core curriculum subjects such as torts, contracts and corporations law. This movement has surely influenced the discourse of the core curriculum more than any other academic/political movement—not only in terms of its influence upon casebooks but also, one suspects, in terms of the frequency with which economic theories and concepts are deployed in classroom conversations.[189]

In addition to the merits of economics, the discipline of law schools suggests three reasons for the success of this movement: the appeal of economic analysis as a more powerful source of authority and expertise than legal doctrine; the parallel structures of economic thought and the discipline's routine intellectual practices; and the tacit reinforcement that economics provides to the discipline's quiet emphasis on property rights.

First, the application of economic reason to questions about the efficiency of legal rules yields "organizing principles" that can help law professors interpret and criticize legal doctrine with authority and ease once they have mas-

---

187. See, e.g., Richard Posner, Economic Analysis of Law (5th ed. 1998).
188. See Lewis A. Kornhauser, *The Great Image of Authority*, 36 Stan. L. Rev. 349, 353–57 (1984).
189. See, e.g., A.T. Kronman, supra note 31, at 166–67; Walter Gellhorn & Glenn Robinson, *The Role of Economic Analysis in Legal Education*, 33 J. Legal Educ. 247 (1983). For an intellectual history of law and economics, see G. Minda, supra note 8, at 83–105.

tered a few basic economic principles.[190] In particular, economic concepts offer instant ad hoc policy arguments that professors and students can use to make quick arguments, interpretations and criticisms of judicial decisions in the caldron of case method classrooms. Economics thus provides some law professors with a new, more powerful form of expertise or new vantage point from which to make judicial criticisms in charismatic or authoritative ways. In an era when many doubts have emerged about the validity of doctrinal analysis, it is not surprising that the promise of a new kind of authority and expertise from law and economics has been relatively successful in influencing the scholarship, casebooks and perhaps teaching methods of many law professors.[191]

Secondly, both economic thought and the discourse of law schools emphasize analysis, an orientation towards "rules" that are abstracted from historical contexts, deductive reasoning from premises, and a certain kind of objectivity. They also share a binary thought process (an act is either efficient or not; a party either has a right or no right) and a rhetoric that denies its rhetorical qualities while trying to vanquish any ambiguous or poetic language that would blur "analysis."[192] In these important ways, economic reasoning fits with the discourse of law schools and provides parallel thought that can reinforce the rhetorical dimensions of the discipline's tacit conceptions of law and lawyers. Law professors and law students who are enamored of "rigor" or "logic," which are common terms in law school discourse, may be especially drawn, tacitly or otherwise, to the organizing principles that can be generated by applying economic reasoning to legal materials.

Thirdly, economic reasoning fits the discipline's tacit emphasis on economic rights and competitive individualism. If, for example, the purposes of property law and tort law are to define and protect economic rights, it will seem *only natural* that the definition and protection of these rights be done *economically*. More generally, if the purposes of most core curriculum subjects are to protect abstract individual rights on an equal basis without distinction between differently situated persons or between persons and organizations, the economic principles of consumer sovereignty and maximum utility may

---

190. See Edward Kitch, *The Intellectual Foundations of "Law and Economics"*, 33 J. Legal Educ. 184 (1983).

191. See Gellhorn & Robinson, supra note 189; Henry Hansmann, *The Current State of Law-and-Economics Scholarship*, 33 J. Legal Educ. 217 (1983); William Lovett, *Economic Analysis and Its Role in Legal Education*, 26 J. Legal Educ. 385 (1974).

192. Compare Donald McCloskey, The Rhetoric of Economics (1985) with Gerald Wetlaufer, *Rhetoric and Its Denial in Legal Discourse*, 76 Va. L. Rev. 1545 (1990).

tacitly seem to constitute the *natural* or *necessary* way to resolve all issues about conflicting legal rights.[193]

These compatibilities between economics and the discipline make one wonder why economic analysis has not become more pervasive in law schools. Law and economics, however, also presents tacit threats to basic disciplinary structures and values. These threats and the discipline's responses help explain why economics has had only a limited attraction for most law professors and students.

While economics provides theory, empirical findings and organizing principles that can supplement and enhance conventional legal methods, it also challenges the primary law school method of analogy that governs much classroom discourse and, importantly, governs issue-spotting on final examinations. Economics, in other words, would replace the "metaphor, analogy, and simile [that] have heretofore been the primary analytic tools of the lawyer."[194] In this sense, economic analysis would threaten to substitute new rules of formation in the discourse of law schools for the tacit rules of "analysis" and "legal authority," and this would transform many classroom practices, final examinations, much conventional scholarship and the tacit ideal of the law professor as a *quick, independent, powerful* advocate/judge who can make many distinctions within legal doctrine and between students. The law professor as economist might be able to wield substantial power over her students and be able to grade economics-oriented examinations under a harsh law school grading curve. But this professor's authority will emanate from an academic discipline with which many students are somewhat acquainted, and her authority will no longer be based on the more mysterious professional craft of advocacy/judging for which law students hunger and to which they become attuned. The law professor's image as a total expert and ideal advocate/judge could be decentered by a radical shift in law schools toward economics.

Law and economics also insists on analyzing social consequences systematically, on prospective rather than retrospective reasoning, on drawing clear distinctions between allocative and distributional consequences, and on limiting analysis to the single factor of resource allocation. These habits too contrast sharply with legal habits of mind.[195] And this contrast may explain the

---

193. See generally R. Posner, supra note 187.

194. Hansmann, supra note 191, at 226. See also Bruce Ackerman, Reconstructing American Law (1984) (arguing that legal discourse should be reformed by economic discourse).

195. See Alan Schwartz, *The Future of Economics in Legal Education: The Prospects for a New Model Curriculum*, 33 J. Legal Educ. 314, 332 (1983).

widespread doubts among law professors about the "usefulness" of economics for teaching doctrine or preparing students for bar examinations and practice.[196] If the brilliant law professor's way of life depends on a mastery of complex doctrinal situations and her ability to shift rapidly among facts, rules and ad hoc policy arguments about fairness or efficiency,[197] economic reasoning may threaten not only the law professor's image before her students but also the very roots of her professional expertise, or even her personhood.[198]

Finally, by asking systematic questions about the social causes and effects of law, economic analysis ultimately threatens the very idea of the law school as a site of professional rather than academic training. This threat challenges the subtle but strong links between the discipline and legal profession, links which support the special economic and social status of law schools within the research university. Thus the discipline has strong incentives to include economic analysis in order to strengthen and legitimate the discipline in unsettling academic times, but it also has strong incentives to limit economics to particular niches in the curriculum and legal scholarship in order to preserve its special sense of professional expertise or autonomy and its rather unique professionally-supported position within the American research university.[199]

The Law and Society Movement

The law and society movement produces research "that explains or describes legal phenomena in social terms."[200] This research is performed by sociologists, historians, political scientists, psychologists, anthropologists and a few socially-minded law professors, and it tends to focus on three basic questions. One is how social or nonlegal events, expectations, thoughts and actions produce or influence legal rules, institutions and practices. The second

---

196. See id.; Gellhorn & Robinson, supra note 189, at 269.

197. See Chapter One's discussion of the case method.

198. Cf. John Mudd, *Academic Change in Law Schools, Part II*, 29 Gonz. L. Rev. 225, 260 (1993/94):

> "to some professors change represents not just a threat to their professional activities, but to their person. For example, to professors who tend to be guarded and distant in personal relations, a change requiring that they have more individual contact with students or become part of a faculty team represents a personal threat."

199. See Chapter Five's discussion of law schools, the organized bar and research universities.

200. Freidman, supra note 174, at 763.

is how the legal system functions in educating lawyers, counseling clients, resolving disputes, managing law firms and making legislative, judicial and administrative decisions. The third is about the impact legal practices have on social events and behavior.[201] Law and society analysts are generally committed to studying law with methods drawn from outside the law (from social and behavioral sciences), to explaining legal events in terms of their social contexts, and to pursuing a positivist notion of social science that avoids normative engagements and concentrates on empirical research.[202]

This movement emerged gradually in the 1950s and 1960s at a few law schools that obtained private grants to support empirical research on the law.[203] Its institutionalization in law schools today is more precarious that that of economics, although the law and society movement has produced well-recognized scholarship,[204] journals,[205] significant casebooks on contracts,[206] and what some contend has been a "dramatic increase" in law and society scholarship within law schools over the past two decades.[207] Yet many experienced participants agree that law schools have not been particularly hospitable to the aims of this movement.[208]

---

201. See id. at 763, 772–73. A related field, but one which does not confront the discipline in the same way law and society research does, is "social science in law." Here the emphasis in both teaching and research is on using social science as an analytical tool of the law, especially in litigation. See John Monahan & Lawrence Walker, *Teaching Social Science in Law: An Alternative to "Law and Society"*, 35 J. Legal Educ. 478 (1985).

202. See Friedman, supra note 174, at 763–64; Trubek, supra note 10, at 33–36; but cf. id. at 41–54 (arguing that law and society analysts should recognize the connections between their normative commitments and their social analysis).

203. See J.H. Schlegel, supra note 18, at 238–51; Bryant Garth and Joyce Sperling, *From Legal Realism to Law and Society: Reshaping Law for the Last Stages of the Social Activist State*, 32 Law & Soc. Rev. 409 (1998).

204. See, e.g., Mark Galanter, *Why the "Haves" Come Out Ahead*, 9 Law & Soc. Rev. 95 (1974); Stewart Macaulay, *Non-Contractual Relations in Business: A Preliminary Study*, 24 Am. Soc. Rev. 55 (1963).

205. Law & Social Inquiry; Law and Society Review.

206. See Stewart Macaulay, John Kidwell, William Whitford & Mark Galanter, Contracts: Law in Action (1995); Ian MacNeil, Contracts: Exchange Transactions and Relations (2d ed. 1977).

207. See William J. Woodward, Jr., *Clearing the Underbrush for Real-Life Contracting*, 24 Law & Soc. Inquiry 99, 137–38 (1999).

208. See, e.g., J.H. Schlegel, supra note 18, at 238–57; Friedman, supra note 174; Trubek, supra note 10. See also Jonathan Simon, *Law after Society* (review of Stewart Macaulay, Lawrence M. Friedman & John Stockey, Law and Society: Readings on the Social Study of Law, 1995), 24 Law & Soc. Inquiry 143 (1999).

The law and society movement's poor fit with most of the discipline's structures help explain its poor reception. First, law and society work has tended to remain disengaged from interpretive and normative questions about legal doctrine.[209] It has thus been quite easy for disciplinarians to ignore or discount this movement, to dismiss it by silence and keep it cabined in the far reaches of legal scholarship. This silence and ignorance have been expressed in faculty hiring, faculty decisions about curriculum and teaching methods, and faculty choices about topics to pursue in their research and writing. The disciplinary practices of publishing frequently with prestigious publishers or law reviews, of publishing work that wins the applause of many peers and is cited in judicial opinions, and of publishing "legal theory" that earns the attention of law school elites all serve to discourage commitments to law and society work, which in contrast to doctrinal work is empirical, "grubby," frustrating and costly.[210] The disciplinary imperatives of demonstrating expertise quickly and frequently before many students and grading large numbers of examinations under law school grading curves also discourage attempts to introduce law and society research into the main arenas of legal education.

Secondly, law and society research raises particularly subversive questions about the discipline's practices in training lawyers and producing scholarship. For example, the law and society analysis of lawyer-client interactions may be more significant than judicial doctrine in understanding the "effective law" that clients experience and lawyers must work with, and this analysis questions the discipline's reliance on teaching subjects like contracts, civil procedure, family law or corporations law as a matter of doctrine and doctrinal analysis.[211] At the very least, it seems, this research supports the introduction of significant clinical considerations into doctrinal classrooms if not the writing of new casebooks, a substantial restructuring of the case method and different kinds of final examinations. These changes, of course, would disrupt the discipline's focus on analysis, rules and abstract notions of clients and lawyers. Similarly, law and society studies of the effects or impact that law has on social behavior reveal substantial gaps between what the rules say and how persons or organizations behave in response to rules. These studies, if introduced widely into law teaching and scholarship, could displace the discipline's

---

209. See Trubek, supra note 10, at 28–36.

210. See Friedman, supra note 174, at 774–75.

211. See, e.g., Galanter, supra note 204; Macaulay, supra note 204; Robert Mnookin & Lewis Kornhauser, *Bargaining in the Shadow of the Law: The Case of Divorce*, 88 Yale L. J. 950 (1979); Austin Sarat & William Felstiner, *Law and Strategy in the Divorce Lawyer's Office*, 20 Law & Soc'y Rev. 93 (1986); Woodward, supra note 207.

normative celebration of conservative, property-oriented doctrines with more critical perspectives.[212] This displacement, of course, would displease those many disciplinarians who are tacitly committed to the discipline's lessons of professional autonomy, competitive individualism and property.

Law and Literature

The law and literature movement developed in law schools in the 1970s and 1980s.[213] By employing literature about law and literary techniques of rhetoric, narrative and interpretation, this diverse movement fundamentally aims to bring ethical contexts and interpretive sophistication to the study of law.[214] In some ways the movement fits rather well with the discipline. In other ways, however, the humanism of law and literature is deeply subversive to the discipline. The discipline accordingly has worked to accommodate the law and literature movement but keep it limited to special courses and to scholarship.[215]

There are affinities between the discipline's focus on the analysis of texts, the analysis of the meanings of rules, the construction of arguments and conservative individualistic values and the attention of law and literature work to language, texts, rhetoric and the ethical values of individualism. Both the discipline and law and literature movement appear to share an intense commitment to authoritative texts and correct methods for reading or interpreting

---

212. See Trubek, supra note 10.

213. See, e.g., G. Minda, supra note 8, at 149–66; Richard Weisberg, *Coming of Age Some More: "Law and Literature" Beyond the Cradle*, 13 Nova L. Rev. 107, 110–113 (1989). For earlier appreciations of literature as training for lawyers, see Benjamin Cardozo, *Law and Literature*, Yale Rev. 699 (1924–25); John Wigmore, *A List of One Hundred Legal Novels*, 17 Ill. L. Rev. 26 (1922). The start of the law and literature movement is usually attributed to the publication of James Boyd White's The Legal Imagination (1973).

214. See, e.g., Martha Nussbaum, Poetic Justice: The Literary Imagination and Public Life (1995) (on the role of literature in bringing ethical considerations to law); James Boyd White, When Words Lose Their Meaning: Constitutions and Reconstitutions of Language, Character, and Community (1984) (reading literary and legal texts to demonstrate their use of "constitutive rhetoric" to address fundamental disagreements within communities); Derrick Bell, Jr., And We Are Not Saved (1987) (using fictional narratives to discuss race and the law); Ronald Dworkin, Law's Empire (1986) (arguing that legal interpretation is "constructive interpretation" like that involved in interpreting any work of art).

215. See G. Minda, supra note 8, at 149–66 (discussing the scholarship); Elizabeth Villiers Gemmette, *Law and Literature: Joining the Class Action*, 29 Val. U. L. Rev. 665 (1995) (describing law and literature courses in law schools).

these texts. Further, much as the case method grants substantial normative discretion to casebook authors and law teachers, the diversity of texts, literary theories and methods in law and literature provides legal humanists with substantial discretion to make persuasive arguments and advance compelling interpretations that are essentially justificatory and conservative of traditional values.[216] Thus the focus of law and literature work on texts and their language may exclude or ignore considerations of broader social contexts, power and politics.[217] Or literature's focus on the conditions of individual lives may tend to recommend individual solutions to social injustice rather than political or collective solutions.[218] Particular approaches to law and literature then are quite capable of tacitly reinforcing the discipline's commitments to authoritative texts, the analysis of texts and language, and individual or conservative values.

At the same time, should law and literature's practices be installed widely in law schools, many disciplinary practices and conceptions might be subverted. The reading of legal texts like literary texts to tease out their ambiguities, multiple meanings, rhetorical structures and contradictory norms or values could wreak havoc upon the discipline's ethic of rule coverage and its practice of instrumentalist or paraphrase reading to determine the single correct rule or holding of any judicial opinion.[219] Literary readings of legal texts would also demand the use of complete texts of judicial opinions rather than excerpts provided by casebooks, and these readings could threaten the discourse of law schools by replacing its tacit rules of analysis, authority and confidence with more open-ended rules of formation that value poetic expres-

---

216. See Susan Mann, *The Universe and the Library: A Critique of James Boyd White as Writer and Reader*, 41 Stan. L. Rev. 959 (1989) (making this argument about the seminal law and literature work of James Boyd White); Thomas Morawetz, *Ethics and Style: The Lessons of Literature for Law*, 45 Stan. L. Rev. 497 (1993) (making a similar argument about Richard Weisberg's Poethics and Other Strategies of Law and Literature (1992)).

217. See Robert Cover, *Violence and the Word*, 95 Yale L. J. 1601 (1986); Allan Hutchinson, *Indiana Dworkin and Law's Empire*, 96 Yale L. J. 637 (1987); Robin West, *Adjudication is Not Interpretation: Some Reservations About the Law-as-Literature Movement*, 54 Tenn. L. Rev. 203 (1986).

218. Compare M. Nussbaum, supra note 214 (arguing that the literary imagination is necessary for good political discourse and decision making although recognizing or worrying about literature's individualizing tendencies) with Lennard J. Davis, *Are Novels Good for Us?*, The Nation, July 15/22, 1996, pp. 40–42 (reviewing Nussbaum and expressing skepticism about literature's likely contributions to collective remedies for social injustice).

219. See, e.g., Philip C. Kissam, *Disturbing Images: Literature in a Jurisprudence Course*, 22 Legal Studies Forum 329 (1998).

sion, creativity, ethics and competing interpretive theories.[220] Law and literature's attention to ethical values and to competing interpretive theories could also modify the discipline's tacit conception of law as something of a muddle between clear binding rules and manipulable rules, thus creating room for a more balanced discussion and consideration of the relative values of competing legal theories.[221] More room in the discipline might also have to be made for a moral analysis of legal rules, and the discipline's rhetoric of unshakeable confidence could be transformed into more tentative, more ambivalent and more dialogical forms of reflection and interpretation.

This mixture of possibilities suggests the discipline's optimum strategy towards law and literature. Confine this movement to scholarship and a few special courses. Without threatening the discipline's structures, this will provide ideological work for both idealist and discontented students and professors of many persuasions. It might also enhance the law school's reputation and legitimacy within the university, particularly among humanistic scholars and students. In the right hands, moreover, the law and literature movement can generate attractive images of law and lawyers that enhance the discipline and the legal profession by depicting lawyers as considerate, sympathetic individuals[222] and by depicting law as a system in which "law works itself pure."[223] Meanwhile the confinement of the movement diminishes its subversive possibilities.

Critical Legal Studies

Critical legal studies (or CLS) was started in the 1970s by law professors who desired to use scholarship, teaching and legal practices to advance a more radical or more egalitarian law, politics and legal education.[224] CLS has been

---

220. Compare J.B. White, supra note 214 (describing law as "constitutive rhetoric") with Chapter One's discussion of the case method and law school examinations.

221. To sample such possibilities, see R. Dworkin, supra note 214.

222. See, e.g., Richard Weisberg, *Three Lessons from Law and Literature*, 27 Loyola L.A. L. Rev. 285, 287–91 (1993).

223. R. Dworkin, supra note 214, at 400.

224. See Robert Gordon, *Brendan Brown Lecture: Critical Legal Studies as a Teaching Method*, 35 Loyola L. Rev. 383, 393 (1989) ("CLS is basically a movement of legal intellectuals, originating in intellectual quarrels with their own legal education.") Duncan Kennedy & Karl Klare, *A Bibliography of Critical Legal Studies* 94 Yale L. J. 461, 461–62 (1984); John Henry Schlegel, *Notes Toward an Intimate, Opinionated, and Affectionate History of the Conference on Critical Legal Studies*, 36 Stan. L. Rev. 391 (1984).

described as a "political location" of law professors and lawyers "on the left,"[225] but it also obtains the rough intellectual coherence of a movement or school of thought from three propositions about law that are widely shared by CLS adherents.[226] First, CLS argues that legal doctrine is significantly indeterminate because of contradictions between legal premises, principles and concepts,[227] or because the conventional methods of legal argument about textual meanings, legislative histories and precedents, which can often be read both broadly and narrowly, can always be used in difficult cases to generate opposing arguments of seemingly equal weight.[228] Second, CLS is committed to understanding law in comprehensive legal and social contexts and to studying "how particular interest groups, social classes, or entrenched economic institutions benefit from legal decisions despite the indeterminacy of the legal doctrines."[229] Third, CLS asks how law as ideology mystifies insiders and outsiders and helps justify the law's generally conservative results as "objective," "neutral" or "natural."[230] In an important sense CLS work has revived and deepened the more radical teaching of Legal Realism, although critical legal studies has seemed more committed to egalitarian politics than Realism.[231]

Critical legal studies bloomed as a reform movement in the 1970s and 1980s. It organized annual conferences, produced prolific and controversial scholarship, and generated noted disputes at particular schools about hiring or granting tenure to critical legal scholars.[232] Its collective activities and energy are less apparent today, but CLS ideas and influence have become well established in the legal academy by the hiring of critical legal scholars at many

---

225. Tushnet, supra note 183, at 1515.

226. See G. Minda, supra note 8, at 107–08; Martha Minow, *Law Turning Outward*, 73 Telos 79, 83–85 (1986); Tushnet, supra note 183, at 1516–18. Duncan Kennedy has claimed recently that CLS as a movement ended in the 1990s although it remains "a school of thought." Duncan Kennedy, A Critique of Adjudication (fin-de-siecle) 9 (1997).

227. See M. Kelman, supra note 176, at 3–4; Duncan Kennedy, *Form and Substance in Private Law Adjudication*, 89 Harv. L. Rev. 1685 (1976); *The Structure of Blackstone's Commentaries*, 28 Buffalo L. Rev. 205 (1979).

228. See the authorities cited in note 182 supra.

229. Minow, supra note 226, at 84–85.

230. See M. Kelman, supra note 176, at 4–6; Minow, supra note 226, at 85; Tushnet, supra note 183, at 1524–26. But cf. Alan Hunt, *The Theory of Critical Legal Studies*, 6 Ox. J. Legal Studies, 1, 11–13 (1986) (noting the lack of empirical evidence and consequent "problematic" assumption by CLS theorists that legal ideology affects social behavior).

231. See James Boyle, *The Politics of Reason: Critical Legal Theory and Local Social Thought*, 133 U. Pa. L. Rev. 685 (1985); Schlegel, supra note 224, at 404–08.

232. See G. Minda, supra note 8, at 110–27.

schools and by the continuing development and influence of CLS scholarship and teaching.[233] Yet the acceptance of CLS has only been a limited one that implies accommodation with the discipline of law schools.

On the one hand, the CLS emphasis on politics and the ideology of law, which clearly has antagonized many in the legal academy, threatens the discipline's rule-orientation, its conventional forms of legal analysis and its tacit messages of professional autonomy and property rights. Yet on the other hand, there are affinities between critical legal studies and the routine practices of the discipline which suggest a substantial compatibility between critical scholars and the discipline's structures of the core curriculum, case method and final examinations.[234] For example, CLS professors like to emphasize to their students that the "paired opposites" of conventional legal methods, such as interpreting a statute by its "plain meaning" or its "purposes," often generate arguments which produce legal indeterminacy, judicial discretion and the opportunity for political decisions by judges.[235] But this teaching may simply inscribe more deeply in many law students the discipline's tacit lessons of unresolved contradictory messages, law as manipulable rules, toughness as a rhetorical style and moral indifference to legal results. The careful analysis of judicial opinions and legal doctrines in much CLS teaching and scholarship is also quite consistent with the discipline's focus upon "analysis" as the primary intellectual method of lawyers and upon a relatively autonomous system of legal rules. CLS scholarship may rely on dense social theory, ideological analysis or the unconventional methods of "deconstruction" or "trashing,"[236] but it also has an essential doctrinal orientation that may entice many CLS law professors into maintaining a doctrinal focus in their teaching within the core curriculum—since teaching doctrine will support their scholarship. CLS scholarship, of course, also can provide useful ideological work for discontented left academics that helps them administer the discipline's routines in

---

233. See id. at 126–27; Tushnet, supra note 183, at 1519–20.

234. Cf. Peter Goodrich, *Sleeping with the Enemy: An Essay on the Politics of Critical Legal Studies in America*, 68 NYU L. Rev. 389 (1991) (arguing that CLS has been captured in general by the politics of the American legal academy); Catherine Hantzis, *Kingsfield and Kennedy: Reappraising the Male Models of Law School Teaching*, 38 J. Legal Educ. 155 (1988) (suggesting that CLS teaching styles tend to replicate the analytical, rule-oriented rhetoric and style of traditional law professors).

235. See, e.g., Boyle, supra note 182; Kennedy, *Politicizing the Classroom*, supra note 182.

236. See, e.g., Jerry Frug, *The Ideology of Bureaucracy in American Law*, 97 Harv. L. Rev. 1276 (1984); Mark Kelman, *Trashing*, 36 Stan. L. Rev. 293 (1984); Kennedy, *The Structure of Blackstone's Commentaries*, supra note 227.

other aspects of their work. In addition to these affinities, there is ample evidence that the discipline has limited the spread of critical legal studies by its simple but powerful techniques of silence, ignorance and marginalization of the movement's members and ideas, especially in terms of appointing no more than one recognized CLS scholar to a particular law faculty.[237]

The relationships between critical legal studies and the discipline are thus rich in irony. The basic CLS propositions about law, should they be implemented widely, would change the discourse of law schools and vanquish any possibility of law school talk about binding rules. But the commitments of CLS scholarship and teaching to the analysis of appellate opinions, legal rules and conventional methods of argument and even the CLS commitment to "theory" are consistent with major disciplinary practices. As long as CLS remains a relatively marginal part of the discipline, then, this reform movement may be tacitly reinforcing the discipline's conceptions of law and lawyers much more than it contests them.

In any event, the optimal strategy of the discipline towards CLS is clear. This movement should be incorporated into the discipline but kept at the margins, for the critical approach can enhance and improve some tacit teaching of the discipline as long as its express ideological threats remain peripheral. The express distress or anger among disciplinarians towards critical legal studies [238] may thus be counter-productive. What better serves the discipline is a general silence and ignorance towards CLS, which allows it to flourish on the margins of law schools but at the same time reinforce the discipline's values. In this situation CLS is enfolded within the discipline, full of subversive intentions, perhaps ambivalent about its oppositional but unachieved promises, and servant to the discipline's subtle power/knowledge relationships.

Feminist Jurisprudence

Feminist jurisprudence involves questioning the law, legal practices and legal education from the perspectives and experiences of women in order to expose and reform any express or implicit advantages that these institutions may confer on males.[239] This movement was recognized in the 1980s as women

---

237. See, e.g., Tushnet, supra note 183, at 1519–23.

238. See, e.g., A. Kronman, supra note 31, at 240–70; Paul Carrington, *Of Law and the River*, 34 J. Legal Educ. 222 (1984); Owen Fiss, *The Death of Law?*, 72 Cornell L. Rev. 1 (1986).

239. See Heather Wishik, *To Question Everything: the Inquiries of Feminist Jurisprudence*, 1 Berkeley Women's L. J. 64 (1986). See also Patricia Smith (ed), Feminist Jurisprudence

became a significant presence in law schools and began to generate prolific and controversial scholarship, law reviews devoted to women's rights and feminist legal thought, and a distinctive critique of male-dominated legal education.[240] Feminist legal scholarship today has many diverse strands, but to explore the relationships between the discipline of law schools and feminist jurisprudence it should suffice to consider just a few of its basic approaches.

"Liberal feminism," broadly speaking, seeks equal rights for men and women under the principle that persons similarly situated should be treated similarly.[241] This theory proceeds by questioning stereotypes, prejudices and misunderstandings about women that support patriarchal advantages in law, and it uses conventional legal methods and the fundamental legal principles of equality and fairness to argue for law that eliminates unjustified discrimination against women.[242] Liberal feminism as practice and scholarship has influenced many legal developments including the Supreme Court's recognition of a woman's right to an abortion[243] and its gradual development of an increasingly careful and demanding review of government gender classifications.[244]

While liberal feminism raises many unsettling questions about law, this approach is generally consistent with the discipline of law schools. It relies on conventional methods and conventional legal discourse, asking only that these methods and discourse be employed to ensure women's legal equality is rethought and implemented free of damaging stereotypes or prejudice. Liberal feminism demands, in other words, that law work itself pure. In this view, as long as legal education is free of such gender discrimination, there is no reason to question the discipline's structures that traditionally have been used to train lawyers. Liberal feminists, however, might decide that the discipline

---

and the Nature of Law (1993); Cynthia Grant Bowman & Elizabeth M. Schneider, *Feminist Legal Theory, Feminist Lawmaking, and the Legal Profession*, 67 Ford. L. Rev. 249 (1998); Robin West, *Jurisprudence and Gender*, 55 U. Chi. L. Rev. 1 (1988).

240. For a survey of feminist legal scholarship, see G. Minda, supra note 8, at 128–48. On the feminist critique of legal education, see, e.g., ABA, Comm'n on Women in the Profession, Don't Just Hear It Through The Grapevine: Studying Gender Questions at Your Law School (1998); Symposium, *Women in Legal Education* supra note 177.

241. See, e.g., P. Smith, supra note 239, at 4–5; Wendy Williams, *The Equality Crisis: Reflections on Culture, Courts, and Feminism*, 7 Women's Rights L. Rev. 175 (1982).

242. See Ruth Bader Ginsburg & Barbara Flagg, *Some Reflections on the Feminist Legal Thought of the 1970s*, 1989 U. Chi. Legal Forum 9; Williams, supra note 241.

243. Roe v. Wade, 410 U.S. 113 (1973); Planned Parenthood of Southeastern Pennsylvania v. Casey, 505 U.S. 833 (1992).

244. See Reed v. Reed, 404 U.S. 71 (1971); Frontiero v. Richardson, 411 U.S. 677 (1973); Craig v. Boren, 429 U.S. 190 (1976); United States v. Virginia 518 U.S. 515 (1996).

incorporates male-oriented stereotypes or provides opportunities for particular individuals to exercise prejudice against women. In this case, liberal feminists might choose to join the feminist critique of legal education that will be considered shortly.

A second important branch of feminist jurisprudence is "cultural" or "relational" feminism. This theory emphasizes gender differences as well as similarities, the interdependence of persons as well as their autonomy, contextuality and an ethics of caring for others, and legal changes that would modify the law's traditional emphasis on bright-line rules and autonomous individuals.[245] Relational feminism could contest the discipline in significant ways. This approach argues that emotions play an important role in acquiring knowledge and making decisions as, for example, when empathy for others helps us understand their experiences, perspectives or arguments and makes us better judges of hard questions as a result.[246] An emphasis on emotions would put in question the discipline's highly rationalized and rule-oriented discourse and rhetoric to say nothing of the disciplinary techniques of personal invisibility and coolness. Relational feminism also argues for highly contextualized and pragmatic forms of inquiry, argument and judgment.[247] Thus relational feminism, together with the other reform movements that emphasize contexts, could challenge the discipline's rule-oriented discourse, its rhetoric of confidence and closure and its tacit lesson of professional autonomy. Relational feminism, as we shall see, also contributes heavily to the explicit feminist critique of legal education.

A third strand of feminist legal thought is more radical. This feminism focuses on male power and the hidden male norms that pervade American institutions, and it perceives law as an instrument that could be used to disrupt

---

245. See, e.g., P. Smith, supra note 239, at 7; Elizabeth Schneider, *The Dialectic of Rights and Politics: Perspectives from the Women's Rights Movement*, 61 N.Y.U. L. Rev. 589 (1986); West, supra note 239. This strand of feminist jurisprudence draws especially on Carol Gilligan's work on the moral psychology of men and women and her articulation of a psychology and ethics of attending to human relations and caring for others. See Carol Gilligan, In a Different Voice: Psychological Theory and Women's Development (1982).

246. See Lynne Henderson, *Legality and Empathy*, Mich. L. Rev. (1987); Robin West, *Love, Rage and Legal Theory*, 1 Yale J. Law & Feminism (1989). See also M. Nussbaum, supra note 214, at 53–78 (discussing "rational emotions"); *The Use and Abuse of Philosophy in Legal Education*, 45 Stan. L. Rev. 1627, 1633–34 (1993) (discussing the role of emotions in developing legal knowledge); Alison Jagger, *Love and Knowledge: Emotion in Feminist Epistemology*, in A.M. Jagger & S.R. Bordo (eds), Gender/Body/ Knowledge: Feminist Reconstructions of Being and Knowing 145 (1989).

247. See, e.g., Katherine Bartlett, *Feminist Legal Methods*, 103 Harv. L. Rev. 829 (1990); Margaret Radin, *The Pragmatist and the Feminist*, 63 S. Cal. L. Rev. 1699 (1990).

this power and contest these norms.[248] Like liberal feminism, radical feminism argues for equality between men and women but radical feminism insists that formal equality in terms of conventional legal discourse, arguments and rights is not sufficient to establish an authentic equality. Instead law must become "substantive" in order to question the vast multiplicity of male norms that continue to advantage men throughout society. Like relational feminism, radical feminism considers relationships and differences as well as similarities between men and women. But radical feminism is skeptical or pessimistic about the values of relational thinking and an ethics of caring, which it views as constructed and dominated by male power and interests. In this perspective, law must first disrupt male power in order to make it possible to think clearly and wisely about the ethics of gender relationships.[249]

The challenges of radical feminism to the discipline are in many ways similar to those of critical legal studies. Like CLS, radical feminism employs much case analysis, pragmatic policy arguments and a charismatic rhetoric about legal doctrine that are generally consistent with the discipline's tendencies. But also like CLS, radical feminism's insistence on making contextual or "substantive" arguments, its use of dense social theory, and its insistence on interrogating politics or power everywhere could transform the discipline's tacit conceptions of rule-oriented law and lawyers. Radical feminism, then, has ambiguous implications for the discipline.

Feminist jurisprudence has developed a relatively systematic critique of legal education that challenges many aspects of the discipline. This critique includes arguments that the core curriculum and casebooks exclude or unfairly present issues and perspectives important to women.[250] It is concerned too about the relative silence or silencing of women students in case method classrooms, a silence which deprives women of an equal opportunity to practice a lawyer's "public speaking" and may diminish their self-esteem or motivation for legal study.[251] This feminist critique of the classroom appears to have contributed

---

248. See, e.g., Catherine MacKinnon, Feminism Unmodified (1989); Diane Polan, *Toward a Theory of Law and Patriarchy*, in The Politics of Law (D. Kairys ed. 1982).

249. See, e.g., Judith Baer, Our Lives Before the Law (1999); MacKinnon, *Difference and Dominance*, in Feminism Unmodified, supra note 248.

250. See, e.g., Mary Coombs, *Crime in the Stacks, or A Tale of A Text: A Feminist Response to a Criminal Law Textbook*, 38 J. Legal Educ. 117 (1988); Nancy Erickson, *Sex Bias in Law School Courses: Some Common Issues*, 38 J. Legal Educ. 101 (1988); Mary Jo Frug, *Re-Reading Contracts: A Feminist Analysis of a Contracts Casebook*, 34 Am. U. L. Rev. 1065 (1985).

251. See, e.g., Tanya Banks, *Gender Bias in the Classroom*, 14 S. Ill. U. L. Rev. 527 (1990); 38 J. Legal Educ. 137 (1988); Lani Guinier, Jane Fine & Micelle Balin, *Becoming*

to the diversification of teaching methods in law schools, particularly by emphasizing student-centered learning and clinical education.[252] Perhaps most fundamentally, feminist scholars have engaged in attempts to measure whether the law school's examination/grading/class ranking system produces unjust grade differences between men and women who begin their legal studies with similar academic credentials.[253] Although such differences have been documented at only a few schools, and the causes of the differences remain a matter of speculation,[254] these studies have generated disturbing evidence that suggests the discipline's most fundamental structure, the final examination system, may be inhospitable to women students in general.[255]

The discipline thus has reasons both to use and to limit feminist jurisprudence. The substantial presence of women faculty and students in the legal academy indicates that some sort of feminist jurisprudence may help legitimate law, lawyers and law schools and provide opportunities for ideological work or dalliances that can mollify alienated or discontented women professors and students. Furthermore, corrections to casebook coverage of women's rights issues and modifications that would include women more comfortably within case method classrooms can only help the discipline operate more efficiently as well as legitimately. At the same time, feminist jurisprudence's more radical questions about the basic nature of large case method classes, the essential nature of final examinations and the conservative, rule-oriented discourse of law schools could, if widely pursued, threaten the discipline's structures. But the discipline has powerful norms and techniques available to dampen these radical criticisms. For example, new women law professors may face not only the usual imperatives to generate prestigious scholarship and earn favorable student evaluations but also the quiet encouragement, steering

---

Gentlemen: Women's Experiences at One Ivy League Law School, 143 U. Pa. L. Rev. 1 (1994); Catherine Weiss & Louise Melling, *The Legal Education of Twenty Women,* 40 Stan. L. Rev. 1299 (1988); Stephanie Wildman, *The Question of Silence: Techniques to Ensure Full Class Participation,* 38 J. Legal Educ. 147 (1988).

252. See Carrie Menkel-Meadow, *Women's Ways of "Knowing" Law: Feminist Legal Epistemology, Pedagogy, and Jurisprudence,* in Knowledge, Difference, and Power: Essays Inspired by Women's Ways of Knowing 57, 57–72 (1996).

253. See ABA, Don't Just Hear It Through The Grapevine, supra note 240; Guinier et al, supra note 251.

254. See, e.g., Guinier, et al, supra note 251 (documenting grade differences at Pennsylvania and speculating that large case method classrooms, which women dislike more then men, as well as blatant prejudices among male students towards women may diminish the self-esteem and motivations of many women law students).

255. See ABA, Don't Just Hear It Through The Grapevine, supra note 240.

or other tacit evaluations from well-intentioned colleagues who wish them to focus on "the more important tasks" of teaching legal doctrine, writing scholarship on doctrinal issues and using conventional legal methods.[256] Women students may be distracted from feminist questions not only by the discipline's imperatives but also by its suasive images of heroic or brilliant litigators whose skill at charismatic oral performances must be mastered to prove oneself a lawyer. These kinds of norms are neither conspiratorial nor intentional but the light, economical tactics of disciplinary power.

Critical Race Theory

Critical race theory has been the most recent academic/political movement to emerge in law schools. This movement has deep historical roots in the civil rights movement, the increasing presence of persons of color in law schools, and the dissatisfactions of many civil rights scholars with the stalling or regression in American civil rights law, the limited effects of mainstream civil rights scholarship and the contemporary discourse about race in law schools, law and politics.[257] Critical race theory questions law from the perspectives and distinctive experiences of persons of color. Its basic goals are to expose the racial contexts and subtexts that underlie the law's rules and to develop better strategies against the pervasive, seemingly endemic racism and indifference to racism that plague modern America.[258]

Critical race theory borrows from many sources and overlaps other academic/political movements, in particular CLS and feminist jurisprudence.

---

256. See Leslie Bender, *For Mary Jo Frug: Empowering Women Law Professors*, 6 Wisc. Women's L. J. 1, 12–13 (1991).

257. See Richard Delgado, *Introduction*, in Critical Race Theory: The Cutting Edge xiii–xv (R. Delgado, ed. 1995).

258. For some representative works of critical race theory scholarship, see Derrick Bell, Jr., And We Are Not Saved (1987); Derrick Bell, *Law School Exams and Minority-Group Students*, 7 Black L. J. 304 (1981); Kimberle Williams Crenshaw, *Foreward: Toward A Race-Conscious Pedagogy in Legal Education*, 11 Nat. Black L. J. 1 (1989); Kimberle Williams Crenshaw, *Race, Reform, and Retrenchment: Transformation and Legitimation in Antidiscrimination Law*, 101 Harv. L. Rev. 1331 (1988); Richard Delgado, *The Imperial Scholar: Reflections on a Review of Civil Rights Literature*, 132 U. Pa. L. Rev. 561 (1984); Mari J. Matsuda, *Public Response to Racist Speech: Considering the Victim's Story*, 87 Mich. L. Rev. 2320 (1989); Symposium, *Critical Race Theory*, 82 Cal. L. Rev. 741 et seq (1994); Symposium, *LATCRIT*, supra note 178.

Critical race theorists, however, have advanced three distinctive positions.[259] First, they question the subtle ways in which racism and a pervasive, often tacit "race consciousness" inform both law and legal education.[260] For example, critical race theorists offer insights into the specially destructive ways in which racist or hate speech harms persons of color differently from any way whites might be said to be harmed by racist speech, and they have advanced innovative theories about free speech and equal rights that would support the regulation of particular types of racist speech.[261]

Second, critical race theorists argue that the special cultures, experiences and perspectives of persons of color generate distinctive voices and special normative insights about race and the law.[262] This claim has been contested by many, including minority scholars.[263] But true or not, these claims have had the salutary effects of generating confidence among critical race theorists in developing their oppositional, dissident scholarship and helping legal scholars focus on ways to consider and evaluate fairly the perspectives, normative claims and different kinds of work by those who are "outsiders" to mainstream legal scholarship.[264]

Third, critical race theorists have particularly emphasized the use of narratives in legal scholarship to convey cultural, personal and imaginative ex-

---

259. For descriptions of critical race theory, see Delgado, *Introduction*, supra note 257, at xiii–xv; Angela Harris, *Foreward: The Jurisprudence of Reconstruction*, 82 Cal. L. Rev. 741, 741–58 (1994); Rachel Moran, *Foreward* to LATCRIT symposium, supra note 178.

260. See, e.g., Crenshaw, *Toward a Race-Conscious Pedagogy*, supra note 258; Charles R. Lawrence, III, *The Id, the Ego and Equal Protection: Reckoning with Unconscious Racism*, 39 Stan. L. Rev. 317 (1987); Matsuda, supra note 258.

261. See Charles R. Lawrence, III, *"If He Hollers Let Him Go:" Regulating Racial Speech on Campus*, 1990 Duke L.J. 431; Matsuda, supra note 258. To date, of course, the Supreme Court has been unresponsive to arguments for validating the regulation of racist speech. See R.A.V. v. City of St. Paul, 505 U.S. 377 (1992).

262. See, e.g., Delgado, *The Imperial Scholar*, supra note 258; Mari J. Matsuda, *Looking to the Bottom: Critical Legal Studies and Reparations*, 22 Harv. Civ. Rts-Civ. Lib. L. Rev. 323 (1987).

263. Compare Randall Kennedy, *Racial Critiques of Legal Academia*, 103 Harv. L. Rev. 1745 (1989) (contesting the "distinctiveness thesis" of critical race theorists), with Robin Barnes, *Race Consciousness: The Thematic Content of Racial Distinctiveness in Critical Race Scholarship*, 103 Harv. L. Rev. 1864 (1990); Richard Delgado, *Mindset and Metaphor*, 103 Harv. L. Rev. 1872 (1990) (responding to Kennedy's criticisms).

264. See Mary Coombs, *Outsider Scholarship: The Law Review Stories*, 63 Col. L. Rev. 683 (1992); Daniel Farber & Suzanna Sherry, *Telling Stories Out of School: An Essay on Legal Narratives*, 45 Stan. L. Rev. 807 (1993); Edward L. Rubin, *On Beyond Truth: A Theory for Evaluating Legal Scholarship*, 80 Cal. L. Rev. 889 (1992).

periences that support their insights, theories and arguments about racism and American law.[265] For example, in his exploration of the stalled, regressive state of American civil rights law, *And We Are Not Saved*, Derrick Bell imagines a civil rights heroine, Geneva Crenshaw, a series of "chronicles" which engage Geneva in several disheartening defeats of civil rights actions, and a series of dialogues between Geneva and a narrator (who is Derrick Bell) about these failed actions that reflect on the limitations of American law and politics. And despite the frustrations and defeats, Geneva and her narrator continue to work with faith, some hope and reason towards developing a vision of a new kind of strategy that might generate an authentic racial justice in our society.[266] The law and literature movement and feminist jurisprudence also have employed narratives to incorporate and convey emotions, personal experience and imagination,[267] but the narratives of critical race theorists seem distinctive in the power of their attempts to capture and convey the special pain, immorality, and corrosive oppression of racism and racism's effects in contemporary American society.

Critical race theorists have also developed a specific critique of legal education. One component involves the articulation of the special discontents, challenges and discrimination that are experienced by minority law professors and students at mostly white law schools.[268] A second component attempts to understand, criticize and promote affirmative action policies in law schools for minority students and law professors.[269] A third aspect of the critique has been innovative work in classrooms and the curriculum to invent and implement new methods and new courses for the more effective study of law and racism by all students. In Kimberle Crenshaw's words, this work is designed

---

265. See, e.g., D. Bell, supra note 258 (using fictional narratives); Matsuda, supra note 258 (using non-fictional narratives).

266. D. Bell, supra note 258.

267. See, e.g., *Pedagogy of Narrative: A Symposium* 40 J. Legal Educ., Issues # 1 & 2 (1991); Kathryn Abrams, *Hearing the Call of Stories*, 79 Cal. L. Rev. 971 (1991).

268. See, e.g., Derrick Bell, Jr., *Strangers in Academic Paradise: Law Teachers of Color in Still White Schools*, 20 U.S.F. L. Rev. 385 (1986); Bell, *Law School Exams and Minority-Group Students*, supra note 258; Crenshaw, *Toward a Race-Conscious Pedagogy*, supra note 258; Richard Delgado, *Minority Law Professors' Lives: The Bell-Delgado Survey*, 24 Harv. Civ. Rts-Civ. Lib. L. Rev. 349 (1989).

269. See, e.g., Derrick Bell, Jr., *Bakke, Minority Admissions, and the Usual Price of Racial Remedies*, 67 Cal. L. Rev. 3 (1979); *Application of the "Tipping Point" Principle to Law Faculty Hiring Policies*, 10 Nova L.J. 319 (1986); *The Final Report: Harvard's Affirmative Action Allegory*, 87 Mich. L. Rev. 2382 (1989). See also Daniel Farber, *The Outmoded Debate Over Affirmative Action*, 82 Cal. L. Rev. 893 (1994) (summarizing the critical race theory literature on affirmative action issues).

to "create spaces" in legal education within which one may question dominant legal frameworks and present relevant personal ideas and experiences without the threat or stigma to these actions that are implicit in the discipline's discourse, rhetoric and other techniques that govern legal education.[270]

Critical race theory thus reinforces and adds new dimensions to the explicit and implicit threats to the discipline from other academic/political reform movements. Much like feminist jurisprudence, this theory calls for inquiries into pragmatic contexts, a caring for other persons and their different experiences, and the legal appreciation of subjectivity as well as objectivity. This movement thus implicitly challenges the discipline's tacit lessons of analysis, rule-orientation and professional autonomy. But this theory's overall relationship to the discipline is ambiguous. The discipline surely benefits from a limited and marginal presence of critical race theory just as it benefits from the marginal presence of law and literature, CLS and feminist jurisprudence. The discipline, moreover, can always employ its policies of silence, ignorance and the tacit steering of faculty and students to keep this new and relatively small movement cabined mostly within the far reaches of legal scholarship and the periphery of the law school curriculum.

———

In summary, what have the academic/political movements accomplished vis-à-vis the discipline? The new movements have modified the discourse of scholarship and the case method. Law journals dedicated to work within particular movements have been started, and some of these journals are edited by professors and select articles by peer review.[271] These movements have also influenced the trend towards publishing "theoretical" articles.[272] But conventional scholarship has expanded at the same time,[273] and the discipline's imperatives for prestigious and large numbers of publications appear to have in-

———

270. Crenshaw, *Toward a Race-Conscious Pedagogy*, supra note 258; see also Frances Ansley, *Race and the Core Curriculum in Legal Education*, 79 Cal. L. Rev. 1511 (1991); Jerome Culp, *Autobiography and Legal Scholarship and Teaching: Finding the Me in the Legal Academy*, 77 Va. L. Rev. 539 (1991).

271. See, e.g., The Clinical Law Review; Harvard Women's Law Journal; Journal of Law and Economics (faculty-edited); Journal of Legal Studies (faculty-edited); La Raza Law Journal; Law and Society Review (faculty-edited); National Black Law Journal; Women's Rights Law Review; Yale Journal of Law and Humanities.

272. See Michael J. Saks, Howard Larsen & Carol J. Hodne, *Is There a Growing Gap Among Law, Law Practice, and Legal Scholarship?: A Systematic Comparison of Law Review Articles One Generation Apart*. 30 Suffolk L. Rev. 353 (1996).

273. See id. at 370–71.

tensified.[274] The new scholarship and new courses developed by the academic/political movements also encourage ideological work by professors and students that can reconcile them to the discipline's basic routines and values. More fundamentally, the core curriculum, casebooks, the case method and final examinations are relatively unchanged from, say, the 1960s. The modern academic/political reform movements have altered the discipline on its surface and at its margins and they remain a source of possible transformation, but the discipline's deep structures also remain firmly in place. These movements, like the professional reforms of legal education, have failed to develop any coherent widely accepted critique of legal education and they have failed to develop the strong counter-hegemonic alliances that might bring about systematic and sustainable change. The discipline has divided and captured them.

---

274. See, e.g., Richard S. Markovits, *The Professional Assessment of Legal Academics: On the Shift from Evaluator Judgment to Market Evaluations*, 48 J. Legal Educ. 417 (1998).

CHAPTER FIVE

FOREIGN RELATIONS

Law school practices are linked to other practices and institutions with varying degrees of fit, and these relationships are important to the discipline. Legal practices in general, corporate law firms, the American judicial system, the organized bar and the American research university place demands on law schools that invite and reinforce the discipline's basic structures. But the generality of these external demands and particular conflicts between them allow the discipline substantial discretion to operate on its own, to serve its own interests and those of law school inhabitants. Thus law schools do not serve "their constituencies" with optimum efficiency and may often disserve them as the discipline functions with its partial but significant autonomy.

This chapter analyzes the connections between law schools and external institutions to ascertain the positive effects by which the discipline and these institutions serve each other and the dysfunctions that these relationships create. This analysis articulates the external constraints on the discipline, particularly those that arise from the disciplines or practices of corporate law firms, the organized bar and American research universities. These constraints are usually general in nature, and the discipline as a system can operate in good part without specific determination or control by insiders or outsiders. There thus appears to be room for instituting significant shifts or modifications to both legal education and the discipline of law schools within the complex and subtle organizational environment or political economy of law schools.

The Diffuse Influence of Legal Practices

Lawyers do many different kinds of things and work in many different fields of law. For example, when John Heinz and Edward Laumann studied the social structure of Chicago lawyers, they sought to determine how lawyers allocated their time between 30 different fields of law. These fields were defined by different legal doctrines aimed at regulating categories of persons or corporate actors and in some cases by adversarial specialties that serve one side of a doctrinal field such as criminal defense lawyers.[1] Lawyers also serve many kinds of clients whose legal problems are embedded in diverse factual contexts. Thus, while most practicing lawyers engage in some kind of problem solving that involves some kind of legal doctrine, the great variety of practices among lawyers makes it difficult to assess the demands that legal practices as a whole place on legal education, or to assess how well law schools serve these practices. But there are three relationships between legal practices and law schools that throw light upon the discipline and its tacit effects.

First, in the nineteenth century, when government regulations were much less significant and litigation practices and common law doctrines constituted the major part of law practices, the discipline's core curriculum of common law and other private law subjects, its focus on the case method, and even the nature of law school examinations appear to have been aimed at training students directly for major aspects of legal practice. This is less obvious today in view of the proliferation of new legal doctrines, most of them involving complex statutory law and many involving the public law of administrative regulations, and the great diversity of modern legal practices in which transactional work outweighs litigation practices. To be sure, the core curriculum, case method and final examinations engage students in *particular kinds* of problem-solving and *particular forms* of reading, writing and thinking. But little of the discipline's work exposes students directly to the kinds of contexts, practical judgments, tacit knowledge or imaginative reflections that can help lawyers engage effectively in the diverse kinds of office counseling, complex negotiations with multiple parties or government administrators and specialized forms of litigation that constitute legal practices today. In light of this mismatch between the discipline and the nature of contemporary legal practices, it is no wonder that many lawyers today, including the hiring partners of large corporate law firms, believe that general abilities in oral and written communication are among the most important skills of lawyers and that law schools should and could be doing a better job of training lawyers in these skills.[2] Moreover, while this complaint does not mention the "practical judgment" or "common sense" of lawyers, it is likely that perceived deficiencies in oral and written communication are often linked to a lack of sound practical judgment or good reflective abilities in the speaker or writer. Thus the discipline deflects attention from important skills that modern lawyers should have.

---

1. See John P. Heinz & Edward O. Laumann, Chicago Lawyers: The Social Structure of the Bar 33–34, 38 (1982).

2. See Bryant G. Garth & Joanne Martin, *Law Schools and the Construction of Competence*, 43 J. Legal Educ. 469 (1993).

Second, it seems relatively clear that the core curriculum, the case method and the final examination/grading/class ranking system primarily serve one sector of legal practice, the practice of corporate law, even if this sector is not served with optimum efficiency. We shall explore the close connections between the discipline and corporate law firms in the next section, but we may note here several ways in which the discipline's structures and lessons promote the corporate practice of law over other legal practices. The core curriculum, as we have seen, includes a number of courses such as corporations law, tax law, the law of commercial contracts and administrative procedure law that are basically concerned with legal doctrines of interest to corporate clients.[3] The discipline's tacit lessons that reduce law to non-binding manipulable laws, privilege property rights over competing claims, and teach the need for deference to professional hierarchies also seem designed to help lawyers work in law firms that represent corporate clients. The discipline's tacit lessons of quick productive analysis and instrumentalist reading and writing seem similarly designed to train corporate lawyers for the rapid production of lengthy complex briefs, merger agreements, securities registration statements and other documents that pervade the practice of corporate law. More generally, the discipline's case method and final examination system may be said to both teach and test for "complex symbolic manipulations" that indirectly approximate the kinds of complex symbolic manipulations that are required in the work that law firms do for corporate clients and wealthy persons. Most fundamentally, the discipline's overall image of the lawyer as an amoral technician may help reconcile many corporate lawyers to the ethical indifference of their organizational clients.

The consequence of this privileging of corporate law firms is that law schools pay much less attention to training lawyers who serve personal clients or work for businesses or government agencies in jobs that demand less in the way of complex symbolic manipulations and more in the way of exercising practical judgment for a larger number of clients in a greater variety of contexts. The discipline's heavy emphasis upon complex symbolic manipulations in the core curriculum, case method and final examinations provides little direct training for lawyers who work, say, in the specialized fields of family law, criminal law, the representation of middle-income persons or the provision of legal aid services to low-income clients. These fields require complex personal skills of many kinds, good oral abilities in a variety of legal and non-legal situations, much common sense and sound practical judgment, but they

---

3. See Chapter One's discussion of the core curriculum.

generally do not involve the kinds of complex symbolic manipulations that serve corporate clients. For example, an ability to win and maintain the confidence of many different clients and perhaps coach these clients in sharing some of the legal work in order to keep their fees down may be necessary to provide legal services successfully to middle-income clients.[4] An ability to understand clients and their problems, identify issues quickly and make persuasive and imaginative oral presentations to government administrators all seem necessary to successful practices for low-income clients.[5] Perhaps the case method in its ideal form can somehow teach these skills indirectly, but we have seen that the realities of the discipline diminish these possibilities.[6]

Third, although many of the diverse fields of contemporary legal practice may not be well served by the discipline of law schools, ironically these fields can impose diffuse pressures on law schools that help maintain the discipline's structures. At many law schools, especially non-elite schools, as new fields of legal doctrine develop it is understandable that practitioners, alumni and students campaign for the inclusion of the new fields within the law school's curriculum. The natural or easy response for the case method/final examination law school is to offer a new case method/final examination course on the doctrine in question. This response extends the discipline and siphons resources away from more effective programs that might help prepare law students for the diversity and complexities of modern law practices.

Corporate Law Firms

Corporate law firms are only one of several sectors of the legal profession that provide employment for law school graduates. But it has long been recognized that corporate firms exercise a disproportionate influence over the law school's curriculum, its teaching methods, its final examination/class ranking/grading system and many of its scholarly practices, especially the presence of student-managed law reviews. This influence is understandable since cor-

---

4. See James Podgers, *Rediscovering the Middle Class: Old-fashioned values and creative thinking are proving to the formulas for success in serving primarily middle-income clients*, ABA Journal, Dec. 1994, pp. 265–72.

5. See David G. Savage, *Everyday People: The work of storefront clinics funded by the Legal Services Corp. is not glamorous—just crucial to those who cannot help themselves*, ABA Journal, May 1995, pp. 280–84.

6. See Chapter One's discussion of the case method and Chapter Three's discussion of the disciplinary techniques of invisibilities, coolness and the examinatorial regime.

porate firms provide the most lucrative and prestigious employment for lawyers, are a primary source of private donations to law schools, constitute a major training ground for law professors and provide the major share of consulting opportunities for law faculty. Moreover the scope and intensity of these relationships have broadened and deepened in recent years. Corporate law firms have expanded dramatically in size and become more specialized and more openly competitive in the past 25 years.[7] The demand of these firms for law graduates who have elite credentials and good work characteristics has increased correspondingly, and the firms have begun to recruit many more law students, including those with lower class ranks at elite schools and those who have earned the best grades at non-elite schools.[8] In the mid-1990s, moreover, a stagnant overall market for lawyers increased employment uncertainties among students at many law schools, including elite schools.[9] It seems essential then to inquire how relationships between corporate law firms and law schools influence and construct the discipline.

Consider first the process by which law students are hired by corporate law firms. These firms desire several qualities in their new lawyers. The new lawyer should have credentials which help build or maintain the reputation of the law firm,[10] and these credentials include the prestige of a lawyer's law school, his or her class rank, his or her participation on a law review and, for some firms, a prestigious judicial clerkship after graduation.[11] The new lawyer should also have a cluster of particular talents or skills, which include good oral and writing abilities, an ability to instill the confidence of others in oneself and an abil-

---

7. See, e.g., Marc Galanter & Thomas Palay, Tournament of Lawyers: Transformation of the Big Law Firm (1991); Robert L. Nelson, Partners with Power: The Social Transformation of the Large Law Firm (1988).

8. See Richard Abel, American Lawyers 166–210 (1989); see also Linda Wightman, Legal Education at the Close of the Twentieth Century: Descriptions and Analyses of Students, Financing, and Professional Expectations and Attitudes 60–84 (1995) (Law School Admission Council) ("The most coveted work settings are large and mid-sized firms, with a full third of the entering class identifying these as their first choice.").

9. See, e.g., Dirk Johnson, "More Scorn and Less Money Dim Law's Lure," NY Times, Sept. 22, 1995, p. 1.

10. On the importance to lawyers and law firms of their *reputations* as providers of high quality legal services, see Smith & Cox, *The Pricing of Legal Services: A Contractual Solution to the Problem of bilateral Opportunism*, 14 J. Legal Studies 167 (1985).

11. See, e.g., Francis Zemans & Victor Rosenblum, The Making of a Public Profession 91–122 (1981); Eaves, Png & Ramseyer, *Gender, Ethnicity and Grades: Empirical Evidence of Discrimination in Law-Firm Interviews*, 7 Law & Inequality 189, 201 (1989); Campbell & Tomkins, *Gender, Race, Grades, and Law Review Membership as Factors in Law Firm Hiring Decisions: An Empirical Study*, 18 J. Contemp. Law 211, 220–23, 234–36 (1992).

ity in "legal analysis and legal reasoning."[12] In addition, corporate firms presumably desire new lawyers who are self-disciplined, confident in themselves, full of initiative, interested in corporate law work, "tough," and capable of mastering diffuse materials and presenting useful summaries and solutions to complex problems in a relatively rapid or productive manner.[13]

The process by which corporate firms seek such lawyers from law schools seems on first impression well designed to achieve these goals. Corporate firms concentrate their recruiting efforts at the most prestigious law schools they can, in part because of the prestige of the schools and in part because these schools admit students with the highest pre-law academic credentials, which indicates that students at these schools are likely to possess talents and skills such as good writing ability, self-confidence and self-discipline.[14] These firms also rely on class ranks and law review participation in their screening decisions,[15] in part because of the prestige of these credentials and in part because these credentials indicate self-discipline, an interest in corporate law subjects, a general competence and taste for competitive activities, and an ability to master diffuse materials and write coherently about such materials in a rapid, productive manner.[16]

As we have seen, corporate law firms employ an elaborate process of student interviews and summer clerkships in order to assess the talents and skills of students that are not easily measured by academic credentials.[17] These firms seek on-campus interviews with many students who meet their academic criteria in order to ascertain the students' apparent interests in corporate law work, their oral abilities, their apparent discipline and taste for collective work within a professional hierarchy, their ability to gain the confidence of others and their "toughness" as well[18] For many law students these interviews typi-

---

12. These four general skills were rated as the most important skills to legal practice in a recent survey of lawyers in Chicago and Missouri. See Garth & Martin, supra note 2, at 472–477.

13. Cf. David B. Wilkins & G. Mitu Gulati, *Why Are There So Few Black Lawyers in Corporate Law Firms? An Institutional Analysis*, 84 Cal. L. Rev. 493, 514–20 (1996) (describing the interest of corporate firms in obtaining new associates who are highly motivated to work effectively with little monitoring by supervisors).

14. See Russell Korobkin, *In Praise of Law School Rankings: Solutions to Coordination and Collective Action Problems*, 77 Tex. L. Rev. 403 (1998).

15. See, e.g., Campbell & Tomkins, supra note 11.

16. See Philip C. Kissam, *Law School Examinations*, 42 Vand. L. Rev. 433 (1989).

17. See Chapter One's discussion of the placement process.

18. See Garth & Martin, supra note 2, at 488–91 (describing the expectations of hiring partners in Chicago law firms that new law firm associates should have several talents and skills not measured by law school grades such as good oral abilities and the ability to gain the confidence of others).

cally occur in the fall semester of their second year, although students who have earned highest grades in the fall of the first year may be interviewed for summer clerkships after their first year, thus lending early prominence within law schools to the hunt for jobs with corporate firms. On-campus interviews are followed by "call backs" for students who are selected to visit law firm sites for more elaborate interviewing. The successful students in first and second year interviews are chosen to work at well-paid clerkships during the summers before their second and third years of law school, and these clerkships often provide an intoxicating combination of law work, a competitive testing of one's abilities against the firm's expectations and other clerks, and the respect, admiration and other blandishments offered by corporate firms to make eventual full-time employment with the firm seem attractive.[19]

Each component of corporate law firm hiring reinforces major elements of the discipline. The concentration of recruiting at the most prestigious schools encourages not only elite schools but also schools seeking corporate law opportunities for their students to admit as students only persons who have the best possible academic credentials, thus ensuring an examination-conscious student body. This concentration also inclines law schools to maintain or seek other factors that help establish a school's reputation. Law schools may only hire faculty who have prestigious credentials such as top law school grades, major law review editorships, prestigious judicial clerkships and experience at prestigious law firms.[20] Schools may encourage their faculty to publish often in prestigious law reviews and encourage their students with top grades to seek prestigious judicial clerkships as additional ways of enhancing their relative standing in the *U.S. News & World Report*'s annual ranking of law schools.[21] These factors reinforce other aspects of the discipline too, in particular its em-

---

19. See Note, *Making Docile Lawyers: An Essay on the Pacification of Law Students*, 111 Harv. L. Rev. 2027, 2034–42 (1998) (describing the qualities of the recruiting process of corporate law firms at Harvard Law School).

20. On the credentials of law professors, see Robert J. Borthwick & Jordan R. Schau, *Gatekeepers of the Profession: An Empirical Profile of the Nation's Law Professors*, 25 U. Michigan J. Law Reform 191 (1991); Donna Fossum, *Law Professors: A Profile of the Teaching Branch of the Profession*, 1980 Am. Bar Found. Research J. 501; Howard Glickstein, *Law Schools: Where the Elite Meet to Teach*, 10 Nova L. Rev. 541 (1986).

21. The academic credentials of law students, the credentials of law faculty, faculty publications and the judicial clerkships of law school graduates are all considered factors which enhance a law school's prestige, and these factors either directly or indirectly influence a law school's ranking in the *U.S. News & World Report*. See W. Scott Van Alstyne, Jr., Joseph R. Julin & Larry D. Barnett, The Goals and Missions of Law Schools 3–24 (1990); Korobkin, supra note 14.

phasis on appellate court decisions, the production of much conventional doctrinal scholarship by student-managed law reviews, and the discipline's examination/grading/class ranking system.

The focus of corporate firms on high class ranks and law review work in hiring lawyers from particular schools will, of course, reinforce the law school's final examination/grading/class ranking system as a necessary utilitarian mechanism that must be perceived to operate accurately and fairly to distribute employment opportunities. This focus also reinforces the perceptions of many students that it is their grades and competitions for law review, not their course work, that count in legal education.[22] In addition, the recent proliferation of multiple student-managed law reviews at individual schools can be explained as the provision of more opportunities for more students to qualify and compete for prestigious and lucrative employment by corporate firms.[23]

The interviewing/summer clerkship process generates more subtle disciplinary lessons too. Most fundamentally, this process can consume a lot of a student's time during the academic year, beginning as early as the spring semester of first year for some students and accelerating in the fall of the second year as corporate firm recruiters swarm around law schools to interview students for clerkships after their second year.[24] This commitment of time by itself forces students to miss numbers of classes, to enter some classes late and leave others early, and to seek short-cuts in academic work that are likely to incline them towards basic disciplinary methods.[25] The time spent on job searches by some students also symbolizes for all students in the law school what is the most important or perhaps only goal of legal education: to get the right job.

This hiring process also forces students to contemplate the issue of how they will present themselves as lawyers to other lawyers. This issue raises sub-

---

22. Cf. Roy Rickson, *Faculty Control and the Structure of Student Competition: An Analysis of the Law Student Role*, 25 J. Legal Educ. 47 (1973) (discovering that law students who score well on law school examinations tend to spend their time studying for examinations instead of preparing for or attending classes).

23. On the proliferation of multiple law reviews at individual schools in recent years, see Michael J. Saks, Howard Larsen & Carol J. Hodne, *Is There A Growing Gap Among Law, Law Practice, and Legal Scholarship? A Systematic Comparison of Law Review Articles One Generation Apart*, 30 Suff. L. Rev. 353, 363 (1996).

24. See, e.g., Note, supra note 19, at 2035.

25. See Rickson, supra note 22; Chapter Two's discussion of the temporal rhythms of law students.

tle questions of appropriate dress, style and demeanor that many law students may not have contemplated before. The conservative answers that are given to these questions intermingle with the discipline's tacit lessons of respect for professional authority, impersonality, coolness and rhetorical toughness.

The search for legal jobs, which is triggered for many students by the hiring process of corporate firms, seems to focus many students upon making the "right choice" of law school courses in their second and third years.[26] Such choices quietly encourage students to enroll in doctrinal courses that feature the disciplinary virtues: casebooks, the coverage of many rules, the case method, and a traditional sort of examination. Such choices also encourage students to study the subjects that demonstrate their interest in corporate law, thereby reinforcing the discipline's lessons of the importance of property rights and the equality between corporations and persons.

Finally, the interviewing/summer clerkship process provides significant psychological rewards or "ego stroking" for individuals who succeed and benefit from this process. These rewards contrast sharply with the impersonality and coolness of routine law school practices, and this contrast may have several tacit effects.[27] One effect is attachment to the idea that corporate law firm work should govern the rest of a student's choices in law school. Another is increasing indifference to further academic studies, with a consequent search by law students for disciplinary shortcuts to finish their required law school work. Yet another effect is the comparison of job opportunities among students, comparisons that are bound to tacitly reinforce the value of grades, law reviews and successful rhetorical styles that have helped individuals win these competitions.[28] The corporate law firm hiring process thus pervades the cul-

------

26. Interview conversations may contemplate a student's course selections if for no other reason than to find a comfortable topic for both the student and interviewer, and such conversations could steer students towards making the "right choice" of courses that meet the expectations of interviewers. See Chapter One's discussion of the placement process. On the other hand, the law student's focus on taking the right courses may result more from contemplation of the interviewing process than from actual experience. Corporate law firms may not place as much emphasis on knowledge of particular substantive and procedural law as many law students and perhaps many professors seem to think. Cf. Garth & Martin, supra note 2 (finding that contemporary Chicago and Missouri lawyers rate knowledge of substantive and procedural law relatively low among "the most important skills" of lawyers).

27. See Note, supra note 19, at 2040–42.

28. The disciplinary lessons from these comparisons may be particularly strong at regional or non-elite law schools where only a fraction of the student body is able to compete successfully for jobs with corporate law firms. But even at schools like Harvard there

tures of elite law schools and many non-elite schools in ways that are closely linked to basic elements of the discipline.

Consider also the relatively direct connections between corporate firms and law faculties. Corporate lawyers and their firms are major sources of private donations to law schools, and these donations, among other things, can support curriculum development, faculty expansion, faculty salaries, and research assistance or monetary rewards for scholarship.[29] Corporate firms also provide much of the post-law school, pre-teaching training of law professors,[30] and they provide a major share of the most remunerative consulting opportunities for law professors. These connections have many purposes but they all tend to reinforce elements of the discipline.

The raising of private funds by American law schools, like corporate firm hiring, is an elaborate, sensitive and important process.[31] Much public relations work is done to convince potential donors, large and small alike, that gifts to the law school are worthy investments. Thus deans talk regularly to alumni (and others) and glossy magazines are mailed regularly to alumni (and others) to promote the virtues of the law school. Not surprisingly, these announcements rely heavily on virtues that can be easily dramatized or reduced to sound bites, and each of these virtues encourages law school inhabitants to attend to elements or practices of the discipline. Among the virtues regularly featured are the strength of the pre-law academic credentials of the study body, which can be expressed numerically by average LSAT scores and undergraduate grades, the prestigious judicial clerkships obtained by recent graduates, the prestigious credentials of new faculty members, and the quantity or prestige of recent faculty publications. This process also features more intimate sorts of contacts by deans, other administrative officials and individual faculty with the potential donors of large gifts in order to propose projects for private funding and "to close the deals" as it were. In these contacts the particular interests of corporate firms in legal education can be recognized and advanced,

---

are subtle if at times subterranean comparisons of this sort taking place. See, e.g., Scott Turow, One L (1977); Note, supra note 19.

29. See, e.g., Joel Seligman, The High Citadel 71–84 (1978) (describing Dean Erwin Griswold's successful fund raising for Harvard Law School in the two decades following World War II); Tamar Lewin, "Georgetown President Ends Push to Replace Law School Dean," NY Times, April 22, 1998, p. E 22 (describing how law school alumni "threatened to withhold $4 million dollars in pledges, nearly half the annual total," to support a dean who had worked to make the law school "as autonomous as possible" from the university).

30. See Borthwick & Schau, supra note 20, on the importance of corporate firm experience in law professors' backgrounds.

31. See, e.g., Lewin, supra note 29.

sometimes by gifts for specific projects that interest corporate lawyers but more often one imagines by understated or tacit exchanges that are related to the general funding of law schools. In these conversations projects involving new faculty appointments, new courses, teaching methods, curriculum reform projects and faculty scholarship can be discussed. These conversations are also excellent forums in which deans and individual faculty members, either explicitly or tacitly, can reassure distinguished and wealthy alumni of their school and other elite lawyers that the law school's curriculum will continue to promote subjects of interest to corporate law firms, that the credentials of students and the school's teaching methods will continue to produce the keen doctrinal analysts corporate firms desire, and that faculty scholarship will continue to enhance the reputation of the school and maintain the development of complex, sophisticated law.[32] Fund raising by law schools thus entrenches the discipline by orienting law schools towards two corporate firm objectives: the production of new corporate lawyers and the production of an increasingly complex, sophisticated law which defines a particular sense of professional expertise that helps legitimate the work of corporate lawyers.[33]

Corporate firms also influence the supply of law professors since many professors work as young associates in these firms before they teach and their work in firms is likely to influence their work as professors. The work of new associates in large corporate law firms tends to be highly specialized, relatively fragmented, and performed under the supervision of hierarchically-ordered teams of attorneys.[34] Will not new law professors coming from corporate law firms be likely to emphasize in their teaching and their scholarship, especially during those intense and formative pre-tenure years, the fragmented analysis of many judicial opinions and specialized doctrinal rules that the discipline's case method invites? Similarly, no matter what fields they specialize in, will not these professors be likely to retain at least implicit presumptions or respect for corporate legal values such as the importance of private property and legal equality between corporations and persons? Large corporate firms may not

---

32. Cf. J. Seligman, supra note 29 (describing Dean Erwin Griswold's successful fund raising at Harvard and the conservative development of the curriculum, teaching methods and faculty during the same period).

33. On the interests of the elite bar in establishing the professional expertise of lawyers as an abstract and theoretical system which provides a kind of scientific legitimacy for their practices, see Ronen Shamir, Managing Legal Uncertainty: Elite Lawyers in the New Deal, esp. 113–18 (1995).

34. See, e.g., Robert Nelson, *Practice and Privilege: Social Change and the Structure of Large Law Firms*, 1981 Am. Bar Found. Research J. 97, 110–26.

provide an ideal training ground for legal educators, who as teachers must educate a diverse lot of beginners in acquiring a somewhat mysterious craft, or for legal scholars who wish to or should be exploring the competing political values of law or performing interdisciplinary scholarship. But corporate law firms do provide excellent training for the discipline of law schools.

Corporate firms also hire many law professors to consult on specialized doctrinal issues that firms need to address. This work surely reinforces the discipline's tacit messages about the importance of case analysis, the coverage of legal rules, corporate legal values and the idea that professional expertise consists of a mastery of complex doctrinal rules. Moreover this work, like the fund raising process, can engage faculty members in many informal exchanges with corporate lawyers which tacitly remind the professors of the special kinds of courses, teaching methods and scholarship that cohere with the interests of the professional elite. It is not surprising that visions of corporate firm partners dominate the thinking of many professors about the nature of the legal practices for which they are educating students,[35] that practice in corporate firms may constitute the norm of highest quality work in law schools,[36] or that the aspirations or propensities of many law professors is "to teach for the lawyer ten years out" by using complex case method tactics rather than teaching basic methods of legal inquiry to beginners.[37] Of course, at elite schools that send most of their graduates to corporate law firms, this kind of teaching may be functional. But the dominance of one sector of the legal profession over major elements of the discipline such as the curriculum, the case method and final examinations suggests at least that there are substantial dysfunctions of the discipline at many law schools.

Let us assess now the positive effects and possible dysfunctions that may arise from relationships between corporate firms, law schools, and the discipline. First, the discipline tacitly legitimates the work of corporate law firms in several ways. The emphasis on complex doctrinal analysis in case method classrooms and final examinations quietly promotes the kind of work in which corporate firms specialize and establishes this "analytical work" as a norm for all lawyering. The emphasis in the law school placement process on obtaining jobs with corporate firms similarly signals that corporate law work is the best

---

35. See Banks McDowell, *The Lawyer as Manipulator: Is This a Useful Model for Legal Education and Practice?*, 31 Washburn L. J. 506, 506 (1992).

36. See Robert Granfield, Making Elite Lawyers: Visions of Law at Harvard and Beyond (1992).

37. I owe this observation to Gordon Shneider of the Northern Illinois University College of Law.

kind of legal practice. Moreover, among both lawyers and the public, the fact that lawyers who work at corporate firms have attended the most prestigious law schools, obtained the highest grades, and participated on law reviews suggests that these lawyers will be perceived as deserving of greater income, more prestige, more respect and more frequent referrals than other lawyers.[38] Furthermore, the discipline's norms or incentives to produce much legal scholarship in general and much "cutting-edge" or "theoretical" scholarship in particular, especially at elite law schools, supports the interest of elite corporate lawyers in establishing a sense among lawyers, their clients and the public that the basic expertise of lawyers is relatively abstract, complex, sophisticated and unattainable by non-lawyers.[39] There is some irony in this connection between scholarship and corporate law firms. Disagreeable theoretical developments in legal scholarship can bring strong protests from members of the elite corporate bar, or judges, to the effect that this scholarship is "too political," "too theoretical," "too abstract" and "not useful to practitioners."[40] Yet this scholarship, at the same time, may be increasing the complexity and sophistication of legal theory and consequently promoting an understanding about the nature of legal expertise that helps legitimate the corporate bar.

Second, the discipline also does a pretty fair job of producing new lawyers for corporate law firms. The discipline's admissions process, which is devoted to obtaining top credentials in entering students, the fundamental distinction between elite and non-elite schools, the final examination/grading/class ranking system and student-managed law reviews generate credentials and provide measures of productivity and quality in doctrinal analysis for new corporate lawyers. The curriculum and case method ensure a substantial introduction to corporate law subjects, corporate legal values and complex doctrinal analysis. The paradigm of good paragraph thinking/ writing that is taught by the

---

38. Cf. Samuel Bowles & Herbert Gintis, Schooling in Capitalist America 98–106 (1976); John W. Meyer, *The Effects of Education as an Institution*, 83 Am J. Soc. 55, 58–70 (1977) (describing how education in general legitimates social roles by allocating persons to different roles on the basis of their relative academic merit or academic accomplishments).

39. See generally Andrew Abbott, The System of Professions: An Essay on the Division of Labor (1988); Magali S. Larson, The Rise of Professionalism: A Sociological Analysis (1977); R. Shamir, supra note 33.

40. On the protests against the work of legal academics that supported New Deal policies, see R. Shamir, supra note 33, at 131–57; on such protests against more recent legal scholarship, see Harry T. Edwards, *The Growing Disjunction Between Legal Education and the Legal Profession*, 91 Mich. L. Rev. 34 (1992); Harry H. Wellington, *Challenges to Legal Education: The "Two Cultures" Phenomenon*, 37 J. Legal Educ. 327 (1987).

examination system would appear to generate a certain kind of instrumentalist productivity that may help corporate lawyers in their work of complex symbolic manipulations. And all these elements together with the discipline's more pervasive techniques tacitly teach rhetorical traits, attitudes, styles and ideological values such as "toughness" and deference within professional hierarchies that train law students in the conventional practices of corporate firms. Corporate law firms, then, appear to have powerful interests in maintaining the discipline's practices that legitimate their power and wealth and produce large numbers of qualified applicants for membership.

Yet there are signs that the discipline contains contradictions and may be dysfunctional towards corporate firms in some important respects. The discipline's incentives to produce large amounts of theoretical, cutting-edge and prestigious scholarship, which have influenced the modern reform movements in legal scholarship and conventional scholarship as well, may in fact have diminished the quantity of scholarship that is useful for corporate law work by making prominent scholarly writing less particularistic, less contextual, less conventional and more openly political than common judicial and legal discourse.[41] Thus, even if modern scholarship enhances the legitimacy of professional expertise and the corporate bar's expertise in a general way, its new forms that are influenced if not dictated by the discipline may be diminishing the overall value of scholarship to the corporate bar. The new "academic" attitudes towards scholarship may also be influencing the qualities of case method instruction, substituting interdisciplinary theories or political analysis for a student's full immersion in the professional craft values of doctrinal analysis, the conventional methods of legal argument and making practical judgments.[42] Most significantly, the discipline's elements and techniques, which seem devoted in particular to producing and legitimating corporate lawyers, limit the possibilities that all students—including those bound for corporate law—will obtain relevant training from law school clinics, ethics courses and writing projects.[43] The discipline's tacit instruction in the limited instrumentalist habits of "paraphrase reading" and "the paradigm of good paragraph thinking/writing" may also limit the abilities of corporate lawyers to engage in work that requires large amounts of reflection, imagination and creativity.[44] Ironically, the hiring partners in contemporary corporate firms

---

41. See Wellington, supra note 40, at 327–29.

42. See, e.g., Anthony T. Kronman, The Lost Lawyer: Failing Ideals of the Legal Profession (1993); Wellington, supra note 40, at 329–30.

43. See Chapter Four's discussion of the professional reforms.

44. See Chapter One's discussion of casebooks and law school examinations.

appear to place a premium on the general oral and writing abilities of new corporate lawyers and believe that law schools to a significant extent should be teaching these abilities.[45] Thus the discipline does not accomplish everything that corporate lawyers desire from legal education.

Nonetheless, corporate law firms provide rich opportunities for many law graduates and for law professors who consult with these firms. These economic links suggest that relationships between corporate firms and law schools help entrench the discipline's elements and techniques rather deeply. Most specifically, the disciplinary structures of the core curriculum, casebooks, case method and final examination/ grading/class ranking system are important to the practices of corporate law firms and thus likely to be among the most difficult structures to change. The related disciplinary techniques of impersonality, coolness, a confessional technology and an examinatorial regime will be similarly resistant to change as they too implicitly serve the culture of corporate law firms.

On this account the discipline is not well-designed to serve the other prominent sectors of the legal profession: solo practitioners, small firm practitioners, government lawyers, criminal lawyers and family law practitioners. Law schools and the organized bar have worked to supplement the discipline's structures in this regard, especially by providing law school clinics and upper class elective courses that are aimed at educating lawyers for work in these other sectors. But we have seen that the discipline constrains clinical programs.[46] The discipline also implicitly subordinates and handicaps these supplemental developments more generally, for example, by making it difficult for law schools and individuals to institute appropriate interdisciplinary training in such subjects as family law and criminal law.[47] The point, of course, is not that law school deans or faculty intentionally discriminate against these other kinds of law work, but that the routine practices, habits and tacit knowledge of the discipline are oriented in a different direction and can thus be substantially dysfunctional for important areas of legal practice.

---

45. See Garth & Martin, supra note 2, at 488–89, 496–98.

46. See Chapter Four's discussion of clinical education.

47. The handicapping of such developments is both subtle and multi-faceted. Barriers to such developments include hiring decisions that favor traditional law faculty credentials over interdisciplinary training and relevant practice experiences, teaching decisions that favor casebooks, the case method and traditional final examinations over more diffuse interdisciplinary approaches, and even subtle administrative barriers to allowing law students to take for law school credit relevant courses elsewhere in the university.

The Judicial System

Judges are the most honored members of the American legal profession. They wield certain kinds of power over society, the lawyers who practice before them and the parties whose disputes they decide. They are perceived by many to work under the ideals of judicial neutrality that place them outside or above normal politics. As a result of this power and these ideals, judges possess a social and political status that is important for the recognition of lawyers as a legitimate and expert profession.[48] The links between the judicial system and law schools are more ideological than material, but these relationships help construct and protect the discipline of law schools in important ways.

Most obviously, judges produce the appellate court decisions and opinions that constitute the main subject of study in law schools. This production continuously creates new opportunities and imposes subtle constraints on law professors and conventional legal scholars who attend to the flow of these opinions. Casebooks and treatises must be supplemented and revised on regular schedules, and these changes must then be incorporated into doctrinal courses and contemplated as "cutting edge" developments by the professors and students who use these texts. The production of new appellate opinions also generates subjects for writing the vast numbers of law review articles that report on and criticize judicial doctrines. Thus the work of judges, especially appellate court judges, tacitly encourages the discipline's focus on casebooks, the case method and the analysis of judicial opinions as the staple of legal thought in law school classrooms and conventional legal scholarship.

Like corporate law firms, the American judicial system trains many law professors. A relatively large number of law professors have clerked for judges, especially Federal judges, and former clerks appear to exercise a disproportionate if tacit influence on the policies and practices of law schools.[49] These professors typically have enjoyed working with "their judges" at least as much as law review members remember their experiences fondly. It would be surprising, then, if former judicial clerks did not implicitly view the practice of appellate courts as *the model* for legal education. If a law professor's most significant professional experience before her first teaching appointment focused

---

48. See, e.g., R. Shamir, supra note 33, at 31–81.

49. See Borthwick & Schau, supra note 20, at 214–217 (in the 1980s nearly 30% of all new law professors hired had judicial clerkship experience, and 61% of the new professors at the seven highest ranked elite law schools had been judicial clerks).

upon the conventional methods of legal research, appellate advocacy and opinion writing, methods which tend to divide problems into many discrete issues and make multiple arguments from rules and prior cases, this professor understandably is likely to emphasize such tactics in teaching prospective lawyers and writing articles, especially in her formative pre-tenure years. Former clerks also may recall their judge's style of questioning litigators from the bench and try to incorporate this style into their classroom discourse, moot court exercises and trial advocacy courses. The style and discourse of American judges undoubtedly casts significant influence upon the construction of the discipline's routine practices and techniques.

American judges also influence the discipline by hiring law students who have the highest grades and best recommendations from their professors to be their clerks. The screening and hiring process for judicial clerks is conducted within law schools more privately than corporate firm hiring, but this process too begins in earnest in the second year of law school and provides significant psychological rewards to those who succeed in the competition of law school grades and style to obtain the more prestigious clerkships.[50] The eventual award of clerkships to a law school's "best students" is also recognized as an important honor to both the students and the school, at least among faculty and alumni if not the student body. The annual hiring of judicial clerks to work with the most honored members of the legal profession surely creates tacit incentives for law professors and at least some students to excel in the case method, final examinations, and the student-managed law reviews of the discipline.

Finally, American judges frequently visit law schools for purposes of teaching courses, conducting moot court or mock trial competitions, conducting sessions of their own courts, or giving public lectures on such subjects such as "the nature of law," "the nature of judging," "the nature of the constitution" or "the importance of the legal profession." These visits and the commitment of judges to teaching law school courses are special events for the discipline, as they invite awe-inspiring displays of professional deference to judges and thus remind students and faculty alike of the power and importance of American judges.[51] While the opinions of judges are often criticized in classrooms and scholarship, their actual presence in law schools is another thing to behold. In these visits, faculty and students tend to honor judges by high praise

---

50. See, e.g., Note, supra note 19, at 2041 (describing the "crushing" disappointments of Harvard law students who fail to obtain prestigious clerkships).

51. See Graham Hughes, *The Great American Legal Scholarship Bazaar*, 33 J. Legal Educ. 424, 427 (1983).

and substantial deference, and this behavior quietly promotes the ideal of "the wise, objectivist, neutral judge" as a good model for lawyers to admire if not emulate.[52]

These relationships between the judiciary and law schools help entrench major aspects of the discipline. Conversely, the discipline tacitly helps to legitimate the judiciary as an independent and powerful government agency, a status which casts indirect honor on the legal profession and law schools. Law professors in their classrooms and conventional scholarship articulate notions of how ideal judges, acting independently from "politics," do or should decide and justify cases. They advance these ideas in two distinct ways: in classroom discourse, which at times may be dismissive of particular opinions but on the whole celebrates judicial opinions by studying them,[53] and in the deferential, objectivist rhetoric of conventional scholarship that is intended to persuade an audience of "ideal judges" to follow the author's recommendations.[54] Within the discipline of law schools, then, the tacit utilitarian Janus-faced image of judges as objectivist or political dissolves at times into an image of the judge as "lawyer-hero."[55] This alternative image instructs students in the appropriate professional respect to be paid to judges in practice that will help them negotiate their ways through our complex judicial system.

The discipline may serve the judicial system more efficiently than it serves any other external constituency, although there is one possible dysfunction. We have seen that the discipline generates resistance to itself and tends to incorporate resistance and reform movements in order to serve its own purposes.[56] In recent decades, the new movements in legal scholarship have generated much abstract, theoretical and openly political scholarship, particularly in the pages of elite law reviews.[57] This development has bothered some judges, for it has tended to deny them both assistance and citations from elite law reviews.[58] But the discipline of law schools otherwise appears to serve the judicial system's interests rather nicely.

---

52. Cf. Chapter Three's discussion of the law school symbol of the Janus-faced neutral/politicized judge under Rituals, Symbols, Myths.

53. See David Riesman, *Toward an Anthropological Science of Law and the Legal Profession*, 57 Am. J. Soc. 121, 122–24 (1951); Chapter One's discussion of the case method.

54. See, e.g., Edward L. Rubin, *The Practice and Discourse of Legal Scholarship*, 86 Mich. L. Rev. 1835, 1847–53 (1988); Pierre Schlag, *Normativity and the Politics of Form*, 139 U. Pa. L. Rev. 801 (1991).

55. See Riesman, supra note 53, at 122.

56. See Chapters One and Four.

57. See, e.g., Edwards, supra note 40; Saks, Larsen & Hodne, supra note 23; Chapter Four's discussion of "The Academic/Political Movements."

58. See, e.g., Edwards, supra note 40.

The Organized Bar

The organized bar consists of the American Bar Association, State Bar Associations and other organizations, including state agencies, that are designed to promote or regulate the work and interests of the legal profession. The relatively specific connections between the organized bar and law schools include the licensure of lawyers, the accreditation of law schools by the ABA, the recurrent studies of legal education conducted by the ABA, and more localized connections such as a state bar's interest in obtaining continuing education services from the faculty of a state law schools. These connections generally reinforce the discipline, although at times they can produce modifications to the discipline as well.

States license lawyers to practice. But the licensing system of the different states is similar and in general implements the organized bar's interests in standardizing the production of lawyers and ensuring that new lawyers satisfy minimum quality standards.[59] State licensing requires that virtually all practicing lawyers must graduate from a law school approved by the ABA and pass a time-limited written examination on certain subjects, an examination which usually lasts for two days and employs both multiple choice and essay questions about law and its applications.[60] These conditions impose several constraints, often tacit ones, on the discipline of law schools.

First, bar examination subjects tend to be subjects which constitute the core curriculum of law schools such as contracts law, torts, property law, constitutional law, evidence and criminal law.[61] This situation imposes at least an ethical duty if not also a market imperative on law schools and their faculty to prepare students in these core curriculum subjects.[62] To be sure, if one assumes that a school's students are quick learners and effective examination-takers, this responsibility rests lightly and need not govern much of the school's curriculum, its discussions in doctrinal classrooms or its final exam-

---

59. See R. Abel, supra note 8, at 14–73.

60. See id. at 62–68, 263–64 (five states still retain a "diploma privilege" that allows the graduates of law schools in these states to obtain licenses without examination, but only a few lawyers are licensed by this route).

61. See, e.g., "41,000 Graduates Await the Test of a Lifetime," NY Times, July 23, 1993, p. B9 (nat. ed.).

62. See, e.g., American Bar Assoc., Standards for Approval of Law Schools and Interpretations, Standard 301 (a) (Oct. 1992) (hereinafter "ABA Standards") ("A law school shall maintain an educational program that is designed to qualify its graduates for admission to the bar.")

inations. But even at elite schools, where this assumption is most prevalent, the influence of bar examination subjects is evident in the required courses, the typical casebook assignments in these core courses, and the nature of final examinations, which deal with the kinds of materials and problems that will appear again on bar examinations.[63] Where the assumption about good student test-taking abilities is not made, the perceived or implicit responsibilities of law schools to prepare students for bar examinations encourage the widespread teaching of the many rules that might be covered on these exams and the widespread use of rule-oriented final examinations that replicate and provide practice for bar examinations.[64]

Secondly, there appear to be both a striking similarity and reciprocal influences between the structure of bar examinations and the structure of law school examinations. Harvard Law School may have introduced its written examinations in 1870 at least in part to improve the performance of its graduates on the written bar examinations that were started by Massachusetts and New York in that year.[65] In turn, the written essay examinations used at Harvard seem to have been the model for the adoption of similar bar examinations by other states in the late nineteenth and early twentieth centuries.[66] And today, the comprehensive nature of modern bar examinations enforces the law school's final examination system in both obvious and subtle ways. Although not often recognized, the provision of comprehensive, end-of-the-semester, time-limited, problem-solving examinations in law schools would seem to be a good way, if not the best way, to provide law students with comprehensive

---

63. See, e.g., David Chambers, *The First-Year Courses: What's There and What's Not*, in Looking At Law School 111 (S. Gillers, ed., 1984); Cynthia H. Cooper, An Insider's Guide to the Top Fifteen Law Schools (2d ed. 1990) (describing the curriculums at 15 elite law schools); E. Gordon Gee & Donald Jackson, Following the Leader? The Unexamined Consensus in Law School Curricula (1975) (describing the influence of bar examination subjects on law school curriculums).

64. Cf. Thomas Shaffer & Robert Redmount, Lawyers, Law Students and People 162–192 (1977) (describing the prevalence of rule-oriented lectures at three Indiana law schools); Kissam, supra note 16, at 463–64 (noting that the increased modern use of multiple choice questions in law school examinations parallels the multiple choice questions on bar examinations). Note too that some law professors teach "bar review courses" as a supplemental project and that this rule-oriented teaching may very well tacitly influence their teaching of doctrinal courses in law schools.

65. See R. Abel, supra note 8, at 62–63; Robert Stevens, Law School: Legal Education in America from the 1850s to the 1980s, p. 94, 105 at n. 20 (1983); Alfred Z. Reed, Training for the Public Profession of the Law 357 (1921).

66. See J. Willard Hurst, The Growth of American Law: The Law Makers 263 (1950).

practice in taking and passing state bar examinations.[67] Indeed, the practice provided by law school examinations may explain why graduates of law schools with experimental or innovative examination systems have experienced special difficulties in passing bar examinations.[68] Reciprocal effects between bar examinations and law school examinations are also evident in the increasing use of multiple-choice questions on both types of examinations.[69] Thus, to the extent law schools take seriously some ethical obligation or market imperative to prepare their students to pass bar examinations, they may wish to continue to examine students throughout the three year curriculum by means of end-of-the-semester, comprehensive, time-limited final examinations. This regimen, of course, is a critical part of the discipline and enforces the tacit lessons of analysis, property rights and an objectivist rhetoric that is grounded firmly in complex legal authorities.[70]

The most pervasive and subtle effect of bar examinations may be the way in which these examinations, as the gateway to professional practice, engender expectations among law students about what should be taught in law school. Law students typically know relatively little about legal education or legal practice when they enter law school.[71] But they do know about bar examinations. The implicit understanding that they will need some kind of comprehensive knowledge of legal rules to pass these examinations combines with our culture's more general notions of "law as rules" and "the rule of law" to produce pervasive expectations among law students that they should be taught legal doctrine rather than, say, legal process, legal theory, legal arguments, in-

---

67. Cf. Paul Carrington, *One Law: The Role of Legal Education in the Opening of the Legal Profession Since 1776*, 44 Fla. L. Rev. 501, 556 (1992) (the law school's institution of examinations was "in some measure, at least…dictated by the development of licensing examinations in the early years of the twentieth century"); Kissam, supra note 16, at 494–96 (describing the value of practice and feedback for improving performance on law school final examinations).

68. See Chester, *Reshaping First-Year Legal Doctrine: The Experience in Law Schools*, 20 Florida State L. Rev. 599, 614–15 (1993); David Margolick, *At the Bar: CUNY Law School, a Trail-blazer in Legal Education, Finds Itself at a Crossroad*, N.Y. Times, Feb. 19, 1988, at B7, col. 1 (reporting on the difficulties that CUNY-Queens law graduates have had in passing the New York state bar examination and the resulting pressure on this innovative law school to provide more traditional kinds of law school examinations).

69. See R. Abel, supra note 8, at 62–68; Kissam, supra note 16, at 463–464, esp. notes 97 & 98; (describing the increased use of multiple choice examinations in law schools); "41,000 Graduates Await the Test of a Lifetime," supra note 61 (current bar examinations typically consist of at least half multiple-choice questions).

70. See Chapter One's discussion of law school examinations.

71. See, e.g., Shaffer & Redmount, supra note 64, at 88.

terdisciplinary inquiry or social policy.[72] These expectations are a powerful force that promotes the discipline's classroom practices and tacit conceptions of law and lawyers. Bar examinations thus influence the law school's teaching methods broadly in ways that entrench the discipline's tacit lessons of analysis and an objectivist, rule-oriented discourse.

In principle, the licensure requirement that lawyers must graduate from an accredited law school grants considerable power to the ABA to regulate legal education. Historically, however, this power has been exercised mostly against marginal law schools attempting to enter or stay in the industry, and established law schools have been left pretty much alone.[73] Yet the ABA's accreditation standards reflect if they do not require crucial aspects of the discipline, and the accreditation process takes place every seven years at each law school. This process includes an elaborate "self-study" report by the law school and a subsequent visit by an accreditation team, and it provides ample opportunities for informal conversations, pointed reminders and tacit signals about the importance to the legal profession of the discipline's structures and practices.

In this perspective, the most important accreditation norms may be those concerning classroom hours and student attendance. These norms reflect and help construct the temporal rhythms of law school, especially the student rhythms of weekly time, semester time and examination time.[74] ABA standards require students to attend on average more than 13 class hours per week during their three years in law school,[75] and each school "has the burden to show it has adopted and enforces policies [which ensure] regular and punctual class attendance."[76] These ideals for legal study are modeled on undergraduate education, not graduate training. These standards probably receive

---

72. See John Henry Schlegel, *Searching for Archimedes—Legal Education, Legal Scholarship, and Liberal Ideology*, 34 J. Legal Educ. 103, 108 (1984) ("Take any group of middle-class, first-year law students and try any other approach than a doctrinal, rule-focused one. They hate the alternatives because the alternatives undercut the notion of law as specialized knowledge available only to, and for sale by, the professional lawyer.").

73. See, e.g., Paul Carrington, *Diversity!*, 1992 Utah L. Rev. 1105; Harry First, *Competition in the Legal Education Industry*, 53 NYU L. Rev. 311 (1978); *Competition in the Legal Education Industry (II): An Antitrust Analysis*, 54 NYU L. Rev. 1049 (1979).

74. See Chapter Two's discussion of the rhythms of student time.

75. ABA Standards, Standard 305. This minimum average may be reduced to about 11 class hours per week for the three year course of study "if the law school has a program that permits or requires student participation in studies or activities away from the law school or in a format that does not involve attendance at regularly scheduled class sessions." Id., Standard 306.

76. Id., Standard 305 (c)).

little formal attention in most accreditation reviews, but they do not need attention because they reflect pervasive and powerful assumptions about how law school courses should be conducted, that is, to include many class hours that allow for the oral coverage of many rules, and how law students should study, that is by attending to the oral discourse of doctrinal masters. The ABA's standards for the structure of courses and class attendance reflect and encourage the discipline's tendencies to teach impulsiveness, speed or productivity, and the instrumentalist methods of paraphrase reading and good paragraph thinking/writing.

The ABA's standards also reflect and enforce the discipline's core curriculum and its comprehensive, end-of-the-semester, time-limited final examinations. ABA standards require that law schools provide a curriculum which includes "those subjects generally regarded as the core curriculum,"[77] that they employ "written examinations" of "suitable length and complexity" to evaluate student work in all courses except clinical courses, research seminars and individual research projects,[78] and that they ensure that applicants take the Law School Admission Test (LSAT) or some other "acceptable test for the purpose of determining apparent aptitude for law study."[79] The accreditation process thus presupposes the core curriculum, which promotes ideas of rule coverage and corporate legal values,[80] and legal studies that are oriented around end-of-the-semester final examinations that lie at the heart of the discipline's tacit lessons.[81]

In addition the accreditation standards require or expect law schools to employ full-time law professors who are committed to scholarship as well as teaching,[82] who have strong academic credentials,[83] and who are permitted to engage in outside consulting work that "relate[s] to major academic interests

---

77. ABA Standards, Standard 302 (a).

78. Id., Standard 304 (b). This examination requirement has been interpreted to mean "either a written examination or term paper." Interpretations to Standard 304.

79. Id., Standard 503.

80. See Chapter One's discussion of the core curriculum.

81. See Chapter One's discussion of law school examinations and Chapter Three's discussion of the examinatorial regime.

82. ABA Standard 403 requires that students at approved law schools "shall receive substantially all of their instruction in the first year" and "a major proportion of their total instruction" from "full-time faculty members." Standard 401 requires that "members of the faculty shall possess a high degree of competence, as demonstrated by education, classroom teaching ability,…and scholarly research and writing," and Standard 404 limits the class hours of law professors to just a few hours per week, thus leaving full-time professors substantial time for scholarship.

83. See ABA Standard 401 as quoted in note 74 supra.

or enrich[es] the faculty member's capacity as scholar and teacher, or [is] of service to the public generally" as long as these consulting activities "do not interfere with one's responsibilities."[84] These standards contemplate or at the least permit a good number of the discipline's routines. Law schools should only hire faculty who have earned the best credentials as law students, which suggests that the masters of law school final examinations are likely to reproduce the same system. These examination-conscious professors should commit only limited time to their teaching, a commitment that attaches them to the discipline's case method and examination system in order to save time for scholarship.[85] Substantial consulting with outside agencies is also allowed if not encouraged, and we have seen how law faculty consulting with corporate law firms can help entrench several aspects of the discipline.[86]

The licensure and accreditation relationships between the organized bar and law schools invite a third relationship: the recurrent efforts by professional organizations and licensing bodies to study and reform legal education, particularly in those moments of "professional crisis" when economic or political conditions threaten the legitimacy and economic interests of lawyers.[87] Over the past 25 years these efforts have included proposals to reform legal education by adding trial advocacy courses, more clinical education, more writing programs, better instruction in legal ethics and better teaching of "legal professionalism."[88] The general fate of these and similar educational re-

---

84. ABA Standard 402 (b).

85. See Chapter One's discussion of the case method, law school examinations and institutions of legal scholarship, and Chapter Three's discussion of the law school's examinatorial regime and confessional technology.

86. See supra text accompanying notes 35–37.

87. See, e.g., Rayman L. Solomon, *Five Crises or One: The Concept of Legal Professionalism, 1925–1960*, in Lawyers' Ideals/Lawyers' Practices 144 (R.L. Nelson, D.M. Trubek, R.L. Solomon, eds, 1992). For a listing of the several ABA-sponsored reports on legal education that were produced from the late 1970s through the early 1990s, see John Mudd, *Academic Change in Law Schools: Part I*, 29 Gonz. L. Rev. 29, 29 n.1 (1993/94).

88. On trial advocacy courses, see, e.g., ABA Section of Legal Education and Admissions to the Bar, Report and Recommendations of the Task Force on Lawyer Competency: The Role of Law Schools 3–4, 17–18 (1979) (the "Cramton Report"); ABA Special Committee for a Study of Legal Education, Law Schools and Professional Education 63–69 (1980); on clinical education and writing programs, see, e.g., ABA Section of Legal Education and Admissions to the Bar, Report of the Task Force on Law Schools and the Profession, Legal Education and Professional Development—An Educational Continuum (the "MacCrate Report"); the Cramton Report, supra, at 3–4, 15–18; on better ethics training, see, e.g., Law Schools and Professional Education, supra, at 55–62; the MacCrate Report, supra, at 235–36; on the teaching of "professionalism," see, e.g., ABA Commission on Pro-

form proposals has been described in Chapter Four, but it is pertinent to note how this process of task force and committee studies generates tacit support for the discipline of law schools. Legal academics, often law school deans, play a substantial role in writing these reports,[89] and the reports tend to assume a common form. First they praise the discipline's core curriculum and case method for teaching the essential skills of "legal analysis" or "legal reasoning" and then, but only then, they propose supplemental additions to the law school curriculum.[90] Moreover, whenever these proposals threaten law school interests, the response of law school leaders tends to re-state the importance of the core curriculum and case method teaching, thus entrenching ideological commitments to the discipline.[91] The profession's attempts to reform legal education function something like the debates within law schools about changing the core curriculum: a hearing is provided for the discontented, relatively minor changes are proposed, and a discourse that emphasizes fundamental commitments to the discipline is maintained.[92]

Local relationships between the bar and law schools also tend to support the discipline.[93] State bars and state regulatory agencies have tried at times to influence the curriculum of local law schools, usually to obtain new required courses or new courses of particular interest to the local bar. State bar associations may seek continuing education programs from the faculty of local schools, thus encouraging lectures by faculty on the recent judicial decisions and the organization of rules in their doctrinal specialties. Local bar organizations also provide regular audiences that the deans and faculty of some schools cultivate as part of a school's fund raising, for student recruitment

---

fessionalism (the "Stanley Commission"), In the Spirit of Public Service: A Blueprint for the Rekindling of Lawyer Professionalism, 112 F.R.D. 243 (1987); the MacCrate Report, supra; ABA Section of Legal Education and Admissions to the Bar, Report of the Professionalism Committee, Teaching and Learning Professionalism (1996).

89. For example, the ABA Task Force that produced the MacCrate Report had two vice chairpersons and a reporter who were law professors, and at least 13 of the 22 members of the Task Force had had substantial experience in law teaching. See MacCrate Report, supra note 88, at v.

90. See, e.g., id. at 243 ("Many aspects of the skill of legal analysis and reasoning, an important element of professional training, have long been effectively taught through appellate case analysis.").

91. See, e.g., John Costonis, *The MacCrate Report: Of Loaves, Fishes, and the Future of American Legal Education*, 43 J. Legal Educ. 157, 167–68 (1993).

92. Cf. Chapter One's discussion of law school debates about the core curriculum.

93. Cf. R. Stevens, supra note 65, at 210 (describing regional and local law schools in the period after World War II as dependent "on the approval of the professional community in and for which it functions").

purposes or other political goals. These conversations are likely to reinforce the discipline by emphasizing student and faculty achievements in easily dramatized statements such as those that concern a rising level of student academic credentials, the quantity of recent faculty publications, or prestigious accomplishments by particular faculty and students. More informal conversations with bar leaders, like informal conversations with corporate lawyers, can also signal to the bar and law faculties that traditional elements of the discipline such as the case method, the core curriculum and the final examination/grading/class ranking system will be continued in ways that assure the public that local law schools are producing high quality lawyers.

Thus the discipline responds in a variety of ways to the concerns of the legal profession. But how well does the discipline serve the entire profession? At least three kinds of dysfunction are apparent. First, as we have seen, the discipline has accepted but substantially constrains the profession's recent calls for more legal writing, more clinics and more ethics training.[94] Second, the ABA's requirements that encourage a lot of scholarship by law professors presupposes, of course, that this scholarship will be largely aimed at serving the profession either directly, by providing legal analysis of practical problems faced by practitioners, or indirectly by enriching the education of future practitioners who are studying the law. As we shall see in the next section, however, the connections between law schools and contemporary research universities may be diverting legal scholarship from these presupposed goals, and some practitioners, like some judges, may reasonably believe that contemporary scholarship disserves their interests. Third, even when law schools comply with professional demands on legal education, this compliance in the disciplinary context may not serve the profession's best interests. Consider, for example, the relative alacrity with which law schools have implemented and expanded trial advocacy programs in response to the profession's demands of the 1970s that law students were not well trained in litigation skills. It has been observed that the overall focus of law schools on adjudication, adversarial procedures and doctrinal complexity may promote a widespread attitude among lawyers that "adversarial legalism" is the most appropriate means of resolving social disputes, an approach which tacitly inclines lawyers to recommend more law and more adversarial procedures to solve their clients' or society's problems notwithstanding the availability of more economic or more effective alternatives.[95] In the disciplinary context, then, what are the effects of adding

---

94. See Chapter Four's discussion of these professional reforms.

95. See, e.g., Robert A. Kagan, *Do Lawyers Cause Adversarial Legalism? A Preliminary Inquiry*, 19 Law & Soc. Inquiry 1 (1994); Jonathan Macey, *Civic Education and Interest*

relatively popular trial advocacy courses to the curriculum? On the one hand, they may provide a valuable form of quasi-clinical legal education. On the other hand, might not these programs help entrench an adversarial legalism that disserves both the legal profession and society?

In summary, the constraints on the discipline from the organized bar lie more deeply in the background than those established by corporate law firms and the judiciary. Moreover, to the extent that corporate lawyers influence or control professional organizations,[96] the interests that bar organizations have in legal education will reflect the interests of the corporate bar. But the organized bar purports to represent an entire profession and the bar's demands on legal education, for example, for more clinical education, may diverge from and even conflict with those from corporate law. These conflicts are evidence of the partial autonomy of law schools and the discipline that to an extent operate on their own, picking and choosing among various external constraints. We shall see in the next section how the American research university complicates this situation, adding additional conflicting demands, constraints and new possibilities for the autonomy of the discipline.

The Research University

Most law schools are located in research universities. Yet law schools appear to operate with substantial autonomy from their universities. The isolating architecture and geographical locations of most law schools support this view, as do certain demands of the legal profession and law school alumni for the law school's autonomy from its university.[97] A closer look, however, reveals significant if subtle relationships between research universities and law schools that have shifted and expanded in recent decades with important implications for the discipline. The connections between research universities and law schools influence law faculty, the abilities and expectations of law students, and the political and economic services that law schools provide to their universities.

Group Formation in the American Law School, 45 Stan. L. Rev. 1937, 1939–46 (1993); Peter H. Schuck, *Legal Complexity: Some Causes, Consequences, and Cures*, 42 Duke L.J. 1 (1992).

96. On the possibility of such control, see Terrence C. Halliday, Beyond Monopoly: Lawyers, State Crises, and Professional Empowerment (1987); R. Shamir, supra note 33.

97. See Chapter Two's discussion of spatial relationships; Lewin, supra note 29 (on alumni demands); text supra at notes 73–94 (on the legal profession's demands).

Research universities have always established general norms that influence law schools. In the late nineteenth century the American research university was founded under the general ideal that universities would become sites of "reason" and "culture." Reason was to be applied by the different academic disciplines to contest traditions and advance knowledge in the enlightenment sense of Kant, and culture was to be pursued in the dual sense of the German university: as the expansion and preservation of knowledge and as the cultivation of young minds.[98] Under this ideal, professors should be both teachers and scholars, they should commit substantial efforts to scholarship—even to give scholarship priority over their teaching, their scholarship and teaching should be integrated somehow, and their scholarship and teaching should be "theoretical" or about "reason" rather than "practical" or "applied".[99]

The modern American law school was grounded in these ideas of reason and culture, and these ideas still reverberate throughout the legal academy. In the late nineteenth century, Langdell at Harvard promoted casebooks and the case method as means of applying reason or theory to legal materials. He advocated hiring full-time professors who did not need substantial practice experience but who instead would be capable of expanding legal knowledge theoretically and teaching students this knowledge by a skillful use of the case method. He also promoted final examinations, another tactic drawn from the university, to force students to take the university study of law seriously.[100] Meanwhile, on the cultural front, Oliver Wendell Holmes, Jr. argued that the law school's mission was to provide "moral education" to an "army of specialists" who would be capable of employing technical legal concepts to restrain "democratic excesses."[101] Today, most law professors hold similar abstract ideals about promoting "theory" by their teaching and their scholarship and about cultivating students' minds by introducing them to theoretical knowledge.[102] These ideals encourage adherence to many elements of the discipline by privileging scholarship over teaching, privileging "theory" over

---

98. See Bill Readings, The University in Ruins 54–88 (1996).

99. See, e.g., Larry Cuban, How Scholars Trumped Teachers: Change Without Reform in University Curriculum, Teaching, and Research, 1890–1990 (1999) (an historical study of Stanford University); B. Readings, supra note 98.

100. See, e.g., William LaPiana, Logic and Experience: The Origin of Modern American Legal Education (1994); R. Stevens, supra note 65, at 52–54; Thomas Grey, *Langdell's Orthodoxy*, 45 U. Pitt. L. Rev. 1 (1983).

101. See Oliver Wendell Holmes, Jr., *The Use of Law Schools*, in The Essential Holmes 224 (R. Posner ed. 1992).

102. See, e.g., Mark Spiegel, *Theory and Practice in Legal Education: An Essay on Clinical Education*, 34 UCLA L. Rev. 577 (1987).

"practice" and committing law professors to the discipline's casebooks, case method and examination system as conventional devices by which they can teach law theoretically while engaging substantially in scholarly work.

In recent decades, the research university and its social norms have been transformed with corresponding implications for the discipline. Since World War II the vast expansion of external funding for university research has substantially increased both the attention and the resources that universities devote to faculty research, scholarship and training graduate students to become university faculty.[103] One consequence has been the strengthening within universities of norms that privilege scholarship over teaching and theory over practice, a process which has left the education of undergraduates by research universities as something of a poor cousin to scholarship and the training of graduate students.[104] These norms have gradually begun to influence how law professors think about their scholarship and teaching.[105] Ideas that legal scholarship must reveal new knowledge about its subject, should have a scientific, empirical or other "theoretical" basis, and is often enhanced by interdisciplinary analysis now pervade legal scholarship and, in fact, have created much controversy and uncertainty about what legal scholarship should be.[106] University norms that favor scholarship and theory are also implicated in the contemporary law professor's attempts to emulate other university professors by publishing vast quantities of scholarship, a phenomenon that surely detracts from new experiments in teaching or from committing time to individualized instruction that could help law students with diverse learning styles acquire much legal knowledge and skills.

---

103. See, e.g., Jonathan R. Cole, Elinor G. Barber & Stephen R. Graubard (eds), The Research University in a Time of Discontent (1994); Hugh Davis Graham & Nancy Diamond, The Rise of American Research Universities: Elites and Challengers in the Postwar Era (1997).

104. See, e.g., Jonathan R. Cole, *Balancing Acts: Dilemmas of Choice Facing Research Universities*, in Cole, Barber & Graubard, supra note 103, at 4, 23–28. See also Ernest L. Boyer, The Undergraduate Experience in America (1987); Scholarship Reconsidered: Priorities of the Professoriate (1990).

105. See, e.g., Christopher Jencks & David Riesman, The Academic Revolution 252–53 (1968); Francis Allen, *Legal Scholarship: Present Status and Future Prospects*, 33 J. Legal Educ. 403 (1983); Thomas Bergin, *The Law Teacher: A Man Divided Against Himself*, 54 Virgina L. Rev. 646 (1968); George Priest, *Social Science Theory and Legal Education: The Law School as University*, 33 J. Legal Educ. 437 (1983).

106. See, e.g., Priest, supra note 105; Chapter Four's discussion of the Academic/ Political Movements.

The American research university has also begun to regulate the teaching and scholarship of law faculties in ways that help entrench tacit lessons of discipline. As research universities have expanded during the past 40 years, they have imposed standards of accountability for scholarship and teaching on decisions by departments and the university that affect tenure, promotion, salary increases, research grants and new appointments.[107] For scholarship, these standards typically emphasize the prestige and quantity of one's publications.[108] For teaching, these standards are typically more open-ended but heavily focused upon numerical scores that are obtained from the formal evaluations of professors and their courses by university students.[109]

These evaluation schemes have been applied directly to law faculties by universities and have served as models for law schools that adopt their own schemes.[110] The emphasis on the quantity of publications, of course, encourages many law professors to produce conventional scholarship and to search for narrow, fragmented doctrinal issues on which they can easily say something "new" or "original." The increased competition for publication in prestigious law journals and the need to produce large amounts of scholarship also encourage legal scholars to stick closely to appellate cases that are presented by casebooks and form the basic structure of a scholarly field. Thus disciplinary practices in scholarship and teaching reinforce each other. The diminished attention to teaching caused by the new privileging of scholarship in law schools also encourages the use of disciplinary devices such as rule-oriented lectures, short answer or multiple choice examinations, and reduced attention to inquiries by students outside the classroom. The new attention to student evaluations of teaching encourages law professors to conform to the tacit disciplinary norms of entertaining students, modeling professional behavior, controlling discussions to provide information that helps students write objectively-scored, rule-oriented final examinations, and adhering to the case method to ensure that the conventional expectations of law students are satisfied. Student evaluations of law teaching thus reinforce many important aspects of the discipline.[111]

Research universities influence the supply of law students in two ways: by the nature of the undergraduate education they provide and, to a lesser ex-

---

107. See generally Joseph Centra, Determining Faculty Effectiveness (1979).

108. See Howard R. Bowen & Jack H. Schuster, American Professors: A National Resource Imperiled 147–50 (1986); Centra, supra note 107, at 11–16; 119–24.

109. See Centra, supra note 107, at 1–46.

110. See, e.g., Richard Abel, *Evaluating Evaluations: How Should Law Schools Judge Teaching?*, 40 J. Legal Educ. 407, 412–13 (1990).

111. See Chapter Three's discussion of the law school's examinatorial regime.

tent, by the influence they cast on the research and teaching orientation of other higher education institutions such as smaller liberal arts colleges that also train future law students.[112] The case method/final examination system of law schools presupposes that university-trained undergraduates will have sufficient aptitudes and skills to engage successfully, with little formal or individualized instruction, in reading and interpreting complex appellate court opinions, in understanding complicated class discussions, and in writing clearly and coherently (at times imaginatively) about legal problems buried in the complicated factual situations of final examinations. But the transformation of research universities suggests that this presupposition may not be as valid as it once was. There is evidence to suppose that many law students today are not particularly well-trained to cope with the demands of the law school's case method or its final examinations, or that they enter law school with the general skills of oral and written communication that law firms desire in their new lawyers. Many law students today may have been trained instead by their undergraduate education to understand and react to the routine practices of law schools in ways that help entrench the tacit lessons of the discipline.

The modern transformation of the American research university has two fundamental aspects: the increasing priority of research over teaching and vast expansion in the size of research universities, especially public universities, as college enrollments in the United States have more than tripled between 1960 and 1990.[113] As a result of these changes, today's research university typically provides large, impersonal classes in many or even most undergraduate subjects, a faculty that is committed primarily to research and training graduate students, an examination system that is heavily oriented towards multiple choice, objective examinations, a substantial impersonality in faculty-undergraduate relationships, and much instruction in basic writing and mathe-

---

112. Liberal arts colleges claim distinction in their attention to teaching undergraduates, but at liberal arts colleges, especially elite ones, there has also been an increasing attention to research in recent decades. See, e.g., C. Jencks & D. Riesman, supra note 105, at 12–27 (describing smaller liberal arts colleges as "university colleges" that operate under the influence of research universities); William H. Honan, "Small Liberal Arts Colleges Facing Questions on Focus," NY Times, Mar. 10, 1999, p. A16 ("The claim [that faculty at small colleges are devoted to teaching and mentoring] is only partly valid, since small college professors, like those at universities, are well aware that throughout academe, professional advancement is largely based on research and publishing and therefore are ignored at one's peril.").

113. See, e.g., George H. Douglas, Education Without Impact: How Our Universities Fail the Young 105–126 (1992); Alan Ryan, *Invasion of the Mind Snatchers*, NY Review of Books, Feb. 11, 1993, p. 13.

matics courses by graduate student teaching assistants.[114] Law students trained in this way are likely to possess significant attitudes and traits that support the discipline.

First, today's law student will have been relatively successful at meritocratic, objectivist evaluation schemes, and they are likely to be well socialized into the idea that higher education's *primary role* is to certify or allocate students into different social roles.[115] Many or most law students may think of legal education simply as a certification or allocation process that should be based upon the most objective evaluation scheme possible, and that their primary if not only purpose in law school is to obtain the best possible certification. Thus once the initial mysteries and uncertainties of learning a new technical vocabulary and grammar are dealt with, these students are likely to accept or even participate enthusiastically in the discipline's regime of final examinations, comparative grading, and precise class rankings.

Second, many law students will have had substantial experience with large classes. Some will have acquired tastes or abilities for competitive performances before authoritative professors and large numbers of peers, and many will be accustomed to attending large lecture classes (with the expectation or hope that the lectures will be entertaining) and taking rapid, voluminous notes. These experiences will have prepared law students to appreciate the kinds of classroom behavior that the discipline encourages: expository and charismatic performances by professors and by some students in large amphitheatre classrooms.[116] They will have prepared law students to take voluminous or verbatim notes in order to master the many doctrinal rules they must be ready use on final examinations. Such undergraduate experiences may be a major reason for the decline of the Socratic method in law school classrooms and its replacement by lecturing or "Socratic monologues."[117] The experiences and tastes of modern undergraduates thus support the discipline's tacit lessons of rule coverage, a rule-oriented rhetoric and charismatic lawyering.

Third, the research university hardens its students to the impersonality of bureaucratic organizations[118] and this hardening clearly supports the disci-

---

114. See, e.g., E.L. Boyer, College: The Undergraduate Experience in America, supra note 104; G.H. Douglas, supra note 113.

115. See C. Jencks & D. Riesman, supra note 105, at 61–154; Meyer, supra note 38.

116. See Chapter One's discussion of the case method.

117. On the apparent decline of the Socratic method and extensive questioning of students in contemporary law schools, see C. H. Cooper, supra note 63; T. Shaffer & R. Redmount, supra note 64 at 162–92.

118. See C. Jencks & D. Riesman, supra note 105, at 35–50; cf. Carnegie Foundation for the Advancement of Teaching, Campus: In Research of Community (1990) (reporting

pline of law schools. As we have seen, law students hesitate to invade their professors' offices, to ask much about examinations or to challenge law professors inside or outside the classroom on matters that the professor signals are within his expertise.[119] But this docility or deference to authority may have become an engrained predisposition among many students even before they enter law school.

Fourth, many law students may arrive from an undergraduate education in the research university that has not provided much experience or practice in speaking before diverse and critical academic audiences, in writing on complex topics or in reading complicated texts. These students are likely candidates for capture by the discipline's instrumentalist habits of paraphrase reading and the paradigm of good paragraph thinking/writing. In sum, the undergraduate education of many contemporary law students may tend to produce law school disciplinarians.

Another link between law schools and their universities concerns university funding and university prestige. University administrators, like law school administrators, are fundamentally engaged in raising money and enhancing the prestige of their institutions.[120] Law schools can play a special role in helping university administrators achieve these goals. Historically law schools, with large student/faculty ratios, appeared as possible "profit centers" for universities in the sense that they might bring extra prestige or extra revenues to the rest of the university by reason of their special status and a collection of revenues that exceeded their costs.[121] This revenue possibility has been limited or offset, of course, by the relatively high salaries that are paid to law professors and the operating autonomy of many law schools.[122] When such profit-taking is realized, however, the university has an incentive to maintain a large law

---

that college students invest a minimum of their time in studies); G. H. Douglas, supra note 113, at 168–82 (describing how most university students find academic work drudgery and "divide" their lives into "the drudgery" of academic work and "the good times" of parties, athletic events and just hanging out).

119. See Chapter One's discussion of the case method and Chapter Three's discussion of the law school's confessional technology.

120. See, e.g., Joan Huber, *Institutional Perspectives on Sociology*, 101 Am. J. Soc., Issue #1, pp. 194, 199–200 (July 1995) ("most academic administrators have two primary goals: to enhance any institution's prestige and ensure its survival").

121. See, e.g., Robert L. Potts, *Too Many Lawyers, Too Few Jobs*, Chron. Higher Ed., Feb. 2, 1996, p. B1, B2 ("a new law school brings to a campus more students, faculty members, money, prestige and affluent alumni....as president of a university without a law school, I can testify that the temptation to create a law school is great").

122. See Carrington, supra note 73, at 1179–93; First, supra note 73, Parts I & II.

student-to-law faculty ratio, and the large classes that ensue help entrench the discipline by inviting the dramatic and sometimes traumatic disciplinary practices of large amphitheatre classrooms and traditional kinds of final examinations. The maintenance of a law school to enhance its university's prestige encourages other disciplinary practices such as the proliferation of law faculty scholarship, an insistence upon high LSAT scores for entering law students and the demand for prestigious academic and professional credentials for new law faculty.

The revenue-raising and prestige-enhancing roles of modern law schools in the research university have more subtle consequences too. For private universities, law school deans and faculty may often be well situated to aid university administrators in the complicated business of university image-making and the solicitation of donations that occur through intimate contacts with distinguished alumni of the university. For public universities, which typically are dependent on state governments for funding, law school deans and professors may be even more essential to university fund raising because of their contacts or consulting work with distinguished members of the state bar and leaders of the state legislature. These special roles in university fund raising invite or sanction law professors who provide substantial amounts of consulting to well-connected law firms or important government agencies and who provide continuing education services to the legal profession. These activities help establish and nurture those delicate political relationships that universities hope to enjoy with their actual and potential funding agents. Such consulting and continuing education work, of course, seems bound to strengthen the doctrinal commitments of law faculty, thus reinforcing the rule-oriented aspects of the discipline and keeping faculty away from any new experiments in teaching or from committing more time to individualized instruction. Thus university fund raising contributes tacitly to the discipline of law schools.

Finally, the dramatic expansion of American universities has supported a concomitant expansion of law schools that has strengthened the discipline in several ways. The enrollment in law schools nearly quadrupled between 1960 and 1990, with much of this expansion taking place at non-elite law schools in the 1960s and 1970s.[123] New and expanding law schools tended to hire new faculty who were graduates of elite law schools, thus incorporating "the theory" of the elite schools in this period, which was the theory of legal process or reasoned elaboration, into both teaching and scholarship

---

123. See R. Abel, supra note 8, at 278–79.

at many non-elite schools.[124] The theory of legal process emphasizes the special character and relative autonomy of legal arguments from social contexts and other academic disciplines, and these ideas have reinforced the disciplinary practices of classrooms, examinations and conventional legal scholarship that display these characteristics. Moreover, the enlarged legal professoriate simultaneously became more productive in its scholarship. This productivity has dramatically increased the competition for publishing articles in prestigious law reviews,[125] to say nothing of competition for appointments to more prestigious or better paying law schools.[126] Thus the new faculty hired by expanding law schools and ensuing competitions among this faculty have strengthened the discipline's tacit privileging of scholarship over teaching and theory over practice. The expansion of law schools itself, like the expansion of American research universities, has helped construct the discipline of law schools.

How well does the discipline serve the research university? The explicit demands that research universities place on law schools (for scholarship, teaching or fund raising) and other relationships between universities and law schools are relatively general and open-ended. Law schools still have substantial discretion to satisfy their universities in a variety of ways, and in this light the discipline probably serves the research university quite adequately. Yet conversely, the relationships or tacit demands that run from the research university directly to the discipline are more specific and capable of influencing numerous aspects of the discipline. Like corporate firms, the judicial system and the organized bar, the practices of the American research university have contributed significantly to the construction of the discipline.

---

124. See Fossum, supra note 20 (describing law faculty recruitment patterns in the 1960s and 1970s); Glicksman, supra note 20 (arguing that the selection of faculty from elite law schools has stifled diversity). On the theory of legal process or reasoned elaboration, which dominated American law schools for 20 to 25 years after World War II, see Edward White, *The Evolution of Reasoned Elaboration: Jurisprudential Criticism and Social Change*, 59 Va. L. Rev. 279 (1973).

125. See, e.g., Erik M. Jensen, *The Law Review Manuscript Glut: The Need for Guidelines*, 39 J. Legal Educ. 383 (1989).

126. See Philip C. Kissam, *The Decline of Law School Professionalism*, 134 U. Pa. L. Rev. 251, 270 (1986). cf. Mark Tushnet, *Legal Scholarship: Its Causes and Cure*, 90 Yale L. J. 1205, 1207 n. 13 (1981) (describing the upwardly-mobile desires of elite law school faculty).

The State and Culture

Legal education responds in diffuse ways to changes and developments in the American state, political culture and social culture. These responses are less tangible, less predictable and often more transient than the responses of law schools to the external institutions we have just examined. But law school responses to these broader influences can affect the discipline, at times in permanent ways and more frequently by altering disciplinary practices for the short term.

Consider first how major changes in the American state and political culture have affected law schools. The ideas of Langdell and Holmes that influenced legal education in the nineteenth century[127] were part of a larger conservative "moral reform" movement in American politics and intellectual life following the Civil War that sought order and discipline in a rapidly changing society.[128] Legal Realism in the 1920s and 30s was influenced by Progressive ideas,[129] and many prominent realist professors worked for the federal government during the New Deal.[130] After World War II, the general political and intellectual optimism in government actions and the social sciences supported development of formal interdisciplinary research programs in law schools.[131] Similarly, contemporary changes in the American state and political culture appear to be having effects on law school practices.

Sometime between the New Deal and 1960s, the discourse of American politics and government shifted basically from "a discourse of law" to "a discourse of economics."[132] That is, the concerns of American politics about limitations imposed on government agencies and private organizations by constitutional and statutory law lost their prominence to competing concerns about individual and corporate self-interests, economic efficiency and eco-

---

127. See supra text accompanying notes 100–01.

128. See George M. Frederickson, The Inner Civil War: Northern Intellectuals and the Crisis of the Union 183–216 (1965).

129. See John Henry Schlegel, *American Legal Realism and Empirical Social Science: From the Yale Experience*, 28 Buffalo L. Rev. 459 (1979).

130. See R. Shamir, supra note 33, at 131–74.

131. See, e.g., John Henry Schlegel, American Legal Realism and Empirical Social Science 238–57 (1995).

132. See Theodore J. Lowi, *The State in Political Science: How We Become What We Study*, 86 Am. Pol. Sci. Rev. 1 (March 1992). Cf. Bruce Ackerman, Reconstructing American Law (1984) (describing how modern federal legislation has brought economic thought into practical legal discourse).

nomic growth. The upper class curriculum of law schools is quite sensitive to changes in statutory law, and the new prominence of economic issues in political discourse has gradually seeped into the discourse of law schools. The precise mechanisms of this dispersal are difficult to trace, as they include political speeches, campaigns, platforms, political news, editorials, social science criticisms of legislation, legislative committee reports, judicial opinions and finally legal scholarship, casebooks and the law and economics movement in law schools. Clearly though a significant consequence of this dispersal has been support for the law and economics movement in establishing its place in contemporary legal scholarship and law school courses.[133] More generally, whenever debates occur about conflicts between economic rights and other rights, in law schools or elsewhere, the emphasis of our contemporary political discourse on "economics" tacitly inclines these debates towards the consideration and protection of economic rights, thus reinforcing the discipline's tacit messages of conservative and corporate legal values.[134]

A more recent change in American political culture may also be affecting the discipline. The historian Charles Maier has recently argued that the end of the Cold War has produced a "moral crisis of democracy."[135] In his view, periods of moral crisis in democracies display three characteristics. These periods "are marked by a feeling of historical aftermath and disorientation" at the end of great world-making events. They reveal "a broad distrust of political representatives regardless of ideology," and "are marked most profoundly by seismic shifts in intellectual orientation and social thought" that cast doubts on social reforms and favor "conservative critiques of mass politics."[136] If Maier is correct and this moral crisis in our political culture is long-lasting, it could have several significant consequences for the discipline of law schools.

First, political and intellectual disorientation and "seismic shifts" in our political culture promise to support the proliferation of diverse intellectual trends in law schools, thus supporting and further fracturing the kinds of academic/political movements we considered in Chapter Four. Disorientation or

---

133. See, e.g., Symposium, *The Place of Economics in Legal Education*, 33 J. Legal Educ. 183 (1983); Chapter Four's discussion of law and economics.

134. Cf. William E. Connolly, Politics and Ambiguity 17–51 (1987) (describing how the policy value of economic growth has become a "system imperative" which automatically trumps competing policy values in modern political discourse).

135. Charles S. Maier, *Democracy and Its Discontents*, Foreign Affairs, July/Aug. 1994, p. 48.

136. Id. at 54–56.

diversity in legal thought is likely to reinforce major aspects of the discipline in two rather different ways. It would presumably increase the unresolved contradictory messages in the discourse of law schools that generate the tacit message "there is no law there." It would also provide new opportunities for dissidents in law schools to work on their special forms of politics without abandoning the tacit values that attach them to the discipline's basic practices.[137]

Secondly, "conservative critiques of mass politics" in our political culture support several disciplinary lessons. Law students enamored of these critiques are likely to pay more attention to the private law curriculum that protects property rights, thus supporting the discipline's teaching of corporate legal values and its implicit privileging of property rights over competing claims. In the public law curriculum of subjects like constitutional law, administrative law and criminal law, both professors and students influenced by the conservative critiques may tend to favor (tacitly if not also expressly) doctrines that resemble "clear" property and contract rules such as the new textualist and new originalist theories of statutory and constitutional interpretation. The influence of conservative critiques also may cause many law students to shy away (at least tacitly) from valuable training in law school clinics, or to ignore or dismiss ethical considerations that would question the discipline's idea of the lawyer as an amoral servant of clients. These conservative critiques also will incline law school debates about what law should be, tacitly if not expressly, towards protecting property rights and ideas of economic efficiency. As William Connolly has argued, a new distinctive ideology has risen across our contemporary political spectrum which promotes economic growth as a "system imperative" that automatically trumps any competing policy values.[138] As a backdrop to the discourse of law schools, this economistic ideology supports the privileging of many of the discipline's tacit conservative values.

There are also more immediate practical relationships between law schools and the State. Legislatures continuously produce statutes and administrative agencies new rules, and these laws, like the appellate opinions of courts, encourage many law professors to pay constant attention to the development of legal doctrines. Legislative committees and administrative agencies also hire law professors for short term work or consulting, which tends to bind professors to the doctrinal knowledge for which they are hired and to the doctrinal developments in which they participate. These relationships, somewhat like

---

137. Cf. Chapter Four's discussion of the academic/political movements in modern law schools.

138. See W. Connolly, supra note 134.

consulting work with private law firms, tacitly encourage commitments to the discipline's lessons of analysis, rule-coverage and rule-oriented rhetoric.[139]

Finally, we should consider the relationships between law schools and social culture. The most significant of these relationships recently have been the effects on law schools of the legal and cultural revolutions in America that brought women, persons of color and other persons with distinctive perspectives into law schools in substantial numbers. The discipline, in other words, has had to confront many persons who are different from the "classic law student" and "classic law professor" who historically were white, male, presumably straight and drawn from the professional and other middle classes of America.[140]

One consequence of this confrontation has been the emergence of movements like feminist jurisprudence and critical race theory. More generally, the presence in law schools of women, persons of color, gays, lesbians and other persons with distinctive backgrounds, styles, interests and perspectives has supported many kinds of resistance to the discipline. Members of these groups have recorded their dissatisfactions with legal education, experimented with new sorts of teaching, and developed prominent critiques of law schools.[141] These critiques focus on how the discipline's case method, its examinations and its discourse tend to alienate "outsiders", to silence them within law schools and possibly to discriminate against them by failing to recognize their

---

139. Cf. R. Shamir, supra note 33, at 131–74 (arguing that Legal Realism as a reform movement lost its intellectual and radical edges when many prominent members of this movement began to work for federal agencies during the New Deal).

140. Compare Wayne Thielens, Jr., The Socialization of Law Students 18–56 (1980) (describing the family backgrounds of the all male entering class of Columbia Law School in 1953) with Richard H. Chused, *The Hiring and Retention of Minorities and Women on American Law School Faculties*, 137 U. Pa. L. Rev. 537 (1988).

141. See, e.g, R. Granfield, supra note 36, at 94–122 (analyzing the contradictions and discomforts experienced by women and working class students at Harvard Law School and finding these concerns associated with a greater idealism among these groups than among other Harvard students); Derrick Bell, Jr, *Law School Exams and Minority-Group Students*, 7 Black L. J. 304 (1981–82) (analyzing cultural limitations on African-American law students); Kimberle Williams Crenshaw, *Foreward: Toward a Race-Conscious Pedagogy in Legal Education*, 11 Nat. Black L. J. 1 (1989) (describing particular hurdles faced by minority law students and a teaching approach to alleviate these hurdles); Lani Guinier, Michelle Fine & Jane Balin, *Becoming Gentlemen: Women's Experiences at One Ivy League Law School*, 143 U. Pa. L. Rev. 1 (1994) (describing and analyzing the experiences of women students at the University of Pennsylvania Law School); Catherine Weiss & Louise Melling, *The Legal Education of Twenty Women*, 40 Stan. L. Rev. 1299 (1988) (describing the alienation of twenty women students at Yale Law School).

interests in law or by distributing disproportionately low grades to particular groups.[142] For example, groups of women students have reported their substantial alienation from the routine practices of law school.[143] The causes of this alienation are undoubtedly complex but they appear to include instances of overt and covert discrimination, much tacit or unconscious discrimination (for example, by questioning or talking with male and female law students in different ways) and perhaps different ways of talking, thinking, reading and writing among men and women.[144]

The relationships between outsider groups and the discipline are thus full of ambivalence and tension. On the one hand, the discipline's norms that tacitly induce conformity to particular attitudes, ideas and behavior can help many law students, including outsiders, begin to acquire certain legal skills and professional conventions in an economical manner.[145] On the other hand, basic elements of the discipline such as large case method classes and final examinations may be important causes of the alienation, low motivation, low self-esteem, silencing and relatively low grades that members of the outsider groups are experiencing. In this situation it is not surprising that the recommendations of outsider critiques, like most reform ideas in law school, tend to call only for supplemental changes at the margins of the discipline such as less use of the case method, smaller classes, experimental seminars and the like.[146]

---

142. For an overview of the specific studies to date of law schools and gender, the alienation that has been reported by women students, and the issue of possible discrimination against women law students in terms of grades, see American Bar Association, Commission on Women in the Profession, Don't Just Hear It Through the Grapevine: Studying Gender Questions at Your Law School (1998).

143. See, e.g., Guinier et. al, supra note 141; Weiss & Melling, supra note 141.

144. See Weiss & Melling, supra note 141; cf. Sandra Janoff, *The Influence of Legal Education on Moral Reasoning*, 76 Minn. L. Rev. 193 (1991) (comparing the "rule-oriented reasoning capabilities" of first year men and women law students at one school, which shows that the rule-oriented capabilities of men exceeded that of women at the beginning of the year but that, by the end of the first year, men and women law students demonstrated no difference in rule-oriented reasoning); Elizabeth Flynn, *Gender and Reading*, 45 College English 236 (1983) (describing male college students as attempting to "dominate" the texts they read while women students try rather to "interact" with the same texts); Elizabeth Flynn, *Composing as a Woman*, 39 College Composition and Communication 423, 427 (1988) (describing narrative writing by male college students as "stories of achievement, of separation" and narrative writing by women college students as "stories of interaction, of connection").

145. See, e.g., Janoff, supra note 144 (describing a tacit acquisition of "rule-oriented reasoning capabilities" by first year women law students equal to those of men).

146. See, e.g., Crenshaw, supra note 141 (experimental seminars); Guinier et al, supra note 141 (less case method and smaller classes).

The modern diversity of law students and law professors may also have been an important if tacit factor in many of the shifts in routine practices of law schools that have occurred gradually in recent decades.[147] One suspects, for example, that much of the expansion in law school writing opportunities and law school clinics has been fueled by the increasing presence of women and persons of color in law schools who have become dissatisfied with more traditional elements of the discipline.[148] Thus, although the discipline appears to erect a variety of special hurdles for outsiders, the discipline has been subject to gradual changes and modifications by these outsiders.

We might conclude that relationships between the discipline and shifts in American culture are too ineffable to support firm conclusions about specific influences or likely changes in the discipline of law schools. It does appear, though, that recent shifts in American politics and culture are providing significant support for disciplinary values and, perhaps, some grounds for transformative changes. This soft conclusion frames the main topics of the next chapter: the possibility for ethical judgments and decisions that might alter the discipline of law schools, and the even more substantial possibility that ethical decisions shaped by the discipline are likely to oppose such changes.

---

147. For a description of these changes, see Jay Feinman, *The Future History of Legal Education*, 29 Rutgers L. J. 475 (1998).

148. Cf. Marina Angel, *The Glass Ceiling for Women in Legal Education: Contract Positions and the Death of Tenure*, 50 J. Legal Educ. 1 (2000); Chused, supra note 140 (describing how much of the recent hiring of women and minority law faculty has occurred disproportionately in clinical and legal writing positions).

Chapter Six

Ethics

"Selfhood and the good, or in another way selfhood and morality, turn out to be inextricably intertwined themes."
— Charles Taylor, Sources of the Self 3

"The self is not a passive entity"
— Anthony Giddens, Modernity and Self-Identity 2

How should we evaluate the discipline of law schools? This will depend, of course, upon the discipline's consequences and the moral perspectives of the evaluator. But evaluation of the discipline by any inhabitant or former inhabitant of law schools is complicated by the fact that the discipline itself may have influenced the self and ethics of the evaluator. There is, in other words, a problem of circularity. This is much like the problem of trying to avoid distortion from one's own ideology when assessing ideologies, because all ideologies distort understanding.[1]

These considerations suggest that we explore the ethics of the discipline in three stages. First, I shall sketch the major consequences of the discipline for lawyers, law students and law professors. Then I will explore several moral perspectives that might be brought to bear in evaluating the discipline, and how the discipline is likely to shape, influence and constrain these perspectives. Significantly, the discipline of law schools appears to shape or reward particular conceptions of the self and ethics that support and reinforce the discipline. These conceptions of the self and ethics favor strictly circumscribed domains of ethical inquiry, domains which allow one to think that virtually all issues about law, lawyering and legal education are technical issues devoid of ethical implications. This view of ethics substantially limits the kinds of questions that are legitimate to ask in evaluating the discipline or law. In this view, the basic purposes and methods of legal education and law are assumed or privileged, and the only legitimate questions tend to be technical questions

---

1. See Paul Ricoeur, Lectures on Ideology and Utopia 21–266 (1986).

about how legal education might make students better analysts of existing legal doctrines or could introduce more rationality into law or law practices.

In the third stage, I shall follow Paul Ricoeur's advice for evaluating ideology and in essence "declare a utopia" in order to evaluate the discipline of law schools, understanding of course that this utopian perspective itself will have been influenced by the discipline.[2] This perspective is based on what we might call *a dissident conception* of the self and ethics, and this evaluation of the discipline will serve two fundamental purposes. One purpose is to suggest *idealistic* but *realistic* pathways towards a more diverse, more effective and more democratic education of lawyers.[3] These alternative pathways will help us evaluate the discipline, and they may also encourage ethical decisions, first by individuals and then by law schools, that could improve legal education. The other purpose is explanatory rather than normative. This utopian contrast to the discipline will help us understand the attractions that the discipline may have for many persons when they are confronted by a stark vision of alternative educational practices.

Major Consequences of the Discipline

We have seen how the routine practices, habits and tacit knowledge of law schools have several significant effects. Some of these will be considered positive effects from just about any moral perspective, while others may usually be thought to have negative value. Still others, perhaps the most important ones, will be evaluated differently depending upon the evaluator's perspective. In this section I shall summarize the major consequences of the discipline without attempting an overall evaluation. Any overall assessment must wait upon the ethical analysis in the subsequent sections of the chapter.

---

2. See id. at 165–80, 269–314. Ricoeur states specifically that

"This is my conviction: the only way to get out of the circularity in which ideologies engulf us is to assume a utopia, declare it, and judge an ideology on this basis. Because the absolute onlooker is impossible, then it is someone within the process itself who takes the responsibility for judgment. It may also be more modest to say that the judgment is always a point of view—a polemical point of view though which claims to assume a better future for humanity—and a point of view which declares itself as such." Id. at 172–73.

3. Ricoeur argues that a useful political utopia "is not only a dream but *a dream that wants to be realized.* It directs itself toward reality; it shatters reality" or, in other words, "all utopias have the ambiguity of claiming to be realizable but at the same time of being works of fancy, the impossible." Id. at 289, 301 (emphasis added).

First, the discipline inculcates a group of intellectual attitudes or skills that appear to be important to conventional legal practices. Among these are the attitudes and skills of *analysis*, that is the skill of dividing legal materials into useful relevant parts, of *precision* in handling complex legal details, of *skepticism* about the meanings of words, intentions or "facts," and of *confidence* in treating and resolving complex or controverted legal issues. The discipline also inculcates an attitude of *toughness* that involves setting aside emotions, personal relationships or ethical qualms in order to get the job done in a technically competent manner. Of course, lawyers at their best will employ these attitudes and skills in combination or in balance with other attitudes and skills such as empathy for other persons, an ability to synthesize or interpret complex events, an aesthetic appreciation for simplicity and a commitment to doctrinal or ethical rules, obligations and aspirations. A major question, then, is whether the discipline's routine practices, habits and tacit knowledge allow and, more importantly, encourage the inhabitants of law schools to acquire appropriate combinations of these manifold skills and attitudes.

Second, the discipline tacitly inculcates the instrumentalist reading and writing habits of *paraphrase reading* and *good paragraph thinking/writing*. These habits are generated by the routines of casebook readings, examination preparations and examination writing, and they are reinforced by the discipline's more general emphases upon productivity and oral performances. These habits provide a certain efficiency in carrying out routine law school work and they may provide a similar efficiency in carrying out many aspects of legal work. But these instrumentalist kinds of reading, writing and thinking need to be balanced with a lawyer's abilities to engage in more complicated sorts of reading, writing and thought. It must be asked whether the discipline encourages law school inhabitants to develop these other skills in appropriate combination with the instrumentalist practices of paraphrase reading and good paragraph thinking/writing.

Third, the discipline tacitly privileges a group of *conservative values*, including the values of property, order, certainty, precedent, technique and the status quo, and a conservative attitude of both skepticism and apathy towards any ideas of binding law, political ideals or ethics. This privileging tacitly inclines participants in law school discussions towards taking conservative positions on many issues without open or full deliberation and tacitly supports the generation of conservative political ideologies. Of course, many express arguments are made in law schools against these conservative values, but the discipline tilts the debate in favor of conservative positions by establishing strong tacit presumptions or burdens of proof that favor these positions.

Fourth, the discipline embodies a rather unruly discourse of *unresolved contradictory messages* about legal rules, legal theories and legal behavior. Understanding and sorting out these kinds of conflicting messages can be an important legal skill. Within the disciplinary context, however, these messages tend to inculcate the powerful tacit message that "there is no law there" in the sense that there are no binding rules or obligations on individuals, lawyers or judges. In this tacit conception, both the dominant view of lawyers as amoral technical servants of their clients and the common view that judges are free to make law politically as they wish flourish and become privileged over other views of the lawyer's and judge's roles that depend on some sense that law obligates persons.[4] In other words, the discipline tacitly or quietly promotes particular contested theories of law and lawyers by first generating and then leaving unresolved a confusing mix of contradictory messages about what law is and what lawyers do.

Fifth, the discipline of law schools promotes *an overall image* of the lawyer as a quick, productive, error-free and tough or combative intellectual warrior, and this image discourages the participation of lawyers in open-ended, risk-taking deliberations about ethical, moral and political issues. This image and the related practices that surround it seem powerful enough to influence the character of many lawyers. Furthermore, as we shall see in the next section, this image is consistent with, supported by and supportive of particular conceptions of the self and ethics that are prevalent in law schools and promoted by the discipline of law schools. These conceptions of the self and ethics, like the overall image of lawyers, discourage the participation of lawyers in open-ended, risk-taking deliberations about ethical, moral and political issues.

Finally, the discipline treats many law students rather poorly. The case method and final examination system appear to confuse and alienate many students. The grading/class ranking system of most law schools provides insufficient and potentially damaging feedback to students about their potential as lawyers and persons. The discipline's practices also may create undue obstacles for many outsiders such as women or persons of color. There is evidence too that many students fail to acquire the basic legal skills of statutory analysis, case analysis and the general communicative/thinking skills that legal employers expect, to say nothing of specific knowledge and experience that would serve lawyers who work outside the realms of corporate law. Most significantly, the discipline tends to impose a one-size-fits-all model of legal ed-

---

4. For different conceptions of lawyers' ethics and how the realist view of law as politically constructed rules supports the dominant view of lawyers as amoral servants of their clients, see William H. Simon, The Practice of Justice: A Theory of Lawyers' Ethics (1998). For a comparison of different conceptions of law and the judge's role, see Ronald Dworkin, Law's Empire (1986).

ucation on all students. This model of technical doctrinal analysis serves corporate law firms, if not optimally, but it tends to ignore the more complicated, more critical and more imaginative methods of law that should be a central part of the general training of all lawyers. It also tends to ignore or discount much training for the diffuse kinds of other legal practices in which many law students, especially those at non-elite law schools, will practice.[5]

In order to evaluate the discipline of law schools and its consequences, we will of course bring our own ethical or moral perspectives to bear on the evaluation. These perspectives, however, can be shaped or influenced by the discipline. Thus, let us consider how the discipline may influence different conceptions of self and ethics before we attempt any overall evaluation.

Possible Selves, Possible Ethics

Charles Taylor has argued that conceptions of the self and ethical perspectives are "inextricably intertwined themes," in essence because ethical conduct is not only justified by ethical thought but also motivated by "moral sources" such as ideas of God, nature and human agency that have a common location in some conception of the self.[6] In his magisterial work, *Sources of the Self*, Taylor articulates several fundamental conceptions of the self and related ethical frameworks that have been developed throughout the history of Western thought.[7] In this section I shall use these conceptions to help clarify how the discipline of law schools can influence ethical evaluations of itself and of other legal matters. Let us consider five basic conceptions of the self and ethics and the likely relationships between these conceptions and the discipline.

Taylor's analysis of eighteenth century thought begins with "the Radical Enlightenment" and its "ideal of the disengaged self."[8] This self attempts to disengage its reasoning from all thoughts and feelings about God, nature, other selves, or one's desires and emotions in order to think in dispassionate, instrumentalist and objective ways about how one best might pursue one's own goals. The moral sources of this Disengaged Self include a deep if tacit faith in the powers of the isolated human individual, and this self's ethics is a type of utilitarianism or the counting of the utilities and disutilities for particular individuals. In Taylor's account, the Disengaged Self and its instrumentalist

---

5. See Chapter Five's discussion of the diffuse influence of legal practices.
6. Charles Taylor, Sources of the Self 3–52, 91–105 (1989).
7. See id.
8. See id. at 21, 321–54.

rationality, disengaged perspectives and utilitarian ethics have been prominent in modern American life, and this conception of the self and ethics has played an important role in the development of modern capitalism, bureaucratic organizations and large-scale politics. Organizations operate efficiently with owners, managers and workers who can apply disengaged or dispassionate means-ends reasoning.[9]

Two other basic conceptions of the self and ethics developed in reaction to the Radical Enlightenment's ideal of the Disengaged Self. One has its roots in Judaic and Christian thought and was given secular form and prominence by Immanuel Kant. We might call this conception the "Moral Self," although this self has two fundamentally different versions that stem from different moral sources. This self views individuals as "moral/rational agents," in other words, as decision-making agents who desire to act morally for good reasons and who possess a rationality that assesses ends as well as means.[10] This self finds its moral sources in different combinations of God, nature and ideas of human agency, and it may have either religious or secular foundations. The Moral Self seeks "moral freedom" by following duties that are prescribed by the rules or principles of moral codes. These codes are developed by reasoning about the principles of justice (the secular or Kantian Moral Self) or by reasoning combined with divine revelation that directs the wills of human agents (the religious Moral Self). The rights and duties under these moral codes are foundational for the Moral Self, and this self too has influenced much Western thought, politics and political philosophy. Taylor, for example, notes the influence of Christian thought about the essential commonality of humans in motivating the English and American abolitionist movements.[11] The influence of Kant's concept of moral/rational human agents on modern theories of political liberalism, the rule of law and social justice is similarly well-recognized.[12]

Disengaged and Moral Selves have some common characteristics that are important to the relationships between them and the discipline. Both conceptions are prominent in public life and public discourse and thus are likely to influence law schools from the outside, for example, by constituting the basic ethical frameworks of many entering students. Both conceptions embody strong notions of rationality, individuality and universality which fit closely with the rule-oriented, analytical and rationalistic practices of the dis-

---

9. See id. at 458.

10. See id. at 363–67.

11. See id. at 397–99.

12. See, e.g., Robert Nozick, Anarchy, State and Utopia (1974); John Rawls, A Theory of Justice (1971); Michael Sandel, Liberalism and the Limits of Justice (1982).

cipline's case method, discourse, final examination/ grading/class ranking system, examinatorial regime and conventional doctrinal scholarship. For instance, the exclusive focus of the Disengaged Self on reasoning about means that best serve given ends approximates the discipline's tacit vision of the lawyer as an amoral technician who serves client interests. The emphasis of the Moral Self on rights and duties under codified rules approximates the discipline's tacit vision of law as infinitely expanding compartments of rules that entail a rule-oriented rhetoric and discourse. The Moral Self's emphasis on the rights and duties prescribed by codified rules also approximates the dominant view of legal ethics that lawyers act ethically as long as they satisfy the rules in professionally sanctioned ethical codes that are emphasized in law school courses on legal ethics. The relationships between Disengaged or Moral Selves and the discipline are thus likely to be mutually reinforcing. Many individuals will bring these conceptions to law school and be inclined to make ethical choices that approve major aspects of the discipline. The discipline's practices in turn will tacitly generate or reinforce these conceptions as "accurate" or "useful" conceptions of what the self and ethics should be.

Disengaged and Moral Selves are also based on the common idea of the "autonomous individual" or "unencumbered self," and they promote the autonomy of individuals by limiting the scope of their ethical rules and duties to relatively narrow "public" or "moral" domains.[13] This limitation significantly creates a relatively large domain of "private" discourse and action in which an individual's choices are solely a matter of personal judgment, interests, tastes or gratification. Disengaged and Moral Selves are thus likely to leave most choices about legal education and the law to the individual judgments or tastes of law professors, students and lawyers, to characterize many ethical or collective deliberations about educational and legal choices as either irrelevant or uninteresting, and to limit ethical deliberations about law school practices to occasional decisions that must be made about the curriculum or basic criteria for hiring faculty or admitting students. Similarly, Disengaged and Moral Selves are likely to ignore many moral and ethical arguments about what the law and ethical lawyering should be or to consign these arguments to "legislative" arenas outside the immediate practice of law by lawyers and judges.

The prevalence of Disengaged and Moral Selves in law schools helps explain the marked tendency of American law professors to perceive their choices about what to teach, how to teach, and what kinds of scholarship or service

---

13. See Seyla Benhabib, Situating the Self: Gender, Community and Postmodernism in Contemporary Ethics 71–76, 89–113, 148–178 (1992); M. Sandel, supra note 12.

to perform as *technical choices* only and not also as *ethical choices* about how one should act towards other persons and define one's self. This tendency allows many educational choices in law schools to be made unreflectively, by instincts, habits and conventions that tacitly support the reproduction of the discipline.[14]

The second fundamental alternative to the Disengaged Self is grounded in the Romantic reaction to the Radical Enlightenment. Like Kant, Jean Jacques Rousseau and the romantic philosophers and artists of the early nineteenth century drew on ideas about nature, including human nature, to articulate their conceptions of the self and ethics. The Romantics, however, looked at nature more broadly and drew more radical conclusions than Kant about human nature and the physical world. Their ideas tended to decenter the rational powers of the self and to emphasize the human emotions, human creativity, imagination, the social and creative roles of language, and the self's relations to other individuals and nature. The Romantics began to conceive of selves as artistic creations that should be aimed at "expressing" the "inner voices" or "impulses" of nature which can disclose truth and make judgments by exercising the passions, imagination and creativity as well as rationality.[15] In Taylor's words, the Romantics recognized "a new and fuller individuation" in the sense that "each individual is different and original, and that this originality determines how he or she ought to live."[16] The ethical frameworks of Romantic or Expressive Selves thus incorporate the emotions, language, aesthetics, historical communities, and relationships with the concretely different Other (that is, other selves or other nature) in addition to reasoning about means and ends. The ethical frameworks of Expressive Selves can also expand the domain of moral deliberations and may blur or break down the boundaries between public and private spheres of thought and action. The ethical prescriptions of Expressive Selves vary more widely than the prescriptions of Disengaged and Moral Selves, who rely exclusively on different forms of reason and draw sharp lines between public and private spheres.

There are certainly traces of romantic ethical thought within the contemporary reform movements in law schools. For instance, the law and literature movement relies on aesthetic principles, ethical principles and a careful attention to human relationships and emotions in reading and interpreting legal

---

14. Cf. Philip C. Kissam, *The Ideology of the Case Method/Final Examination Law School*, 70 U. Cinn. L. Rev. 137 (2001) (analyzing the ideological factors that help reproduce the discipline's case method and final examinations).

15. C. Taylor, supra note 6, at 355–63, 368–90.

16. Id. at 375.

texts.[17] Clinical legal education emphasizes the individualized features of lawyer-client and student-supervisor relationships and incorporates concerns about the emotions, "original individuals" and the ethical obligations that are implicated by face-to-face relationships between concretely different individuals.[18] The interests of critical race theory and feminist jurisprudence in writing narratives about concrete situations to illuminate, criticize and reform law[19] and in emphasizing the role of emotions in making legal arguments or judgments[20] are other important instances that reveal the influence of romantic ethics and the Expressive Self.

The possibilities for Expressive Selves and Romantic ethical thought in American life and law schools are significantly constrained, however, by another fundamental conception of the self. Charles Taylor describes John Stuart Mill's attempt to reconcile the demands that Mill felt "for the most austere disengaged reason," which he inherited from Jeremy Bentham's utilitarianism, with his need "for a richer sense of meaning, which he ultimately found through the Romantic poets."[21] Mill's resolution of this dilemma, Taylor says, was to adopt a conception of the Disengaged Self and its instrumental reasoning for the *public spheres* of commerce and politics while reserving personal space for an Expressive Self and its aesthetics, sentiment and passion for the Other in the *private spheres* of Mill's life. Mill's resolution, we might say, was to construct a Dualistic Self that combined a Disengaged Self for action in public spheres with an Expressive Self for one's life in private spheres. This Dualistic Self, in Taylor's words, represents "one form of a widespread attempt to integrate Romantic notions of personal fulfillment into the private lives of the denizens of a civilization run more and more by the canons of instrumental reason."[22] In this way, "the wheels of industry [that are guided by the instrumentalist reasoning and utilitarian calculus of Disengaged Selves] turn

---

17. See, e.g., R. Dworkin, supra note 4; Martha C. Nussbaum, Poetic Justice: The Literary Imagination and Public Life (1995); James Boyd White, When Words Lose Their Meaning: Constitutions and Reconstructions of Language, character, and Community (1984).

18. See, e.g., Philip Meltsner, Rowan & Givelber, *The Bike Tour Leader's Dilemma: Talking About Supervision*, 13 Vt. L. Rev. 399 (1989); Nina Tarr, *The Skill of Evaluation as an Explicit Goal of Clinical Training*, 21 Pac. L. J. 967 (1990).

19. See Chapter Four's discussion of feminist jurisprudence and critical race theory.

20. See, e.g., Lynne Henderson, *Legality and Empathy*, 85 Mich. L. Rev. 1574 (1987); Robin West, *Love, Rage and Legal Theory*, 1 Yale J. Law & Feminism 101 (1989).

21. C. Taylor, supra note 6, at 458.

22. Id. Cf. S. Benhabib, supra note 13, at 158 (describing a split in the "male ego" between "the public person and the private individual" or, in other words, a split between

in order to give individuals the means for a rich and satisfying private life [that may, if needed, be guided by the aesthetic principles and passion of Expressive Selves]."[23]

This idea of the Dualistic Self allows law school disciplinarians and lawyers to tacitly combine ideas of the Disengaged Self or Moral Self in their work with ideas from the more open-ended perspectives of an Expressive Self in their personal lives. The idea of a Dualistic Self also allows law school inhabitants and lawyers to compartmentalize their professional work by using the ideas of a Disengaged Self for some functions while employing a Moral or Expressive Self for other functions. Imagine, for example, a law professor who combines a Disengaged Self for the instrumentalist pursuit of her career goals with a specific Moral Self (say a Kantian, Hegelian, Marxist or Aristotelian self) for choosing the topics, perspectives, and voice in her scholarship. Or imagine a law professor who adopts a Disengaged Self's instrumentalism in pursuing career goals, an Expressive Self's charismatic style in classroom work, and a Moral Self in producing scholarship.[24] The basic point here is that many law school inhabitants may feel uncomfortable or even express dissident views about aspects of the discipline while all the time working to maintain the discipline's basic structures under the overall governorship of a Disengaged Self.

This possible combination or compartmentalization of selves suggests that diverse ethical discourses can coexist easily with disciplinary structures. Disengaged Selves fit well with the instrumental rationality of the case method classroom and final examinations, the demand on law professors to publish frequently in prestigious places, and the insistent search for employment with corporate law firms. At the same time, some professors may discover that the assumption of a Moral or Expressive Self for scholarly work can provide more satisfaction and better results in terms of the ideological ends they wish to pursue or in terms of criticizing judicial opinions from external standpoints. Some professors may find that a Moral or Expressive Self and its ethical qual-

---

"the public sphere of justice, in which history is made, and the atemporal realm of the household, in which life is reproduced").

23. C. Taylor, supra note 6, at 458. Cf. Elinor G. Barber, The Bourgeosie in 18th Century France 45–46 (1955) ("Businessmen especially, but lawyers also, had managed to compartmentalize their values, restricting the 'new' secular ones to the occupational sphere of their activities, and keeping their private and family life in the framework of the old religious definition of the meaning of life and death.").

24. Cf. Michael Walzer, Thick and Thin: Moral Argument at Home and Abroad 85–104 (1995) (contrasting the pluralistic "divided selves" of roles, identities and values which reside in modern societies with "thin selves" that tend to pursue one dominant value).

ities are more satisfying for classroom work in terms of delivering charismatic, aesthetic performances or providing a caring teaching style that appeals to a diverse range of students. Dualistic Selves of various kinds thus join together with Disengaged Selves and Moral Selves in generally supporting and protecting the discipline of law schools.

The combination or compartmentalization of possible selves would also seem useful to the professional work of practicing lawyers. The Disengaged Self supports the idea of the lawyer as an amoral technician who is ready to make any kind of legal argument on behalf of any kind of client, thus holding himself out for a maximum of business. Meanwhile, the Moral Self could help the writing of insightful rule-oriented briefs for rationalistic judges, while the expressions of a more romantic Expressive Self could help in appealing to jurors, empathizing with clients and making public policy arguments on behalf of clients before public bureaucracies. A divided self, in other words, can help the lawyer make instrumental uses of different ethical perspectives as needed in different aspects of her professional work.

There is, finally, the possibility of a fifth conception in which the self attempts to integrate rather than compartmentalize the Enlightenment and Romantic concepts of self and ethics. This concept can be detected in the recent work of several ethical and political theorists who are trying to combine Enlightenment and Romantic ethics in order to create an ethics that is sensitive to the concretely different Other.[25] This ethics is based on the conception of a Dialectical or Dialogical Self, a self that is dialectical internally between its different components and dialectical externally in its relationships with the concrete Other. Internally, this self attempts to oscillate between or integrate other conceptions of the self (say, for example, a Kantian Moral Self and a Romantic Expressive Self) in order to balance our thought and emotions in ethical thought and actions. Externally, this self attempts to engage in either actual or simulated "moral conversations" or "artistic dialogues" with "concrete others" in order to develop persuasive ethical positions that respect the autonomy and concrete diversity of humans. To construct these conversations, the Dialogical Self recognizes that participants must observe certain moral or procedural constraints such as a "universal moral respect" for others and an "egal-

---

25. I have drawn the concept of a Dialectical or Dialogical Self and its ethical perspective largely from the work of three political theorists: Seyla Benhabib, supra note 13; Romand Coles, Self/Power/Other: Political Theory and Dialogical Ethics (1992); Stephen K. White, Political Theory and Postmodernism (1991). See also Martha Minow, Making All the Difference: Inclusion, Exclusion and American Law (1990) (developing a legal theory of difference based on sensitivity to relationships between concretely different persons).

itarian reciprocity" between the participants to the conversation. These constraints allow each participant equal substantive rights to engage in the moral conversation. They enjoin the participants to take account of different standpoints or the perspectives of others by practicing an "enlarged thinking" or a "reversibility of perspectives" that would articulate and judge issues from the viewpoints of persons who have concretely different experiences and values from one's own.[26]

The Dialogical Self recognizes that a person's relationships with concrete others are important sources of ethical responsibilities in addition to moral rules or principles based on consent or reason.[27] In Stephen White's terms, the Dialogical Self "oscillates" between two different senses of ethical responsibility: a "responsibility to action," which involves providing sound moral-pragmatic reasons for one's actions, and a "responsibility to otherness," which entails contemplating and recognizing ethical duties that are based upon historically-embedded relationships with other persons and nature.[28] This recognition of associational or relational duties in addition to duties based on rules and principles brings to the Dialogical Self's ethics a flexibility and expansiveness as well as sensitivity to the ethical positions of others that are missing from the narrower, rule-oriented ethics of Disengaged and Moral Selves. At the same time, the requirement of dialogical ethics that one must provide persuasive moral-pragmatic reasons for one's actions ensures a continuing respect for individual autonomy and interests.[29]

---

26. See S. Benhabib, supra note 13, at 8–9, 30–32, 121–141.

27. See id.; Nel Noddings, Caring: A Feminine Approach to Ethics and Moral Education (1984); S. K. White, supra note 25.

28. S. K. White, supra note 25, at 19–23.

29. See S. Benhabib, supra note 13; S. K. White, supra note 25. Both Benhabib and White attempt to combine or work between the communicative or discourse ethics of Jurgen Habermas, which specifies universal procedures for normative debates about principles of justice, and the contrasting normative positions of difference feminists, communitarian philosophers and postmodern theorists who contest universalist theories of ethics and instead emphasize the concrete differences, embedded historical situations and character, emotions and language of human agents who make moral or ethical judgments. Benhabib and White thus rely on both Kantian ideas of moral/rational agency, which lie at the basis of Habermas' discourse ethics, and ideas of a Romantic or Expressive Self that would employ passion, aesthetics and narrativity about experiences, contexts and history together with practical reason in an effort to articulate ethical and political responsibilities we owe to concretely different other persons.

Habermas' discourse ethics holds that moral reasons for actions must be reasons provided under the conditions of an "ideal speech situation," or a situation in which everyone participates equally in a "fair debate" seeking agreement on moral principles by engaging

The general notion of a Dialogical Self and its relational ethics may underlie many of the developments in law school reform movements that are promoting more pluralistic and more inclusive views about law, lawyers and legal education. Many aspects of clinical education, law school writing programs, the new teaching and scholarship about professional ethics and the new movements in legal scholarship are consistent with the Dialogical Self's ethical concerns for concretely different persons. For example, both clinical education and writing programs are designed in part to provide a more diverse education that can be especially productive for students with different learning styles

---

in such speech acts as initiating topics, questioning premises or the evidence of other participants, and even questioning the basic presuppositions of the conversation. See Jurgen Habermas, Moral Consciousness and Communicative Action 43–196 (1990).

Benhabib argues that discourse ethics, in order to provide for the possibility of agreements on moral principles, retains some of the rigidity of earlier universalistic and rationalist moral theories, including both inattention to the emotional or affective bases of moral judgments and the maintenance of a *sharply limited public sphere* within which moral conversations are limited to seeking agreement on principles of social justice. Discourse ethics, in her view, thus provides an inadequate moral account of the concrete, historically embedded experiences and perspectives of persons whose lives and conceptions do not fit those of the Kantian "moral/rational agent" or "generalized others," in particular persons like women, workers, and racial minorities whose life experiences tend to be radically different from those of white upper class males in modern Western societies. She thus proposes that discourse ethics should incorporate "moral conversations" between "concretely different" persons. See S. Benhabib, supra note 13, at 49–53, 107–13, 148–98.

White argues that Habermas' theory is designed to articulate procedures for establishing principles of our "responsibility to action" or, in other words, our duty to give persuasive moral-pragmatic reasons for actions we take that affect others. But White also argues that Habermas' theory ignores our ontological and ethical "responsibility to otherness," as well as our needs for "poetic" or "world-disclosing" language to serve this responsibility to otherness. He maintains that this responsibility to otherness, as articulated by Heidegger, postmodernist theorists like Richard Rorty, Michel Foucault, and Jacques Derrida, and difference feminists such as Carol Gilligan and Seyla Benhabib, appears when we dwell on human limits, our finitude, our death, and our face-to-face relationships with concretely different persons. These considerations, which are missing from Habermas' moral theory and systematically subordinated by modern systems of rational moral-pragmatic action, drive us toward attempts to understand and care for the Other, or persons and things who are not us. White argues that this ethical responsibility to otherness is an essential corrective to universalistic moral theories, although he sees no way to integrate these considerations with Habermas' theory of discourse ethics as Benhabib does. White calls instead for maintaining a "fruitful tension" between these two quite different senses of ethical or moral responsibility. See S. K. White, supra note 25, at 19–28, 55–74, 90–113, 115–47. In essence, both Benhabib and White propose theories to repair Habermas' discourse ethics by taking into account the concrete experiences, perspectives and goals of the Other.

who do not flourish in the case method/final examination system.[30] Feminist jurisprudence and critical race theory have each developed critiques of law and legal education that focus on obstacles faced by women and persons of color.[31] The Dialogical Self, then, would appear to be a good source of both actual and potential resistance to the discipline that strives to make legal education more effective and more diverse. Moreover, because of its substantial expansion of the ethical domain, the Dialogical Self would also appear to be a good source of motivations to improve the ethical nature of American law and American legal practices.

In the next section, we shall examine how a Dialogical Self might think ethically about the discipline of law schools. First, however, we should consider how the ideal-types of selves we have been considering can be affected by certain phenomenological aspects of the discipline. Anthony Giddens has described how modern social institutions shape our ideas of self-identity by creating certain "dilemmas" or "tribulations" for the self, which produce normal healthy reactions in some persons but "pathologies" for others when a self reacts excessively and fails to preserve a coherent narrative of self-identity.[32] Several of these dilemmas are presented by the discipline of law schools and these can be especially acute dilemmas, since many law students experience the discipline at "fateful moments" in their young adult lives, fateful moments at which the self is particularly susceptible to external influence.[33] It appears, moreover, that both the normal and pathological reactions to these social tribulations can generate tacit ideas of the self and ethical behavior which support the discipline in a variety of ways.

Giddens argues that the complex social institutions of the modern world tend to separate the self from its sense of community, its passions, and the "existential questions" or "moral experiences" of death, external nature and our relations with other persons. This separation results in "an evaporation of morality, particularly in so far as moral outlooks are integrated in a secure way with day-to-day practice," or in a "sequestration of moral experiences."[34]

---

30. This purpose or effect is not often talked about openly in law school circles. To do so, of course, would be to lower the status of clinics and writing programs within disciplinary law schools. But consider the special growth of clinics at regional and local law schools and the common notion at these schools that clinics can help "non-law review students" obtain their first employment upon graduation.

31. See Chapter Four's discussion of feminist jurisprudence and critical race theory.

32. Anthony A. Giddens, Modernity and Self-Identity (1991).

33. See id. at 112–14.

34. Id. at 52–54, 144–69.

In the relentless rationality, impersonality, and conflicting messages of the discipline, we can observe just this kind of sequestration of self from community, passion and morality. Furthermore, the separation of the ethical from day-to-day practices favors Disengaged, Moral and Dualistic Selves who are capable of limiting their moral domains to narrow spheres of discourse while leaving most discourse and choices by individuals unconstrained by ethical deliberations. Thus modernity and the discipline of law schools together tend to promote ideas of self-identity that are congruent with the discipline and its separation of technique from ethics.

One distinctive tribulation faced by the modern self, according to Giddens, is the tension between authority and uncertainty. This tension results from the absence in modernity of "determinant authorities" and the presence of "diverse, mutually conflicting authorities" such as religion, community and expert systems, and this dilemma normally is "resolved through a mixture of routine and commitment to a certain form of lifestyle, plus the vesting of trust in a given series of abstract systems."[35] The discipline of law schools certainly entails tension between authority and uncertainty, as it presents many authoritative legal rules together with the many uncertainties of case method discourse and final examinations. It appears too that many law students and professors tend to resolve this dilemma "normally," as Giddens would say, through "a mixture of routine and commitment" to the discipline's conventions or lifestyle and "the vesting of trust" in "abstract systems" such as those provided by legal treatises or legal theories. One of the pathologies that results from this dilemma is "dogmatic authoritarianism," in which a person "essentially gives up faculties of critical judgement in exchange for the convictions supplied by an authority whose rules and provision cover most of the aspects of his life," and others include "pathological states in which individuals are virtually immobilized through a tendency towards universal doubt."[36] One observes these pathologies in the discipline, for example, when students tacitly accept the case method professor as both the model and authority for how to practice law or when students (and professors) become consumed with a pervasive skepticism towards moral values and the idea of any binding law. The dilemma of authority versus uncertainty within the discipline thus promotes important tacit lessons and tends to reproduce the discipline.

A second tribulation is the tension between powerlessness and appropriation or, in other words, the tension between an individual's experience of

---

35. Id. at 194–96.
36. Id. at 196.

"powerlessness in relation to a diverse and large-scale social universe" and her "reappropriation" of power from modern institutions by mastering their complex resources and relationships.[37] The discipline exposes beginning law students to a strong sense of powerlessness in terms of legal techniques, and then expects them to master a complex set of technical resources in the course of their education.[38] The pathologies of this dilemma are "engulfment," where the "individual feels overwhelmed by a sense of powerlessness in the major domains of his phenomenal world," and "omnipotence," where the individual's "ontological security is achieved through a fantasy of dominance; the phenomenal world feels as if it is orchestrated by that person as a puppeteer."[39] Within the discipline, young adult students are plunged into a complex and competitive environment and they would seem to be ripe candidates for *engulfment* by the discipline and its tacit conceptions.[40] The discipline also may often incite attitudes of *omnipotence* or *fantasies of dominance* by providing opportunities to demonstrate a mastery of complex legal doctrines in classroom discussions, final examinations or scholarship.[41] These pathologies of engulfment and omnipotence surely help maintain the discipline in place as they produce different kinds of surrender to the discipline's conventions.

A third tribulation for the modern self concerns the self's capacity to maintain a coherent self-narrative in the face of contradictory social pressures towards both "unification" of the self and "fragmentation" of the self as it engages in diverse actions, contexts and roles. Normally, Giddens argues, these forces are "positively incorporated" into distinctive, healthy self-identities.[42] The discipline tacitly imposes such contradictory pressures on law school selves as legal education invites law students to develop a comprehensive view of themselves as lawyers, even perhaps as ethical lawyers, and at the same time to contemplate participation in the diverse and different roles of law student, litigator, counselor, and judge. There are pathological reactions to this dilemma that strengthen the discipline in specific ways. One reaction is that of the "rigid traditionalist," a person "who constructs his identity around a

---

37. Id. at 191–94.

38. See Chapter One.

39. A. Giddens, supra note 32, at 193–94.

40. See Alan Stone, *Legal Education on a Couch*, 85 Harv. L. Rev. 392 (1971).

41. See Chapter One's discussion of the opportunities to demonstrate the mastery of doctrinal materials in classrooms, examinations and conventional scholarship. Cf. Derrick Bell, Jr., Confronting Authority 44–45, 76–80 (1994) (describing what he calls the excessive commitment of the law faculty at Harvard to hiring only new faculty who have obtained the very best grades from the most elite law schools).

42. A. Giddens, supra note 32, at 189–91.

fixed set of commitments, which act as a filter through which numerous different social environments are reacted to or interpreted."[43] Within the discipline, such rigid traditionalists can be seen as those tacit formalists who become excessively committed to a rule-oriented discourse in classrooms, conventional scholarship and especially final examinations. The other pathological reaction is that of "authoritarian conformity" in which a person "adopts entirely the kind of personality offered to him by cultural patterns" and "becomes exactly as all others are and as they expect him to be."[44] Within the discipline, this behavior occurs in many forms, as students model themselves on or seek the authority of their professors or treatises and as law professors commit themselves unreflectively to the discipline's strong conventions of case method teaching, final examinations and doctrinal scholarship.

To summarize: The discipline and prevailing conceptions of the self in American society and in law schools are compatible and mutually reinforcing. The discipline's pressures on individuals stimulate a series of "pathological reactions" that also support the discipline in various ways. These prevailing concepts of self and ethics and pathological reactions to the tribulations of the discipline also support the lawyer's generally conservative approach to law, lawyering and legal ethics.

Yet the discipline entertains and tolerates resistance to its power, and prominent forms of contemporary resistance to the discipline's practices suggest that dissident types of Expressive and Dialogical Selves are present in law schools as well. To help evaluate the discipline, then, let us contemplate a particular utopian vision of legal education based on such dissident ideas.

The Ethics of a Dialogical Self

How should we assess the discipline and its manifold routines, habits and tacit effects? An observer who stands outside the discipline of law schools will bring his or her conception of self and its related ethical framework to bear in this evaluation. Enough has been said about the discipline and its consequences to let these evaluations begin. But observers like this writer, who stand partially or wholly within the discipline, face a special problem. Our sense of self and ethics has been influenced, tacitly of course, by the routine practices, habits and tacit knowledge of the discipline that we would evaluate. How can we make any judgment about the discipline that is not some-

---

43. Id. at 190.
44. Id. at 190–91.

how distorted by our own experiences within the discipline? Paul Ricoeur's advice on the similar problem of evaluating ideologies is that one can only declare one's utopia and use utopian ideals to evaluate an ideology with the belief that ultimately some kind of oscillation between utopia and the reality it seeks to shatter may produce useful evaluations.[45] In this view, it makes sense to pursue the ethics of a Dialogical Self and evaluate the discipline from this perspective for two separate reasons. First, this ethics supports visions of legal education and law that are quite different from the views of legal education and law that are promoted by the discipline and its consorting selves: Disengaged Selves, Moral Selves and Dualistic Selves. This difference should help others develop their own ethical judgments by offering them a substantial or radical alternative to the discipline. Second, the ethics of a Dialogical Self supports visions of legal education and law that would be more diverse, more effective and more inclusive than the standard model of education that is promoted by the current discipline of law schools. Dialogical ethics is thus worth pursuing for these ends even if ultimately this ethics too is likely to be captured or limited by discipline and incapable of establishing systemic reform.

What would the law school ethics of a Dialogical Self be? How might this self think ethically about the discipline under an expanded notion of moral domains, a desire to engage in moral conversations with concrete others, and a commitment to making legal education more inclusive, more pluralistic and more effective? We may begin by noting the broad parameters of a "moral conversation" about the discipline of law schools that might occur between a Dialogical Self and representatives of concretely different other persons to whom law school work relates.[46] We should then try to imagine such a moral conversation. This conversation, as I imagine it, will lead us first to *deconstructing* the discipline and then to *reconstructions* of the discipline that promise more diverse, more effective and more democratic forms of education. In the end, of course, these arguments may constitute little more than a small part of the reform tradition in law schools that helps legitimate the discipline.[47] But at least we will have examined a

---

45. See P. Ricoeur, supra note 1, at 172–73, 309–12.

46. Cf. Jerry Frug, *Review Essay: McCarthyism and Critical Legal Studies*, 22 Harv. Civ. Rts.-Civ. Lib. L. Rev. 665, 690–701 (1987) (urging conversations within the university that would engage persons of different persuasions in discussions of fundamental academic issues).

47. See Chapter Four's discussion of the reform tradition in law schools.

substantial alternative that will help us appreciate the attractions of the discipline.

The Moral Conversation

Who should participate in an actual or simulated "moral conversation" about law school ethics with the Dialogical Self? One should start with representatives of the many different kinds of students who are in face-to-face relationships with law professors at particular law schools. For the Dialogical Self, face-to-face relationships are a primary source of ethical duties.[48] This conversation should thus include representatives of all students who might bring different kinds of talents, experiences, backgrounds, perspectives and learning styles to the law school as well as representatives of the school's students who will practice in several different sectors of the legal economy. This conversation should also include representatives of women students, working class students, racial minorities and gay and lesbian students not only because these groups bring different experiences and perspectives to their legal studies but also because of the accumulating evidence and reasonable suspicions that the discipline may in fact disadvantage these groups.[49]

This conversation should also include representatives of the different kinds of clients that a school's students are likely to or should serve in their legal practices. Representatives of different kinds of employers of the school's graduates, different alumni who have interests in maintaining the reputation of their school or making donations and, for state law schools, different kinds of citizens and taxpayers of the state should also be included. Consumers of the scholarship and other public services that a school's faculty produces, or should produce, also deserve representation. Relationships between law schools and these concrete others are less direct and less tangible than the face-to-face relationships between law professors and their students, but these

---

48. See N. Noddings, supra note 27 (on the importance to education of "caring for" as opposed to "caring about" one's students); Paul Savoy, *Toward a New Politics of Legal Education*, 79 Yale L. J. 444, 448 (1970) ("If any real learning is to go on in our schools..., then our first responsibility must be to the human beings who live in our academic house, not to the Bar, or the profession, or the alumni.").

49. See, e.g., Lani Guinier, Michelle Fine & Jane Balin, *Becoming Gentlemen: Women's Experiences at One Ivy League Law School*, 143 U. Pa. L. Rev. 1 (1994); Chapter Four's discussion of the feminist and critical race theory critiques of legal education.

groups too are affected by legal education and their interests surely deserve recognition in the ethics of a Dialogical Self.

Representatives of the legal profession as a whole and of different kinds of law faculty should participate as well. These representatives, however, may be included in a special or limited way, at least to start with. This moral conversation begins by focusing on questions of individual ethical choice: that is, upon questions for individuals about how to teach, how to study, what scholarship to do and, importantly, how a law professor should allocate her time between teaching and scholarship. In this initial stage the conversation need not be concerned with collective law school decisions about what the curriculum should be, what the criteria for student admissions or faculty hiring should be, what a school's grading system should look like, or what an entire faculty's scholarly program should be. These questions are relevant to individual ethical choices, to be sure, but these questions about collective choices may be suspended or deferred at first. The choices that individual faculty make in terms of their teaching and scholarship can have effects upon the teaching and scholarship of others and the legal profession. But initially the weight given to the views of other faculty or the profession may be significantly less than that given to the views of those who have face-to-face relationships with the Dialogical Self or are otherwise specifically related to her work. The moral conversation should first help a Dialogical Self make decisions about her own teaching and scholarship, and only after this process is well underway need we consider collective choices by law schools that would promote the same goals and enrich the lives of Dialogical Selves.

What kinds of selves should be imputed to the "others" in this moral conversation? Some mixture of selves is appropriate in order to provide a pragmatic or realistic view of law school relationships, responsibilities and possibilities. Moreover, substantial majorities should undoubtedly be awarded to the more atomistic conceptions of Disengaged, Moral and Millian Dualistic Selves in order to replicate the probable mix of selves around American law schools, at least until ethical decisions about law school practices should begin to take hold and possibly influence or alter this mix of selves.

Two general obligations or constraints are likely to be recognized by all the participants to this conversation, although each is an open-ended constraint that leaves substantial discretion to individuals who must make ethical choices about their law school work. First, each law professor surely has some obligation to help prepare her students to pass their bar examinations and acquire basic knowledge and skills that will help them begin legal practice. This obligation includes providing ample opportunities for students to study and review legal doctrine, especially in subjects covered by bar examinations, ample opportunities to practice for the bar exam by taking examinations which simulate bar examinations,[50] and ample opportunities to acquire the common analytical and problem-solving skills that are used in a variety of legal practices. This obligation, however, is both general and limited. For example, some rough judgment about what constitutes "ample opportunities" for most students to prepare for bar examinations and acquire beginning practice skills must be made, and any such judgment will depend on a professor's assessment of her students' abilities to learn things on their own. Further, there are no studies which demonstrate the superiority of particular teaching methods or examination techniques in preparing students for bar examinations or diverse legal practices.[51] There are "rational myths" about law teaching, that the case method or final examination system is a superior form of education, but these are abstract myths or conventions and there is no empirical documentation or validation of these ideas.[52] The obligation to prepare students for bar examinations and legal practices leaves the Dialogical Self with substantial discretion to choose her teaching methods.

The participants in the moral conversation would probably also agree that any professor, at least if she is a traditional classroom teacher, has some obligation to allocate her professional efforts between teaching and something else, whether this is scholarship, the continuing education of lawyers or other public service. Conventionally the major external constituencies of law schools such as corporate law firm partners, judges and other leaders of the bar have expressed interests or been understood to have interests in a law faculty's scholarship and other non-teaching work. Research universities that house most law schools also have a general interest in law school scholarship. This work is desired by these groups for a variety of reasons: because it promotes law reform, because it constitutes evidence of sound teaching, because it may establish better professional practices, or because it helps maintain the reputation of a particular law school which is in the interest of its alumni, university or state.[53] The Dialogical Self will thus want to commit to both teaching and some kind of scholarship or other public service in a general way. But this

---

50. See Philip C. Kissam, *Law School Examinations*, 42 Vand. L. Rev. 433, 463–465 (1989).

51. See David Bryden, *What Do Law Students Learn? A Pilot Study*, 34 J. Legal Educ. 479 (1984); Paul Teich, *Research on American Law Teaching: It There A Case Against the Case System?*, 36 J. Legal Educ. 167 (1986).

52. See Chapter Three's discussion of the case method as a "rational myth" under Rituals, Symbols, Myths.

53. See Chapter Five's discussion of corporate law firms, the organized bar and research universities.

obligation, like the obligation to prepare students for bar exams and practice, grants substantial discretion to the Dialogical Self. Neither law schools nor their external constituencies have imposed many constraints on the *specific kinds* of scholarship or other services they expect of tenured law professors or on the *division of time* they expect between law teaching and other professional services,[54] except perhaps for the Research University's expectation that professors should publish quantities of scholarship for their own professional advancement and the reputation of the university.[55]

This moral conversation, once constructed, must now take up the primal question of the Dialogical Self's ethical responsibilities to "concrete others" in her teaching and her scholarship. Different kinds of students will desire or need different kinds of instructional assistance. Different kinds of future clients and different state citizens will desire or need a broad variety of skills and knowledge in their lawyers and be interested in different kinds of law reform projects. The question is complicated further by the Dialogical Self's recognition of ethical responsibilities to her own self and self-interests, since caring for one's self is both necessary and important to caring for others.[56] This primal question raises a wide swath of conflicting responsibilities that cut across the teaching and scholarly work of law professors, and more individualistic selves may understandably seek to rely on the discipline's conventions and its discretion for individuals in answering (or avoiding) this question. But a Dialogical Self will want to explore and reflect deeply about these ethical cross-currents. To avoid hiding behind the routines, habits and tacit knowledge of the discipline, which is the subject of evaluation, the Dialogical Self will first want to question everything about the discipline.

In this perspective, the techniques of *deconstruction* may be an economical way to interpret and interrogate the discipline of law schools. Deconstruction's project is to question and undermine "the metaphysics of presence" or, in other words, to question our usual desires for foundational principles in order to disclose the internal contradictions and exclusionary effects of these principles and to facilitate other ways of thinking, feeling and acting.[57] The discipline's structures of the core curriculum, the case method, the examina-

---

54. See, e.g., Terrence Sandalow, *The Moral Responsibility of Law Schools*, 34 J. Legal Educ. 163 (1984).

55. See Chapter Five's discussion of the Research University.

56. See N. Noddings, supra note 27.

57. See, e.g., Madan Sarup, An Introductory Guide to Post-Structuralism and Post-modernism 35–38 (2d ed. 1993); Jack Balkin, *Deconstructive Practice and Legal Theory*, 96 Yale L. J. 743, 746–51 (1987).

tion/grading/class ranking system, and conventional legal scholarship certainly have foundational or even metaphysical qualities. So does the discipline's implicit overriding purpose of training students to be technically adept lawyers. Trying to read and deconstruct the discipline as if it were a literary text may help us understand the discipline, its dysfunctions and the value of alternative strategies that could subvert the discipline's purpose and structures, open them up, and make possible a more effective and more humane discipline.

Deconstructing the Discipline

Deconstruction is "a method of reading a text so closely that the author's conceptual distinctions on which the text relies are shown to fail on account of the inconsistent and paradoxical use made of these very concepts within the text as a whole."[58] Three techniques of this method are prominent and seem sufficient to deconstruct the discipline's basic structures.[59] First, the reader must identify a text's significant *hierarchical oppositions* or, in other words, its distinctions between favored and disfavored concepts that give a text force and apparent meaning. One expects to find hierarchical oppositions in any text or rational system because of our desires, at least in Western culture, for foundational principles and the determinate meaning of texts. The reader then must deconstruct these hierarchical relationships by showing that different properties ascribed individually to favored and disfavored concepts in fact belong to each concept in a pair. This *deconstructive reversal* indicates that the favored concept depends on the disfavored concept as much as the disfavored concept depends on the privileged one. Such reversals frequently are accomplished by identifying "traces" of the disfavored concept that appear in the favored concept and suggest the dependence of the favored concept on the disfavored one. Finally, to explore the possible benefits from rehabilitating the disfavored concept, the deconstructive reader should *invert* or *temporarily reverse* the hierarchical opposition by imagining a world dominated by the disfavored concept rather than the favored one. The point of the inversion is to stimulate our imagination and thereby enlarge our understanding, our ethical debates and our possible actions.

Significant hierarchical oppositions structure the discipline of law schools. The case method is privileged over other instructional methods, and the final

---

58. M. Sarup, supra note 57, at 34.

59. The following discussion is based upon Jack Balkin's description of three major techniques in deconstructive readings or interpretations. See Balkin, supra note 57, at 746–67.

examination system privileges a particular kind of examination and evalua-tion over alternative methods.[60] The discipline also privileges speech and speech-like writing on final examinations over more critical forms of reading and writing.[61] Scholarship is privileged over teaching for a number of reasons, which include the greater intellectual excitement of scholarship that many pro-fessors experience and the bureaucratic demands from both law schools and research universities for the production of scholarship to earn individual re-wards and enhance a school's reputation.[62] More fundamentally, if elusively, the discipline tacitly privileges "theory" over "practice"[63] and "law" over "pol-itics."[64] But a deconstruction of the case method, final examinations, the priv-ileging of speech over writing, and the privileging of scholarship over teach-ing should be sufficient to reveal the values of radically different forms of legal education.

The more difficult tasks of deconstructive reading remain. For each hier-archical opposition, we need to identify the specific relationships and com-mon properties that are shared between the favored and disfavored concepts in order to tease out the hidden contradictions in the favored concept. We also need to invert the favored and disfavored concepts and imagine the possible benefits from rehabilitating the disfavored concept. The point of these rever-sals is to illuminate the disfavored concepts and practices as sites of potentially productive resistance to the discipline or as reformative concepts that may be of special interest to Dialogical Selves.

The case method relies on casebooks for the assigned readings in doctrinal courses and on the dissection of judicial opinions and hypothetical problems in class discussions that often are conducted by question-and-answer dialogues between professors and students.[65] This method is thought to promote many values. These include the skill of a careful, skeptical reading and analysis of

---

60. See Chapter One's discussion of the case method and final examinations and Chap-ter Four's discussion of the professional reforms of legal education.

61. See Chapter One's discussion of the case method and final examinations; Chapter Two's discussion of amphitheatre classrooms and Moot Court; and Chapter Three's dis-cussion of the hedonic pleasure of the law school's oral culture.

62. See Chapter One's discussion of the institutions of legal scholarship; Chapter Three's discussion of the examinatorial regime; Chapter Five's discussion of the American research university.

63. See Mark Spiegel, *Theory and Practice in Legal Education: An Essay on Clinical Ed-ucation*, 34 UCLA L. Rev. 577 (1987).

64. On the origins of this distinction, see Paul Carrington, *William Gardiner Hammond and the Lieber Revival*, 16 Cardozo L. Rev. 2135, 2149–50 (1994).

65. See Chapter One's discussion of casebooks and the case method.

judicial opinions, practice at applying precedents and rules to novel situations, an objective knowledge of the leading cases, rules and principles in major doctrinal areas, and good practice at public speaking and making practical judgments of the kinds that lawyers will face in their practices.[66] The case method is privileged over at least three other educational methods: the systematic study of legal doctrine by treatises, lectures and writing projects; the study of "complete case materials" as these are developed and worked on by practicing lawyers; and theoretical approaches to understanding law such as those provided by law and economics, law and social science, or critical legal studies.

In the deconstructive mode, we may ask: Why is the case method more fundamental or foundational to these alternative methods? Does the case method come close to accomplishing its purported goals? Is the case method coherent or comprehensible to most students as it operates within the discipline's comprehensive web of routine practices and tacit norms?

Consider the traces of alternative methods within the case method. Systematic statements of legal doctrine are often employed by law professors in the classroom to demonstrate "expert" or "correct" readings of cases, and such statements are eagerly sought by law students from their professors or treatises in order to prepare for their examinations. Faint traces of a "complete case method" are suggested by the very excerpts of appellate opinions in casebooks and may be found in occasional admonitions or questions by law professors about how lawyers might have avoided litigation in a particular case. Theoretical approaches also creep into the case method. Indeed, the law professor's use of some kind of "theory" to explain and criticize judicial opinions, whether the theory is Langdellian formalism, policy-oriented legal realism, or one of the new academic/political reform movements, is what provides law professors with their epistemological and normative authority that helps them maintain control in the classroom and respect for their expertise.[67] The case method thus depends on alternative but disfavored teaching methods.

Why are these alternative methods disfavored, feared and not generally recognized as appropriate teaching methods? Do the traces of these other methods within the case method suggest that the case method is failing to accomplish its goals? Consider, for example, that when a professor begins to rely on making systematic statements of legal doctrine in the classroom, her students

---

66. See, e.g., Anthony Kronman, The Lost Lawyer: Failing Ideals of the Legal Profession (1993); Paul Carrington, *Hail! Langdell!*, 20 Law & Social Inquiry 691 (1995); Chapter One's discussion of the case method.

67. See Chapter One's discussion of the case method.

may stop reading casebook opinions altogether, preferring to have the opinions read for them by the professor. This of course defeats the knowledge and skills goals of the case method. Or consider that when theory is employed to establish a professor's criticism of particular cases, the professor's students may lose any sense that legal doctrine and legal methods can be objective or systematic. Furthermore, the casual use of theory within the case method to criticize judicial opinions often may have the effect of "smuggling in," by simple assertion, the "truthfulness" of general normative propositions in the guise of examining isolated instances,[68] thus defeating the case method's skills of skeptical and critical reading. The case method appears to be at war with itself, or at least at war with these alternative methods.

Inverting this hierarchical opposition is relatively easy because some law professors and at least one law school are already experimenting with alternative instructional methods.[69] Imagine what a law school would look like if its first and second year doctrinal courses were to "cover" the necessary doctrine systematically outside the classroom by assigning treatise readings and providing tests on this material without devoting much class time to doctrinal coverage.[70] Class time could then be devoted to other kinds of learning exercises, which could include both practice examinations and other types of writing projects, studying complete case materials in ways that project different models of lawyering, more comprehensive and more theoretical studies of legal doctrine, and more elaborate discussions of the methods of legal argument, legal interpretation and judicial decisionmaking.[71] To be sure, there would be objections from disciplinarians, some theoretical—that these other methods would destroy a *necessary focus* on the case method[72]—and others practical—about the impossibility of maintaining "objective" and "fair" grading procedures or student evaluations of teachers when radically different

---

68. See Nikolaus Benke, *Women in the Courts: An Old Thorn in Men's Sides*, 3 Mich. J. of Gender & Law 195, 202–03 (1995).

69. See Jay Feinman, *The Future History of Legal Education*, 29 Rutgers L. J. 475, 482 (1998) (describing alternative instructional methods at play in today's case method/final examination law school). The George Mason Law School has implemented a law and economics approach throughout its curriculum.

70. See James Boyd White, *Doctrine In a Vacuum: Reflections On What A Law School Ought (And Ought Not) To Be*, 36 J. Legal Educ. 155 (1986).

71. Such teaching, of course, would require many new kinds of teaching materials and would be enhanced by substantial alterations to the typical law school casebook. See generally Alan Watson, Law Out of Context 140–55 (2000).

72. See, e.g., Mary Ann Glendon, A Nation Under Lawyers 177–253 (1994); A.T. Kronman, supra note 66.

methods are employed.[73] There also would be objections about retooling time and the extra teaching time that law teachers would need to employ more complicated alternative methods, time that would have to be taken from their "primary purpose" of producing scholarship.[74] But a Dialogical Self might think that her dual ethical responsibilities to action and otherness dictate a priority to providing effective learning for her diverse kinds of students and entail a displacement of the case method. This self might be willing therefore to endure the practical difficulties and discomforts of implementing different methods, administering more complicated grading systems, and receiving student evaluations of her non-conventional, non-comparable teaching methods and style.

Final examinations are commonly thought to measure and help instruct law students in the internalization of legal doctrine, the identification of legal issues, the application of legal rules, analogies and disanalogies to novel situations, and writing productively to convey legal analysis efficiently and clearly to others.[75] The discipline's system of single, end-of-the-semester final examinations is privileged over alternative learning and evaluation devices such as practice examinations, mid-term examinations, oral examinations, analytical papers and research papers. These alternative practices are disfavored because of disciplinary fears about their "subjectivity," their ineffectiveness at teaching "legal analysis," their apparent demands for extra professorial time in advising and evaluations, and—importantly—the special difficulties that each of these alternative practices presents for dispensing many different grades that facilitate administration of law school grading curves. Practice examinations and practice obtained by taking mid-terms may make it much more difficult to establish the multiple grading distinctions of grading curves in assessing examination performances.[76] Oral examinations and student papers do not generate multiple grading distinctions as easily as written final examinations because of the different nature of the student work and evaluation processes

73. Cf. Jay Feinman & Marc Feldman, *Pedagogy and Politics*, 73 Geo L. J. 875 (1985) (describing a faculty's termination of a first year teaching experiment that involved significant departures from the case method/final examination system).

74. On the primacy of scholarship over teaching in law schools, see infra note 101 and the accompanying text.

75. See Kissam, supra note 50; Chapter One's discussion of law school examinations.

76. See Feinman & Feldman, supra note 73; Kissam, supra note 50, at 494–96; Gary A. Negin, *The Effects of Test Frequency in a First-Year Torts Course*, 31 J. Legal Educ. 673 (1981); Owen Roberts, *Methods for Review and Quiz in "Case System" Law Schools*, 1 Am. L. Sch. Rev. 222, 224 (1904).

in these cases.[77] And each of these other practices could easily require law professors to allocate more time to their teaching.

But are law school final examinations any more fundamental than, or deservedly privileged over, these alternative examining techniques? Do final examinations accomplish the law school's educational goals? The final examination system certainly accomplishes the *allocation goal* of establishing grading curves and class ranks, but might not this system hinder the writing abilities of those very law students who are employed by law firms who desire high class ranks let alone the writing/thinking abilities of all lawyers?[78] Does the final examination system, then, not contain contradictory, paradoxical qualities which may defeat law school goals to a significant extent and promote substantial dysfunctions?

Consider the traces of practice examinations, mid-term examinations, oral examinations and even research papers that are present in the final examination system. Practice examinations are a means of encouraging risk-taking or mistakes by practicing legal analysis repeatedly, under supervision, and with feedback. Traces of these practices may be found in the frequent use by law students of a professor's old exam questions or other practice questions to help prepare for final examinations. Traces may also be found in the occasional provision of practice examinations in one or more first semester courses. Mid-term examinations offer educational values by reducing the scope of necessary reviews, which can allow for more in-depth review, by providing helpful repetitions, and by providing specific feedback to students about how they might improve their work on later examinations. Traces of these practices can be found in the periodic reviews that individual students and student study groups engage in throughout the semester, and in the limited but intensely sought "feedback" that grades on final examinations provide to students. Oral examinations provide the extra evidence of an oral exchange that can help students interpret complex questions or allow examiners to ask follow-up questions which probe a student's knowledge more deeply and effectively.[79] In the

---

77. See, e.g., John Burman, *Oral Examinations as a Method of Evaluating Law Students*, 51 J. Legal Educ. 130 (2001); Steven Friedland, *Towards the Legitimacy of Oral Examinations in American Legal Education*, 39 Syracuse L. Rev. 627 (1988); Philip C. Kissam, *Seminar Papers*, 40 J. Legal Educ. 339 (1990).

78. See Bryant G. Garth & Joanne Martin, *Law Schools and the Construction of Competence*, 43 J. Legal Educ. 469 (1993) (describing the high value placed on the skills of written communication by both lawyers and hiring partners and their beliefs that law schools could do a better job in providing new lawyers with better writing skills).

79. See Burman, supra note 77; Friedland, supra note 77. European law schools have relied on oral examinations for just these reasons.

final examination system, traces of these values may be found in the significance that students give to reviewing and interpreting their class notes for clues
about possible examination questions or answers. They can be found in those
classic faculty-student exchanges about "what will be on the examination" or
how a student performed on a particular examination. In these exchanges, the
student presses for helpful information while the faculty member simulates a
helpful response while trying to avoid giving away too much or spending too
much time with the individual student.[80] Final examinations even have traces,
however faint, of research papers since final examination answers, like research
papers, are typically graded on the basis of their "comprehensiveness" in identifying and treating many legal issues more than on their insight, imagination
or coherence.[81]

If the final examination system depends on the values of these alternative
practices to function effectively, why are the alternative practices disfavored and
largely absent as such from the formal teaching and evaluation by most law professors? Does not their absence suggest that the final examination system may
fail substantially to accomplish its goals of teaching or measuring students in
their abilities to analyze legal problems, employ internalized doctrine, or engage in productive instrumentalist writing? For many or most students, the final
examination system may teach only the most limited kind of legal analysis, the
memorization and restatement of doctrine rather than skillful applications.[82]
This system also tacitly teaches and privileges the paraphrase reading of complex legal texts and the instrumentalist thinking and writing habits of the paradigm of good paragraph thinking/writing, thus limiting a lawyer's reflective,
imaginative and critical reading and writing skills.[83] The Dialogical Self will want
to weigh these concerns against the values of establishing class ranks easily and
preserving time for scholarship that the final examination system produces.

We should now invert this hierarchical opposition. What would law schools
look like if most doctrinal courses featured practice or mid-term examinations
with individualized feedback to students on this work in addition to final ex-

---

80. See Philip C. Kissam, *Conferring With Students*, 65 UMKC L. Rev. 917, 920–26
(1997).

81. See Kissam, supra note 50, at 444–52.

82. See Bryden, supra note 51; Janet Motley, *A Foolish Consistency: The Law School
Exam*, 10 Nova L.J. 723 (1986).

83. See Elizabeth Fajans & Mary R. Falk, *Against the Tyranny of the Paraphrase: Talking Back to Texts*, 78 Cornell L. Rev. 163, 163–70 (1993) (describing law students' paraphrasing of judicial opinions and their inability to engage in critical readings of these texts);
Kissam, supra note 50 (describing the limited nature of the instrumentalist paradigm of
good paragraph thinking/writing that is induced by law school final examinations).

aminations?[84] What would law schools look like if research, writing and drafting projects were added to or substituted for final examinations in major doctrinal courses?[85] Disciplinarians will object that these alternatives will not fairly test students in their comprehensive knowledge of subjects, and that "objective" and "fair" grading standards can not be maintained in evaluating these kinds of student work.[86] They will also object that alternative examining devices require extra professorial time, thus limiting the primary purpose of law professors to publish. Dialogical Selves, on the other hand, might conclude, at least temporarily or long enough to try these alternative practices, that these inversions might provide more effective and more egalitarian education for many students who have different learning styles and experiences. Furthermore, these alternative practices might provide a better education in basic legal analysis and writing skills for all law students.[87]

Underlying the privileged positions of the case method and final examination system is a deeper but more subtle hierarchical opposition. The discipline privileges speech acts over writing in several tacit but distinctive ways. Brilliant or authoritative discourse in law school classrooms, especially by professors, is privileged over the casebooks, course outlines and treatises that students read or are expected to read. This speech is viewed as the model of "what lawyers are like" and as the best source of "what the professor really wants" on examinations.[88] The discipline celebrates oral heroism in moot court exercises too, by providing more attention and applause to oral advocacy, especially successful oral advocacy, than to the accompanying written briefs that are duly filed as part of these exercises.[89] Writing speech-like final examinations is also privileged over other forms of student writing. Law school examination writing approximates a special kind of one-way oral discourse in which, given the

---

84. See Jay Feinman & Marc Feldman, *Achieving Excellence: Mastery Learning in Legal Education*, 35 J. Legal Educ. 528 (1985).

85. See, e.g., Kathleen Bean, *Writing Assignments in Law School Classes*, 37 J. Legal Educ. 276 (1987); Philip C. Kissam, *Teaching Constitutional Law Differently*, 9 Const. Comment. 237 (1992).

86. See Feinman & Feldman, supra note 73; Philip C. Kissam, *Thinking (By Writing) About Legal Writing*, 40 Vand. L. Rev. 135, 158–63 (1987).

87. See, e.g., Peter Gross, *On Law School Training in Analytic Skill*, 25 J. Legal Educ. 261 (1973) (writing tasks should be given more emphasis in order to teach legal analysis effectively); Carol McCrehan Parker, *Writing Throughout the Curriculum: Why Law Schools Need It and How to Achieve It*, 76 Neb. L. Rev. 561 (1997).

88. See Chapter One's discussion of the case method and law school examinations.

89. See Kissam, supra note 86, at 142–43; Chapter Two's discussion of law school courtrooms and moot court exercises.

time pressure of final examinations, students are expected to react to complicated questions and factual situations, think quickly "on their feet" so to speak and respond as a good oral advocate might by writing roughly-organized paragraphs that each identify a discrete issue and apply a rule both quickly and confidently.[90]

Our culture's traditional privilege of speech over writing lies at the heart of the discipline's speech/writing opposition. We tend to believe that "speech is connected more closely to the immediate thoughts of the communicator than is writing" and that "writing is only a method of representing speech."[91] But these speech/writing distinctions are easily undermined. As Jacques Derrida has shown, speech and writing have similar properties and evidence traces of each other since each form of communication consists of signs which are separate from the intentions of authors and accessible to listeners or readers only under the influence of distortions from the perspectives of the listeners and readers.[92] Furthermore, writing can do much more than convey a speaker's thoughts because the writing process itself generates and shapes our thinking.[93] The privileging of speech over writing thus has significant exclusionary effects in law schools. With this privilege, both students and professors are free to ignore critical, reflective and imaginative readings of written texts in favor of "instrumental" or "paraphrase" readings, readings which teach bad habits but are often quite sufficient to support brilliant classroom performances, successful examination performances and the prolific production of conventional scholarship.[94] Both students and professors are thus free to ignore the process of "critical writing" which, in contrast to instrumental writing, provides both internal and external feedback to writers in ways that help develop imaginative, critical, well-constructed texts.[95] The exclusion of criti-

---

90. See Kissam, supra note 50; Chapter One's discussion of law school examinations.

91. Balkin, supra note 57, at 756. See Jacques Derrida, Of Grammatology (1976); Writing and Difference (1978); Lisa Eichhorn, *Writing in the Legal Academy: A Dangerous Supplement?* 40 Ariz. L. Rev. 105 (1998); see also Kissam, supra note 86, at 141–45 (describing the celebration of oral heroism in law schools and how this celebration reinforces misunderstanding of the writing process as the mere conveyance of a speaker's fully formed thoughts).

92. See Balkin, supra note 57, at 757.

93. See, e.g., George Rideout & Jill Ramsfield, *Legal Writing: A Revised View*, 69 Wash. L. Rev. 35 (1994).

94. Cf. Fajans & Falk, supra note 83; Philip C. Kissam, *The Evaluation of Legal Scholarship*, 63 Wash. L. Rev. 221, 247–50 (1988) (both describing differences between instrumental, reflective and critical readings).

95. See Kissam, supra note 86; Rideout & Ramsfield, supra note 93.

cal and reflective reading and writing practices by the privileging of speech over writing thus teaches poor habits while supporting the discipline, its tacit conceptions and its tendency to subjugate passion, imagination, reflection, interpretation and the development of coherent moral, social and legal thought.

Inverting writing over speech could open the discipline to more pluralistic, more effective and more egalitarian education. Imagine doctrinal courses where students spend less time in class, less time preparing for exams, and more time drafting legal documents or writing papers, short analytical papers as well as longer research papers, with some subjects assigned, other subjects chosen by students on the basis of individual interests, and much individualized feedback to students on these kinds of written work.[96] Imagine too doctrinal classrooms where discussion begins with written statements or written questions about the readings submitted by students in order to orient the discussion around student understandings of texts rather than the professor's.[97] And imagine legal scholarship which is published only after many readings and comments from other experts, both informal and formal peer reviewers, instead of the practice of law reviews in which most publishing and editing decisions are made by upper class students.

In this imaginary domain, where writing is privileged over speech, the intensity and diversity of writing and learning by many different students could be substantially enhanced and the quality and depth of professorial scholarship, if not its quantity, might be improved.[98] To be sure, disciplinarians would object to both pedagogical and scholarly aspects of this domain. Pedagogically, widespread writing by students in lieu of speech by professors would threaten the control and self-identities of law professors as omniscient experts, because research projects and even short written statements about assigned readings tend to make the student "the expert" on a particular subject rather than the professor. Disciplinarians might also complain about the time involved in work with individual students[99] or about the possibilities for unfairness and excessive conformity in scholarship that is subject to regular peer

96. See, e.g., Bean, supra note 85; Kissam, supra note 85; Parker, supra note 87.

97. See Kissam, supra note 86, at 157.

98. On writing by law students, see, e.g., Kissam, supra note 50, at 500–02; Kissam, supra note 86; on writing by law faculty, see James Lindgren, *Reforming the American Law Review*, 47 Stan. L. Rev. 1123 (1995); Richard Posner, *The Future of the Student-Edited Law Review*, 47 Stan. L. Rev. 1131 (1995).

99. See, e.g., Patrick J. Schiltz, *Legal Ethics in Decline: The Elite Law Firm, the Elite Law School, and the Moral Formation of the Novice Attorney*, 82 Minn. L. Rev. 705, 747–56 (1998) (describing the legal academy's "materialism" that is oriented towards scholarship).

review.[100] But many Dialogical Selves and perhaps other selves too might decide that promoting diverse writing experiences instead of speech acts would generate a richer, more diverse teaching and learning environment than that which is made available by the current discipline of law schools.

The previous oppositions are tied, somewhat paradoxically, to another important hierarchical opposition: the primacy of scholarship over teaching.[101] Disciplinarians will sense in deep tacit ways and will even argue that the case method, final examinations and any consequent privileging of speech over writing in law teaching support their commitments to scholarship and other non-teaching activities. The former practices help generate ideas for scholarship, especially conventional doctrinal scholarship, and, most importantly, they also provide the legal scholar with much time and energy to engage in extensive research and writing. Yet many traces of law teaching appear in legal scholarship. These traces range from the substantial attention that is paid by legal scholars to the leading issues presented by casebooks, to similar uses of the case method in both classroom and scholarly work, to the close analytical attention that is paid to legal doctrine in much of the scholarship of the new academic/political movements. More fundamentally, law teaching makes legal scholarship possible by justifying the legal scholar's salary. Which is foundational then, teaching or scholarship?

To imagine the inversion of teaching over scholarship is quite easy. Law professors would have more time to consult with individual students about their work, to provide practice exams and other writing or quasi-clinical exercises that supplement and enrich the study of legal doctrine, to bring more theory into classrooms and even to teach additional courses, thus offering a broader curriculum for students preparing to enter diverse kinds of practices. Disciplinarians would have objections of course. Teaching would lose its "critical edge" if teachers "abandoned" scholarship (although inversion does not call for abandonment). "The law" would suffer from losing a large body of critical or reformist literature. Law schools would lose their reputations, at least relative to others, if faculties reduced their scholarly output. Still, there is little evidence to support these claims, and Dialogical Selves might conclude

---

100. See, e.g., Paul Carrington, *The Dangers of the Graduate School Model*, 35 J. Legal Educ. 11 (1986).

101. On the presence of this hierarchical opposition in law schools, see John S. Elson, *The Case Against Legal Scholarship or, If the Professor Must Publish, Must the Profession Perish?*, 39 J. Legal Educ. 343 (1989); Marin Roger Scordato, *The Dualist Model of Legal Teaching and Scholarship*, 40 Am. U. L. Rev. 367 (1990); Schiltz, supra note 99, at 747–56; Chapter One's discussion of the institutions of legal scholarship; Chapter Five's discussion of the research university.

that the primacy of scholarship over teaching is yet another rational myth of the discipline: if everybody believes and acts upon this myth it will seem effective. In any event, Dialogical Selves might be tempted to surrender their tacit attachments to the primacy of scholarship and commit to providing a richer, more diverse kind of law teaching and perhaps a different kind of scholarship as well.

Reconstructions

The methods and ethics of deconstruction are designed to interrogate our foundational concepts, expand our understandings of texts or social practices, and enrich our ethical debates. The techniques of deconstruction, however, do not determine the actions one should take, and any action suggested by deconstruction should itself be subject to the continuous reflexivity of further deconstructions.[102] Yet the Dialogical Self enters the moral conversation for the purpose of seeking guidance in making ethical choices about her actions, and at some point she must suspend her deconstructive questioning and choose to act in accordance with her ethical judgments.[103] Dialogical law professors who deconstruct the discipline are thus like architects who deconstruct architectural practices but are committed to designing buildings that work.[104]

The deconstruction of the discipline has suggested many practices that might open the discipline to more pluralistic, more democratic and more effective forms of legal education. Limited resources, however, will cause the Dialogical Self to seek pragmatic guidance about where to start and what to emphasize in constructing her ethical practices. Let us imagine a Dialogical Self who is interested in challenging the discipline across a relatively broad front in order to maximize opportunities for subjugated values and subjugated persons in her teaching and scholarship. She will seek principles of pragmatic guidance in order to draw feasible plans and ideas from her interrogations and inversions of the discipline. The implementation of these principles, of course, must be integrated with the concrete situations of different persons and particular law schools, and this implementation should strive to be realistic in two senses: it should build upon existing law school practices and not assume

---

102. See, e.g., Balkin, supra note 57.

103. Cf. id. (regarding the deconstruction of legal doctrine and taking legal actions).

104. See Susan McLeod, *Architecture and Politics in the Reagan Era: From Postmodernism to Deconstructivism*, 8 Assemblage, Feb. 1989, pp. 23, 45–50; Witold Rybcinski, *Pale Fire*, NY Rev. of Books, Nov. 19, 1992, pp. 43, 46.

extra resources. But these principles provide a heuristic summary of the general implications of the Dialogical Self's dual ethical responsibility to action and otherness in her law school work.

In essence, these principles should promote three kinds of educational diversity in contradistinction to the discipline's standard model of legal education. One kind of diversity would respect the different learning styles of law students, for some learn best by listening and talking, sometimes in crowds and sometimes in more intimate settings, others learn best by reviewing for and taking comprehensive final examinations, and still others learn best from the writing, feedback from texts and others, re-visioning and rewriting of a complex writing process. The second kind of diversity would provide equal time and equal respect for the plurality of intellectual methods that lawyers should be trained in. In other words, methods of synthesizing complex materials in coherent and persuasive ways, interpreting difficult legal authorities, and constructing complex or imaginative legal arguments should not be tacitly subordinated to the discipline's privileged method of analysis. The third educational diversity (this diversity may depend more on collective action by law schools and less on individual ethical decisions) would attempt to provide equal time and respect for different models of lawyering. That is, in addition to the discipline's model of highly skilled doctrinal analysts who best serve large corporate law firms, a reconstructed legal education should bring other models of the lawyering process from the margins of contemporary legal education into its center. Thus, for example, models of ethical corporate lawyering,[105] of small business firm lawyering, of transactional and litigation work for personal clients[106] and of public regulation lawyering need somehow to be brought fully into the first and second year curriculums and not reserved, as they tend to be under the discipline, for special courses and clinics in the final year of law school. These manifold diversities may seem like a very tall order for an individual Dialogical Self, or even an entire law faculty, but there are a few principles or methods that could make this all work, if worked at hard enough and long enough by many persons.

---

105. See, e.g., W.H. Simon, supra note 5; Robert Gordon, *Corporate Law Practice as a Public Calling*, 49 Md. L. Rev. 255 (1990); William H. Simon, *Ethical Discretion in Lawyering*, 101 Harv. L. Rev. 1083 (1988).

106. See, e.g., James Podgers, *Rediscovering the Middle Class: Old-fashioned values and creative thinking are proving to be the formulas for success in serving primarily middle-income clients*, ABA Journal, Dec. 1994, pp. 265–72; David G. Savage, *Everyday People: The work of storefront clinics funded by the Legal Services Corp. is not glamorous—just crucial to those who cannot help themselves*, ABA Journal, May 1995, pp. 280–84.

Here are four such principles. First, the concrete, face-to-face nature of human relationships between law students and law teachers should establish a strong priority for the education of students.[107] This education, moreover, should be student-centered rather than faculty-centered and, importantly, individualized as much as possible in order to engage individual student strengths, weaknesses and different learning styles. There is the general obligation of law professors to both teaching and some form of non-teaching work, to be sure, but in the case of major conflicts or trade-offs the Dialogical Self should favor serving the concrete others of students and their future clients over the more diffuse values of scholarship.

A second principle of the Dialogical Self's teaching should be to promote *critical reading* and *critical writing* habits among all law students. This goal cannot be achieved by lecturing students to engage in these practices on their own, or by somehow increasing the "rigor" of the case method or final examinations, because the discipline teaches the *instrumentalist* ways of paraphrase reading and good paragraph thinking/writing that need to be decentered or balanced with more critical forms of reading and writing. This second principle in other words can be applied only by decentering the case method and final examinations with alternative writing and reading exercises throughout the curriculum. In this displacement, one should begin with writing exercises that stimulate students to engage in the imaginative and critical readings of texts for, as Ann Berthoff suggests, "the old formula—students can only write as well as they can read—may be reversed as teachers come to understand what it means to say that writing is a mode of learning: *students can read only as well as they can write.*"[108] The Dialogical Self, in other words, should contemplate transplanting methods from the American university's writing-across-the-curriculum movement to legal education.[109] This self's slogan might become: abandon classrooms and conference with individual students on their writing projects.[110]

These writing exercises should provide ample opportunities for imaginative and critical readings and imaginative and critical writings that explore the

---

107. See supra note 48 and accompanying text.

108. Ann Berthoff, *I.A. Richards* in Traditions of Inquiry 50, 52 (J. Brereton ed. 1985) (author's emphasis).

109. For discussions of the potential values to be achieved by this transplantation, see Philip C. Kissam, *Lurching Towards the Millennium: The Law School, The Research University, and the Professional Reforms of Legal Education,* 60 Ohio St. L. J. 1965 (1999); Parker, supra note 87.

110. On the values of conferring with law students, see Kissam, supra note 80.

language, relationships, contexts and ethical possibilities of law and lawyering, and they should provide much individualized feedback from professors to students. They thus would contribute much to the effectiveness of teaching basic analytical skills by respecting different learning styles of students. These writing exercises should also be used to promote the second and third kinds of educational diversity: the equality of pluralistic intellectual methods and the equality of different models of lawyering.[111] In other words, learning by writing could become a flexible method of achieving several different purposes in the reconstructed law school.

A third heuristic principle for our Dialogical Self would be to bring new contexts to the legal doctrine that is studied in law schools: factual contexts, historical contexts, social contexts, theoretical contexts and even the *doctrinal contexts* of the leading cases that are excerpted in the typical casebook.[112] Using these contexts will help the Dialogical Self, her students and readers of her scholarship to interrogate and modify the exclusion of values and subjugation of persons that the discipline tacitly promotes by privileging the acquisition and analysis of legal doctrine. This principle will also help implement the second and third kinds of educational diversity: pluralistic legal methods and different models of lawyering. To be sure, this principle may be difficult to follow in a democratic, pluralistic way because so many contexts are relevant to law and because time, energy and other resources are limited. How does one "cover" the necessary doctrine in any basic law course and still present balanced contextual perspectives that engage, inform and question many students who bring their own varied experiences and perspectives to class? In teaching or scholarship, how does one avoid the messy but inherent confusions of multiplicity? There are no easy responses to this dilemma for the Dialogical Self who wishes to employ multiple contexts. Writing exercises, which individualize learning by causing students to work on their own, student-teacher interactions in conferences, and other individualized feedback to students can be helpful in resolving this dilemma. Multiple contexts, practical questions and theoretical questions about legal doctrine can be introduced and examined with more intensity by complex writing projects than by the basic disciplinary practices of the case method and final examinations.[113] But the dilemma of how to present adequately balanced contexts for both classroom

---

111. See supra text accompanying notes 105–06.

112. On the absence of these contexts, including doctrinal contexts, from law school casebooks, and the problems this creates for teaching legal interpretation and argumentation, see A. Watson, supra note 71, at 140–55.

113. See, e.g., Kissam, supra note 85.

teaching and questioning doctrine through writing projects will surely not disappear.

Finally, the Dialogical Self will want to commit herself to non-teaching work that serves otherness or, in other words, work that serves persons and values which are subjugated by the discipline, the American legal system or our social institutions. Implementing this principle will depend on the contingencies of each individual's interests, talents, values, experiences and professional situation. Bringing contexts to doctrine and experimenting with non-conventional forms of scholarship or service that resist or invert disciplinary structures are means to this end. But conventional kinds of doctrinal scholarship and public service, if aimed at the proper subjects, can serve this ethical responsibility of the Dialogical Self just as well. In essence, the Dialogical Self will want to substitute a new principle of *public service* or *the public good* for the principle of productive and prestigious scholarship that is promoted by the discipline. This new principle encompasses scholarship but it is scholarship of the sort that Rennard Strickland has called "public service scholarship"[114] and John Elson "social welfare scholarship."[115] This would be scholarship that is aimed, either directly or indirectly, at societal ills that are "most in need of redress and most likely to benefit from scholars' attention."[116] In other words, the scholarship of a Dialogical Self should in some significant respect concern issues that relate either to persons who are outsiders or disadvantaged in American society or to institutions that lack adequate resources to develop satisfactory arguments for the redress or mitigation of pressing social problems. This scholarship may approach its problems from conservative, liberal or radical perspectives, but it should be designed for audiences who are likely to have some kind of impact or interest in changing social conditions in ways that would promote the public good.

The moral conversations of Dialogical Selves with other selves should never end, of course, for Dialogical Selves will want to experiment, change and grow, and other selves may change as well. Further, any actions suggested by deconstructive interrogations of the discipline must remain open to deconstructive interrogations themselves, and any new actions will constitute parts of a reformulated discipline, not a utopia. If individualized writing projects

---

114. In his inaugural address as President of the American Association of Law Schools, Orlando, January 1994.

115. John S. Elson, *Why and How the Practicing Bar Must Rescue American Legal Education from the Misguided Priorities of American Legal Academia*, 64 Tenn. L. Rev. 1135, 1138–41 (1997).

116. Id. at 1140.

should decenter the discipline's case method and examination/grading/class ranking system, the power/knowledge relations that bind law professors and their students would not disappear, they would merely shift and reappear in the more subjective, and perhaps more dangerous, arenas of individual student-teacher conferences and faculty evaluations of individual projects. When law professors bring non-doctrinal contexts to their classrooms or scholarship, they may stumble dangerously as non-experts and may exert even more power over their students than before by displaying, no matter how unconsciously, an apparent expertise about both legal doctrine and non-doctrinal subjects. Yet Dialogical Selves who care about their dual ethical responsibilities to action and otherness will entertain these challenges, continue to experiment in their teaching, scholarship and other public services, and continue to interrogate these experiments. At the same time, these Dialogical Selves would be changing the discipline of law schools in ways that promise to support more diverse of kinds of selves and more diverse kinds of ethics among law students and lawyers, a greater willingness to tolerate ethical considerations in law and lawyering, and more effective and more democratic forms of legal education.

Ultimately, in this Utopia, one may contemplate opening up the moral conversation to collective decisions about curriculum design, grading/class ranking systems and other issues that would enhance the attempts of Dialogical Selves to promote more diverse and more effective forms of legal education. Three kinds of changes seem critical here.

The first and second year curriculums should be reorganized to teach the skills of critical reading and writing about law and establish competing models of lawyering on an equal basis within the law school's core curriculum. This would entail constructing courses that employ diverse teaching materials, diverse teaching methods and diverse forms of evaluation. In this process, for example, the "problem method" might replace the "case method" as the major technique in a majority of first and second year courses,[117] advocacy exercises and other kinds of "clinical simulations" might appear in many doctrinal courses,[118] and—most importantly—many varied writing projects, including practice examinations, mid-term examinations, drafting legal documents and writing reflectively and critically about difficult issues of interpretation or ethics, should supplement and in some instances replace the writing of end-

---

117. See John S. Elson, *The Regulation of Legal Education: The Potential for Implementing the MacCrate Report's Recommendations for Curricular Reform*, 1 Clin. L. Rev. 363, 383–87 (1994).

118. See Russell Weaver, *Langdell's Legacy: Living with the Case Method*, 36 Vill. L. Rev. 517, 574–76 (1991).

of-the-semester final examinations.[119] Another important principle of this re-organization should be to provide each student with substantial supervised practice and individualized feedback while making his or her initial attempts to read, think, talk and write about using the law in diverse ways to solve diverse practical problems. In other words, all three education diversities need to be implanted firmly within the law school's core curriculum.

In this Utopia, law schools would also abandon or substantially modify the discipline's final examination/grading/class ranking system in favor of more particularized evaluations of law student work. This does not mean that examinations or other student work should be ungraded, or that grading curves should not be employed to evaluate the work in particular courses where grading curves are important, for student performances on all kinds of work vary and differential grades can provide both stimulation and a kind of feedback to many students. But utopian law schools would not impose particular grading categories and grading curves upon all or most course work in order generate the discrete class ranking systems of most law schools. The fundamental problem with the discipline's final examination/grading/class ranking system is that it creates perverse incentives for law teachers not to provide individualized instruction to students about the development of their legal skills, either because of the fear that this would unfairly place some students ahead of others in the competitive race for grades or because of the instinctive fear that supervised practice and feedback for students would make the imposition of a law school's mandatory grading curve more difficult.[120] The consequences of these perverse incentives include the apparent unwillingness of many professors to help individual students very much outside the classroom,[121] a similar tendency among law professors to limit their cooperation with students in improving the first drafts of writing projects in order to be able to grade the final product *as the student's work*,[122] and the more general tendency of law professors to disparage or avoid teaching courses with writing projects that fit poorly with mandatory grading curves.[123]

---

119. See, e.g., Bean, supra note 85; Feinman & Feldman, supra note 84; Kissam, supra note 85; Kissam, supra note 109, at 2009–13; Parker, supra note 87.

120. Cf. supra note 76 and accompanying text (noting that practice examinations may make the imposition of grading curves on final examinations more difficult).

121. See Kissam, supra note 80, at 920–21.

122. See Kissam, supra note 109, at 1991.

123. The abandonment or substantial modification of grading curves and class ranking systems need not leave students and their prospective employers without evaluative information that could be developed and utilized with relative ease. Many law firms today ask for writing samples, professorial recommendations and evidence of law review status

Finally, as a necessary support for the previous two changes, the discipline's strong priority for scholarship over teaching should be substantially modified by the collective action of law faculties in order to provide the resource of extra teaching time that would encourage law professors to teach a reconstructed curriculum. To be sure, disciplinary law professors tend to overestimate the time they need to supervise student writing projects,[124] and upper class law students can be employed very effectively in many instances to help review law student writing projects and thereby reduce the pressure upon professorial time.[125] But helping students engage in much critical reading and writing and providing them with supervised practice in alternative models of lawyering should replace legal scholarship as the major priority among law professors if their ethical responsibilities to concrete others, especially their students, are to be fulfilled by some reorganization of the curriculum as suggested above. Thus law faculties in this utopia will be motivated to abandon the discipline's somewhat mechanical obsession with the quantities of law faculty scholarship and substitute more qualitative assessments of scholarship that take account of scholarship's appropriate relationships to effective law teaching.

---

or performance in particular courses, and law professors without much extra effort should be able to provide written evaluations of law student work in smaller classes and of student writing projects that could help legal employers screen their applicants, perhaps even more effectively that they can with class ranks and grades alone.

124. Cf. Kissam, supra note 109, at 2009–13 (describing several low cost ways to implement writing projects in large law school classes).

125. See Jay M. Feinman, *Teaching Assistants*, 41 J. Legal Educ. 269 (1991); Leon Trakman, *Law Student Teachers: An Untapped Resource*, 30 J. Legal Educ. 331 (1979).

EPILOGUE

OUR DISCIPLINARY FUTURE

"The question whether some forms of resistance are more effective than others is a matter of social and historical investigation and not of a priori announcement."[1]

Where does this leave us? The inherent attractions and positive functions of the discipline, the organizational environment of law schools, and the prevailing concepts of self and ethics in American society and law schools are likely to support the elements and techniques of the discipline for a long time to come. The discipline has absorbed many changes and reform ideas in the past 130 years and its structures have remained largely the same. Dissident selves and dissident ethics that would mount any sustained resistance or subversion to the discipline would appear to face major obstacles.

To be sure, predictions about the discipline's future are complicated by the current restructuring of the American economy and corresponding shifts that are occurring in corporate law firms, the American judicial system, research universities and law schools. Several shifts of this sort are worth noting. Each shift contains possibilities for reinforcing the discipline and modifying or disrupting it. In light of the discipline's history, however, the discipline appears likely to incorporate major features of these changes and muffle the disruptive tendencies.

Law schools today are increasingly in competition with each other, especially for students and for reputation in terms of rankings like those provided by the *U.S. World and News Report*.[2] On the one hand, this competition between law schools for new students, especially at non-elite law schools, could cause increasing experimentation that brings diversity to both curriculums and educa-

---

1. Jana Sawicki, Disciplining Foucault 26 (1991).
2. See, e.g., Jan Hoffman, "Judge Not, Law Schools Demand of a Magazine That Ranks Them," NY Times, Feb. 19, 1998, p. A1 (describing the public relations concerns of law school deans, including their unhappiness with the *U.S. World and News Report* rankings, in the face of a recent 30% decline in law school applications).

tional methods as individual schools try to distinguish themselves from others or serve students with particular interests.[3] On the other hand, like the television networks, law schools traditionally have tried to serve the broad center of their marketplace, and there is a good reason for this because most law students choose to specialize only after finding their first specialist job. The traditional mission of providing generalist training together with a school's limited resources is likely to encourage most law schools to engage in less expensive competition by focusing on public relations rather than educational reforms. In this approach, the curriculum, teaching methods and examination system would not change, and law schools would compete more strenuously for relative reputations and rankings in the *U.S. World & News Report* and other comparative forums. This kind of competition supports the discipline's practices of admitting students with the highest LSAT scores and undergraduate grades whose expectations in turn support the final examination/grading/class ranking system. This kind of competition also intensifies the pressure on law faculties to publish frequently in prestigious places in order to enhance the relative reputations of their law schools.[4] Law school competition, then, on balance is likely to be discipline-reinforcing rather than discipline-shifting.

The competition between and commercialization of law firms are also likely to increase. We have seen that the expansion and commercial practices of contemporary law firms have increased the pressure on law schools to generate both class rank and law review credentials for prospective law firm employees.[5] The competition among students for these credentials requires the dispensation of many different grades that can be easily explained to law students by their professors, and this requirement undergirds the discipline's final examination system and its retention of large case method classes.[6] At the same time, the commercialization of law firms may be causing firms to try to shift their training costs to law schools or more simply to diminish their training

---

3. Consider the George Mason Law School in Virginia that emphasizes a law and economics curriculum and the Vermont Law School that emphasizes environmental law.

4. See Chapter One's discussion of elite and non-elite law schools. The real possibility of new or intensified pressures on law professors to publish frequently and in prestigious places is evident in the proliferation in recent years of glossy law school brochures that trumpet the recent publications and reputations of law school faculty members. These brochures are distributed widely with the apparent intent, among other purposes, of enhancing the reputation of the school among legal academics and among judges and lawyers, two factors that figure in the *U.S. World & News Report*'s law school rankings.

5. See Chapter Five's discussion of the case method and corporate law firms.

6. See Chapter One's discussion of the case method and examinations.

of new associates,[7] thus demanding implicitly or expressly that law schools provide more comprehensive education than they traditionally have. This development could encourage law schools to expand their writing and other practice-oriented courses, especially to improve the skills of their graduates in general oral and written communication.[8] But this demand is more diffuse than the demand for law school credentials. Moreover, it is not clear that much law firm training of associates, which is often firm specific, could be delegated to law schools. Thus the commercialization of law firms seems likely to strengthen the discipline on balance.

Another potentially transformative force in legal education consists of the new computer technology and information highways. This new technology has the potential to open up the discipline and to make possible more and different kinds of research, more writing and more individualized feedback to students than is provided by the case method/final examination system. Yet this technology may reinforce important disciplinary routines. For example, the internet provides low cost rapid access to much greater amounts of relevant legal information, but will discovering and reading such information on small screens change the way one processes or understands the information? Will this kind of reading make us more critical or less critical readers? Similarly, the internet classroom, with its elaborate electronic communications among faculty and students, promises more individualized student-faculty contacts which could enhance individualized learning by students with different learning styles.[9] Might not the internet classroom, however, tend also to discipline students into undertaking more exhaustive (or more exhausting) reading, reading which is instrumental in nature, as they pursue the many leads of hypertext assignments? Similarly, laptop computers allow students to take verbatim notes much more easily, and this kind of note taking surely feeds

---

7. Compare Mary A. McLaughlin, *Beyond the Caricature: The Benefits and Challenges of Large-Firm Practice*, 52 Vand. L. Rev. 1003, 1010 (1999) (large law firms provide "one-on-one mentoring" by "excellent lawyers"), with Patrick J. Schiltz, *Provoking Introspection: A Reply to Galanter & Palay, Hull, Kelly, Lesnick, McLaughlin, Pepper, and Traynor*, 52 Vand. L. Rev. 1033, 1037-38 (1999) (the commercialization of law firms is reducing the mentoring of new lawyers).

8. Cf. Bryant G. Garth & Joanne Martin, *Law Schools and the Construction of Competence*, 43 J. Legal. Educ. 469 (1993) (describing the desire of hiring partners that law students bring with them better skills in general oral and written communication).

9. See William R. Slomanson, *Electronic Lawyering and the Academy*, 48 J. Legal Educ. 216 (1998); Desktop Colleague, A Technology Newsletter for Law Faculty from West Group, Vol. 3, Issue 2 (1998) (describing Professor Philip Bouchard's internet classroom at the Western New England College School of Law).

the disciplinary law student's penchant for noting the many bits of positive information that may be helpful on examinations. Furthermore, word processors can facilitate writing, re-vising, and re-writing complicated texts, but word processors on balance may merely invite more instrumentalist writing of more frequent, more complex and longer texts that fail to improve one's writing or thought.[10] Students trained on computers and the information highway may thus become more adept at securing the rules and other bits of positive law they need to compete for grades on final examinations and no more interested in attending to the complex practices of critical reading, critical writing, making practical judgments and ethical contemplation than today's disciplined law students. This seems a likely result when we take into account the major imperatives of the discipline, for students to obtain jobs by competing for the best grades and for professors to establish their reputations by publishing frequently, as the basic context for this technology.

Finally, we should consider the possible effects on the discipline of an apparent change in the ethos of contemporary research universities. Bill Readings argued recently that the historical emphasis on reason and culture in university education has given way to a new university ideology of "excellence."[11] This ideology is fundamentally non-referential: that is, in the university of excellence one may be excellent in many things or anything, and reason or culture need have little or nothing to do with this excellence. One may be academically excellent in using reason or in cultivating minds, but one may also be academically excellent in obtaining good grades or publishing in prestigious journals without any necessary reference to the reason or culture of the work. Thus, one may be an "excellent student" by getting top scores on aptitude tests and top grades in courses, no matter what subjects are studied or what learning process is pursued, and this excellence may have nothing to do with a person's reading and writing abilities or intellectual curiosity and experience. One can be an "excellent teacher" by earning top scores in student evaluations without reference to other criteria of good teaching such as the development of a student's reasoning skills or cultivation of good writing habits.[12] One can be

---

10. Cf. Jeff Madrick, *Computers: Waiting for the Revolution*, NY Rev., March 26, 1998, pp. 29, 31 ("Why haven't computers dramatically augmented productivity? Some analysts believe that the enormous power of computers is often superfluous. For example, law briefs are now much thicker and more detailed than they once were, thanks to word processing and the greater ease in obtaining supporting documents. But this does not mean that law is being practiced more efficiently; perhaps just the opposite is true.").

11. See Bill Readings, The University in Ruins (1996).

12. See Joseph Centra, Determining Faculty Effectiveness 1-46 (1979) (describing a marked increase in the use of student evaluations of teaching by American universities in

an "excellent scholar" by producing large quantities of publications or prestigious publications no matter what the subject or quality of the scholarship.[13] This ideology of excellence is not merely reductive, however, as these examples suggest. The governing idea of excellence allows the university, or "multiversity" as Clark Kerr called it, to take on as legitimate many different tasks just as long as the endeavor is perceived as striving for some kind of excellence.[14] The university of excellence can thus embrace innovative, non-traditional ideas about teaching and scholarship as long as these ideas are perceived as excellent in some way. The new university ethos, like other potentially transformative shifts, could support significant changes to the discipline.

The university of excellence has replaced the older university of reason and culture for a number of reasons. The expansion of universities, especially public universities, and vast increase in funding for university research in basic sciences, medical sciences and defense-related research since World War II are major causes, and the new openness of research universities to the financial, political and ideological influence of business corporations is certainly another.[15] The bureaucratization of the research university, in order to deal with external influences and apply "rigorous" measures of accountability to faculty performances, has also supported the displacement of reason and culture by the ideology of excellence. But whatever its causes, the university of excellence clearly has shifted power and influence from faculty members, who specialized in reason and culture, to administrators and other policymakers who specialize in establishing the "objective criteria" of "excellence" for teaching, research and scholarship.[16]

---

the 1970s and attributing this to the need of university administrators to make more discriminating choices about tenure, salary increases and other employment matters); Richard L. Abel, *Evaluating Evaluations: How Should Law Schools Judge Teaching?*, 40 J. Legal Educ. 407 (1990) (describing the bureaucratic development of student evaluations of law teaching); Richard S. Markovits, *The Professional Assessment of Legal Academics: On The Shift from Evaluator Judgment to Market Evaluations*, 48 J. Legal Educ. 417 (1998) (describing an increased emphasis on student evaluations in the law school's evaluation of law teaching).

13. See, e.g., H. Graham & N. Diamond, The Rise of American Research Universities: Elites and Challengers in the Postwar Era (1997) (relying heavily on "publication counts" as a means of ranking American research universities); Markovits, supra note12 (describing the increased attention of law professors in evaluating their own work and the work of their colleagues to the prestige of law reviews in which articles are published).

14. See Clark Kerr, The Uses of the University (3rd ed. 1982); B. Readings, supra note 11, at 28-43.

15. See H. Graham & N. Diamond, supra note 13; B. Readings, supra note 11.

16. See B. Readings, supra note 11.

The new ethos of excellence may contribute to diminished interests in reading, writing and intellectual exploration among law students who learn, as undergraduates and law students, to pursue excellence rather than reason or culture. The university of excellence also may contribute by ideology and bureaucratic accountability to the rather marked tendency among law professors today to commit their all to scholarship, consulting and their specialized subdisciplines while leaving aside questions about what should be done to provide good training for new lawyers.[17] These two tendencies also combine in something of a pincers movement to restrict the quality of legal education. Law students trained in the university of excellence may be less capable and less interested in learning the skills of the traditional case method or learning to write competently about complex matters without extensive instruction or practice. Meanwhile law professors are committed by the university of excellence to obtaining marks of excellence for their scholarship (or their consulting or teaching special subjects), and they will want to rely on the case method, which includes much lecturing and "Socratic monologues" about the cases, and traditional final examinations in order to preserve their time and energy to pursue such excellence.[18] Thus the university of excellence may very well support the major disciplinary practices on balance.

Notwithstanding a continuation of the discipline in similar forms, the discipline will continue to generate resistance, contradictions and open spaces in the margins of its practices. These phenomena are resources for establishing subversive practices that can challenge the discipline's values if not also its structures. One of Michel Foucault's infrequent statements about the overall effects of disciplinary power provides a good description of the possibilities:

> "Are there no great radical ruptures, massive binary divisions, then? Occasionally, yes. But more often one is dealing with mobile and transitory points of resistance, producing cleavages in a society that shift about, fracturing unities and effecting regroupings, furrowing across individuals themselves, cutting them up and remolding them, marking off irreducible regions in them, in their bodies and minds."[19]

---

17. On this tendency, see John S. Elson, *The Case Against Legal Scholarship or, If the Professor Must Publish, Must the Profession Perish?*, 39 J. Legal Educ. 343 (1989); Terrence Sandalow, *The Moral Responsibility of Law Schools*, 34 J. Legal Educ. 163 (1984); Patrick J. Schiltz, *Legal Ethics in Decline: The Elite Law Firm, the Elite Law School, and the Moral Formation of the Novice Attorney*, 82 Minn. L. Rev. 705, 747-56 (1998).

18. See Chapter Three's discussion of the discipline's examinatorial regime.

19. Michel Foucault, The History of Sexuality, Vol. I, 96 (Robert Hurley trans. 1978).

At its best, then, this book should perhaps be thought of as a furrowing and report on other furrowings within the discipline of law schools. The most likely effect of these furrowings, of course, like other reform ideas, may only be to help legitimate the discipline by pacifying the discontented and by offering modest supplements that the discipline can use to justify itself. Thus, for the discipline's future, we may predict a muddle, a disciplinary muddle to be sure, but one that could be interesting and productive for individual law professors and law students who continue to explore points of resistance to the discipline and the furrowings that can result from this exploration.

In any event, we should by now have a much better understanding of the law school's paradoxes. The contentious political disputes against the basic conservative values of law schools are maintained or even generated by the discipline of law schools as a form of *useful resistance*, and these disputes in fact serve the conservative values of law and law schools by helping legitimate law schools and their disciplinary practices. The case method/final examination system powerfully and tacitly inculcates some important skills and attitudes. But the case method/final examination system does this to an excess that causes unhappiness among students, treats them in inhumane ways, and diminishes or fails to promote adequately the basic case method skills that law students are expected to acquire, to say nothing of disfavoring other important legal skills and instincts. The disciplinary law school also serves corporate law firms but does this in a contradictory fashion. The case method/final examination system generates class rank credentials and productive "symbolic analysts" which are both desirable to corporate law firms. Yet at the same time, the discipline of law schools limits the capacities of American law schools to train corporate lawyers in ways that would engage them in more comprehensive forms of reading, thinking and writing about the law. Finally, the legal profession and law schools promise ethical training for lawyers but the discipline then limits this training and tacitly instructs its students to keep their ethical instincts and thoughts largely removed from their legal selves. The law school's paradoxes are part and parcel of the discipline of law schools.

Index

277